Embedded Computing
for High Performance

Embedded Computing for High Performance

Efficient Mapping of Computations Using Customization, Code Transformations and Compilation

João M.P. Cardoso

José Gabriel F. Coutinho

Pedro C. Diniz

MORGAN KAUFMANN PUBLISHERS

AN IMPRINT OF ELSEVIER

Morgan Kaufmann is an imprint of Elsevier
50 Hampshire Street, 5th Floor, Cambridge, MA 02139, United States

Library of Congress Cataloging-in-Publication Data
A catalog record for this book is available from the Library of Congress

British Library Cataloguing-in-Publication Data
A catalogue record for this book is available from the British Library

ISBN: 978-0-12-804189-5

For information on all Morgan Kaufmann publications
visit our website at https://www.elsevier.com/books-and-journals

Working together
to grow libraries in
developing countries

www.elsevier.com • www.bookaid.org

Publisher: Jonathan Simpson
Acquisition Editor: Jonathan Simpson
Editorial Project Manager: Lindsay Lawrence
Production Project Manager: Punithavathy Govindaradjane
Cover Designer: Mark Rogers

Typeset by SPi Global, India

Dedication

We dedicate this book to:

our parents
our families

To Teresa, Rodrigo, Frederico, and Dinis.
To my grandmother Amélia.
To Rafael Nuno, who over the last years has endured so much more than he should have.

Contents

About the Authors

João M.P. Cardoso is a full professor at the Department of Informatics Engineering, Faculty of Engineering of the University of Porto, Porto, Portugal and a research member at INESC TEC. Before, he was with the IST/Technical Univ. of Lisbon (UTL) (2006–08), a senior researcher at INESC-ID (2001–09), and with the University of Algarve (1993–2006). In 2001/2002, he worked for PACT XPP Technologies, Inc., Munich, Germany. He received his PhD degree in electrical and computer engineering from IST/Technical University of Lisbon in 2001. He served as a Program Committee member, as General Co-Chair, and as Program Co-Chair in many international conferences. He has (co-)authored over 150 scientific publications on subjects related to compilers, embedded systems, and reconfigurable computing. In addition, he has been involved in several research projects. He is a senior member of IEEE, a member of IEEE Computer Society, and a senior member of ACM. His research interests include compilation techniques, domain-specific languages, reconfigurable computing, application-specific architectures, and high-performance computing with a particular emphasis in embedded computing.

José Gabriel F. Coutinho is an associate researcher working in the Custom Computing Research Group at Imperial College London. He received his M. Eng. degree in computer engineering from Instituto Superior Técnico, Portugal in 1997. In 2000 and 2007 he received his MSc and PhD in computing science from Imperial College London, respectively. Since 2005, he has been involved in United Kingdom and EU research projects, including FP6 hArtes, FP7 REFLECT, FP7 HARNESS, and H2020 EXTRA. In addition, he has published over 50 research papers in peer-referred journals and international conferences and has contributed to four book publications. His research interests include reconfigurable computing, HPC platforms, cloud computing platforms, high-level compilation techniques, programming models, and domain-specific languages.

Pedro C. Diniz received his MS in electrical and computer engineering from the Technical University in Lisbon, Portugal and his PhD in computer science from the University of California, Santa Barbara in 1997. Since 1997 he has been a research associate with the University of Southern California's Information Sciences Institute (USC/ISI) and a research assistant professor of Computer Science at USC in Los Angeles, California. He has participated and/or led various research projects in the area of compilation for high-performance computing, mapping and synthesis for reconfigurable computing architectures, and more recently resilient computing. He has also been heavily involved in the scientific community having participated as part of the technical program committee of over 20 international conferences in the area of high-performance computing, reconfigurable and field-programmable computing.

Preface

Over the last decades, computer users have enjoyed the benefits of a seemingly unbounded availability of transistors on a die, with every new microprocessor design exhibiting performance figures that dwarfed previous generations. Computing platforms evolved from a single processor core to general-purpose multicores and specialized cores, such as graphics processing units (GPUs), delivering unprecedented performance thanks to the high degree of parallelism currently available. More recently, energy efficiency has become a major concern, prompting systems to include custom computing engines in the form of field-programmable gate arrays (FPGA) and other forms of reconfigurable computing devices.

All these computing platforms trends are permeating the embedded computing domain, especially in high-performance embedded computing systems. Still, these advanced architectures expose an execution model that is far detached from the traditional sequential programming paradigm that programmers have been accustomed to when developing their extensive code base, and which they rely on when reasoning about program correctness. As a natural consequence of this gap between architectures and high-level programming languages, developers must understand the basic mapping between the application and the target computing architectures to fully exploit their capabilities. To help mitigate the complexity of this mapping and optimization problem, many high-level languages now include language extensions and compiler directives that allow applications to make more effective use of parallel architectures, for instance, to exploit multithreading on multiple cores. Given the stringent requirements of current embedded computing platforms in terms of latency, throughput, power and energy, developers need to further master this mapping process.

This book provides a comprehensive description of the basic mapping techniques and source code transformations for computations expressed in high-level imperative programming languages, such as C or MATLAB, to high-performance embedded architectures consisting of multiple CPUs, GPUs, and reconfigurable hardware (mainly FPGAs). It is therefore meant to help practitioners in the area of electrical, computer engineering, and computer science to effectively map computations to these architectures.

This book also covers existing compilers and their transformations outlining their use in many mapping techniques. These include the classical parallel-oriented transformations for loop constructs, but equally important data-oriented and data-mapping transformations that are key in the context of GPU-based systems. As such, this book is aimed to help computer engineers and computer scientists, as well as electrical engineers, who are faced with the hard task of mapping computations to high-performance embedded computing systems. Given the comprehensive set of source code and retargeting transformations described here, this book can be effectively used as a textbook for an advanced electrical, computer engineering, and computer science course focused on the development of high-performance embedded systems.

We are very conscious about the difficulty of presenting in a single book, and in a cohesive form, all the topics we consider important about the process of mapping computations to high-performance embedded computing platforms. However, we believe that the topics presented in this book should be mastered by the next generation of developers.

We hope you enjoy reading this book, and that it contributes to increasing your knowledge about developing efficient programs on high-performance embedded platforms, and that it serves as an inspiration to your projects.

João M.P. Cardoso
José Gabriel F. Coutinho
Pedro C. Diniz

Acknowledgments

We would like to acknowledge Walid Najjar, from the University of California Riverside, United States, for reading a previous version of Chapter 2 and for providing important feedback and suggestions for improving it.

We would like to acknowledge all the members of the SPeCS group[1] for their suggestions and discussions, namely, João Bispo, Tiago Carvalho, Pedro Pinto, Luís Reis, and Ricardo Nobre. We are also grateful to all of them for reviewing previous versions of this book's chapters and for their valuable feedback that undoubtedly helped to improve the book.

Students of the PhD Program on Informatics Engineering (ProDEI) of the Faculty of Engineering of the University of Porto (FEUP) have also been a source of helpful feedback regarding some of the contents of this book, as earlier revisions from selected chapters were used as part of the class material for the High-Performance Embedded Computing (CEED) course.

In addition, we would also like to acknowledge the support given by the following companies. Xilinx Inc.[2] (United States) provided, through their University Program, FPGA-based development boards and software licenses including Vivado and Vivado HLS. ARM Ltd.[3] (United Kingdom) provided, through its ARM University Program, a sample ARM Lab-in-a-Box on Efficient Embedded Systems Design and Programming.

João M.P. Cardoso would like to acknowledge the support of the Department of Informatics Engineering of the Faculty of Engineering of the University of Porto, of INESC TEC, and the partial support provided by the following research projects: ANTAREX (H2020 FETHPC-1-2014, ref. 671623), CONTEXTWA (FCT PTDC/ EEI-SCR/6945/2014), and TEC4Growth—RL1 SMILES (NORTE-01-0145-FEDER-000020). José Gabriel F. Coutinho would like to acknowledge the support of Wayne Luk, the Department of Computing at Imperial College London, United Kingdom, and the partial support of the EXTRA research project (H2020 FETHPC-1-2014, ref. 671653).

We would like to acknowledge Elsevier for giving us the opportunity to write this book. A warm acknowledgment and appreciation to Lindsay Lawrence, our Elsevier editor, for her belief in this project since the very beginning, as well as her direction which helped us finish this book project.

Last but not least, we would like to thank our families for their support and understanding for the countless hours we had to devote to this book.

---

[1]SPeCS (Special Purpose Computing Systems, Languages and Tools) Research Group: http://www.fe.up.pt/~specs/.
[2]Xilinx Inc., http://www.xilinx.com.
[3]ARM Ltd., http://www.arm.com/.

Abbreviations

ACPI	advanced configuration and power interface. A standard promoted by Intel, Microsoft, and Toshiba
ADC	analog-to-digital converter
AMD	advanced micro devices
AOP	aspect-oriented programming
API	application programming interface
ARM	advanced RISC machines
ASIP	application-specific instruction-set processor
AST	abstract syntax tree
AVX	advanced vector extensions
BRAM	block RAM
CD	computing device
CDFG	control/data flow graph
CFG	control flow graph
CG	call graph
CGRA	coarse-grained reconfigurable array
CISC	complex instruction set computer
CLB	configurable logic block
CMP	chip multiprocessor
COTS	commercial off-the-shelf
CPA	critical path analysis
CPU	central processing unit
CU	computing unit
DAC	digital-to-analog converter
DAG	directed acyclic graph
DDG	data dependence graph
DDR	double data rate
DFG	data flow graph
DFS	dynamic frequency scaling
DPM	dynamic power management
DRAM	dynamic random-access memory (RAM)
DSE	design space exploration
DSL	domain-specific language
DSP	digital signal processing
DVFS	dynamic voltage and frequency scaling
DVS	dynamic voltage scaling
EDA	electronic design automation
EDP	energy delay product
EEMBC	embedded microprocessor benchmark consortium
FMA	fused multiply-add

FPGA	field-programmable gate array
FPS	frames per second
FSM	finite state machine
GA	genetic algorithm
GCC	GNU compiler collection (originally named GNU C Compiler)
GPGPU	general-purpose graphics processing unit (also known as general-purpose computing on graphics processing unit)
GPIO	general-purpose input/output (IO)
GPU	graphics processing unit
HLS	high-level synthesis
HPC	high-performance computing
HPEC	high-performance embedded computing
HPF	high performance Fortran
ICC	Intel C/C++ compiler
IDE	integrated design environment
ILP	instruction-level parallelism or integer-linear programming
IO	input/output
IOB	input/output block
IR	intermediate representation
ISA	instruction set architecture
LDG	loop dependence graph
LLVM	low level virtual machine
LOC	lines of code
MIC	many integrated core
MPI	message passing interface
MPSoC	multiprocessor SoC (system-on-a-chip)
NFRs	nonfunctional requirements
NUMA	nonuniform memory access
OpenACC	open accelerators
OpenCL	open computing language
OpenMP	open multiprocessing
PC	personal computer
PCI	peripheral component interconnect
PCIe	peripheral component interconnect express
PE	processing element
QoE	quality of experience
QoS	quality of service
QPI	Intel QuickPath interconnect
RAM	random-access memory
RISC	reduced-instruction set computer
ROM	read-only memory
RTOS	real-time operating system
SA	simulated annealing

SDR	single data rate
SDRAM	synchronous dynamic random-access memory
SIMD	single instruction, multiple data
SIMT	single instruction, multiple thread
SLP	subword-level parallelism
SMT	simultaneous multithreading
SNR	signal-to-noise ratio
SoC	system-on-a-chip
SPIR	standard portable intermediate representation
SPM	ScratchPad memory
SPMD	single program, multiple data
SRAM	static random-access memory (RAM)
SSA	static single assignment
SSE	streaming SIMD extensions
TG	task graph
TMR	triple-module redundancy
UART	universal asynchronous receiver/transmitter
UMA	uniform memory access
UML	unified modeling language
USB	universal serial bus
VL	vector register length
WCET	worst-case execution time

Introduction

1

1.1 OVERVIEW

Embedded computing systems permeate our lives from consumer devices, such as smartphones and game consoles, to less visible electronic devices that control, for instance, different aspects of a car's operation. Applications executing on current embedded systems exhibit a sophistication on par with applications running on desktop computers. In particular, mobile devices now support computationally intensive applications, and the trend points to a further increase in application complexity to meet the growing expectations of their users. In addition to performance requirements, energy and power consumption are of paramount importance for embedded applications, imposing restrictions on how applications are developed and which algorithms can be used.

Fig. 1.1 presents a generic and simplified architecture of an embedded computing system. A key distinguishing feature of an embedded system lies in the diversity of its input and output devices, generically known as *sensors* and *actuators*, fueled by the need to customize their use for each specific domain. In this diagram, we have a bus-based computing core system consisting of a RAM, ROM, and a processor unit. The computing core system interacts with its physical environment via a set of actuators and sensors using Analog-to-Digital (ADC) and Digital-to-Analog (DAC) converter units. At the software level, the operating system and application software are stored in ROM or in Flash memory, possibly running a customized version of the Linux operating system able to satisfy specific memory and/or real-time requirements [1] and can support additional software components, such as resident monitors, required by the embedded system.

Developing applications in heavily constrained environments, which are typical targets of embedded applications, requires considerable programming skills. Not only programmers need to understand the limitations of the underlying hardware and accompanying runtime support, but they must also develop solutions able to meet stringent nonfunctional requirements, such as performance. Developing these interdisciplinary skills is nontrivial and not surprisingly there is a lack of textbooks addressing the development of the relevant competences. These aptitudes are required when developing and mapping high-performance applications to current and emerging embedded computing systems. We believe that this textbook is a step in this direction.

1

Embedded Computing for High Performance. http://dx.doi.org/10.1016/B978-0-12-804189-5.00001-6

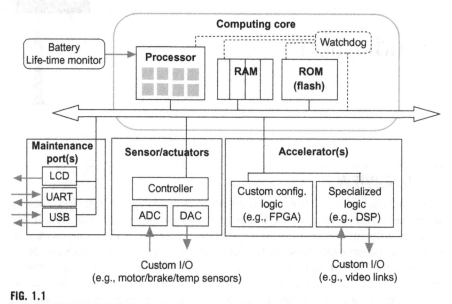

FIG. 1.1

Block diagram of a typical embedded computing system.

1.2 EMBEDDED SYSTEMS IN SOCIETY AND INDUSTRY

While not necessarily comprehensive, Fig. 1.2 illustrates the diversity of the domains and environments in which embedded systems operate. At home, embedded systems are used to control and monitor our appliances from the simple stand-alone microwave oven, washing machine, and thermostat, to the more sophisticated and sensitive security system that monitors cameras and possibly communicates with remote systems via the Internet. Embedded systems also control our vehicles from the fuel injection control to the monitoring of emissions while managing a plethora of information using visual aids to display the operation of our vehicles. In our cities, embedded systems monitor public transportation systems which are ubiquitously connected to central stations performing online scheduling of buses and trains and provide real-time updates of arrival times across all stops for all transportation lines. At the office, embedded systems handle small electronic devices such as printers, cameras, and security systems as well as lighting.

Moreover, today's smartphones are a marvel of technological integration and software development. These high-end embedded systems now include multicore processor(s), WiFi, Bluetooth, touch screens, and have performance commensurate to the performance of high-end multiprocessing systems available just a few years ago to solve scientific and engineering computing problems.

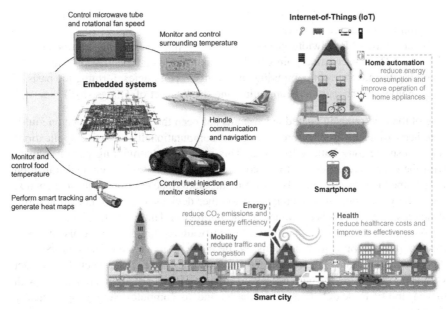

FIG. 1.2

Embedded computing in every daily life.

1.3 EMBEDDED COMPUTING TRENDS

Over the last decades, the seemingly limitless availability of transistors has enabled the development of impressive computing architectures with a variety and heterogeneity of devices. This resulted in the ability to combine, on a single integrated circuit, computing and storage capacity, previously unimaginable in terms of raw hardware performance and consequently in terms of software complexity and functionality. Various empirical laws have highlighted and captured important trends and are still relevant today in the context of embedded systems. These empirical laws include:

- Moore's Law—"The number of components in integrated circuits doubles every 18 months." Moore's Law is one of the driving forces leading to the miniaturization of electronic components and to their increasing complexity;
- Gustafson's Law—"Any sufficiently large problem can be efficiently parallelized." Due to the increasing complexity of embedded applications, the potential to use the many- and multicore architectures has also increased;
- Wirth's Law—"Software gets slower faster than hardware gets faster." This observation is supported by the fast advances of multicore systems and custom computing and hardware accelerators when compared with the availability of

effective development tools and APIs (Application Programming Interfaces) to exploit the target architectures;

- Gilder's Law—"Bandwidth grows at least three times faster than computer power." This observation points to the advances in data transmission which amplify the advances of computing and storage technologies, forming the basis of technologies such as cloud computing and the Internet of Things (IoT).

One of the key trends in embedded systems has been the growing reliance on multi-core heterogeneous architectures to support computationally intensive applications while ensuring long battery lifetimes. This increase in computing power coupled with the ever increase desire to be connected has fueled a fundamental transition from embedded systems, mostly operating in stand-alone environments, to a context where they are ubiquitously connected to other devices and communication infrastructures, in what has been coined as the Internet of Things (IoT).

As with the evolution of hardware, IoT software requirements have also evolved to support more application domains. While in the past years, the focus has been on digital signal and image processing, embedded systems are now expected to interact with other devices on the network and to support a variety of applications, e.g., with the capability to search remote databases and to compute using geographically distributed data.

Not surprisingly, the computational demands of mobile applications have also increased exponentially [2], thus exacerbating the complexity of mapping these applications to mobile architectures. It is believed (see, e.g., [3]) that in some domains neither hardware scaling nor hardware replication is enough to satisfy the performance requirements of advanced mobile applications. Therefore, in addition to the research and development of next-generation hardware architectures, it will be critical to revisit the development and mapping process of applications on resource-constrained devices. In particular, a key step ahead, when considering algorithmic and/or target hardware system changes, is the evaluation of code transformations and compiler optimizations that fully leverage the acceleration capabilities of the target system.

Another critical issue for companies is time-to-market [4] (see Fig. 1.3). Delays entering the market mean smaller overall sales as products have less time to benefit from the market before it starts to decline. Thus, a fast and efficient process to develop applications is one of the key factors for success in such competitive markets.

1.4 EMBEDDED SYSTEMS: PROTOTYPING AND PRODUCTION

Fig. 1.4 illustrates a design flow for embedded systems. Developing a high-performance application for an embedded platform requires developers to exploit sophisticated tool flows and to master different levels of abstraction across the various stages of application development, including deployment and maintenance.

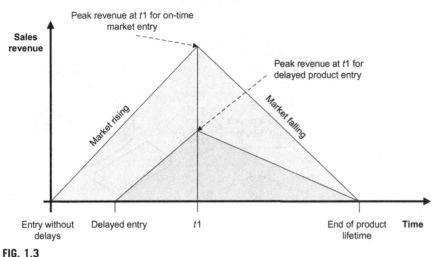

FIG. 1.3

Simplified sales model and marketing entry.

Based on Vahid F, Givargis T. Embedded system design: a unified hardware/software introduction. 1st ed. New York, NY: John Wiley & Sons, Inc.; 2001.

In our example, the development flow begins by capturing the user requirements followed by the actual development of the application. A first proof-of-concept prototype is usually validated on a desktop computer, possibly using a programming language with features that facilitate early prototyping such as MATLAB, and relying on the emulation of external interfaces (e.g., instead of using the real camera, one can use prerecorded videos or simple sequences of images stored as files). If this initial prototype does not meet its functional requirements, the developer must iterate and modify the application, possibly changing its data types (e.g., converting double to single floating-point precision), and applying code transformations and/or refactoring code to meet the desired requirements. This process is guided by developers' knowledge about the impact of these modifications on the final embedded version. Depending on the project at hand, the prototype may be developed in the same programming language used for the embedded version, but possibly using different APIs.

    The next step of the development process involves modifying the prototype code to derive an embedded code implementation. This includes using emulators, simulators, and/or virtual platforms to validate the embedded version and to optimize it if needed. At this stage, developers must consider the full set of nonfunctional requirements. It is also typical at this stage to explore and test hardware accelerators. This step partitions and maps the selected computations to available accelerators. If this validation stage is successful, the application is then deployed to the target embedded system or to a hardware system emulator, and a second stage of validation is

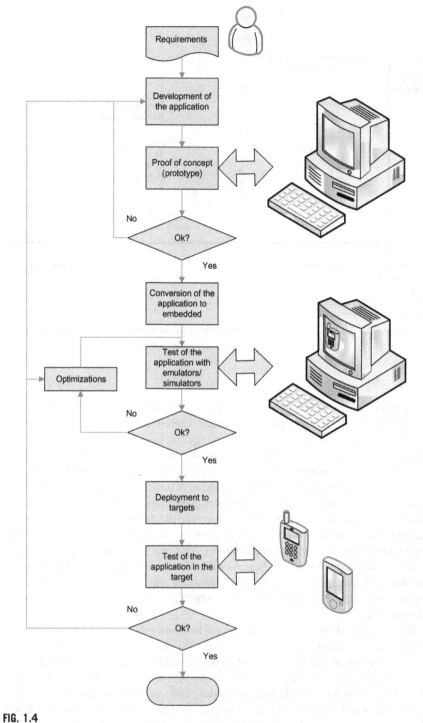

FIG. 1.4

An example of a design flow for developing an embedded application.

performed. If this second level validation is successful, then the application is ready to be deployed as a product.

Depending on the application, target system requirements and nonfunctional requirements (in some of the development stages described earlier) might be merged. One of the barriers preventing an effective integration of these development stages is the lack of interfaces between the corresponding tools to allow them to be truly interoperable. This limitation forces developers to manually relate the effects of the transformations and analyses across them, in an error-prone process.

The development and mapping of applications to high-performance embedded systems must consider a myriad of design choices. Typically, developers must analyze the application and partition its code among the most suitable system components through a process commonly known as hardware/software partitioning [5]. In addition, developers have to deal with multiple compilation tools (subchains) for targeting each specific system component. These problems are further exacerbated when dealing with FPGAs (Field-Programmable Gate Arrays), a technology for hardware acceleration and for fast prototyping as it combines the performance of custom hardware with the flexibility of software [5,6]. As embedded platforms are becoming increasingly more heterogeneous, developers must also explore code and mapping transformations specific to each architecture so that the resulting solutions meet their overall requirements.

One of the key stages of the mapping process is to profile the code to understand its behavior (see, e.g., [7]), which is commonly achieved by extensive code instrumentation and monitoring. In addition, the development of applications targeting high-performance embedded systems leads to source code transformed by the extensive use of architecture-specific transformations and/or by the use of tool-specific compilation directives. Such practices require developer expertize in order to understand when transformations may limit portability, as otherwise when the underlying architecture changes, developers may need to restart the design process. Another issue contributing to development complexity is the presence of different product lines for the same application in order to support multiple target platforms and/or multiple application scenarios.

A key aspect for enhancing performance is exploiting parallelism available in the computing platform. In this context, when improving the performance of an application, developers need to consider Amdahl's law [8,9] and its extensions to the multicore era [10,11] to guide code transformations and optimizations, as well as code partitioning and mapping.

1.5 ABOUT LARA: AN ASPECT-ORIENTED APPROACH

LARA is an aspect-oriented language able to express code transformations and mapping strategies, allowing developers to codify nonfunctional concerns in a systematic fashion, which can be subsequently applied in an automated way on their application code.

The use of Aspect-Oriented Programming (AOP) mechanisms allows LARA descriptions to be decoupled from the application code itself—an important feature to improve maintainability and program portability across target platforms. In addition, LARA descriptions can be easily composed to create increasingly sophisticated design space exploration (DSE) strategies using native LARA looping and reporting analysis constructs. In short, LARA provides a more formal vehicle to specify the strategies for the various stages of an application's design flow, in what can be seen as executable strategies.[1]

Many of the descriptions of code instrumentation and transformations in this book use the LARA language [12]. Despite the many advantages of LARA as a transformation description language, this book is not about LARA. In other texts, many if not all of the mapping techniques and code transformations used when targeting high-performance embedded systems have been described in an informal, often ad hoc fashion, using abstractions of the underlying hardware and even runtime systems. The LARA descriptions presented in this book can thus be viewed as a vehicle to help the reader to clearly and unambiguously understand the various code and data transformations used in a complex mapping process. Furthermore, LARA has been developed and validated in the context of many research projects targeting real computing systems, and supports popular languages such as C and MATLAB to target heterogeneous systems including both GPUs and FPGAs.

1.6 OBJECTIVES AND TARGET AUDIENCE

This book aims at providing Informatics Engineering, Computer Science, Computer Engineering undergraduate and graduate students, practitioners, and engineers with the knowledge to analyze and to efficiently map computations described in high-level programming languages to the architectures used in high-performance embedded computing (HPEC) domains. The required skills are transversal to various areas encompassing algorithm analysis, target architectures, compiler transformations, and optimizations. This book has also been designed to address specific trends regarding technical competences required by industry, and thus prepare computer science and informatics engineering students with the necessary skills.

This book focuses mainly on code transformations and optimizations suitable to improve performance and/or to achieve energy savings in the context of embedded computing. The topics include ways to describe computations in order for compilers

---

[1]Readers will have the opportunity to use LARA strategies with the online tools provided as part of the online materials for this book.

and mapping tools to exploit heterogeneous architectures and hardware accelerators effectively. Specifically, the book considers the support of data and task parallelism provided by multicore architectures and the use of GPUs and FPGAs for hardware acceleration (via C and OpenCL code).

In the description of the various topics, it has been our intention to focus on concepts rather than on actual implementations using current technologies to avoid making the contents of this book obsolete in the short term. Still, we provide over the various chapters "sideboxes" with specific examples to connect the concepts to current implementations or technologies. In addition, we also provide complementary online material regarding each chapter, including in many cases complete source code examples, highlighting in more depth the use of the concepts using today's technologies.

1.7 COMPLEMENTARY BIBLIOGRAPHY

Although there exists a number of technical textbooks (e.g., [4,13–15]) supporting embedded system courses, the topics covered in this book are only partially addressed by other volumes. Conversely, other texts, such as Refs. [16–18], cover complementary topics not addressed in this text.

The texts about compilation techniques for high-performance systems [14], embedded computing [19], performance tuning [20], high-performance computing [21], the AOP approach provided by LARA [22], hardware/software codesign [23], and reconfigurable computing [5,24], also address topics relevant to the topics addressed in this book and can thus serve as complementary bibliography.

Other relevant texts in the context of optimizations for high-performance computing (HPC) include the books from Crawford and Wadleigh [25], from Garg and Sharapov [26], and from Gerber et al. [27].

1.8 DEPENDENCES IN TERMS OF KNOWLEDGE

In order to follow the topics addressed in this book, readers should have basic knowledge on high-level programming, data structures and algorithms, digital systems, computer architecture, operating systems, and compilers. Fig. 1.5 illustrates the dependences between these topics in general, and high-performance embedded computing (HPEC) in particular. Topics related to parallel computing and reconfigurable computing are seen as complementary, and readers with those skills are able to work on more advanced HPEC projects and/or to focus their work on specific technologies.

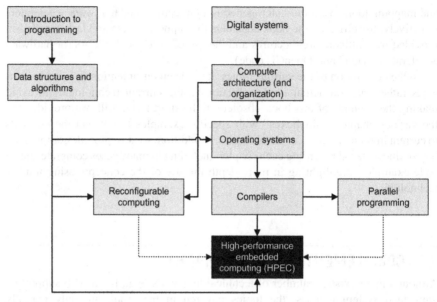

FIG. 1.5

Block diagram showing dependences between topics. Note that to simplify the interconnections we omit dependences not creating additional ordering, such as the one between Computer Architecture and HPEC.

1.9 EXAMPLES AND BENCHMARKS

While the computing industry uses commercial benchmarks such as the ones provided by EEMBC,[2] there are, however, several benchmark repositories that can be used and have been adopted by many research groups. The most used benchmarks are MiBench[3] [28], MediaBench[4] [29], PolyBench,[5] SNU-RT,[6] HPEC Challenge Benchmark Suite[7] [30], CHStone,[8] UTDSP,[9] and SD-VBS[10] [31]. All of them include the source code and input/output data.

In order to provide examples and to draw the attention of the readers to specific optimizations while illustrating their impact in terms of performance, this book

---

[2]EEMBC—The Embedded Microprocessor Benchmark Consortium, http://www.eembc.org/.
[3]MiBench version 1, http://www.eecs.umich.edu/mibench/.
[4]MediaBench II, http://euler.slu.edu/~fritts/mediabench/.
[5]PolyBench/C, http://web.cse.ohio-state.edu/~pouchet/software/polybench/.
[6]SNU Real-Time Benchmarks, http://www.cprover.org/goto-cc/examples/snu.html.
[7]Benchmarks, http://www.omgwiki.org/hpec/files/hpec-challenge/info.html.
[8]CHStone: A Suite of Benchmark Programs for C-based High-Level Synthesis, http://www.ertl.jp/chstone/.
[9]UTDSP Benchmark Suite, http://www.eecg.toronto.edu/~corinna/DSP/infrastructure/UTDSP.html.
[10]The San Diego Vision Benchmark Suite, http://parallel.ucsd.edu/vision/.

sometimes uses code kernels and/or applications from these benchmark repositories. Accompanying material provides full source code for illustrative examples, allowing readers to work with fully functional versions of the sample applications or code kernels.

1.10 BOOK ORGANIZATION

This book consists of eight chapters. Each chapter provides a selection of references we think can be used as complementary reading about specific topics. In each chapter (except this one), we include a "Further Reading" section where we give references and paths for readers interested to know more about specific topics. It is in these sections that we make the connection to research efforts and findings. In addition to the eight chapters, we include a Glossary to briefly describe relevant terms and concepts present through the book.

The eight chapters of the book are as follows:

- Chapter 1 introduces embedded systems and embedded computing in general while highlighting their importance in everyday life. We provide an overview of their main characteristics and possible external environment interfaces. In addition to introducing these topics, this chapter highlights the trends in terms of target architectures and design flows. The chapter explains the objectives of the book, its major target audience, the dependences in terms of prior knowledge, and using this book within different contexts and readers' aptitudes.

  Keywords: Embedded computing, Embedded systems, High-performance embedded computing, Embedded computing trends.

- Chapter 2 provides an overview of the main concepts and representative computer architectures for high-performance embedded computing systems. As the multicore and manycore trends are shaping the organization of computing devices on all computing domain spectrums, from high-performance computing (HPC) to embedded computing, this chapter briefly describes some of the common CPU architectures, including platforms containing multiple cores/processors. In addition, this chapter introduces heterogeneous architectures, including hardware accelerators (GPUs and FPGAs) and system-on-a-chip (SoC) reconfigurable devices. The chapter highlights the importance of the Amdahl's law and its implications when offloading computations to hardware accelerators. Lastly, this chapter describes power/energy and performance models.

  Keywords: Computer architectures, Hardware accelerators, FPGAs, GPUs, Profiling, Amdahl's law.

- Chapter 3 focuses on the need to control and guide design flows to achieve efficient application implementations. The chapter highlights the importance of starting and dealing with high abstraction levels when developing embedded computing applications. The MATLAB language is used to illustrate typical development processes, especially when high levels of abstraction are used in a first stage of development. In such cases, there is the need to translate these models to programming languages with efficient toolchain support to target common embedded computer architectures. The chapter briefly addresses the mapping problem and highlights the importance of hardware/software partitioning as a prime task to optimize computations on a heterogeneous platform consisting of hardware and software components. We motivate the need for domain-specific languages and productivity tools to deal with code maintenance complexity when targeting multiple and heterogeneous architectures. We also introduce LARA, an aspect-oriented domain-specific language used throughout the remaining chapters to describe design flow strategies and to provide executable specifications for examples requiring code instrumentation and compiler transformations.

Keywords: Models, High levels of abstraction, Prototyping, MATLAB, LARA, Optimization strategies, Hardware/software partitioning.

- Chapter 4 describes source code analysis and instrumentation techniques to uncover runtime data later used to decide about the most suitable compilation and/or execution strategy. We describe program metrics derived by static analysis and runtime profiling. This chapter introduces data dependence analysis and graph-based representations to capture both static and dynamic program information. Finally, we highlight the importance of customized profiling and present LARA examples that capture customized profiling strategies to extract complex code metrics.

Keywords: Instrumentation, Profiling, Software metrics, Code analysis, Data dependences.

- Chapter 5 describes relevant code transformations and optimizations, and how they can be used in real-life codes. We include descriptions of the various high-level code transformations and their main benefits and goals. We emphasize on the use of loop and function-based transformations for performance improvement using several illustrative examples. We include code specialization as one of the most important sources of performance improvements. In addition, the chapter describes some of the most representative transformations regarding data structures. Our goal in this chapter is to provide a comprehensive catalog of code transformations and to serve as a reference for readers and developers needing to know and apply code transformations. Finally, we include a set of LARA strategies to exemplify possible uses of LARA regarding the main topics of this chapter.

Keywords: Code transformations, Code optimizations, Loop transformations, Code refactoring.

- Chapter 6 focuses on the problem of mapping applications to CPU-based platforms, covering general code retargeting mechanisms, compiler options and phase ordering, loop vectorization, exploiting multicore/multiprocessor platforms, and cache optimizations. This chapter provides the fundamental concepts used for code targeting for shared and/or distributed memory architectures including the use of OpenMP and MPI, and thus covers important and actual topics required by programmers when developing or tuning applications for high-performance computing systems. We consider the topic of code retargeting important, as most high-level languages such as C/C++ do not have the adequate compiler support to automatically harness the full computational capacity of today's platforms.

Keywords: Loop vectorization, Targeting multicore and multiprocessor architectures, Compiler options, Compiler flags, Phase ordering, Directive-driven programming models, OpenMP, MPI.

- Chapter 7 covers code retargeting for heterogeneous platforms, including the use of directives and DSLs specific to GPUs as well as FPGA-based accelerators. This chapter highlights important aspects when mapping computations described in C/C++ programming languages to GPUs and FPGAs using OpenCL and high-level synthesis (HLS) tools, respectively. We complement this chapter by revisiting the roofline model and describing its importance when targeting heterogeneous architectures. This chapter also presents performance models and program analysis methodologies to support developers in deciding when to offload computations to GPU- and FPGA-based accelerators.

  Keywords: FPGAs, GPUs, Reconfigurable fabrics, Directive-driven programming models, High-level synthesis, Hardware compilation, Accelerator code offloading, OpenCL.

- Chapter 8 describes additional topics, such as design space exploration (DSE), hardware/software codesign, runtime adaptability, and performance/energy autotuning (offline and online). More specifically, this chapter provides a starting point for developers needing to apply these concepts, especially in the context of high-performance embedded computing. More specifically, this chapter explains how autotuning can assist developers to find the best compiler optimizations given the target objective (e.g., execution time reductions, energy savings), and how static and dynamic adaptability can be used to derive optimized code implementations. Furthermore, it covers simulated annealing, which is an important and easily implementable optimization technique that can be used in the context of DSE and offline autotuning. In addition, this chapter covers multiobjective optimizations and Pareto frontiers which we believe provides a foundation for readers and developers to deal with more complex DSE problems. Although we cannot possibly cover all of the aforementioned topics in detail due to their nature and complexity, we expect that this chapter provides a useful introduction to them, and as the final chapter to this book, that it brings interesting points of discussion on top of topics presented in previous chapters.

  Keywords: Design space exploration (DSE), Autotuning, Runtime adaptivity, Simulated annealing, Multiobjective optimization, Multicriteria optimization, Multiversioning.

1.11 INTENDED USE

This book has multiple intended uses. Readers with a solid background on computer architecture, hardware accelerators, and energy and power consumption may skip Chapter 2. Readers with an interest on code transformations, compiler optimizations, and the use of directive-driven programming models or directives to guide tools may focus on Chapters 5, 6, or 7, respectively. Chapter 8 describes advanced topics, such as design space exploration, runtime adaptivity, and autotuning, which may be of interest to readers as an introduction to those topics. Lastly, while we have used LARA specifications throughout this book, readers without a particular interest in this DSL, which is used to capture and automate strategies, can still grasp the concepts of this book by following the examples described in this language.

1.12 SUMMARY

This chapter introduced the high-performance embedded computing topics covered in this book, which places a strong emphasis on the interplay between theory and practice with real-life examples and lab experiments. This book has been designed to address competences that are becoming of paramount importance and are not commonly addressed by courses in the curricula currently offered by most Informatics Engineering, Computer Engineering, and Computer Science programs.

REFERENCES

[1] Stankovic JA, Rajkumar R. Real-time operating systems. Real-Time Syst 2004;28 (2–3):237–53.
[2] Canali C, Colajanni M, Lancellotti R. Performance evolution of mobile web-based services. IEEE Internet Comput 2009;13(2):60–8.
[3] Park Y, Park JJK, Mahlke SA. Efficient performance scaling of future CGRAs for mobile applications. In: International conference on field-programmable technology (FPT'2012), Seoul, Korea (South), December 10–12; 2012. p. 335–42.
[4] Vahid F, Givargis T. Embedded system design: a unified hardware/software introduction. 1st ed. New York, NY: John Wiley & Sons, Inc.; 2001.
[5] Hauck S, DeHon A. Reconfigurable computing: the theory and practice of FPGA-based computation. San Francisco, CA: Morgan Kaufmann Publishers Inc.; 2007. November.
[6] Cardoso JMP, Diniz P, Weinhardt M. Compiling for reconfigurable computing: a survey. ACM Comput Surv (CSUR) 2010;42(4):1–65. Article 13.
[7] Tu C-H, Hsu H-H, Chen J-H, Chen C-H, Hung S-H. Performance and power profiling for emulated android systems. ACM Trans Des Autom Electron Syst 2014;19(2) Article 10, 25 pages.
[8] Amdahl GM. Computer architecture and Amdahl's Law. Computer 2013;46(12):38–46.
[9] Amdahl GM. Validity of the single processor approach to achieving large scale computing capabilities, In: Proceedings AFIPS spring joint computer conference; 1967. p. 483–5.
[10] Hill MD, Marty MR. Amdahl's Law in the multicore era. IEEE Comput 2008;41:33–8.
[11] Cassidy AS, Andreou AG. Beyond Amdahl's Law: an objective function that links multiprocessor performance gains to delay and energy. IEEE Trans Comput 2012;61(8):1110–26.

[12] Cardoso JMP, Carvalho T, Coutinho JGF, Luk W, Nobre R, Diniz P, et al. LARA: an aspect-oriented programming language for embedded systems, In: Proceedings of the 11th annual international conference on aspect-oriented software development (AOSD'12). New York, NY: ACM; 2012. p. 179–90.

[13] Marwedel P. Embedded system design – Embedded Systems Foundations of Cyber-Physical Systems. 2nd ed. Netherlands: Springer; 2011.

[14] Wolfe M. High-performance compilers for parallel computing. 1st ed. Boston, MA: Addison-Wesley Longman Publishing Co., Inc.; 1995. June.

[15] Lee EA, Seshia SA. Introduction to embedded systems, a cyber-physical systems approach. 2nd ed. Cambridge, MA: MIT Press; 2017.

[16] Wolf M. High-performance embedded computing: applications in cyber-physical systems and mobile computing. 2nd ed. San Francisco, CA: Morgan Kaufmann; 2014. April 15.

[17] Allen R, Kennedy K. Optimizing compilers for modern architectures: a dependence-based approach. 1st ed. San Francisco, CA: Morgan Kaufmann; 2001. October 10.

[18] Cardoso JMP, Diniz PC. Compilation techniques for reconfigurable architectures. New York, NY: Springer; 2008. October.

[19] Fisher JA, Faraboschi P, Young C. Embedded computing: a VLIW approach to architecture, compilers, and tools. San Francisco, CA: Morgan Kaufmann; 2004. December.

[20] Bailey DH, Lucas RF, Williams S, editors. Performance tuning of scientific applications. Boca Raton, London, New York: Chapman & Hall/CRC Computational Science, CRC Press; 2010. November.

[21] Hager G, Wellein G. Introduction to high performance computing for scientists and engineers. 1st ed. Boca Raton, London, New York: Chapman & Hall/CRC Computational Science, CRC Press; 2010. July 2.

[22] Cardoso JMP, Diniz P, Coutinho JG, Petrov Z, editors. Compilation and synthesis for embedded reconfigurable systems: an aspect-oriented approach. 1st ed. New York, Heidelberg, Dordrecht, London: Springer; 2013. May.

[23] Schaumont P. A practical introduction to hardware/software codesign. 2nd ed. New York, Heidelberg, Dordrecht, London: Springer; 2012. December.

[24] Cardoso JMP, Huebner M, editors. Reconfigurable computing: from FPGAs to hardware/software codesign. 1st ed. New York, Heidelberg, Dordrecht, London: Springer; 2011. September.

[25] Crawford I, Wadleigh K. Software optimization for high performance computing: creating faster applications. Upper Saddle River, NJ: Prentice Hall; 2000.

[26] Garg RP, Sharapov I. Techniques for optimizing applications: high performance computing. Palo Alto, CA: Sun Microsystems Press; 2002.

[27] Gerber R, Bik AJC, Smith KB, Tian X. The software optimization cookbook: high-performance recipes for IA-32 platforms, 2nd ed. Hillsboro, OR: Intel Press; 2006, ISBN 0-9764832-1-1. Copyright © 2006 Intel Corporation. https://software.intel.com/sites/default/files/m/0/9/e/toc-swcb2.pdf.

[28] Guthaus MR, Ringenberg JS, Ernst D, Austin TM, Mudge T, Brown RB. MiBench: a free, commercially representative embedded benchmark suite. In: Proc. of the IEEE international workshop on workload characterization, (WWC'01). Washington, DC: IEEE Computer Society; 2001. p. 3–14.

[29] Lee C, Potkonjak M, Mangione-Smith WH. MediaBench: a tool for evaluating and synthesizing multimedia and communications systems. In: Proceedings of the 30th annual ACM/IEEE international symposium on microarchitecture (MICRO'30). Washington, DC: IEEE Computer Society; 1997. p. 330–5.

[30] Haney R, Meuse T, Kepner J, Lebak J. The HPEC challenge benchmark suite. In: Proc. of the ninth annual high-performance embedded computing workshop (HPEC'2005), Lexington, MA, USA, September; 2005.

[31] Venkata SK, Ahn I, Jeon D, Gupta A, Louie C, Garcia S, et al. SD-VBS: the San Diego vision benchmark suite. In: Proc. IEEE intl. symp. on workload characterization (IISWC'09). Washington, DC: IEEE Computer Society; 2009. p. 55–64.

High-performance embedded computing

2

2.1 INTRODUCTION

Embedded systems are very diverse and can be organized in a myriad of ways. They can combine microprocessors and/or microcontrollers with other computing devices, such as application-specific processors (ASIPs), digital-signal processors (DSPs), and reconfigurable devices (e.g., FPGAs [1,2] and coarse-grained reconfigurable arrays—CGRAs—like TRIPS [3]), often in the form of a System-on-a-Chip (SoC). In the realm of embedded systems, and more recently in the context of scientific computing (see, e.g., [4]), the use of hardware accelerators [5] has been recognized as an efficient way to meet the required performance levels and/or energy savings (e.g., to extend battery life). Although the focus of this book is not on GPU computing (see, e.g., [6–8]), the use of GPUs is also addressed as one possible hardware accelerator in high-performance embedded systems.

Fig. 2.1 presents the main drivers that helped improve the performance of computing systems over the last three decades as well as the trends for the upcoming years. Clearly, frequency scaling was the main driver for improving performance until the mid-2000s. Since then, more complex technologies have been employed to increase the computational capacity of computing platforms, including more aggressive pipelining execution, superscalar execution, multicore architectures, single instruction, multiple data (SIMD) support, fused multiply-add (FMA) units, and chip multiprocessors (CMPs). The combination of hardware accelerators with many-core architectures is currently an important source of performance gains for emerging high-performance heterogeneous architectures accelerators, and we believe will continue to be prominent in the upcoming years.

In general, when requirements for a given application and target embedded computing system, such as execution time, power dissipation, energy consumption, and memory bandwidth, are not met, engineers and developers often resort to one or more of the following techniques:

- Perform code optimizations to reduce the number of executed instructions or replace expensive instructions with instructions that use fewer resources while producing the same results.
- Parallelize sections of code by taking advantage of the lack of control and data dependences, thus enabling the parallel execution of instructions by multiple functional units or multiple processor units.

Embedded Computing for High Performance. http://dx.doi.org/10.1016/B978-0-12-804189-5.00002-8

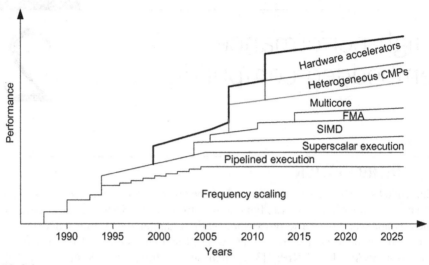

FIG. 2.1

Indicative computer architecture trends in terms of performance enhancements.

Based on Lecture materials for "CSE 6230—High Performance Computing: Tools and Applications" course (Fall 2013): "Performance Tuning for CPU: SIMD Optimization", by Marat Dukhan, Georgia Institute of Technology, United States.

- Find the best trade-off between accuracy and other nonfunctional requirements by reducing computation requirements of specific calculations while meeting numerical accuracy requirements, for example.
- Migrate (also known as offloading) sections of the code from the host CPU to one or more hardware accelerators (e.g., GPUs, FPGAs) to meet nonfunctional requirements, such as performance and energy efficiency.

In some instances, developers may simply consider the use of a more suitable hardware platform, which includes microprocessors, peripherals, and accelerators with more powerful computing capabilities.

2.2 TARGET ARCHITECTURES

A recent trend in embedded computing platforms involves the inclusion of multiple computing components that are either homogeneous or heterogeneous, and are connected using traditional bus systems or using more advanced communication systems based on networking such as those found in network-on-a-chip (NoC) devices. Typically, these architectures include multiple distributed memories, in addition to shared memories, at distinct levels of the memory hierarchy and with different address space views.

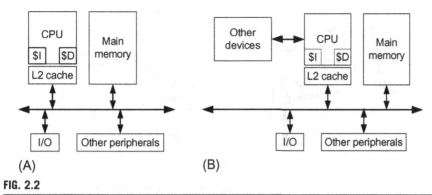

FIG. 2.2

Block diagram of typical single CPU/single core architectures: (A) with all devices connected through a system bus; (B) with the possibility to have devices connected to the CPU using direct channels.

The simplest embedded computing system consists of a single CPU/core with a system bus that connects all the system devices, from I/O peripherals to memories, as illustrated by the block diagram in Fig. 2.2A. In some cases, computing devices (e.g., the CPU) have direct access to other components using point-to-point channels (Fig. 2.2B). In other cases, all the components are accessed using a memory-mapped addressing scheme where each component is selected and assigned to a specific region of the global address space.

In most high-performance systems, the CPU uses a hierarchical memory cache architecture. In such systems, the first level of memory has separate instruction and data caches [9]. For instance, in the system depicted in Fig. 2.2, the memory is organized as a level one (L1) instruction ($I) and data ($D) caches, a second level of cache (L2) and the main memory. However, there are cases, such as low-performance and safety-critical systems, where the system only supports one level of memory. This is because most safety-critical systems with stringent real-time requirements may not cope with the variability of the execution time that cache memories introduce. In particular, a system may not meet its real-time requirement as dictated by the worst-case execution time (WCET) when using cache memories, and therefore these systems may not include them.

2.2.1 HARDWARE ACCELERATORS AS COPROCESSORS

Simple embedded systems, such as the ones depicted in Fig. 2.2, can be extended by connecting the host CPU to coprocessors acting as hardware accelerators. One type of hardware accelerator is the FPGA, which is a reprogrammable silicon chip that can be customized to realize any digital circuit. Other examples of hardware accelerators include GPUs and network coprocessors (i.e., coprocessors specially devoted to the network interface and communication).

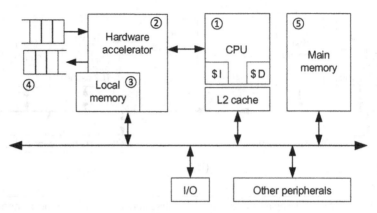

FIG. 2.3

Block diagram of a typical single CPU/single core architecture extended with hardware accelerators.

Fig. 2.3 presents a block diagram of an architecture consisting of a CPU (①) and a hardware accelerator (②). Depending on the complexity of the hardware accelerator and how it is connected to the CPU (e.g., tightly or loosely coupled), the hardware accelerator may include local memories (③: on-chip and/or external, but directly connected to the hardware accelerator). The presence of local memories, tightly coupled with the accelerator, allows local data and intermediate results to be stored, which is an important architectural feature for supporting data-intensive applications.

At a programmatic level, an important aspect to consider when using hardware accelerators is the data movement cost between the accelerator and the host processor. Often, the accelerator only has control of its local storage, and data communication between the host processor and the accelerator is accomplished explicitly via data messaging. Despite its conceptual simplicity, this organization imposes a significant communication overhead if the CPU must be involved in transferring data from the main memory (⑤) to the accelerator (②). An alternative arrangement that incurs in a much lower communication overhead relies on the use of direct memory access (DMA), as the accelerator can autonomously access data in the main memory (②↔⑤). In this case, only the data location needs to be communicated between the host CPU and the accelerator (①↔②). In addition, and depending on the system-level connectivity of the input/output devices, the hardware accelerator may be directly connected to input/output channels (④↔②, e.g., using FIFOs) thereby bypassing the host CPU altogether.

Hardware accelerators are also used in desktops and servers, and are commonly connected to the CPU via a PCI-express (PCIe) bus. Although PCIe provides a dedicated connection, it still imposes a high data transfer latency and exhibits low throughput. Thus, only computationally intensive regions of code where the ratio

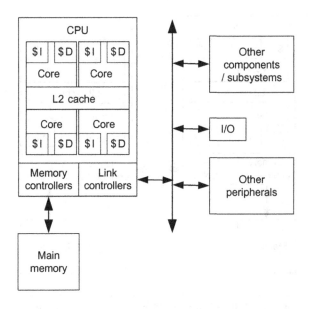

FIG. 2.4

Block diagram of a typical multicore architecture (quad-core CPU).

of computational effort to data transferred is high may profit from offloading them to hardware accelerators.

2.2.2 MULTIPROCESSOR AND MULTICORE ARCHITECTURES

Modern microprocessors are based on multicore architectures consisting of a number of processing cores. Typically, each core has its own instruction and data memories (L1 caches) and all cores share a second level (L2) on-chip cache. Fig. 2.4 presents a block diagram of a typical multicore (a quad-core in this case) CPU computing system where all cores share an L2 cache. The CPU is also connected to an external memory and includes link controllers to access external system components. There are, however, multicore architectures where one L2 cache is shared by a subset of cores (e.g., each L2 cache is shared by two cores in a quad-core, or is shared by four cores in an octa-core CPU). This is common in computing systems with additional memory levels. The external memories are often grouped in multiple levels and use different storage technologies. Typically, the first level is organized using SRAM devices, whereas the second level uses DDRAMs.

COMBINING CPUs WITH FPGA-BASED ACCELERATORS

Several platforms provide FPGA-based hardware extensions to commodity CPUs. Examples include the Intel QuickAssist QPI-FPGA [10], IBM Netezza [11], CAPI [12], and Xilinx Zynq [13]. Other platforms, such as Riffa [14], focus on vendor-independent support by providing an integration framework to interface FPGA-based accelerators with the CPU system bus using the PCI Express (PCIe) links.

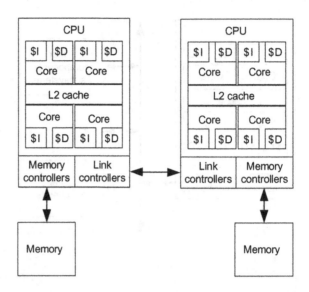

FIG. 2.5

Block diagram of a typical multiple CPU/multiple cores architecture (with two quad-core CPUs) using a distributed memory organization.

Other system components, such as GPIO, UART, USB interface, PCIe, network coprocessor, and power manager, are connected via a fast link possibly being memory mapped. In other architectures, however, the CPU connects to these subsystems (including memory) exclusively using fast links and/or switch fabrics (e.g., via a partial crossbar), thus providing point-to-point communication channels between the architecture components.

In computing systems requiring higher performance demands, it is common to include more than one multicore CPU (e.g., with all CPUs integrated as a CMP[1]). Figs. 2.5 and 2.6 illustrate two possible organizations of CMPs, one using a distributed memory organization (Fig. 2.5) and another one using a shared memory organization (Fig. 2.6).

Fig. 2.5 presents an example of a nonuniform memory access architecture (NUMA). In such systems, the distributed memories are viewed as one combined memory by all CPUs; however, access times and throughputs differ depending on the location of the memory and the CPU. For instance, the memory accesses of the CPU located at the opposite side of where the target memory is located incurs in a larger latency than the accesses to a nearby memory.

CPUs also provide parallel execution support for multiple threads per core. Systems with more than one multicore CPU have the potential to have many concurrently executing threads, thus supporting multithreaded applications.

---

[1]CMP: chip multiprocessor.

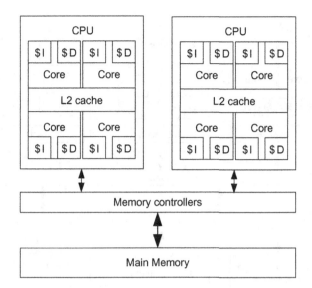

FIG. 2.6

Block diagram of a typical multiple CPU/multiple cores architecture (with two quad-core CPUs) using a shared memory organization.

MOST INTERCONNECTION OF THE CPUs AND OTHER COMPONENTS

The type of interconnections used in a target architecture depends on the level of performance required and the platform vendor.

An example of a switch fabric is the TeraNet,[a] and an example of a fast link is HyperLink.[a] They are both used in some ARM-based SoCs proposed by Texas Instruments Inc,[a] providing efficient interconnections of the subsystems to the ARM multicore CPUs and to the external accelerators.

In Intel-based computing systems, the memory subsystem is usually connected via Intel Scalable Memory Interfaces (SMI) provided by the integrated memory controllers in the CPU. They also include a fast link connecting other subsystems to the CPU using the Intel QuickPath Interconnect (QPI),[b] a point-to-point interconnect technology. AMD provides the HyperTransport[c] technology for point-to-point links.

[a]Texas Instruments Inc. AM5K2E0x multicore ARM KeyStone II system-on-chip (SoC). SPRS864D—November 2012—revised March 2015.
[b]Intel Corp. An introduction to the Intel QuickPath interconnect. January 30, 2009.
[c]API networks accelerates use of hypertransport technology with launch of industry's first hypertransport technology-to-PCI bridge chip. (Press release). HyperTransport Consortium. 2001-04-02.

2.2.3 HETEROGENEOUS MULTIPROCESSOR/MULTICORE ARCHITECTURES

A current trend in computing organization is the Heterogeneous System-on-a-Chip (SoC) with multiple independent and distinct CPUs, where each processor has an arbitrary number of cores and other computing devices such as hardware accelerators. Fig. 2.7 shows a block diagram of an architecture with two distinct CPUs

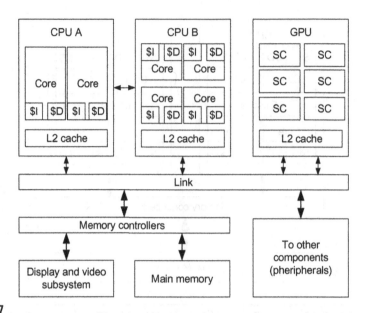

FIG. 2.7

Block diagram of a typical heterogeneous architecture.

(one with two cores and the other with four cores) and a GPU. This computer organization is similar to the one used in mobile devices such as smartphones (see Heterogeneous SoCs).

2.2.4 OpenCL PLATFORM MODEL

Currently, parallel computing architectural models are being extensively used in part due to the existence of hardware implementations supporting them. One well-known example is the computing model proposed in the context of OpenCL (Open Computing Language) [15,16] and instances of the model are herein referred as OpenCL computing devices. This model is supported by a wide range of heterogeneous architectures, including multicore CPUs, and hardware accelerators such as GPUs and FPGAs. In the OpenCL approach, a program consists of two parts: the host program running on the CPU, and a set of kernels running on OpenCL-capable computing devices acting as coprocessors. Chapter 7 provides details about the OpenCL language and tools.

HETEROGENEOUS SoCs

An example of a SoC with organization similar to the one presented in Fig. 2.7 is the Exynos 7 Hexa 7650 (Exynos 7650)[a] designed and manufactured by Samsung Electronics for some of the Samsung smartphones. The SoC includes one 1.8 GHz ARMV8A dual-core Cortex-A72, one 1.3 GHz ARMV8 quad-core Cortex-A53 (and with seamless support of 32-bit and 64-bit instruction sets), and one Mali-T860MP3 GPU.

[a]https://en.wikipedia.org/wiki/Exynos.

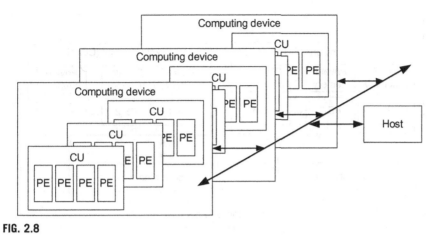

FIG. 2.8

High-level block diagram of the OpenCL platform model.

Fig. 2.8 shows a high-level block diagram of a typical OpenCL platform which may include one or more computing devices. Each device includes several Computing Units (CUs) and each Computing Unit consists of several Processing Elements (PEs). A single kernel can execute in one or more PEs in parallel within the same CU or in multiple CUs. The computing devices (e.g., a GPU board with support to OpenCL) are connected to a host CPU via a shared bus.

PEs are typically SIMD units responsible for executing sequences of instructions without conditional control flow. In some cases, control flow can be supported by applying if-conversion and/or by executing both branches and then selecting the required results by multiplexing the values provided by the different branches.

As depicted in Fig. 2.9, an OpenCL computing device may also include a hierarchical memory organization consisting of private memories (registers) tightly coupled to the PEs (one memory per PE), a local memory per CU, a global read-only memory that can be written by the host CPU but only read by the computing device, and a global memory read/written by the computing device and by the host CPU. Each CU's local memory is shared by all the CU's PEs.

The OpenCL kernels execute through parallel work items (each one with an associated ID and seen as hardware threads) and the work items define groups (known as work groups). Each work group executes on a CU and its associated work items execute on its PEs.

The OpenCL platform is very suitable for computations structured in SIMT (Single Instruction, Multiple Thread) as is the case when targeting GPUs. Recently, the main FPGA vendors have adhered to the OpenCL model and provide toolchain support to map the model to the FPGA resources (i.e., making FPGAs OpenCL computing devices).

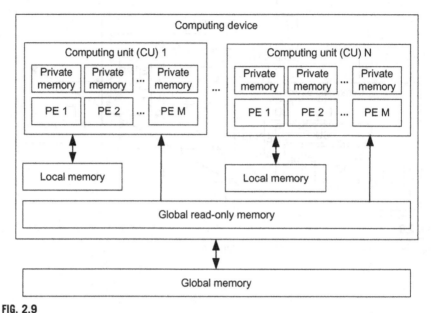

FIG. 2.9

Block diagram of the OpenCL model [15].

2.3 CORE-BASED ARCHITECTURAL ENHANCEMENTS

In addition to the recent multicore trend, CPU cores have also been enhanced to further support parallelism and specific type of computations. This includes the use of SIMD, FMA units, and support for multithreading.

2.3.1 SINGLE INSTRUCTION, MULTIPLE DATA UNITS

Single Instruction, Multiple Data (SIMD) units refer to hardware components that perform the same operation on multiple data operands concurrently. Typically, a SIMD unit receives as input two vectors (each one with a set of operands), performs the same operation on both sets of operands (one operand from each vector), and outputs a vector with the results. Fig. 2.10 illustrates a simple example of a SIMD unit executing four operations in parallel (as represented as follows).

```
C[3:0] = A[3:0] op1 B[3:0];
```

SIMD UNITS

SIMD units have been available in Intel microprocessors since the advent of the MMX, SSE (Streaming SIMD Extensions), and AVX (Advanced Vector Extensions) ISA extensions [17]. The MMX extensions were initially included to speed up the performance of multimedia applications and other application domains requiring image and signal processing.

ARM has also introduced SIMD extensions to ARM-Cortex architectures with their NEON technology. The NEON SIMD unit is 128-bit wide and includes 16 128-bit registers that can be used as 32 64-bit registers. These registers can be thought as vectors of elements of the same data type, being the data types signed/unsigned 8, 16, 32, 64-bit, and single precision floating point. The following example shows how a vector statement involving single-precision floating-point data can be implemented in a Cortex-A9 using the SIMD unit.

```
A[3:0] = B[3:0] x C[3:0];
// assembly:
vldmia.32   r0!, {s15}
vldmia.32   r1!, {s14}
vmul.f32    s15, s15, s14
vstmia.32   r2!, {s15}
```

Typically, the operations in SIMD units include basic arithmetic operations (such as addition, subtraction, multiplication, negation) and other operations such as absolute (abs) and square root (sqrt).

Another factor contributing to the increased performance of SIMD units is the fact that multiple data items can be simultaneously loaded/stored from/to memory exploiting the full width of the memory data bus. Fig. 2.11 depicts a simple illustrative example using SIMD units and vector processing. As can be seen in Fig. 2.11C, the code using SIMD units executes ¼ of the instructions in ¼ of the clock cycles when compared with code executing without SIMD units (Fig. 2.11B).

To exploit SIMD units, it is very important to be able to combine multiple load or store accesses in a single SIMD instruction. This can be achieved when using contiguous memory accesses, e.g., in the presence of unit stride accesses, and when array elements are aligned. In the previous example, arrays *A*, *B*, and *C* are accessed with unit stride and we assume they are aligned (i.e., the base address of each element

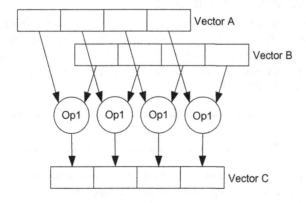

FIG. 2.10

Example of a SIMD unit, executing in this example the same four operations (w/different operands) in parallel.

```
A[i]   = B[i]+C[i];          t1 = LD B, i          v1 = LD B, i, 4
A[i+1] = B[i+1]+C[i+1];      t2 = LD C, i          v2 = LD C, i, 4
A[i+2] = B[i+2]+C[i+2];      t3 = t1 + t2          v3 = v1 + v2, 4
A[i+3] = B[i+3]+C[i+3];      ST A, i, t3           ST A, i, 4, v3
                             t1 = LD B, i+1
                             t2 = LD C, i+1
                             t3 = t1 + t2
                             ST A, i+1, t3
                             t1 = LD B, i+2
                             t2 = LD C, i+2
                             t3 = t1 + t2
                             ST A, i+2, t3
                             t1 = LD B, i+3
                             t2 = LD C, i+3
                             t3 = t1 + t2
                             ST A, i+3, t3
```

(A)   (B)   (C)

FIG. 2.11

Example of the use of a SIMD unit: (A) simple segment of code; (B) symbolic assembly without using SIMD support; (C) symbolic assembly considering SIMD support.

starts in the beginning of a word, i.e., the memory address is a multiple of 4 in a byte-addressable 32-bit machine). When dealing with nonaligned arrays inside loops, it is common to align the addresses (and thus enable the use of SIMD instructions) by applying loop peeling transformations (see Chapter 5). In addition, and to match the array dimensions to the SIMD vector lengths, compilers often apply partial loop unrolling. We provide more details about how to exploit vectorization in high-level descriptions in Chapter 6.

2.3.2 FUSED MULTIPLY-ADD UNITS

Fused Multiply-Add (FMA) units perform fused operations such as multiply-add and multiply-subtract. The main idea is to provide a CPU instruction that can perform operations with three input operands and an output result. Fig. 2.12 shows an example of an FMA unit. In this example, we consider the support of instructions $D = A*B + C$ and $D = A*B - C$.

```
D[3:0] = A[3:0] * B[3:0] + C[3:0];

D[3:0] = A[3:0] * B[3:0] - C[3:0];
```

It is also common for FMA units to support single, double precision floating-point and integer operations, and depending on the data types, to include a rounding stage following the last operation (single rounding step as opposed to two rounding steps) when not using fused operations.

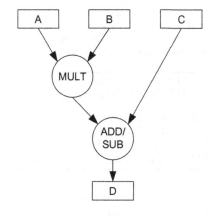

FIG. 2.12

An example of an FMA unit.

Depending on the processor architecture, the input/output of the FMA units might be associated with four distinct registers or three distinct registers, with one register shared between the result and one of the input operands of the FMA unit. The latter is depicted in the FMA unit in Fig. 2.12 when D is one of A, B, or C (depending of the FMA instruction).

In addition to the SIMD hardware support, some recent processor architectures not only include FMA units but also FMA vector operations (an example is the Intel 64 and IA-32 Architectures [18] and the ARM Cortex). In this case, a single SIMD instruction may perform the same fused operation over multiple data inputs, as represented by the following vector forms for $D = A*B + C$ and $D = A*B - C$:

FMA UNITS

The FMA units recently included in Intel microprocessors are able to perform fused operations such as multiply-add, multiply-subtract, multiply add/subtract interleave, signed-reversed multiply on multiply-add and on multiply-subtract. These recent FMA extensions [18] provide 36 256-bit floating-point instructions to compute on 256-bit vectors, and additional 128-bit and scalar FMA instructions.

There are two types of FMA instructions: FMA3 and FMA4. An FMA3 instruction supports three input operands (i.e., three registers), and its result must be stored in one of the input registers. An FMA4 instruction, on the other hand, supports three input operands with the result stored in a dedicated output register. For instance, the Intel FMA instruction VFMADD213PS (FMA3) computes $\$0 = \$1 \times \$0 + \$2$ while the instruction VFMADDPS (FMA4) is able to compute $\$0 = \$1 \times \$2 + \$3$. Most recent processors implement FMA instructions using the FMA3 type.

High-performance ARM microprocessors also include FMA support with the Vector Floating Point (VFP) unit [19]. The following example shows how two vector statements involving single-precision floating-point data and a temporary vector E (not live after these two statements) can be implemented in a Cortex-A9 using fused operations and SIMD.

```
E[3:0] = B[3:0] x C[3:0];
D[3:0] = E[3:0] + C[3:0];
// assembly:
vldmia.32   r0!, {s13}
vldmia.32   r1!, {s14}
vmla.f32    s15, s13, s14
vstmia.32   r2!, {s15}
```

It is possible that the numerical results of FMA instructions differ from the results using non-FMA instructions due to the different numerical rounding schemes used in intermediate values. For instance, the floating-point expression d=a*b+c; implies in the case of an FMA instruction that the multiplication a*b is performed with higher precision, and the result of the addition is rounded to produce the desired floating-point precision (i.e., the precision associated to the floating-point type of d). This computation is performed differently when using non-FMA instructions, which would first compute t=a*b with the same floating-point type for t, a, and b, and then compute d=t+c. In this case, the use of an FMA instruction may produce results with a higher accuracy than the corresponding non-FMA instructions.

2.3.3 MULTITHREADING SUPPORT

Modern microprocessors support simultaneous multithreading (SMT) by providing multiple cores and by duplicating hardware in a single core to allow native support of parallel thread execution. The execution of multiple threads within the same core is realized by time multiplexing its hardware resources and by fast context switching. The Intel Hyper-Threading[2] is an example of such technology, which efficiently supports the balanced execution of two threads on the same core. Processors without multithreading, on the other hand, execute threads sequentially without interleaving their execution. Chapter 6 (Section 6.5) explains how to exploit multithreading using OpenMP.

2.4 COMMON HARDWARE ACCELERATORS

Common hardware accelerators come in many forms, from the fully customizable ASIC designed for a specific function (e.g., a floating-point unit) to the more flexible graphics processing unit (GPU) and the highly programmable field programmable

---

[2]www.intel.com/content/www/us/en/architecture-and-technology/hyper-threading/hyper-threading-technology.html.

gate array (FPGA). These devices require different programming models and have distinct system-level interfaces which, not surprisingly, exhibit different trade-offs between generality of use, performance, or energy. In the following subsections, we focus on GPU- and FPGA-based hardware accelerators.

2.4.1 GPU ACCELERATORS

Originally used exclusively for the acceleration of graphical computation (e.g., shading), graphics processing units (GPUs) have evolved in terms of flexibility and programmability to support many other compute-intensive application domains, such as scientific and engineering applications. Internally, GPUs consist of many lightweight cores (sometimes referred as *shader* cores) and on-chip memories which provide native support for high degrees of parallelism. Hence, the single program, multiple data (SPMD) paradigm is often used to program GPUs.

For embedded devices, GPUs have a relatively simple organization as illustrated by the example in Fig. 2.13, whereas for high-end computing a typical internal organization is depicted in Fig. 2.14. Naturally, the GPU used for embedded applications illustrated in Fig. 2.14 has a relatively "flat" hierarchical organization with multiple GPU cores sharing their access to an internal memory or L2 cache. Conversely, high-end GPUs have a much more complex internal architecture where cores are organized hierarchically in clusters, each of which have local nonshared and shared resources, such as for example, constant caches and L1 caches as illustrated in Fig. 2.14. Regarding their intended target applications, the diversity of the embedded domains has led to a greater diversity of embedded GPU configurations with varying characteristics (e.g., size of caches, number of *shader* cores, number of ALUs per *shader* core). On the other hand, high-end GPUs exhibit less architectural diversity as they are mostly designed to serve as hardware accelerators, providing architectures with many cores and vast on-chip memory resources.

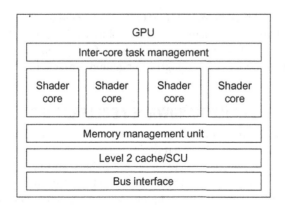

FIG. 2.13

Block diagram of a GPU for embedded devices (in this case representing an ARM Mali high-performance GPU).

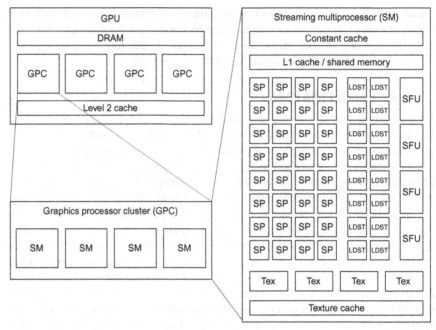

FIG. 2.14

Block diagram of a high-end GPU-based accelerator (in this case representing an NVIDIA Fermi GPU). SP identifies a stream processor, LDST identifies a load/store unit, SFU identifies a special function unit, and Tex identifies a Tex unit.

It should be clear that the earlier two GPU organizations exhibit very different performance and energy characteristics. For mobile devices, the GPU is primarily designed to operate with very low power, whereas for high-end scientific and engineering computing the focus is on high computation throughput.

2.4.2 RECONFIGURABLE HARDWARE ACCELERATORS

Given the ever-present trade-off between customization (and hence performance and energy efficiency) and generality (and thus programmability), reconfigurable hardware has been gaining considerable attention as a viable platform for hardware acceleration. Reconfigurable devices can be tailored (even dynamically—at runtime) to fit the needs of specific computations, morphing into a hardware organization that can be as efficient as a custom architecture. Due to their growing internal capacity (in terms of available hardware resources), reconfigurable devices (most notably FPGAs) have been extensively used as hardware accelerators in embedded systems.

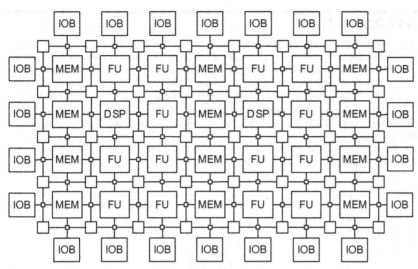

FIG. 2.15

Simplified block diagram of a typical reconfigurable fabric.

Fig. 2.15 illustrates the organization of a typical reconfigurable fabric. It consists of configurable logic blocks (CLBs), input/output blocks (IOBs), digital signal processing (DSP) components, block RAMs (BRAMs), and interconnect resources (including switch boxes). The extreme flexibility of configurable (and reconfigurable) fabric lies in the ability to use its components to build customized hardware, including customizable memories (e.g., both in terms of number of ports and size), customizable datapaths, and control units. With such configurable fabric, developers can thus implement hardware designs that match the characteristics of the computations at hand rather than reorganizing the software code of their application to suit a specific computing architecture. The on-chip memory components (BRAMs or distributed memories) can be grouped to implement large memories and/or memories with more access ports than the two access ports provided by default. This is an important feature as memory components can be customized as needed by the application.

More specifically, reconfigurable architectures allow hardware customization by providing hardware structures to implement functions with an arbitrary number of input bits; bit-level registers; bit-level interconnect resources; resource configuration to support shift registers, FIFOs, and distributed memories; and high-performance built-in arithmetic and memory components that can be configured, for instance, to implement mathematical expressions (e.g., similarly to FMA units) and to support local storage.

FPGA DSP UNITS

An example of built-in components is the XtremeDSP DSP48 slices provided by Xilinx FPGAs (see an example in the following figure). These DSP48 slices can implement functions such as multiply, multiply accumulate (MACC), multiply add/sub, three-input add, barrel shift, wide-bus multiplexing, magnitude comparator, bit-wise logic functions, pattern detect, and wide counter. The DSP48 slices included in high-end FPGAs include logical functions as ALU operations, a 3- or 4-input 48 bit adder, and a 25 or 27 × 18 bit multiplier. The number of DSP slices depends on the FPGA model, but current models provide from about 1,000 to 10,000 DSP slices.

Below we present an FPGA DSP slice showing its basic components: (Xilinx UltraScale DSP48E2, From: Xilinx Inc. UltraScale architecture DSP slice. User Guide, UG579 (v1.3) November 24, 2015.):

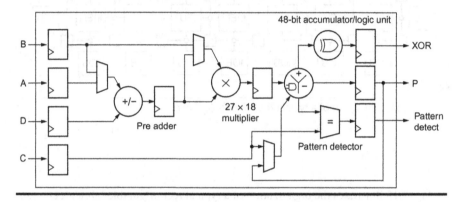

All these hardware resources allow the implementation of sophisticated hardware accelerators, possibly including one or more computing engines, interconnected by the most suitable communication structure (e.g., RAM, FIFO), and with the possibility to natively support data streaming computations. As an illustrative example, Fig. 2.16 depicts a hardware accelerator implemented on a reconfigurable fabric (such as an FPGA[3]), which consists of two computing engines, on-chip RAMs and FIFOs. These customized hardware resources enable the implementation of architectures with significant performance improvements even at low clock frequencies and with high energy efficiency.

The extreme flexibility of reconfigurable hardware, such as FPGAs, however, comes at a cost. First, they are not as computationally dense internally in terms of transistor devices and are thus less "space efficient" when compared to its ASIC or GPU counterparts. Second, and more importantly, due to the lack of a "fixed structure," they require the use of hardware synthesis tools to derive a configuration

---

[3]This "emulation" of a coarse grain architecture over a fine-grained reconfigurable fabric, such as the one offered by existing FPGA devices, is often referred to as an "overlay" architecture as described next.

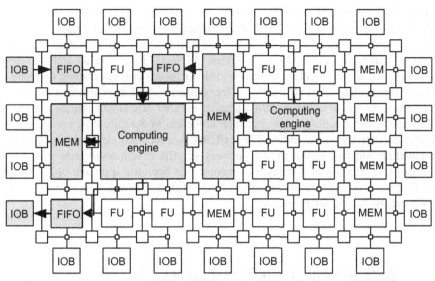

FIG. 2.16

Block diagram of an example of a hardware accelerator implemented in a reconfigurable fabric (i.e., by reconfigurable hardware).

file that defines the actual architecture logic. As a result, reconfigurable hardware accelerators impose an additional burden to the programmer, often requiring the learning of hardware-oriented programming languages and the mastering of low-level hardware details about their physical architecture. Despite these perceived difficulties, recent advances in high-level synthesis (term used to identify compilers that generate a configuration file from a high-level program description) have provided more efficient methods for mapping C and/or OpenCL descriptions to hardware. FPGA vendors also provide integrated design environments (IDEs) which can increase programming productivity by offering a sophisticated set of tools.

The FPGA designs obtained by synthesizing OpenCL code may also exploit the customization features inherent in reconfigurable hardware. Examples include the customized hardware communication mechanisms between computing units (CUs) of the OpenCL model and the use of specialized CUs depending on the data types and operations at hand. Another important feature, when in the presence of SoC devices composed of a CPU and reconfigurable hardware, is the possibility of the hardware accelerator to include direct access to the main memory and to shared data, which might have a significant performance impact as the communication using the CPU is simply avoided.

An alternative approach to realize reconfigurable hardware accelerators is the use of overlay architectures. In this case, reconfigurable hardware resources are used to implement architectures that do not directly result from hardware synthesis over the native FPGA fabric. Examples of overlay architectures include coarse-grained reconfigurable arrays (CGRAs), which typically consist of an array of ALUs (word-length width), memories, and interconnect resources each of which is synthesized using the native FPGA resources. As such, these overlay architectures provide a higher architectural abstraction that exposes coarser-grained elements. This higher architectural abstraction offers shorter compilation times, as the mapping problem has to contend with a smaller number of coarser-grained compute units and simpler control logic, but such reduction in compile time comes at the cost of customization flexibility. These CGRAs are typically designed for specific application domains and/or implement very specific execution models (e.g., systolic arrays). The use of overlay architectures has been the approach of choice of the Convey computer platforms with its Vector Coprocessors [20] which are especially suited for vector processing.

2.4.3 SoCs WITH RECONFIGURABLE HARDWARE

Recent commercial SoCs also include reconfigurable hardware fabrics (i.e., die areas with reconfigurable logic), which are able to implement custom hardware accelerators and/or other system functions as is the example of the Xilinx Zynq device [21,13]. Fig. 2.17 presents the block diagram of a Zynq device which includes a dual-core ARM CPU, on-chip memory, peripherals, reconfigurable hardware, transceivers, I/Os, ADCs, and memory controllers. These devices allow tightly hardware/software solutions in a single chip, and are examples of the need to apply hardware/software codesign approaches (see Chapter 8) and hardware/software partitioning. In this case, the developer needs to identify the components of the application that may run on the CPU (i.e., as a software component) and in the reconfigurable hardware (i.e., as a hardware component and/or as processor softcore). The extensive progress in high-level compilation and hardware synthesis tools for reconfigurable architectures substantially simplifies the development of embedded applications targeting these systems and shortens the time to market of these applications.

In these SoCs, the reconfigurable hardware resources can be used to implement custom hardware accelerators (i.e., hardware accelerators specifically designed to execute part of the application), domain-specific hardware accelerators (i.e., hardware accelerators with possibility to be used by different applications and/or sections of the application due to their programmability support), and even architectures consisting of multiple processors implemented using softcore CPUs (i.e., a CPU implemented using the reconfigurable hardware resources, as opposed to a hardcore CPU which is implemented at fabrication time). The recent increases in device capacity have even enabled these SoCs to morph into MPSoCs (Multiprocessor SoCs) and recent Xilinx Zynq devices, such as the Zynq UltraScale+ [21], even include a GPU core coupled with the CPU.

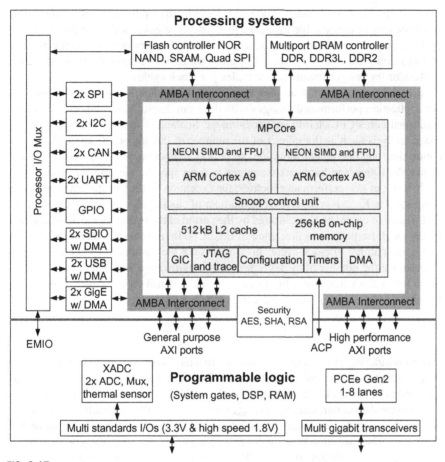

FIG. 2.17

Block diagram of the Zynq-7000 device [21]: an example of a SoC with reconfigurable hardware.

2.5 PERFORMANCE

In the embedded systems domain, an important challenge for developers is to meet nonfunctional requirements, such as execution time, memory capacity, and energy consumption. In this context, a developer must consider and then evaluate different solutions to optimize the performance of a system. As part of this evaluation, it is important for developers to identify the most suitable performance metrics to guide this process.

The performance of an application is defined as the arithmetic inverse of the application's execution time. Other common metrics involve the identification of the number of clock cycles used to execute a function, a specific code section, or the entire application. Additionally, metrics can be driven by the application's non-functional requirements, for instance: *task latency* measures the number of clock cycles required to perform a specific task, and *task throughput* measures the number of tasks completed per time unit. Common measures of throughput also include packets or frames per second and samples per clock cycle.

Scalability is also often an important design consideration as it highlights how the application performance changes with different dataset sizes and/or when using additional cores/CPUs/hardware accelerators. Scalability drives common resource usage analysis such as the impact of the number of threads on the application execution time and energy consumption, and is key to understanding the required level of parallelization and hardware resources to meet specific performance goals.

In terms of raw performance metrics, the execution time of an application or task, designated as T_{exec}, is computed as the number of clock cycles the hardware (e.g., the CPU) takes to complete it, multiplied by the period of the operating clock (or divided by the clock frequency) as presented in Eq. (2.1). In most cases, when dealing with CPUs, the number of clock cycles measured is not the number of CPU clock cycles elapsed, but the number of cycles reported by a hardware timer, which executes at a much lower clock frequency. In this case, Eq. (2.1) is still valid but the period (T) or the clock frequency (f) must reflect the hardware timer used.

$$T_{exec} = N_{cycles} \times T = \frac{N_{cycles}}{f} \qquad (2.1)$$

When considering offloading computations to a hardware accelerator, the execution time is affected by the three main factors in Eq. (2.2), namely the execution time of the section of the application running on the CPU (T_{CPU}), the execution time associated to the data communication (T_{Comm}) between the CPU and the hardware accelerator (HA), and the execution time of the section of the application running on the HA (T_{HA}). The execution time model reflected by Eq. (2.2) considers no overlap in terms of the execution of the CPU of the hardware accelerator and data communication, i.e., the CPU is stalled while the hardware accelerator is executing. Still, it is possible to consider a full/partial overlap between data communications and HA execution and/or between CPU execution and HA execution in the model reflected by reducing the values of the terms T_{Comm} and T_{HA} in Eq. (2.2) to account for the observed overlap.

$$T_{exec} = T_{CPU} + T_{Comm} + T_{HA} \qquad (2.2)$$

When considering hardware accelerators, Eq. (2.1) measures T_{CPU}, which is the time the application spends on CPU execution (including multiple CPUs and/or many-cores). The number of elapsed clock cycles is measured from the beginning of the execution until the end, which is a reliable measurement as this is the component where the execution starts and finishes.

Another useful metric in many contexts is the speedup of the execution which quantifies the performance improvement of an optimized version over a baseline implementation. Eq. (2.3) presents how the speedup can be calculated with an optimized version ($Perf_{optimized}$) and the baseline performance ($Perf_{baseline}$), i.e., the performance achieved by the application and/or system we want to improve.

$$\text{Speedup} = T_{baseline}/T_{optimized} = Perf_{optimized}/Perf_{baseline} \qquad (2.3)$$

When focusing on performance improvements, it is common to first identify the most critical sections (*hotspots*) of the code and then attempt to optimize these sections. The identification of these critical sections is usually based on the use of profiling tools (e.g., GNU gprof) and/or of code analysis (see Chapter 4), as well as performance models. A well-known rule of thumb (known as the 90/10 locality rule [9]) states that "90% of the execution time of an application is spent in 10% of the code." In other words, the critical sections of the applications are in approximately 10% of the code, most often in the form of loops.

2.5.1 AMDAHL'S LAW

Amdahl's law [22,23] states that the performance improvement of a program is limited by the sections that must be executed sequentially, and thus can be used to estimate the potential for speeding up applications using parallelization and/or hardware acceleration. In short, Amdahl's law states that the speedup achieved by accelerating portions of an application is limited by the code sections that are not accelerated. More formally, the achievable performance speedup is limited by the fraction of the sequential (not improved) execution time of the application $(1-f)$ and by the actual speedup (s) one can achieve for the fraction remainder fraction f of the application's execution. This application speedup can thus be expressed by Eq. (2.4).

$$\text{Speedup} = \frac{1}{(1-f)+\dfrac{f}{s}} \qquad (2.4)$$

This relation thus indicates that one must improve significant fractions of the application's execution f that represent a significant fraction of the global execution time if we are to attain substantial overall performance improvements. Also, this relation reveals that if a computation has a substantial fraction f that cannot be (or is not) improved, that fraction f limits the achievable speedup of the overall application. As the performance speedup s of the fraction f increases, possibly using additional resources[4] and/or by the use of advanced compiler transformations, the overall application speedup will asymptotically tend to the values given by Eq. (2.5).

$$\text{Speedup} = \frac{1}{1-f} \qquad (2.5)$$

Fig. 2.18 shows the speedup limit when considering different fractions f being accelerated and considering s as infinite. As can be observed, to attain a speedup of 2, the

---

[4]Under the assumption that there are no hardware resources dependences or data dependences precluding the effective use of these resources for concurrent execution.

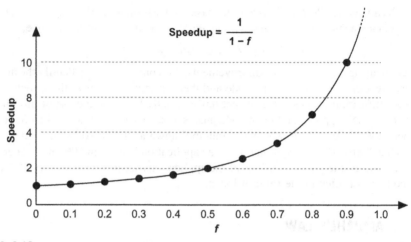

FIG. 2.18

Speedup limit with respect to the fraction of the execution time of the application being accelerated (considering the theoretical case of reducing to 0 s of execution time those fractions, e.g., by using infinite hardware resources).

fraction f of the original application code whose execution time needs to be reduced to a negligible amount is 50%. To attain a speedup of 10, the fraction f needs to be 90%. So, higher performance improvements can only be achieved if an increasingly large section of the code has their execution time substantially reduced. In other words, the maximum achievable performance is thus limited by the intrinsically sequential sections of the applications' code that cannot or are simply not subject to optimizations.

This speedup analysis, while theoretical, is in practice very important as it can provide insights into the speedup limits, thus providing an early cost-benefit analysis for programmer effort and/or additional hardware resource use.

As an example of the usefulness of such a performance model, even if simplified, we consider the Libmad[5] library for MP3 decoding and its theoretical limits for possible acceleration. Fig. 2.19 shows the profiling results when running this program in a typical desktop PC. Using the idealized performance model with no communication cost, we would expect a maximum speedup of 1.11 × when considering the hardware acceleration of *dct32*, a function very amenable to hardware implementation. To achieve a 10 × speedup, we must consider accelerating at least the top 9 functions revealed by the profiling results, which represent over 90% of the overall program's execution time. A plot of the maximum attainable speedup is depicted in Fig. 2.20. Here, the speedup is computed by the cumulative optimization of the first most

---

[5]http://www.underbit.com/products/mad/.

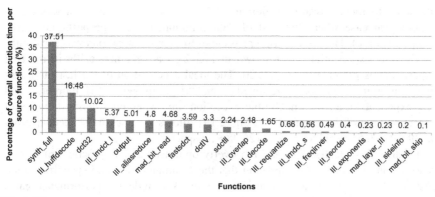

FIG. 2.19

Profiling results for the Libmad library for MP3 decoding considering the 20 most time-consuming functions.

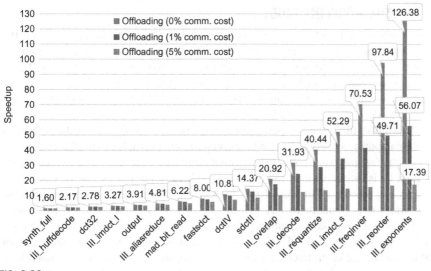

FIG. 2.20

Maximum attainable speedup for various communication cost scenarios when cumulatively optimizing each source code function of the libmad library code (note that this is simply indicative and assumes that all the selected functions can be offloaded to hardware accelerators and their implementation in those accelerators have negligible execution time).

time-consuming functions in the Libmad library. This plot captures the results of three experiments. The first experiment reveals an idealized speedup assuming no communication cost with a hardware accelerator nor any other source of overhead. The second experiment assumes the communication cost is, for each function offloaded to the hardware accelerator, 1% of its execution time (assuming an hypothetical case where the cost of data communication is proportional to the computing time). The last experiment assumes this communication overhead climbs to 5%. The exponential effect shown in Fig. 2.18 is very noticeable in the first experiment as presented in Fig. 2.20. The ideal acceleration of the last three less time-consuming functions presented (i.e., "III_freqinver," "III_reorder," and "III_exponents"), all with negligible execution time when considering the overall execution time of the program (see Fig. 2.19), allows to increase the speedup from $52.29 \times$ to $70.53 \times$, $97.84 \times$, and $126.38 \times$, respectively.

Clearly, this idealized scenario is overly optimistic and in practice infeasible. Also, it can be immediately apparent that the communication and synchronization costs need to be kept to a minimum as they quickly erode any performance gains due to acceleration of even a substantial fraction of the application's execution time. Yet, even a simple model can help developers choose a feasible section of the application's source code to improve on.

2.5.2 THE ROOFLINE MODEL

The roofline model [24,25] is an increasingly popular method for capturing the compute-memory ratio of a computation and hence quickly identify if the computation is compute or memory bound. The roofline model is often represented as a two-dimensional plot with Performance (Flops/Cycle or Flops/s) in the Y-axis and operational (also known as arithmetic or numeric) intensity (Flops/Byte) in the X-axis, as depicted in Fig. 2.21.

This plot delimits various performance regions based on the architectural features of the computing system at hand where computational kernels can be placed depending on the features used and compiler transformations exercised. Clearly, the region labeled ⓪ is infeasible as it implies bandwidth values beyond what the computing system can provide. The line labeled "peak stream bandwidth" thus identifies the bandwidth upper-bound for any given code design. The plot also contains other "upper-bound" lines corresponding to the use of architectural features or elements. For instance, the line labeled "without software prefetching" indicates that codes not taking advantage of prefetching cannot move beyond this performance bound line. Similarly, other horizontal lines bound the performance of a code design if these do not use SIMD instructions or simply do not take advantage of instruction-level parallelism (ILP). Ideally, developers would want to have their code reach as high as possible, and break some of these ceilings, by using compiler transformations and code restructuring to exhibit the highest possible performance rate.

In short, the goal of the roofline model is to set expectations for performance for specific architectures and specific code to guide the developers to tune their code and take advantage of the target computing systems. This model can also be used to expose performance bottlenecks and to guide code transformations. For codes that

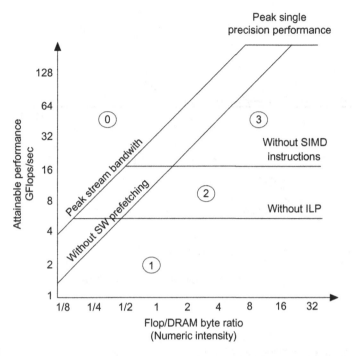

FIG. 2.21

Illustrative roofline model plot with several architectural bandwidth bounds and instruction optimization bounds.

are inherently compute bound, i.e., they have a high operational intensity, they can be "pulled" from region ① to region ③ with the use of source and compiler optimizations. However, if the code is inherently memory bound (lower operational intensity), the most effective performance improvement may be to engage in transformations that reduce or hide the latency of the memory operations by prefetching or exploiting application-level data reuse (in effect eliminating memory accesses). As an example, we depict in Fig. 2.22 [26] the roofline plots for three representative Intel MKL (Math Kernel Library) kernels ("daxpy," "dgemv," "dgemm") and an FFT kernel for various input dataset sizes and considering sequential and parallel versions of the code executing in an i7 Core Sandy Bridge E system.

The peak performance and memory bandwidth depicted in the roofline plots are estimated using specific microbenchmarks on single and multicore platforms and exercising different memory access patterns. The use of multicores in Fig. 2.22B from a single-core execution in Fig. 2.22A has two major effects. First, it increases the maximum performance ceiling from 8 to 48 Flops/Cycle, as expected due to the use of multiple independent cores. Second, it increases the peak bandwidth from 6.2

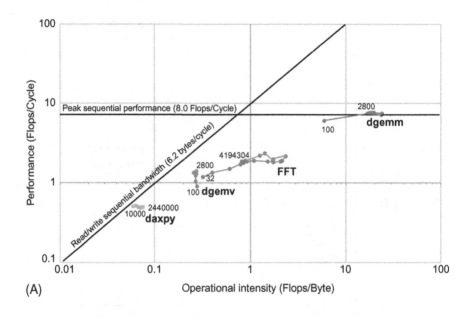

(A)

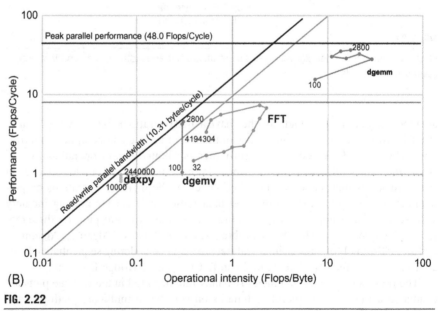

(B)

FIG. 2.22

Examples of roofline plots for Intel MKL BLAS 1–3 and FFT kernels on an i7-3930 K Core Sandy Bridge E system: sequential code (A) and parallel code (B).

From Ofenbeck G, Steinmann R, Cabezas VC, Spampinato DG, Püschel M. Applying the roofline model, In: IEEE international symposium on performance analysis of systems and software (ISPASS'2014), Monterey, CA, March 23–25, 2014. p. 76–85.

to 10.31 Bytes/Cycle, likely due to optimized memory management techniques used in NUMA architectures where memory is allocated "near" the core where the thread is executed (e.g., first-touch policy). Kernels daxpy and dgemv are memory bound (low operational intensity) in both sequential and parallel cases, while dgemm is compute bound reaching close to the peak performance in both cases. The FFT kernel, on the other hand, went from compute bound in the sequential version to memory bound in the parallel version, which means that any optimization applied to the FFT kernel aiming to improve its performance will first hit the bandwidth ceiling.

2.5.3 WORST-CASE EXECUTION TIME ANALYSIS

In other contexts, it is required that specific sections of the code or tasks execute within prescribed time bounds. As such, one must model its execution time. This is the case with many embedded systems such as real-time and safety-critical systems, which require that the execution of specific tasks be time bounded so as to ensure the correct behavior per system requirements (see, e.g., [27], Chapter 10). As an example, in an auto engine, specific operation controls must occur within very stringent timing constraints. Similarly, in a nuclear reactor software, safety-related control actions have to take place at precise time once alarm conditions are triggered. In these contexts, developers must guarantee the worst-case execution time (WCET) for specific tasks to be below a specific time bound so that, and it is common practice, they can execute within the schedule time slot allocated to them by the underlying real-time operating system (RTOS).

Embedded software developers have resorted to a combination of static analysis (instruction counting and execution path coverage analysis) and restriction on the sharing of resources with other tasks, or even preemption, so that feasible execution time upper bounds can be derived (see e.g., [28]).

The existence of architectural elements, such as cache memories and branch prediction with nondeterministic timing behavior, renders the estimation of WCET, even for input bounded code, very complex (see e.g., [29]). Because of these limitations and in instances where satisfying strict timing deadlines are of paramount importance, e.g., in safety applications, software developers opt to use hardware components which do not exhibit nondeterministic behavior often at the expense of lower expected average performance.

2.6 POWER AND ENERGY CONSUMPTION

As power dissipation and energy consumption are critical concerns in most embedded systems, it is important to be aware of techniques that impact and most importantly that reduce them. Dynamic voltage and frequency scaling (DVFS) [30], dynamic frequency scaling (DFS), dynamic voltage scaling (DVS), and dynamic power management (DPM) are techniques related to architectures and hardware to reduce energy/power consumption.

Power consumption is represented in watts (W), which directly affects system heat (temperature) and the possible need for cooling schemes. The total power consumption[6] of a CMOS integrated circuit (IC) is the sum of the static power and the dynamic power as represented by Eq. (2.6).

$$P = P_{\text{static}} + P_{\text{dynamic}} \tag{2.6}$$

Short circuits and leakage currents are responsible for power consumption even when transistor devices are not switching. The static power consumption (P_{static}) can be calculated by Eq. (2.7), where V_{cc} represents the supply voltage (sometimes also represented as V_{dd}) and I_{cc} (sometimes represented as I_{sc}) represents the overall current flowing through the device which is given by the sum of the leakage currents. The static power depends mainly on the area of the IC and can be decreased by disconnecting some parts of the circuit from the supply voltage and/or by reducing the supply voltage.

$$P_{\text{static}} = V_{cc} \times I_{cc} \tag{2.7}$$

The dynamic power (P_{dynamic}) consumption can be calculated by Eq. (2.8), where V_{cc} represents the supply voltage, β represents the activity factor, C_L represents the load capacitance, and f denotes the clock frequency at which the device is operating. P_{dynamic} is proportional to the switching activity of the transistors in the IC. Thus, one way to reduce the dynamic power is to make regions of the IC nonactive and/ or to reduce V_{cc} and/or f.

$$P_{\text{dynamic}} = \beta \times C_L \times V_{cc}^2 \times f \tag{2.8}$$

When reducing the dynamic power by reducing the frequency and/or the supply voltage, it is common to attempt to reduce the value of the supply voltage as its value impacts in a quadratic way the dynamic power $\left(P_{\text{dynamic}} \propto V_{cc}^2\right)$. Reducing the clock frequency clearly has a negative impact on execution time as the components will operate at a lower clock frequency thus translating into longer execution times, increased latencies, or lower throughputs. Moreover, reducing the supply voltage may also imply a reduction of the clock frequency. Typically, the system provides a table of discrete values of supply voltages that they can operate under along with the corresponding maximum clock frequencies (known as frequency-voltage table). Thus, the supply voltage (V_{cc}) can be seen as a linear function of the clock frequency as depicted in Eq. (2.9) and the dynamic power consumption is directly proportional to the cube of the clock frequency ($P_{\text{dynamic}} \propto f^3$), as shown in Eq. (2.10).

---

[6]Although the term "power dissipation is more appropriate," the term "power consumption" is widely used.

FREQUENCY-VOLTAGE PAIRS

The operating performance points (OPPs) depend on the components (e.g., CPUs) and the support included in the system implemented in the IC.

For example, the Texas Instruments OMAP-L138[a] IC includes an ARM9 RISC processor and a VLIW DSP. The following table presents the OOPs for three subsystems of the IC, the ARM processor, the DSP, and the RAM.

Subsystem	Frequency (MHz)	Voltage (V)
DSP C674x and ARM926EJ-S	456	1.3
	375	1.2
	200	1.1
	100	1.0
DDR2	312	1.3
	312	1.2
	300	1.1
	266	1.0

Intel also has provided control over the processor's operating frequency and supply voltage with the Enhanced Intel SpeedStep Technology.[b]

[a]Texas Instruments Inc., OMAP-L138 C6000 DSP+ARM Processor, SPRS586I—June 2009—Revised September 2014.
[b]Intel Corp. Enhanced Intel SpeedStep Technology for the Intel Pentium M Processor, White Paper, March 2004.

The tuple consisting of the voltage and the corresponding maximum clock frequency is known as the operating performance point (OPP), OPP = (f,V). Table 2.1 presents an example of four OOPs of a hypothetical processor. This example considers the processor can operate with a supply voltage of 1 V at a maximum clock frequency of 300 MHz, or 1.2 V at 600 MHz, or 1.3 V at 800 MHz, or at 1.4 V at 1 GHz. These OOPs can be managed by the operating system (OS) and/or by the application via system library functions.

$$V_{cc} = \alpha \times f \tag{2.9}$$

$$P_{dynamic} = \beta \times C_L \times \alpha^2 \times f^3 \tag{2.10}$$

To reduce dynamic power and static power consumption, two main mechanisms can be used, namely, dynamic voltage and frequency scaling (DVFS) and dynamic power management (DPM), respectively. These two techniques are described in the following subsections.

Table 2.1 Example of frequency-voltage table (representing OPPs)

Frequency (MHz)	Supply voltage (V)
300	1.0
600	1.2
800	1.3
1,000	1.4

The energy consumed, represented in Joules (J), during a period of activity is the integral of the total power dissipated (Eq. 2.6 for CMOS ICs) over that period. Eq. 2.11 represents in a simplified way the total of energy consumed during a period T (in seconds) as the product of the average power dissipated over that period (P_{avg}) by T. For a given application, one can save energy if power consumption/dissipation is reduced and the execution time is not increased as much, or conversely if the execution time is reduced without a large increase in power dissipation.

ACPI: ADVANCED CONFIGURATION AND POWER INTERFACE

ACPI[a] is a standard interface specification supported by hardware and software drivers. Usually the operating system uses this API to manage power consumption, but the API can also be used by applications.

ACPI considers four global states (from G0 to G3, with a subdivision in six sleep states S0 to S5), performance states (base on the possible OPPs), known as P-states (and from P0 to P15 at maximum, being P0 the state operating at maximum clock frequency and resulting in the highest power dissipation), Processor states, known as C-states (and usually from C0 to C3, but depending on the processor). The C-states represent operating (C0), Halt (C1), Stop-Clock (C2), and Sleep (C3) states.

[a]Unified EFI Inc. Advanced configuration and power interface specification ACPI overview. Revision 5.1 [July, 2014] http://www.uefi.org/sites/default/files/resources/ACPI_5_1release.pdf.

$$E = P_{avg} \times T \tag{2.11}$$

Energy consumption is not directly associated with heat but affects battery usage. Thus by saving energy one is also extending the battery life or the length of the interval between battery recharges. On the other hand, energy efficiency is a term related to performing the work needed with as less energy as possible, sometimes being quantified by the work done per Joule (e.g., samples/J, Gbit/J, and frames/J). Two common metrics used to represent the trade-off between energy consumption and performance are the energy delay product (EDP) and the energy delay squared product (ED^{2}P). EDP is obtained by multiplying the average energy consumed by the computation time required [31]. Both EDP and ED^{2}P give more importance to the execution time than to the energy consumed. Compared to EDP, by squaring the computation time required, the ED^{2}P metric gives even more importance to execution time than to energy consumption. One can give even more importance to performance by powering the computation time required by values >2.

2.6.1 DYNAMIC POWER MANAGEMENT

Dynamic power management (DPM) techniques [32] use the various operating CPU modes such as sleep (*idle*) and active (*running*) to dynamically reduce power and possibly energy consumption. These techniques need to take into account the switch cost, in terms of time and energy, between those modes. Fig. 2.23 presents an example of a power state machine representing a microprocessor with three power states (RUN, IDLE, and SLEEP). Each state dissipates a certain level of power. The

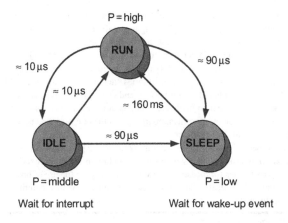

P = high

RUN

≈ 10 µs   ≈ 90 µs

≈ 10 µs

≈ 160 ms

IDLE   ≈ 90 µs   SLEEP

P = middle   P = low

Wait for interrupt   Wait for wake-up event

FIG. 2.23

Example of a power state machine for a StrongARM SA-1100 processor.

transitions between states show the delays associated to the transition between power states. The RUN state may also have different levels according to the support of DVFS, DVS, or DFS.

2.6.2 DYNAMIC VOLTAGE AND FREQUENCY SCALING

Dynamic voltage and frequency scaling (DVFS) is a technique that aims at reducing the dynamic power consumption by dynamically adjusting voltage and frequency of a CPU [33]. This technique exploits the fact that CPUs have discrete frequency and voltage settings as previously described. These frequency/voltage settings depend on the CPU and it is common to have ten or less clock frequencies available as operating points. Changing the CPU to a frequency-voltage pair (also known as a CPU frequency/voltage state) is accomplished by sequentially stepping up or down through each adjacent pair. It is not common to allow a processor to make transitions between any two nonadjacent frequency/voltage pairs.

MEASURING POWER AND ENERGY

Power dissipation can be monitored by measuring the current drawn from the power supply to the system or to each device. There are specific boards providing this kind of measurements but this scheme requires access to the power rails for the inclusion of a shunt resistor from the V_{cc} supplied and the device/system under measurement (note that $P = V_{cc} \times I_{cc}$). This is typically a problem and only useful in certain conditions or environments. Another possibility is to use pass-through power meters as the ones provided for USB interfaces.

Some computing systems provide built-in current sensors and the possibility to acquire from the software side the power dissipated. Examples of this are the support provided by the ODROID-XU3,[a] which includes four current/voltage sensors to measure the power dissipation of the ARM Cortex big.LITTLE A15 and A7 cores, GPU and DRAM individually, and the NVIDIA Management Library (NVML)[b] which allows to report the current power draw in some of their GPU cards.

By measuring the average current and knowing the voltage supply we can derive the average power dissipated and the energy consumed during a specific execution period.

A software power model based on hardware sensing is used in the Running Average Power Limit (RAPL)[c] driver provided for Intel microprocessors since the Sandy Bridge microarchitecture.[d] The measurements are collected via a model-specific microprocessor register.

Recent versions of platform-independent libraries such as the performance API (PAPI)[e] also include support for RAPL and NVML-based power and energy readings in addition to the runtime performance measurements based on hardware counters of the microprocessors. Monitoring power in mobile devices can be done by specific support such as the one provided by PowerTutor[f] in the context of Android-based mobile platforms.

One important aspect of monitoring power dissipation is the power sampling rate (i.e., the maximum rate possible to measure power) which can be too low in some contexts/systems.

Finally, other possibilities for measuring power and energy are the use of power/energy models for a certain platform and application and/or the use of simulators with capability to report estimations of the power dissipated.

[a]ODROID-XU3. http://www.hardkernel.com/.
[b]NVIDIA Management Library (NVML)—Reference manual, NVIDIA Corporation, March 2014, TRM-06719-001 vR331. https://developer.nvidia.com/nvidia-management-library-nvml.
[c]Intel Corp. Intel 64 and IA-32 architectures software developer's manual, vol. 3B: System Programming Guide, Part 2, September 2016.
[d]Intel Corp. Intel Xeon processor. http://www.intel.com/xeon, 2012.
[e]Weaver VM, Terpstra D, McCraw H, Johnson M, Kasichayanula K, Ralph J, et al. PAPI 5: measuring power, energy, and the cloud. In: IEEE Int'l symposium on performance analysis of systems and software; April 2013.
[f]PowerTutor: A power monitor for android-based mobile platforms, http://ziyang.eecs.umich.edu/projects/powertutor/.

Dynamic frequency scaling (DFS) and dynamic voltage scaling (DVS) are techniques to reduce the power dissipation when voltage and frequency ranges are not fully interdependent, i.e., when changes in clock frequency do not imply (up to a certain point) changes in the supply voltage and vice versa. Decreasing the clock frequency without changing the supply voltage (possibly maintaining it to the level needed to operate at the maximum clock frequency) implies a decrease of power dissipation but may lead to insignificant changes in energy consumption (theoretically we would expect the same energy consumption). Decreasing the supply voltage without changing the operating frequency implies both power and energy reductions.

The DVFS technique can be seen as a combination of DFS and DVS and when the interdependence between power supply and operating frequency is managed in a global way. However, in CPUs where the voltage-frequency interdependence exists, DFS, DVS, and DVFS are often used with the same meaning, i.e., the dynamic scaling of voltage-frequency.

2.6.3 DARK SILICON

The end of Dennard scaling [34], which argued that one could continue to decrease the transistor feature size and voltage while keeping the power density constant, has raised a big challenge for large transistor count IC designs. At the core of the issue of power density is the fact that with the growing number of increasingly smaller transistors, the aggregate leakage current, if unchecked, is large enough to create the threat of thermal runaway. This is particularly serious in devices with many cores where the execution of all the cores at maximum or acceptable speed is unfeasible.

To cope with this issue, ICs may have resorted to "Dark Silicon" [35] techniques that under-power or under-clock regions of an IC whenever they are not being used. To support these techniques, ICs have to provide low-level mechanisms that allow the monitoring of the thermal conditions of specific regions of the IC, e.g., of a coprocessor or hardware accelerator and provide an interface with which a runtime environment or a scheduler can reduce the associated clock rate or even temporarily power down that unit for the sake of power dissipation. The impact on the ability of compilers to statically schedule the execution of selected computations on such devices is substantial. Execution predictability and hence nonfunctional requirements guarantees such as latency and throughput are, in this context, harder to ensure. Another possibility is to map and schedule the computations at runtime using OS, middleware, or application-level support.

2.7 COMPARING RESULTS

When comparing execution times, power dissipation, and energy consumption, it is common to compare the average (arithmetic mean) results of a number of application runs. This reduces the impact of possible measurement fluctuations as most of times measurements can be influenced by unrelated CPU activities and by the precision of the measuring techniques. Depending on the number of measurements, it might be also important to report standard deviations. When comparing speedups and throughputs, however, it is convenient to compare the geometric mean of the speedups/throughputs achieved by the optimizations or improvements for each benchmark/application used in the experiments, as opposed to the use of arithmetic mean for speedups which may lead to wrong conclusions.[7] In most cases, the measurements use real executions in the target platform and take advantage of the existence of hardware timers to measure clock cycles (and correspondent execution time) and of the existence of sensors to measure the current being supplied. Most embedded computing platforms do not include current sensors and it is sometimes needed to use a third-party board that can be attached to the power supply (e.g., by using a shunt resistor between the power supply and the device under measurement).

There are cases where performance evaluations are carried out using cycle-accurate simulators (i.e., simulators that execute at the clock cycle level and thus report accurate latencies) and power/energy models. Cycle-accurate simulations can be very time-consuming and an alternative is to use instruction-level simulators (i.e., simulators that focus on the execution of the instructions but not of the clock

[7]How did this get published? Pitfalls in experimental evaluation of computing systems. Talk by José Nelson Amaral, Languages, Compilers, Tools and Theory for Embedded Systems (LCTES'12), June 12, 2012, Beijing.

cycles being elapsed) and/or performance/power/energy models. Instruction-level simulators are used by most virtual platforms to simulate entire systems, including the presence of operating systems, since they provide faster simulations.

The comparison of results is conducted in many cases using metrics calculated from actual measurements. The most relevant example is the speedup which allows the comparison of performance improvements over a baseline (reference) solution. In the case of multicore and many-core architectures, in addition to the characteristics of the target platform (e.g., memories, CPUs, hardware accelerators) it is common to report the number of cores and the kind of cores used for a specific implementation, the number of threads, and the clock frequencies used.

Regarding the use of FPGAs, it is common to evaluate the number of hardware resources used and the maximum clock frequency achieved by a specific design. These metrics are reported by vendor-specific tools at more than one level of the toolchain, with the highest accuracy provided by the lower levels of the toolchain. Typically, the metrics reported depend on the target FPGA vendor or family of FPGAs. In case of Xilinx FPGAs, the metrics reported include the number of LUTs (distinguishing the ones used as registers, as logic, or as both), slices, DSPs, and BRAMs.

2.8 SUMMARY

This chapter described the main architectures currently used for high-performance embedded computing and for general purpose computing. The descriptions include multicore and many-core integrated circuits (ICs) and hardware accelerators (e.g., GPUs and FPGAs). We presented aspects to take into account in terms of performance and discussed the impact of offloading computations to hardware accelerators and the use of the roofline model to reveal the potential for performance improvements of an application. Since power dissipation and energy consumption are of paramount importance in embedded systems, even when the primary goal is to provide high performance, we described the major contributing factors for power dissipation and energy consumption, and some techniques to reduce them.

2.9 FURTHER READING

This chapter focused on many topics for which there exists an extensive bibliography. We include in this section some references we believe are appropriate as a starting point for readers interested in learning more about some of the topics covered in this chapter.

Readers interested in the advances of reconfigurable computing and reconfigurable architectures can refer to, e.g., [1,36–38]. An introduction to FPGA architectures is provided in Ref. [2]. The overviews in Refs. [39,40] provide useful information on code transformations and compiler optimizations for reconfigurable architectures in the context of reconfigurable computing. Overlay architectures provide interesting approaches and have attracted the attention of academia as well as of industry (see, e.g., [20,41]).

A useful introduction about GPU computing is presented in Ref. [6]. In addition, there have been several research efforts comparing the performance of GPUs vs FPGAs (see, e.g., [42]).

Computation offloading has been focus of many authors, not only regarding the migration of computations to local hardware accelerators but also to servers and/or HPC platforms. Examples of computation offloading include the migration of computations from mobile devices to servers (see, e.g., [43]).

Exploiting parallelism is critical for enhancing performance. In this context, when improving the performance of an application,[8] developers should consider Amdahl's law and its extensions to the multicore era [44,45] to guide code transformations and optimizations, as well as code partitioning and mapping.

There have been many approaches proposed to reduce power and energy consumption using DVFS (see, e.g., [46]). A recent and useful survey about DVFS and DPM is presented in [47]. Readers interested in power-aware computing topics are referred to Ref. [48]. Mobile devices have typically strict power and energy consumption requirements. Thus several approaches have addressed APIs for monitoring power dissipation in mobile devices. An energy consumption model for Android-based smartphones is PowerTutor [49]. Readers interested in self-build energy model approaches can refer to Ref. [50].

While the use of simple performance models is well understood for single-core architectures, further understanding is needed to extend or revisit Amdahl's law and its main lessons and extensions to the multicore era as addressed by recent research [44,45]. The complexity of emerging architectures with processor heterogeneity and custom processing engines will also likely lead to advances in more sophisticated models such as the roofline model [51,25] briefly described in this chapter.

---

[8]Note that the Amdahl's law can be also applied to other metrics such as power and energy consumption.

REFERENCES

[1] Pocek K, Tessier R, DeHon A. Birth and adolescence of reconfigurable computing: a survey of the first 20 years of field-programmable custom computing machines. In: The highlights of the first twenty years of the IEEE intl. symp. on field-programmable custom computing machines, Seattle, WA, April; 2013.

[2] Kuon I, Tessier R, Rose J. FPGA architecture: survey and challenges. Found Trends Electron Des Autom 2008;2(2):135–253.

[3] Burger D, Keckler SW, McKinley KS, Dahlin M, John LK, Lin C, et al. Scaling to the end of silicon with EDGE architectures. Computer 2004;37(7):44–55.

[4] Weber R, Gothandaraman A, Hinde RJ, Peterson GD. Comparing hardware accelerators in scientific applications: a case study. IEEE Trans Parallel Distrib Syst 2011;22 (1):58–68.

[5] Ogawa Y, Iida M, Amagasaki M, Kuga M, Sueyoshi T. A reconfigurable java accelerator with software compatibility for embedded systems. SIGARCH Comput Archit News 2014;41(5):71–6.

[6] Owens JD, Houston M, Luebke D, Green S, Stone JE, Phillips JC. GPU computing. Proc IEEE 2008;96(5):879–99.

[7] Nickolls J, Dally WJ. The GPU computing era. IEEE Micro 2010;30(2):56–69.

[8] Mittal S, Vetter JS. A Survey of CPU-GPU heterogeneous computing techniques. ACM Comput Surv 2015;47(4). Article 69, 35 pages.

[9] Hennessy JL, Patterson DA. Computer architecture—a quantitative approach. 5th ed. San Francisco, CA, USA: Morgan Kaufmann; 2012.

[10] Oliver N, Sharma RR, Chang S, Chitlur B, Garcia E, Grecco J, et al. A reconfigurable computing system based on a cache-coherent fabric. In: Proceedings of the international conference on reconfigurable computing and FPGAs (Reconfig'11). Washington, DC: IEEE Computer Society; 2011. p. 80–5.

[11] Singh M, Leonhardi B. Introduction to the IBM Netezza warehouse appliance. In: Litoiu M, Stroulia E, MacKay S, editors. Proceedings of the 2011 conference of the center for advanced studies on collaborative research (CASCON'11). Riverton, NJ: IBM Corp; 2011. p. 385–6.

[12] Stuecheli J, Bart B, Johns CR, Siegel MS. CAPI: a coherent accelerator processor interface. IBM J Res Dev 2015;59(1)7:1–7:7.

[13] Crockett LH, Elliot RA, Enderwitz MA, Stewart RW. The Zynq book: embedded processing with the ARM cortex-A9 on the Xilinx Zynq-7000 all programmable SoC. UK: Strathclyde Academic Media; 2014.

[14] Jacobsen M, Richmond D, Hogains M, Kastner R. RIFFA 2.1: a reusable integration framework for FPGA accelerators. ACM Trans Reconfig Technol Syst 2015;8(4):22.

[15] Howes L. The OpenCL specification. Version: 2.1, document revision: 23, Khronos OpenCL Working Group. Last revision date: November 11, 2015. https://www.khronos.org/registry/cl/specs/opencl-2.1.pdf.

[16] Kaeli DR, Mistry P, Schaa D, Zhang DP. Heterogeneous computing with OpenCL 2.0. 1st ed. San Francisco, CA: Morgan Kaufmann Publishers Inc.; 2015.

[17] Kusswurm D. Modern X86 assembly language programming: 32-Bit, 64-Bit, SSE, and AVX. 1st ed. Berkely, CA: Apress; 2014.

[18] Intel Corp., Intel® 64 and IA-32 architectures optimization reference manual. Order number: 248966-033; June 2016.

[19] Langbridge JA. Professional embedded ARM development. 1st ed. Birmingham: Wrox Press Ltd.; 2014.

[20] Bakos JD. High-performance heterogeneous computing with the convey HC-1. Comput Sci Eng 2010;12(6):80–7.

[21] Xilinx Inc., Zynq-7000 all programmable SoC overview. Product specification, DS190 (v1.10); September 27, 2016.

[22] Amdahl GM. Computer architecture and Amdahl's law. Computer 2013;46(12):38–46.

[23] Amdahl GM. Validity of the single processor approach to achieving large scale computing capabilities. In: Proceedings AFIPS spring joint computer conference; 1967. p. 483–5.

[24] Williams S, Waterman A, Patterson D. Roofline: an insightful visual performance model for multicore architectures. Commun ACM Apr. 2009;52(4):65–76.

[25] Williams S. The roofline model. In: Bailey DH, Lucas RF, Williams S, editors. Performance tuning of scientific applications. Boca Raton, FL, USA: Chapman & Hall/CRC Computational Science, CRC Press; 2010. p. 195–215.

[26] Ofenbeck G, Steinmann R, Cabezas VC, Spampinato DG, Püschel M. Applying the roofline model. In: IEEE International Symposium on Performance Analysis of Systems and Software (ISPASS'2014), Monterey, CA, March 23–25; 2014. p. 76–85.

[27] Kopetz H. Real-time systems: design principles for distributed embedded applications. New York, NY, USA: Springer; 2011.

[28] Altmeyer S, Gebhard G. WCET analysis for preemptive scheduling. In: Proc. of the 8th intl. workshop on worst-case execution time (WCET) analysis; 2008.

[29] Hardy D, Puaut I. WCET analysis of instruction cache hierarchies. J Syst Archit 2011;57(7):677–94. ISSN: 1383–7621.

[30] Le Sueur E, Heiser G. Dynamic voltage and frequency scaling: the laws of diminishing returns. In: Proceedings of the 2010 International conference on power aware computing and systems (HotPower'10). Berkeley, CA: USENIX Association; 2010. p. 1–8.

[31] Laros III J, Pedretti K, Kelly SM, Shu W, Ferreira K, Vandyke J, et al. Energy delay product. In: Energy-efficient high performance computing. Springer briefs in computer science. London: Springer; 2013. p. 51–5.

[32] Benini L, Bogliolo A, De Micheli G. A survey of design techniques for system-level dynamic power management. In: De Micheli G, Ernst R, Wolf W, editors. Readings in hardware/software co-design. Norwell, MA: Kluwer Academic Publishers; 2001. p. 231–48.

[33] Jha NK. Low power system scheduling and synthesis. In: Proceedings of the IEEE/ACM international conference on computer-aided design (ICCAD'01). Piscataway, NJ: IEEE Press; 2001. p. 259–63.

[34] Dennard RH, Gaensslen FH, Rideout VL, Bassous E, LeBlanc AR. Design of ion-implanted MOSFET's with very small physical dimensions. IEEE J Solid State Circuits 1974;SC–9(5):256–68.

[35] Esmaeilzadeh H, Blem E, St. Amant R, Sankaralingam K, Burger D. Dark silicon and the end of multicore scaling. SIGARCH Comput Archit News 2011;39(3):365–76.

[36] Trimberger S. Three ages of FPGAs: a retrospective on the first thirty years of FPGA technology. Proc IEEE 2015;103:318–31.

[37] Hauck S, DeHon A, editors. Reconfigurable computing: the theory and practice of FPGA-based computation. San Francisco, CA, USA: Morgan Kaufmann/Elsevier; 2008.

[38] Najjar WA, Ienne P. Reconfigurable computing. IEEE Micro 2014;34(1):4–6. special issue introduction.

[39] Cardoso JMP, Diniz PC. Compilation techniques for reconfigurable architectures. New York, NY, USA: Springer; 2008. October.

[40] Cardoso JMP, Diniz PC, Weinhardt M. Compiling for reconfigurable computing: a survey. ACM Comput Surv 2010;42(4):1–65.

[41] Rashid R, Steffan JG, Betz V. Comparing performance, productivit and scalability of the TILT overlay processor to OpenCL HLS. In: IEEE Conference on field-programmable technology (FPT'14); 2014. p. 20–7.

[42] Cope B, Cheung PYK, Luk W, Howes LW. Performance comparison of graphics processors to reconfigurable logic: a case study. IEEE Trans Comput 2010;59(4):433–48.

[43] Kun Y, Shumao O, Hsiao-Hwa C. On effective offloading services for resource-constrained mobile devices running heavier mobile internet applications. IEEE Commun Mag 2008;46(1):56–63.

[44] Hill MD, Marty MR. Amdahl's law in the multicore era. IEEE Comput 2008;41:33–8.

[45] Cassidy AS, Andreou AG. Beyond Amdahl's law: an objective function that links multiprocessor performance gains to delay and energy. IEEE Trans Comput 2012;61(8):1110–26.

[46] Saha S, Ravindran B. An experimental evaluation of real-time DVFS scheduling algorithms. In: Proc. of the 5th annual international systems and storage conf. (SYSTOR'12). New York, NY: ACM; 2012. Article 7, 12 pages.

[47] Bambagini M, Marinoni M, Aydin H, Buttazzo G. Energy-aware scheduling for real-time systems: a survey. ACM Trans Embed Comput Syst 2016;15(1):1–34.

[48] Melhem R, Graybill R, editors. Power aware computing. Norwell, MA, USA: Kluwer Academic/Plenum Publishers; May, 2002.

[49] Zhang L, Tiwana B, Qian Z, Wang Z, Dick RP, Morley Mao Z, et al. Accurate online power estimation and automatic battery behavior based power model generation for smartphones. In: Proc. of the 8th Int. conf. on hardware/software codesign and system synthesis (CODES+ISSS 2010), Scottsdale, AZ, October 24–28; 2010. p. 105–14.

[50] Dong M, Zhong L. Self-constructive high-rate system energy modeling for battery-powered mobile systems. In: Proceedings of the 9th international conference on Mobile systems, applications, and services (MobiSys'11). New York, NY: ACM; 2011. p. 335–48.

[51] Williams S, Waterman A, Patterson D. Roofline: an insightful visual performance model for multicore architectures. Commun ACM 2009;52(4):65–76.

Controlling the design and development cycle

3

3.1 INTRODUCTION

The availability of rich programming and visualization environments has allowed the development of high-performance embedded systems using the so-called fourth-generation programming languages such as MATLAB [1] and Simulink [2]. This development approach, in its basic form, starts with a model specification where end-to-end functions are verified taking into account internal feedback loops and specific numeric variable precision requirements. Once this first functional specification is complete, designers and developers can focus on meeting additional specification requirements. These requirements typically involve performance and/or energy goals, and in some extreme cases where Application-Specific Integrated Circuits (ASICs) are sought, design area constraints for specific clock rate ranges. To keep design options open for later phases of the implementation of a design, it is common to encapsulate expensive arithmetic operations as abstract operators at behavioral level. Even for integer value representations, there is a wide variety of implementations for basic operators such as addition and multiplication. This exploration of suitable operator implementations is largely guided by performance factors such as clock rate and timing.

Common design space exploration (DSE) approaches lack the language mechanisms that allow designers to convey specific target requirements, as well as the lack of tools that can use the information conveyed by different stages of the design flow to effectively explore and derive efficient design solutions. While there are tools that perform hardware DSE, they tend to be tightly integrated in a hardware synthesis toolchain (e.g., [3]), or only allow the exploration using a limited set of parameters (such as the unroll loop factor), and thus do not provide the flexibility to explore alternative and potentially more optimized solutions. Other tools focus exclusively on the exploration of arithmetic precision concerns to meet specific algorithmic-level requirements (e.g., noise level).

To make matters worse, these hardware designs often need to be certified for timing requirements and integrated in the context of complex systems-on-a-chip (SoC), in many cases executing under the supervision of a Real-Time Operating System (RTOS). The validation and certification of such systems is extremely complex. While specific hardware designs can meet stringent timing targets, their inclusion in real-time systems requires a perfect synchronization of the timing and the priorities of multiple threads on computing cores with nondeterministic execution. It is

Embedded Computing for High Performance. http://dx.doi.org/10.1016/B978-0-12-804189-5.00003-X

57

common for designers in this case to settle for the worst-case execution time scenarios, which often leads to an increase in resource usage and to suboptimal energy-wise design solutions.

Most of the complexity in designing these systems stems from the fact that it is extremely hard to trace the original project design goals, such as overall energy or timing requirements, to individual design components. As it is common in many areas of engineering, designers organize their solutions into a hierarchy of logically related modules. Tracing and propagating down these requirements across the boundaries of the hierarchy is extremely complex as multiple solutions may exhibit feasible individual design points but when put together, the combined design may not meet its requirements. Thus, exposing requirements at a higher design level and allowing a tool to understand how these requirements can be translated up and down the module hierarchy is a critical aspect of modern high-performance embedded systems design.

In the remainder of this chapter, we address this need using a series of design specifications and examples assuming that readers are familiar with imperative programming languages such as C and MATLAB.

3.2 SPECIFICATIONS IN MATLAB AND C: PROTOTYPING AND DEVELOPMENT

The language used to program an application, a model, an algorithm, or a prototype greatly influences the effort required to efficiently map them to the target computing system. High-level abstraction languages typically promote design productivity while also increasing the number of mapping solutions of the resulting designs without requiring complex code restructuring/refactoring techniques. In the following sections, we use MATLAB [1] and C [4] programming languages to describe the prototyping and the programming development stages.

3.2.1 ABSTRACTION LEVELS

Programming languages such as C are usually considered low level as algorithms are implemented using constructs and primitives closer to the target processor instructions, since most operations, such as arithmetic, logical, and memory accesses, are directly supported by the microprocessor instruction set. For instance, if a low-level programming language does not directly support matrix multiplication or sort operations (either natively or through a library), developers are forced to provide their own implementations using low-level operations. Such low-level implementations can constrain the translation and mapping process of the computation defined at this level of abstraction, since the compiler is naturally limited to a narrow translation and mapping path, leaving relatively little room for high-level optimizations.

Alternatively, developers may use programming languages with higher levels of abstraction which natively support high-level operations such as matrix

`D=A*B*C;`	`D=mult(mult(A,B),C);`

(A)   (B)

FIG. 3.1

Simple MATLAB example (A); C example considering the existence of the function "mult" (B).

multiplication and sorting. This is the case of MATLAB [1], Octave [5], and Scilab [6] which natively support a wide range of linear algebra matrix operations (overloaded with common arithmetic operators on scalars). Fig. 3.1A presents an example of a MATLAB statement using matrix multiplications. This native support makes the code simpler and more concise, allowing the compiler to easily recognize the operation as a matrix multiplication, and thus associate the best algorithm to implement it (e.g., based on the knowledge of whether the matrices are sparse or not). Fig. 3.1B presents a possible equivalent C statement considering the existence of the "mult" function and a data structure to store matrices (including also the size and shape of the matrix). For a compiler to recognize that the "mult" function is an actual implementation of a matrix multiplication operation, it requires a mechanism for programmers to convey that information, e.g., through code annotations.[1]

The abstractions provided by matrix-oriented programming languages, such as MATLAB, are helpful in many situations. Herein we use the *edge detection* application provided by the UTDSP benchmark repository [7], and compare several MATLAB implementations against the corresponding C implementations available in this repository, highlighting possible mappings.

The *edge detection* application uses a function to convolve two input matrices. Fig. 3.2 presents an excerpt of a possible MATLAB code to implement the 2D convolution. In this example, the natively supported dot product ".*" is used to calculate the multiplications of the pixels in a window of $K \times K$ size with the `kernel` matrix. Fig. 3.3 shows a MATLAB code, very similar to the C code present in the repository, which does not use the ".*" operator.

```
% Convolve the input image with the kernel.
  for r = 0:1:(N-K)
    for c = 0:1:(N-K)
      sum1 = sum(sum(input_image(r+1:r+K,c+1:c+K).*kernel));
      output_image(r+dead_rows+1,c+dead_cols+1) = (sum1 / normal_factor);
    end
  end
```

FIG. 3.2

MATLAB code using the native dot product operation for a 2D convolution of an input image with a kernel (matrix of coefficients).

---

[1]Note that languages like C++ support operator overloading, which would allow the code to be as simple as the MATLAB code presented in Fig. 3.1, however the developer must still provide an implementation or use a domain-specific library.

```
%   /* Convolve the input image with the kernel. */
  for r = 0:1:(N-K)
    for c = 0:1:(N-K)
      sum1 = 0;
      for i = 0:1:K-1
        for j = 0:1:K-1
          sum1 = sum1 + input_image(r+i+1, c+j+1) * kernel(i+1,j+1);
        end
      end
      output_image(r+dead_rows+1, c+dead_cols+1) = (sum1 / normal_factor);
    end
  end
```

FIG. 3.3

MATLAB code for a 2D convolution of an input image with a kernel (matrix of coefficients).

```
function [ image_buffer3 ] = combthreshold(image_buffer1, image_buffer2, T)
  N = length(image_buffer1); % for now images are squares

  % pre-allocation and zeroing of the output image
  image_buffer3 = zeros(N); % for now images are squares

  image_buffer3(max(abs(image_buffer1), abs(image_buffer2))>T) = 255;
  % statement below is not needed when considering the pre-allocation and zeroing
  %image_buffer3(max(abs(image_buffer1), abs(image_buffer2))<=T) = 0;
end
```

FIG. 3.4

MATLAB code to assign black or white to each pixel of the output image based on the threshold T and on the individual pixels of two input images.

Other sections of the *edge detection* benchmark include (a) the merging of two images resulting from two convolutions that use different `kernel` values in a single image and (b) the generation of a B&W image (0 or 255 values) based on a threshold (`T`). Both computations are implemented in the *combthreshold* function shown in Fig. 3.4. The code for this function relies on MATLAB's ability to use matrices and to specify logical indexing. While this code version is very compact, it requires the use of temporary matrices to store intermediate results. The MATLAB statement `max(abs(image_buffer1), abs(image_buffer2))` returns a matrix whose elements are the maximum values between the respective elements of `abs(image_buffer1)` and `abs(image_buffer2)`. The result of `max(abs(image_buffer1), abs(image_buffer2))>T` provides a matrix of 1's and 0's indicating whether each element of the matrix `max(abs(image_buffer1), abs(image_buffer2))` is larger than `T` or not.

Thus, in this example, four temporary matrices are used (including the two temporary matrices resultant from `abs(image_buffer1)` and `abs(image_buffer2)`). A translation pass from MATLAB to C would have to decide whether to use these temporary matrices, or instead decompose operations in a way that element-wise operations can be used, thus reducing memory use since the temporary matrices would not be needed. Fig. 3.5 presents another version of the *combthreshold* function, similar to the original C code, and Fig. 3.6 shows a MATLAB version obtained by a statement-by-statement translation from the original C code. These two versions make use of element-wise operations.

```
function [ image_buffer3 ] = combthreshold(image_buffer1, image_buffer2, T)
  N = length(image_buffer1); % for now images are squares

  % pre-allocation of output image
  image_buffer3 = zeros(N); % for now images are squares

  for i = 1:N
    for j = 1:N
      temp1 = abs(image_buffer1(i,j));
      temp2 = abs(image_buffer2(i,j));

      if(temp1 > temp2)
        temp3 = temp1;
      else
        temp3 = temp2;
      end

      if(temp3 > T)
        out = 255;
      else
        out = 0;
      end
      image_buffer3(i,j) = out;
    end
  end
end
```

FIG. 3.5

A second version of the MATLAB code to assign black or white values to each pixel of the output image based on the threshold T and on the individual pixels of two input images.

```
function [ image_buffer3 ] = combthreshold(image_buffer1, image_buffer2, T)
  N = length(image_buffer1); % for now images are squares

  % pre-allocation of output image
  image_buffer3 = zeros(N); % for now images are squares

  for i = 1:N
    for j = 1:N
      temp1 = abs(image_buffer1(i,j));
      temp2 = abs(image_buffer2(i,j));

      if(max(temp1, temp2) > T)
        out = 255;
      else
        out = 0;
      end
      image_buffer3(i,j) = out;
    end
  end
end
```

FIG. 3.6

A third version of the MATLAB code to assign black or white values to each pixel of the output image based on the threshold T and on the individual pixels of two input images.

There are plenty of abstractions that may help to program applications and models. In addition to the inherent support for matrix operations as highlighted in this example, the support for regular expressions is another abstraction that provides enhanced semantic information in a compact form to a compiler. Recognizing a regular expression allows compilers to generate the most efficient implementation considering the target architecture, input data, and regular expression complexity. When direct support for regular expressions is not available, an implementation needs to be provided, which constrains the code transformations and optimizations of a compiler, and reduces opportunities for further transformations.

The use of higher abstraction levels allows the code to capture a specification rather than an implementation. As a specification, it focuses on the operations that need to be done (*what*), as opposed to the way they are done (*how*). As a result, code using low-level abstractions and close to a target implementation may make it difficult to identify alternative implementation paths. Domain-Specific Languages (DSLs) [8] allow the level of abstraction to be increased by providing domain-specific constructs and semantics to developers with which they can convey critical information that can be directly exploited by compilers in pursuit of optimized implementations for a given design.

The use of modeling languages and model-driven approaches has many benefits. Visual modeling languages such as Unified Modeling Languages (UMLs) [9] provide high abstraction levels and a specification of the application/system. They are, however, dependent on the capability of tools to generate efficient code and the availability of environments to simulate these models.

High levels of abstraction can also be provided by environments such as Simulink [2] and Ptolemy [10]. These can be seen as component-based simulation and development frameworks where visual languages (e.g., structuring a program in terms of components) are mixed with textual languages (e.g., to program the behavior of each component). These environments provide the capability to mix different components, such as parts of the computing system and emulator interfaces to these environments, while using models for each component. They also provide the possibility to describe each component with different levels of abstractions, e.g., using high- or low-level descriptions of the behavior, within the same framework. For instance, a system can be simulated such that one or more components use a high-level language description of the computation or can be simulated using a cycle-accurate model of a microprocessor. In some environments, one may simulate the system mixing models with "hardware in the loop" (i.e., using hardware for some of the components) [11].

Higher levels of abstraction can be provided in traditional textual languages such as C/C++ and Java using specific Application Programming Interfaces (APIs) and/or embedded DSLs [33]. An example of an API that provides high levels of abstraction is the regular expression APIs available for programming languages without native support for regular expressions (such as is the case of the Java language[2]).

---

[2]https://docs.oracle.com/javase/8/docs/api/java/util/regex/package-summary.html.

3.2.2 DEALING WITH DIFFERENT CONCERNS

During the design cycle, developers may have to deal with different concerns that include emulating the input/output of the system, providing timing/energy/power measurements, and monitoring capabilities. These concerns might translate to specific code that must be introduced in the application, but ultimately removed in the final implementation and/or when deploying it to the target system. Timing and measuring the power and energy consumption of an application are examples of concerns typically considered during the design cycle. Figs. 3.7 and 3.8 present examples of code inserted in the application to provide such measurements. Both include calls to specific function libraries (APIs) to interface with hardware components (e.g., a timer and a power sensor).

The high abstraction level provided by programming languages such as MATLAB allows the specification of simulation models that take into account the connections to input/output components, but usually impose code to emulate certain features of the system. This code is in a later step removed from the application code. One example is the emulation interface to an input camera which loads images from files instead of connecting to a real camera. In some prototypes and production embedded implementations, these codes interface with a real camera.

```
...
    #include "time.h"
...
    clock_t begin, end;
...
    begin = clock();  // number of CPU clock cycles
    // code section under timing measurements
    end = clock();    // number of CPU clock cycles
...
    printf("Elapsed #clock cycles: %d\n", (int) (end-begin));
    // CLOCKS_PER_SEC is the CPU number of clock cycles per second
    printf("Elapsed time: %f (sec)\n", (double) (end-begin)/CLOCKS_PER_SEC);
...
```

FIG. 3.7

Timing a section of an application.

```
...
    #include "energy.h"
...
    double begin, end;
...
    begin = energy_start();
    // code section under energy measurements
    end = energy_end();
...
    printf("Consumed energy: %d (J) ", (end-begin));
...
```

FIG. 3.8

Measuring energy for a section of an application.

It is common with programming languages such as C to use the preprocessor capabilities and the use of #ifdef and #define constructs to statically configure different versions of the application. This however pollutes the code and makes it difficult to maintain different versions, especially when dealing with many concerns that require many intrusive code changes. Figs. 3.9 and 3.10 present two examples of the use of #ifdef preprocessor directives to configure a section of an application

```
...
#ifdef FROM_FILE
    int image_in[N*N];
    input_from_file(image_in, N*N, "image1.dat");
#endif
#ifdef FROM_H
    #include "image.h" // image.h defines the array of constants const_array
    int *image_in = const_array;
#endif
#ifdef FROM_MEMIO  // memory mapped I/O device
    // assuming 0x0FFF0000 as the memory address used for mapping the real camera
    volatile int *image_in = (volatile int *) 0x0FFF0000;
#endif
...
```

FIG. 3.9

Using #define and #ifdef for configuring the code version to be used at a certain time.

```
...
#ifdef TIMING
    #include "timing.h"
#endif
...
double EucledianDistanceInt(int *str1, int *str2, int size){
  int i, n;
  double sum, dist;

#ifdef TIMING
    start_timer();
#endif

  sum = 0.0;
  for(i = 0; i < size; i++){
    dist = (double)(str1[i] - str2[i]);
    sum += (dist*dist);
  }
  dist = sqrt(sum);

#ifdef TIMING
    showtiming(timer());
#endif

  return dist;
}
...
```

FIG. 3.10

Using #ifdef for enabling the timing of a section of an application.

according to the concern being addressed at a certain design point. The example in Fig. 3.9 shows C code and preprocessing directives that configure the way the input image is acquired: from a data file, from a memory mapped I/O, or defined by an initialization in a header file (".h"). The options to read the image from a file or to define it as a ".h" file representing possible testing and evaluating scenarios are commonly defined before the deployment of the application to the target platform. In the example of Fig. 3.10, the preprocessing directives are used to configure the timing of the function using instrumentation (calls to functions of a timing library). Depending on how the library implements these functions, this example can even measure timing by using the hardware timers available in many microprocessors.

It is common to see preprocessing directives in most real-life C code, especially in the embedded programming domain. Developers use them to configure applications according to their particular needs. The selection of a particular configuration is done by changing the specific values or definitions directly in the source code or by using the support given by the compiler to control the preprocessor via command line options (e.g., GNU gcc supports the –D option to define values of #define preprocessor directives).

PREPROCESSING DIRECTIVES

The C programming language has support for directives that are resolved during the preprocessing phase[a] (i.e., by a preprocessor) of the compilation. The preprocessor returns the source code to be input to the C compiler.

The set of directives include #include, #define, #ifdef, #else, #if, #elif, #ifndef, #undef, #error, etc. The directive #define can be used to define a constant or to define a macro. Following are two examples, one defining a constant and the other defining a macro to return the maximum of two values:

```
#define LIMIT 10
#define MAX(a, b) ((a) > (b) ? (a) :
(b))
```

With GNU gcc, the result of the preprocessing phase can be output using the –E option (e.g., gcc –E file.c).

[a]The C Preprocessor, Copyright © 1987–2016 Free Software Foundation, Inc., https://gcc.gnu.org/onlinedocs/cpp/

One possibility to help the global design/development cycle is to use an Aspect-Oriented Programming (AOP) approach [12,13] to provide the modularity level needed to configure the application and the different stages of the design/compilation flow (including different target languages), according to the requirements of each particular stage. The different code versions associated with a particular application concern can be programmed in separate modules called *aspects*, and a tool (known in the AOP community as *weaver*) is responsible to weave the application code with the aspects to automatically produce different code versions (e.g., one for modeling and simulation, one for prototyping, and multiple ones for implementation). Fig. 3.11 presents an AOP inspired example, considering the same

```
select beginning of file including the call to "EucledianDistanceInt"
    insert "#include "timing.h""

select beginning (after declarations) of function "EucledianDistanceInt"
    insert "start_timer();"

select end (before return statement) of function "EucledianDistanceInt"
    insert "showtiming(timer());"
```

FIG. 3.11

AOP example.

configuration requirements of the first example that was previously presented to illustrate the use of #ifdef preprocessor directives (see Fig. 3.9). This example selects target elements of the program related to the concerns (such as the code to be timed) and specifies actions that include inserting target language code (in this case related to the use of a timing library). Although the application of this example is tied to a function named EucledianDistanceInt, the name of the function can actually be a parameter of the aspect shown in Fig. 3.11, making this *aspect* reusable for every function that needs to be timed via instrumentation.

3.2.3 DEALING WITH GENERIC CODE

When developing a model using a high-level abstraction language, it is often desirable to reuse the model in various projects and applications. With this goal in mind, the code is developed in a more generic way, usually by providing certain options as parameters. This is common when programming for modularity and reusability. For instance, a function to sort a list of numbers is usually programmed to sort N numbers and not a specific number, e.g., 1000, that might be required for a particular application being developed. When considering MATLAB code, it is very common to develop code as generic as possible, taking into account various usage scenarios. This is also true in the context of the functions in the libraries that maximize reusability if provided with many usage scenarios in mind.

ASPECT-ORIENTED PROGRAMMING

"AOP is a programming paradigm that aims to increase modularity by allowing the separation of cross-cutting concerns. It does so by adding additional behavior to existing code (an advice) without modifying the code itself, instead having a separate description that captures which code is modified via a «pointcut», such as «log all function calls when the function's name begins with 'set'». This allows behaviors that are not central to the business logic (such as logging) to be added to a program without cluttering the code core to the functionality. AOP forms a basis for aspect-oriented software development." (in[a])

A well-known AOP language is AspectJ[b] which provides AOP concepts to the Java Programming language.

---

[a]Aspect-Oriented Programming. https://en.wikipedia.org/wiki/Aspect-oriented_programming.
[b]AspectJ. https://en.wikipedia.org/wiki/AspectJ.

```
1.  function [cim, r, c] = harris(im, sigma, thresh, radius, disp)
2.  error(nargchk(2,5,nargin));
3.
4.      dx = [-1 0 1; -1 0 1; -1 0 1]; % Derivative masks
5.      dy = dx';
6.
7.      Ix = conv2(im, dx, 'same');    % Image derivatives
8.      Iy = conv2(im, dy, 'same');
9.      % Generate Gaussian filter of size 6*sigma (+/- 3sigma) and of
10.     % minimum size 1x1.
11.     g = fspecial('gaussian',max(1,fix(6*sigma)), sigma);
12.
13.     Ix2 = conv2(Ix.^2, g, 'same'); % Smoothed squared image derivatives
14.     Iy2 = conv2(Iy.^2, g, 'same');
15.     Ixy = conv2(Ix.*Iy, g, 'same');
16.
17.     cim = (Ix2.*Iy2 - Ixy.^2)./(Ix2 + Iy2 + eps); % Harris corner measure
18.
19.     if nargin > 2   % We should perform nonmaximal suppression and threshold
20.         % Extract local maxima by performing a grey scale morphological
21.         % dilation and then finding points in the corner strength image that
22.         % match the dilated image and are also greater than the threshold.
23.         sze = 2*radius+1;                    % Size of mask.
24.         mx = ordfilt2(cim,sze^2,ones(sze)); % Grey-scale dilate.
25.         cim = (cim==mx)&(cim>thresh);        % Find maxima.
26.         [r,c] = find(cim);                   % Find row,col coords.
27.
28.         if nargin==5 & disp      % overlay corners on original image
29.             figure, imagesc(im), axis image, colormap(gray), hold on
30.             plot(c,r,'ys'), title('corners detected');
31.         end
32.     else  % leave cim as a corner strength image and make r and c empty.
33.         r = []; c = [];
34.     end
35. end
```

FIG. 3.12

A possible MATLAB specification of the Harris corner detection algorithm. eps is a constant with value 2.2204e−16.

From http://slazebni.cs.illinois.edu/spring16/harris.m.

To illustrate this point, we present in Fig. 3.12 a MATLAB code of an image corner detector based on the Harris algorithm [14] widely used in vision-based navigation systems. Line 2 of this code checks if the number of arguments for each call of the function is between 2 and 5. If not, it reports an error. Since MATLAB functions can be called with a variable number of arguments, this kind of code, which checks the number of arguments, is very common (*nargin* is a system MATLAB variable with information about the arguments of the function). In line 19 there is once again a test to the number of arguments. If the function is not called with more than two arguments, r and c are returned empty (line 33), i.e., nothing is to be done and no corner is identified. This code is tangled with other nonfunctional concerns. For instance, lines 29–30 plot the resulting image and the corners. The function includes a parameter, disp, to control the plot.

```
1. function [cim, r, c] = harris(im, sigma, thresh, radius)
2.
3.    dx = [-1 0 1; -1 0 1; -1 0 1]; % Derivative masks
4.    dy = dx';
5.
6.    Ix = conv2(im, dx, 'same');    % Image derivatives
7.    Iy = conv2(im, dy, 'same');
8.
9.    g = fspecial('gaussian',max(1,fix(6*sigma)), sigma);
10.
11.   Ix2 = conv2(Ix.^2, g, 'same'); % Smoothed squared image derivatives
12.   Iy2 = conv2(Iy.^2, g, 'same');
13.   Ixy = conv2(Ix.*Iy, g, 'same');
14.
15.   cim = (Ix2.*Iy2 - Ixy.^2)./(Ix2 + Iy2 + eps); % Harris corner measure
16.
17.   sze = 2*radius+1;                  % Size of mask.
18.   mx = ordfilt2(cim,sze^2,ones(sze)); % Grey-scale dilate.
19.   cim = (cim==mx)&(cim>thresh);      % Find maxima.
20.   [r,c] = find(cim);                 % Find row,col coords.
21. end
```

FIG. 3.13

A possible MATLAB specification of the Harris corner detection algorithm after removing of some concerns.

These two examples illustrate the inclusion of code that increases the usability of the function in a number of different scenarios/applications. Some of the included functionalities will hardly be present in the final system or product. Fig. 3.13 presents the code of the function without this additional code. The original function is now clearer as it only has the functionalities intended to be used in the final system.

We note however that the code is still in a generic form, and with ample potential for performance improvement via specialization.[3] Specifically, there are code sections that can be evaluated at compile time. For instance, `dy=dx';` assigns to `dy` a matrix which is a transpose of the matrix of constants `dx`. Thus one possibility is to assign to `dy` the matrix of constants (i.e., `dy=[-1 -1 -1; 0 0 0; 1 1 1]`) instead of deriving it at runtime from `dx`. Another example consists on calculating `g`: `g=fspecial('gaussian', max(1,fix(6*sigma)), sigma)`. It is common to call the algorithm with a specific value for sigma (1, 2, or 3) for a certain application. In each case, the statement on line 9 can be substituted by the assignment of the respective matrix of values according to the value of sigma. In a more generic implementation, but less generic than the one provided, one can substitute line 9 with one of the three matrices according to the value of sigma.

The code includes invocations to MATLAB functions provided by the MATLAB environment, such as `conv2`. Since `conv2` is a library function, it is also a generic

---

[3]Code specialization is the act of defining a code version that executes only for specific input values, providing better performance for those values compared to a generic version.

```
1. function [cim, r, c] = harris(im)
2.
3.     dx = [-1 0 1; -1 0 1; -1 0 1]; % Derivative masks
4.     dy = [-1 -1 -1; 0 0 0; 1 1 1]; % Transpose of derivative masks
5.
6.     Ix = conv2_same(im, dx);    % Image derivatives
7.     Iy = conv2_same(im, dy);
8.
9.     g=[0.0003    0.0023    0.0062    0.0062    0.0023    0.0003;…
10.        0.0023    0.0168    0.0458    0.0458    0.0168    0.0023; …
11.        0.0062    0.0458    0.1244    0.1244    0.0458    0.0062; …
12.        0.0062    0.0458    0.1244    0.1244    0.0458    0.0062; …
13.        0.0023    0.0168    0.0458    0.0458    0.0168    0.0023; …
14.        0.0003    0.0023    0.0062    0.0062    0.0023    0.0003];
15.
16.    Ix2 = conv2_same(Ix.^2, g); % Smoothed squared image derivatives
17.    Iy2 = conv2_same(Iy.^2, g);
18.    Ixy = conv2_same(Ix.*Iy, g);
19.
20.    cim = (Ix2.*Iy2 - Ixy.^2)./(Ix2 + Iy2 + eps); % Harris corner measure
21.
22.    mx = ordfilt2(cim,9,[1 1 1; 1 1 1; 1 1 1]); % Grey-scale dilate.
23.    cim = (cim==mx)&(cim>1000);      % Find maxima.
24.    [r,c] = find(cim);               % Find row,col coords.
25. end
```

FIG. 3.14

A possible MATLAB specification of the Harris corner detection algorithm after removing of some concerns and performing specialization (eps $= 2.2204e-16$).

function providing the selection of the function code to be executed as its third parameter. In this case, all calls to conv2 in the code use 'same' as the third argument (in conv2(A, B, 'same')) and this means that conv2 returns the central part of the convolution of the same size as A. Thus, one can specialize a version of conv2 related to the 'same' case.

Fig. 3.14 shows a possible code version after specialization considering sigma and radius equal to one and thresh equal to 1000. Matrix *g* is now a matrix of constants and can even be moved inside function conv2_same thus enabling further optimizations in that function. The function ordfilt2 can be also specialized by moving the two arguments' constants inside the function.

As can be seen in this example, the potential for specialization when considering models and generic code can be very high. In Chapter 5, we describe code transformations that can be helpful for code specialization, e.g., in terms of performance and energy/power consumption.

3.2.4 DEALING WITH MULTIPLE TARGETS

It is common to develop code that needs to be evaluated on different architectures in order to decide the target processing component to be used for each function or specific region of code, e.g., when targeting heterogeneous multicore architectures

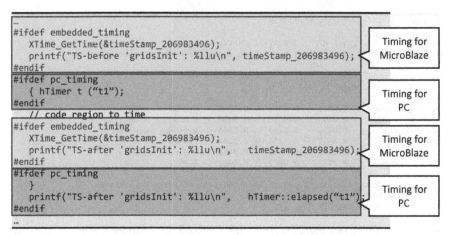

```
...
#ifdef embedded_timing
    XTime_GetTime(&timeStamp_206983496);
    printf("TS-before 'gridsInit': %llu\n", timeStamp_206983496);
#endif
#ifdef pc_timing
    { hTimer t ("t1");
#endif
    // code region to time
#ifdef embedded_timing
    XTime_GetTime(&timeStamp_206983496);
    printf("TS-after 'gridsInit': %llu\n",    timeStamp_206983496);
#endif
#ifdef pc_timing
    }
    printf("TS-after 'gridsInit': %llu\n",    hTimer::elapsed("t1"));
#endif
...
```

Timing for MicroBlaze

Timing for PC

Timing for MicroBlaze

Timing for PC

FIG. 3.15

Example using preprocessor directives for considering code for measuring the execution time considering multiple targets.

and/or architectures providing hardware accelerators, or when implementing products[4] using different computing systems characteristics (e.g., when targeting different mobile devices).

The use of preprocessing directives is very common when developers need to have multiple implementations of certain regions of code, functions, constant values, options, etc. The options can be selected at the preprocessing stage and according to the target architecture. For instance, consider the example in Fig. 3.15, which measures the execution time of a region of code in a Personal Computer (PC) or in an embedded system. This example captures in the same source code: (1) the measurements of the execution time in a PC and (2) in an embedded system using a Xilinx MicroBlaze microprocessor implemented in an FPGA. In this example, depending on the definition (using #define) of "embedded_timing" or "pc_timing," the preprocessor will select one of the code versions for measuring the execution time.

Even when a region of code is implemented using a particular hardware accelerator, different directives may have to be applied according to the toolchain used. Fig. 3.16 illustrates an example where a function is implemented on an FPGA-based hardware accelerator and different directives are used to instruct the target tool to convert the C function code into a custom hardware implementation. In this example, we consider Catapult-C (see, e.g., [15]) and Vivado HLS [16] as the target high-level synthesis (HLS) tools.

Similar examples can be provided when using different compilers (e.g., GCC, LLVM, ICC) or when using the same compiler but considering different target architectures.

---

[4]For example, in the context of software product lines (SPLs).

```
...
#define CATAPULT_SYN
// #define VIVADO_SYN

...
#if defined(CATAPULT_SYN) && defined(VIVADO_SYN)
   #error Only one of the tools at a time.
#endif
...
#ifdef CATAPULT_SYN
   #pragma hls_design top
#endif

...
   #ifdef CATAPULT_SYN
        #pragma hls_pipeline_init_interval 1
   #endif
   for (i=0;i<N;i++) {
      #ifdef VIVADO_SYN
          #pragma HLS PIPELINE II=1
      #endif
      y[i] = 0;
      #ifdef CATAPULT_SYN
        #pragma hls_unroll yes
      #endif
      for (j=0; j<8;j++) {
         #ifdef VIVADO_SYN
            #pragma HLS unroll
         #endif
         y[i] += z[i][j];
      }
   ...
```

FIG. 3.16

Example using preprocessor directives to support multiple tools.

MULTITARGET/MULTITOOLCHAINS USING LARA

In the case of the LARA language, directives that are required in the code can be moved to LARA aspects, so that a weaver can inject the required code depending on the option provided by the user, as shown in the following example.

```
...
select
function.loop.body.first_stmt end
apply

...
  if(option=="VivadoHLS") {
    insert before %{
      #ifdef VIVADO_SYN
         #pragma HLS PIPELINE II=1
      #endif
    }%;
  }
...
end
condition $loop.is_outermost end
...
```

3.3 TRANSLATION, COMPILATION, AND SYNTHESIS DESIGN FLOWS

Given a high-level description of a computation to be mapped to a hybrid software/hardware execution platform, designers need to master a set of tools, namely:

- *Compilers*: These tools translate code described in a high-level imperative programming language, such as C, into assembly code targeting one or more cores, and using concurrency management primitives such as the ones offered by the OpenMP library (see Chapter 7). When interfacing with hardware or GPU devices, the code needs to include specific library and runtime environments for accessing the devices for data and computation synchronization.
- *Synthesis tools*: These tools translate a description in a hardware-centric language such as Verilog/VHDL, describing hardware behavior at Register-Transfer Level (RTL), to a target-specific representation suited for the mapping to, e.g., an FPGA device.

Fig. 3.17 depicts the general organization of the tools and the overall compilation and synthesis flow. At the core of this mapping process there is the need to interface the data and the control between the generated components, namely the software component where the control exists in a sequential or concurrent structure, and is defined by the semantics of the specific concurrency execution environment and the target hardware devices.

When targeting GPU devices, vendors offer libraries and interfacing environments that are still high level and map well to the abstractions of memory and control of traditional execution environments. Typically, the GPU interfaces have been structured around the abstraction of a coprocessor model, where input data is transferred to the device prior to execution followed by the corresponding transfer of results to the host processor address space. Vendors provide library functions to perform copy operations and provide compilers that translate high-level code to GPU assembly code. From a developer's perspective, the intellectual effort includes the encapsulation of which computation needs to be captured as a "kernel" and how to stage the data to and from the device to maximize performance. For many popular computations, such as Fast Fourier Transformations (FFTs) and linear Algebra functions, vendors even provide libraries that facilitate the access to highly tuned implementations of specific functions. Overall these approaches greatly simplify the reasoning of the program execution and hence the development and verification of concurrent codes.

Conversely, when targeting a hardware-centric device, such as an FPGA, there are significant differences in the compilation flow. While the data staging has been captured using the same approach of copying data to and from the device, the actual computation now requires the translation of the computation from a high-level programming language such as C to a hardware-oriented programming language such as Verilog or VHDL. Once the identification of the computation to be mapped to the

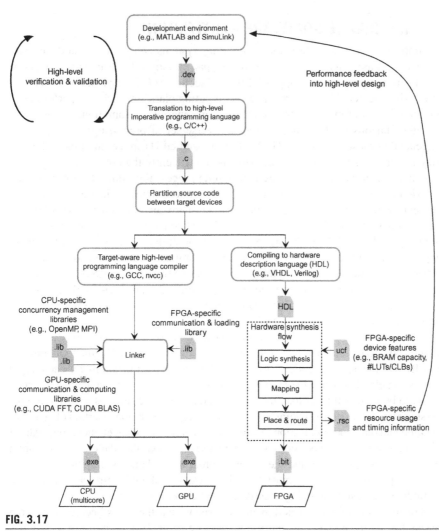

FIG. 3.17

Typical design flow.

device is done, the programmer must use a synthesis tool that will ultimately generate the programing binary file (a bitstream file, in the case of an FPGA device). The hardware design still needs to interface with a section of the FPGA that implements the data communication and synchronization protocols to be integrated with the execution of the host processor. In this context, and from the point of view of the host processor, the notion of a hardware thread has been exploited to facilitate not only the integration of the hardware devices but also its correct execution.

3.4 HARDWARE/SOFTWARE PARTITIONING

An important task when targeting computing systems consisting of hardware and software components is hardware/software partitioning. Hardware/software partitioning is the process of mapping different sections of an application to distinct processing elements in a heterogeneous computing platform, such that performance and/or other nonfunctional requirements, e.g., energy consumption, can be met. A heterogeneous platform may harbor a diverse set of processing elements, such as general purpose processors (GPPs), FPGAs, and GPUs, and each of these devices may handle specific types of workloads more efficiently than others.

An efficient hardware/software partitioning process thus aims at distributing the workload among the most appropriate computation elements in a heterogeneous computing platform consisting of software and hardware components. This process can be considerably complex, as hardware platforms are becoming increasingly more specialized thus requiring enhanced programmer expertize to effectively exploit their built-in architectural features. Examples of heterogeneous hardware platforms include embedded systems consisting of Multiprocessor System-on-Chips (MPSoCs) provided by devices such as Zynq UltraScale+, the new Intel Xeon CPUs with integrated FPGAs, and emerging heterogeneous cloud platforms that offer on-demand computation resources.

The partitioning process identifies computations, described as sections of the application code, to be mapped to the different processing elements. The mapping process usually requires specific code generators and compiler optimizations for each target processing element. Once the mapping process is defined, the main application code needs to be modified to offload the computations and code sections to different processing elements. This offloading process, typically, involves the insertion of synchronization and data communication primitives. As each processing element may exhibit different energy/power/performance characteristics and the data communication between a host processor and the different processing elements may have different costs, the partitioning process must deal with a design exploration process with the goal of finding the best partitioning according to given requirements.

Given its importance, it is thus not surprising that there has been considerable research in hardware/software partitioning (see, e.g., [17]). The choice of techniques and algorithms depend on a number of factors, including:

- The number of candidate program partitions derived from an application description. We consider a partition to be a self-contained program module with well-defined inputs and outputs. Since each partition can be potentially executed on a different processing element, the mapping process needs to take into account the communication overhead between partitions when they are mapped on different processing elements. A partition can be defined by a program function or a subprogram module. However, a function may be further partitioned to find regions of code that are prime candidates for hardware acceleration, for instance, loop statements identified as hotspots in a program.

- The number of processing elements available for the mapping process, their corresponding architecture type, and interprocessor communication model. In particular, processing elements may communicate with each other by storing and accessing data through shared memory. Alternatively, in the case of heterogeneous architectures, each processing element may have its own local memory, and communication might be performed through shared memory and/or communication channels. In the case of non-existent shared memory, the mapping process becomes less flexible, with partitions that share the same data having to be possibly mapped to the same processing element.

In general, we can divide the hardware/software partitioning process in two broad categories: static and dynamic. The static partitioning process is determined at compile time and remains unchanged at runtime. In a dynamic partitioning process, the mapping is determined at runtime taking into account existing workload and device availability. In the remaining subsections, we describe design flows that support these two categories of hardware/software partitioning.

3.4.1 STATIC PARTITIONING

A typical design flow performing static partitioning is illustrated in Fig. 3.18 and consists of the following steps:

1. Refactoring the application to uncover candidate partitions. This involves merging and splitting functions from the original code to find a good set of partitions. Profiling can be performed to find hotspots and regions of code that may be accelerated, as well as to extract data communication patterns between different regions of code. Additional heuristics, based on source code inspection and profiling, can be applied to find partitions with minimized interdependences.

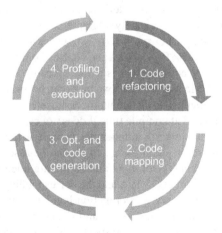

FIG. 3.18

Hardware/software partitioning steps in a static design flow.

Furthermore, partitions can be identified to uncover more opportunities for mapping a partition to different types of processing elements, thus increasing the chances of optimization.

2. Once a set of partitions is derived, the next problem consists in finding an efficient mapping. This usually involves employing a metaheuristic search algorithm, such as tabu search or simulated annealing, where the goal is to satisfy an overall nonfunctional performance goal. To achieve this, a cost model is required to estimate the performance of a particular mapping configuration, and guide the subsequent steps in the optimization process. This cost model may consider possible optimizations in the code for a particular processing element. For instance, loops can be pipelined to increase throughput if mapped onto an FPGA.

3. Once a mapping solution is found, the code may still be optimized to take into account the specific architecture of the processing element chosen. The optimization can be performed at source code level or at a lower intermediate representation (IR) level. Furthermore, as previously mentioned, the code is modified with synchronization and data communication primitives to offload computation between different processing elements. Once the final code is generated, it is compiled and linked by the different subtoolchains.

4. Finally, the generated application can be profiled on the target platform (or by simulation) to ensure it meets the application requirements. If not, then one can run the partitioning process from step 1. In this context, the synthesis and profiling reports are fed back to the refactoring (1), mapping (2), and optimization and code generation (3) steps to refine the hardware/software partitioning process.

The partitioning process also depends on the programming and execution models. Next we look at a typical example where a C application is mapped onto an heterogeneous embedded platform which hosts a CPU and an arbitrary number of hardware accelerators. We consider C functions to define partitions (note that other granularities may be used). Once the code is adequately refactored, a mapping process inspects the code and generates a *static call graph* $G = (N, E)$, where nodes N represent function calls and edges E correspond to flow of data and control from one node to another. We consider that each function call instantiates a *task*. Because a single function can be invoked at different points in the program, two tasks can be instantiated from the same function and potentially mapped to different processing elements. Note that because a static call graph is generated at compile time it does not capture the number of tasks that are executed at runtime since this number may depend on runtime conditions, such as input data. Furthermore, in a call graph, edges can be associated with data flow information, such as the data type of input and output arguments.

Consider the C program in Fig. 3.19A and the corresponding call graph presented in Fig. 3.19B. As can be seen, the `main` function invokes functions (tasks) a and d, and function a invokes functions (tasks) b, c and d. The invocations of function d in the call graph are identified as d_1 and d_2, respectively, as they correspond to two distinct invocation sites.

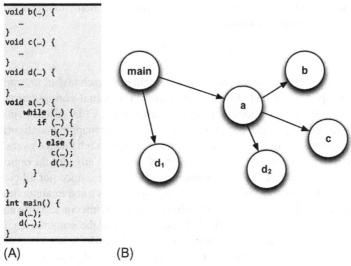

```
void b(…) {
    …
}
void c(…) {
    …
}
void d(…) {
    …
}
void a(…) {
    while (…) {
        if (…) {
            b(…);
        } else {
            c(…);
            d(…);
        }
    }
}
int main() {
    a(…);
    d(…);
}
```

(A)   (B)

FIG. 3.19

Code example and its call graph: (A) C code; (B) Static Call Graph generated from the code in (A). Each node corresponds to a task, with edges denoting the control and data flow between tasks.

Once a call graph has been derived, the next step is to map it to the target heterogeneous architecture. We describe this mapping process for an illustrative heterogeneous embedded platform depicted in Fig. 3.20. This platform contains a CPU as the host processor and a set of hardware accelerators as coprocessors. Each processor has its own local memory with no global shared memory, hence communication is only allowed between the CPU and any of the accelerators. With this type of platform, the CPU runs the application with specific parts of the code (hotspots) offloaded to hardware accelerators to minimize overall execution time.

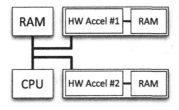

FIG. 3.20

Block diagram of a possible heterogeneous embedded platform.

The task mapping process needs to find a configuration that minimizes the overall cost to meet a given performance goal:

$$\min \sum_{\text{task}\in\text{App}} \text{cost}(PE_{\text{task}},\text{task})$$

where PE_{task} corresponds to the processing element onto each *task* of the application (App) is mapped for a particular configuration. The initial configuration, which serves as the baseline partitioning, places all tasks in the CPU. At each subsequent mapping step, the mapping algorithm tries to find a better mapping configuration by mapping one or more tasks from one processor to another, such that the overall cost is lower than the cost of the previous configuration. One challenge for the optimization process is to find a set of feasible mapping configurations, since not all configurations are valid. For instance, in our previous example, tasks *a* and *b* cannot be mapped to two distinct hardware accelerators, as in our target architecture, hardware accelerators cannot communicate directly with each other. For the same reason, if task *b* cannot be mapped to a hardware accelerator, then task *a*, which invokes task *b*, must also be mapped to the CPU. Hence, a search optimization algorithm, such as simulated annealing, can be associated with a constraint solver to find candidate mapping solutions. Also note that the *cost* estimation function must take into account not only the computation cost of migrating a task to a hardware accelerator, but also the communication overhead between the CPU and the hardware accelerator. Fig. 3.21 depicts a mapping solution for the previous example, where tasks *a*, *b*, *c*, and *d₂* are mapped to hardware accelerator #1 and the remaining tasks to the CPU.

3.4.2 DYNAMIC PARTITIONING

The underlying assumption of static hardware/software partitioning is that the mapping solution derived at compile time is resilient to changing runtime conditions. This may not be true for all classes of applications. Consider the *AdPredictor* machine learning algorithm [34] used to rank web execution for the Bing search engine, so that only *ads* with the highest probability of being clicked are presented.

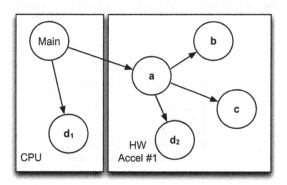

FIG. 3.21

Hardware/software partitioning solution.

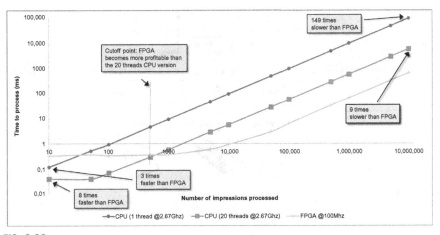

FIG. 3.22

Performance of three *AdPredictor* model training implementations.

This algorithm's training phase takes as input *ad impressions*. Each *ad impression* captures the user session (IP, geographical location, search terms) and whether the corresponding *ad* was clicked or not. With each set of *ad impressions*, the training process updates a Bayesian model and improves its accuracy in ranking web *ads*.

Fig. 3.22 shows the performance of the training process using three implementations: a single-threaded CPU, a 20-threaded CPU, and an FPGA implementation. It can be seen from this figure that the most performant implementation depends on the job size, in this case, the number (volume) of *ad impressions* to be processed. The input size in this case matters because the FPGA design supports a deep streaming architecture which requires enough processing data to hide pipeline latency.

If the job size is only known at runtime, and the most efficient processing element depends on data size or other runtime conditions, then it may be preferable to perform the mapping process at runtime. One possible runtime management system is shown in Fig. 3.23. Here, the application explicitly invokes managed tasks, which are dispatched to the *Executive* process. This *Executive* process determines, based on several factors, which available processing element the task should be executed on.

As with static partitioning, dynamic partitioning relies on the cost estimation model to determine the most efficient processing element for a particular job. A cost model can be built offline by profiling implementations with different data inputs. Since it is unfeasible to profile all combinations of inputs, an estimation model can be derived through regression and further improved by monitoring the application during execution.

One implication of the dynamic partitioning process is that all the application code, except for managed tasks, is handled by the host CPU. A managed task, however, is handled by the *Executive* process, and its execution depends on available task implementations and computing resources. In particular, a task can be associated to

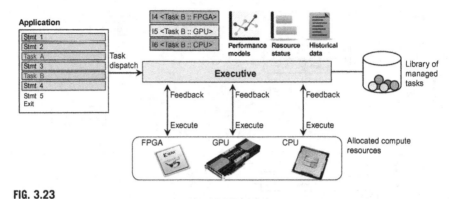

FIG. 3.23

A Runtime management system for dynamic partitioning.

multiple implementations each of which can be executed on a specific type of processing element. Hence, if a heterogeneous computing platform includes N homogeneous processing elements, then in the presence of an implementation of that type, there is a choice of N processing elements it can be executed on. In this context, a central repository or library will store (at runtime) metadata associated with each implementation and accessed by the *Executive* process to make a mapping decision at runtime, in particular:

- *Implementation characterization*. Each implementation must be associated with metadata information, which includes preconditions and performance models. Preconditions allow the *Executive* process to filter out implementations unsuited to run a particular task, for instance, a hardware sorting implementation that only supports integer numbers up to 256. Preconditions can be expressed as a set of predicates, which must all evaluate to true to be considered for execution. A performance model allows the *Executive* process to estimate the baseline performance of an implementation when executing a task given a set of input attributes, such as data size and data type. In Fig. 3.24 we can see that if an incoming task has a volume of 100 *ad impressions*, then the *Executive* process may choose the multithreaded CPU implementation and thus avoiding to offload the computation onto a hardware accelerator, whereas a task with 100 thousand *impressions* would in principle execute faster on an FPGA.
- *Resource availability*. A performance model might not be enough to estimate the fastest processing element given a particular task. For instance, the fastest executor (as identified by using a performance model) may be busy and is only able to execute a task at a later stage, thus executing slower than a potential earlier executor. Hence, to select the most efficient processing element, the *Executive* also needs to estimate how long a task will wait until it is actually

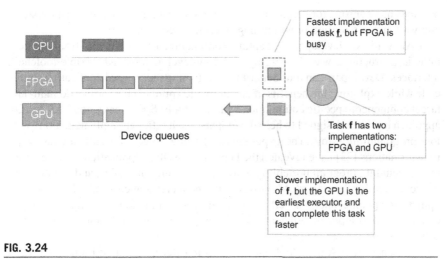

Fastest implementation of task **f**, but FPGA is busy

Task **f** has two implementations: FPGA and GPU

Slower implementation of **f**, but the GPU is the earliest executor, and can complete this task faster

Device queues

FIG. 3.24

Dispatching a task to a processing element.

executed. This is done by inspecting the size of the device queue associated to each processing element and the cost of each task execution currently in the queue. Once an implementation and a processing element are chosen, they are pushed into the corresponding device queue (see Fig. 3.24).

Recent research in this area has led to the development of several dynamic mapping approaches targeting heterogeneous platforms, including StarPU [35], OmpSs [18], MERGE [36], SHEPARD [37], and Elastic Framework [19]. These approaches offer similar runtime mapping mechanisms with differences on the programming and execution models used, how implementations and computing resources are characterized, the target platforms supported, as well as scheduling strategies to optimize workload distribution. For instance, OmpSs supports explicit annotations of task dependences in the source code, allowing the runtime management system to execute tasks asynchronously (and potentially in parallel) while satisfying their dependences.

3.5 LARA: A LANGUAGE FOR SPECIFYING STRATEGIES

LARA [21, 38] is an AOP language [22, 39] specially designed to allow developers to describe: (1) sophisticated code instrumentation schemes (e.g., for customized profiling); (2) advanced selection of critical code sections for hardware acceleration; (3) mapping strategies including conditional decisions based on hardware/software resources; (4) sophisticated strategies determining sequences of compiler optimizations, and (5) strategies targeting multicore architectures. Furthermore, LARA also provides mechanisms for controlling tools of a toolchain in a consistent and systematic way, using a unified programming interface (see, e.g., [20]).

LARA allows developers to capture nonfunctional requirements from applications in a structured way, leveraging high/low-level actions and flexible toolchain interfaces. Developers can thus benefit from retaining the original application source code while exploiting the benefits of an automatic approach for various domain- and target component-specific compilation/synthesis tools. Specifically, the LARA AOP approach has been designed to help developers reach efficient implementations with low programming effort. The experiences of using aspects for software/hardware transformations [23] have revealed the benefits of AOP in application code development, including program portability across architectures and tools, and productivity improvement for developers. Moreover, with the increasing costs of software development and maintenance, as well as verification and validation, these facets of application code development will continue to be of paramount significance to the overall software development cycles.

In essence, LARA uses AOP mechanisms to offer in a unified framework: (a) a vehicle for conveying application-specific requirements that cannot otherwise be specified in the original programming language, (b) using these requirements to guide the application of transformations and mapping choices, thus facilitating DSE, and (c) interfacing in an extensible fashion the various compilation/synthesis components of the toolchain.

LARA support is provided by a LARA interpreter and weavers. Examples of tools using the LARA technology are the following four compilers[5]: MATISSE (a MATLAB to C compiler), Harmonic (a source-to-source C compiler), MANET (a source-to-source C compiler), ReflectC (a CoSy-based C compiler), and KADABRA (a source-to-source Java compiler).

We briefly present in this section the main constructs of the LARA language and how it can be used to modify the code of a given application to meet certain requirements.

The LARA code is modular and organized around the concept of aspects. Aspect definitions can invoke other aspects, and thus, a set of LARA aspects can be applied to a given input program. A special tool, called a weaver, executes these aspects and weaves the input program files according to the actions expressed in the aspects to produce new files. Fig. 3.25 shows the inputs/outputs of two kinds of source-to-source compilers. The first (Fig. 3.25A) which is common, considers the control via directives and/or command line options. The second (Fig. 3.25B) is extended to support LARA. In this case, the output console shown is mainly used to print the messages from LARA aspects (e.g., via LARA *println* statements). We note that other uses of LARA can include the control of a compiler in the context of machine code generation.

---

[5]Harmonic is being developed at Imperial College London, United Kingdom, while the other compilers are being developed at University of Porto, Portugal.

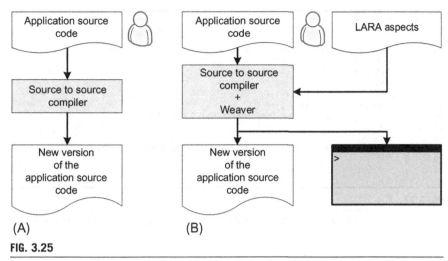

FIG. 3.25

A Source-to-Source compiler: (A) with possible control based on directives and/or command line options; (B) aided with Weaving controlled by LARA.

3.5.1 SELECT AND APPLY

An important feature of LARA is its ability to `query` program elements using a method similar to database queries. Fig. 3.26 shows a simple example of a `select` construct for querying loops in the input source code. The elements of the program queried by a LARA `select` statement are named join points, and a list of supported join points is defined for each target programming language. One can select a specific program element in the code according to its position (e.g., in terms of nested structure) in the code. For instance, we are able to select a specific loop in a specific function for a given file. The `loop` word used in this example refers to the loop join point in all programming languages currently supported by LARA. If this `select` is applied to the C code presented in Fig. 3.27, the result is a list of the 4 loops in the code. Each LARA join point includes a set of attributes which are associated to properties of a specific program element. For instance, some of the attributes associated to the *loop* join point are *is_innermost*, *is_outermost*, *line*, and *type*. We can use the attributes to verify certain characteristics of the associated program element. For instance, *select loop{type=="for"} end* selects only loops of type `for` in the code.

Once the program elements have been selected, we can also apply actions to each of them. For this, the LARA language provides the `apply` statement. Usually, each `select` has an associated `apply` section. The `apply` section supports JavaScript

```
select loop end
```

FIG. 3.26

Querying program elements (loops in this case).

```
//File: convolve.c
//Function: conv2d
…
10. /* Convolve the input image with the kernel. */
11.  for(int r = 0; i<N-K+1, i++) {
12.    for(int c = 0; c<N-K+1; c++) {
13.      sum1 = 0;
14.      for(int i = 0; i<K; i++) {
15.        for(int j = 0; i<K; j++) {
16.          sum1 = sum1 + input_image[r+i][c+j] * kernel[i][j];
17.          }
18.        }
19.      output_image[r+dead_rows][c+dead_cols] = (sum1 / normal_factor);
20.    }
21.  }
…
```

FIG. 3.27

C code section for the MATLAB code for a 2D convolution of an input image with a kernel.

```
select loop end
apply
   println("Found loop of type:" + $loop.type);
end
```

FIG. 3.28

Querying loops and reporting their type (i.e., for, while, do while).

code mixed with specific LARA constructs. Fig. 3.28 shows an example where for each loop in the code the weaver prints to the console the type of each loop found. To access information about the program element, the join point can be used in the apply section by prefixing its name with $ ($loop in the example shown). In order to access an attribute of a specific join point, the name of the attribute prefixed by "$" must be followed by "." and by the name of the attribute (e.g., $loop.type). When the aspect is applied to the code in Fig. 3.27, the output is as follows:

```
Found loop of type: for
Found loop of type: for
Found loop of type: for
Found loop of type: for
```

If the println statement is replaced by *println("Is innermost? " +$loop.is_innermost);* the result is as follows:

```
Is innermost? false
Is innermost? false
Is innermost? false
Is innermost? true
```

The semantics of a select-apply section resembles that of a query language. For each program element found by the select statement, the corresponding code of the apply section is executed. In the example shown in Fig. 3.28, the code does not

```
aspectdef ReportLoops
  /*select*/
  select file.function.loop end
  /*apply*/
  apply
      println("Found loop:");
      println("\tFile name: "+$file.name);
      println("\tFunction: "+$function.name);
      println("\tFunction line number: "+$function.line);
      println("\tLoop line number: "+$loop.line);
      println("\tLoop type: "+$loop.type);
      println("\tLoop number of iterations: "+$loop.num_iterations);
      println("\tControl value: "+$loop.control_var);
      println("\tIncrement value: "+$loop.increment_value);
      println("\tLoop rank: "+$loop.rank);
      println("\tNested level: "+$loop.nested_level);
      println("\tIs innermost? "+$loop.is_innermost);
      println("\tIs outermost? "+$loop.is_outermost);
  end
end
```

FIG. 3.29

Querying loops and reporting about them.

modify the program but outputs messages to the console. This is an important mechanism to report program characteristics determined by a static inspection and/or analysis of the input program.

The `select-apply` constructs are required to be part of an `aspect` module. Each `aspect` module begins with the LARA keyword `aspectdef` followed by the name of the `aspect` and ends with the keyword *end*. Fig. 3.29 shows an example of a LARA `aspect` that reports properties for each loop found in the code. We note that in this example the `select` continues to query for loops but in this case we expose the chain of join points `file.function.loop` to access attributes of `file` (e.g., `$file.name`) and `function` (e.g., `$function.name`), besides the ones related to the `loops` (e.g., `$loop.type`, `$loop.num_iterations`, `$loop.rank`, `$loop.is_innermost`, `$loop.is_outermost`).

When the aspect in Fig. 3.29 is applied to the code of Fig. 3.27 when N and K are equal to 512 and 3, respectively, it yields the output as follows:

```
Found loop:
        File name: convolution.c
        Function: conv2
        Loop line number: 11
        Loop type: for
        Loop number of iterations: 510
        ...
        Is innermost? false
        Is outermost? true
...
Found loop:
        File name: convolution.c
        Function: conv2
```

```
Loop line number:15
Loop type: for
Loop number of iterations: 3
...
Is innermost? true
Is outermost? false
```

We can also use variables in LARA `aspects`. They can be global to the `aspect` or local to each `apply` section. Fig. 3.30 presents the use of a global `aspect` variable to count the number of `for`-type loops in a program.

In addition to the ability to query loops of a certain type using the `select` statement (e.g., `select loop{type=="for"} end`), LARA also supports the `condition` statement which filters the join points that are processed in the `apply` section. Conditions can be expressed using complex Boolean expressions, while `select` filters only allow Boolean comparison of an attribute against an expression. Another possibility is to use if statements in the `apply` section. Fig. 3.30 shows three cases of LARA code, which produce the same results.

Each LARA `aspect` module definition can have multiple `select-apply` statements and these behave using a declarative semantic. More specifically, the `aspect` statements are executed in sequence as they occur in the LARA file. It is thus the responsibility of programmers to ensure that dependences are satisfied by placing

```
aspectdef countFORloops
    var num_for_loops = 0;
    select loop{type=="loop"} end
    apply
        num_for_loops = num_for_loops + 1; // count number of loops FOR
    end
    println("Number of loops: "+num_for_loops); // this is a use not suggested
end

aspectdef countFORloops
    var num_for_loops = 0;
    select loop end
    apply
        num_for_loops = num_for_loops + 1; // count number of loops FOR
    end
    condition $loop.type == "for" end
    println("Number of loops: "+num_for_loops); // this is a use not suggested
end

aspectdef countFORloops
    var num_for_loops = 0;
    select loop end
    apply
        if($loop.type == "for") {
            num_for_loops = num_for_loops + 1; // count number of loops FOR
        }
    end
    println("Number of loops: "+num_for_loops); // this is a use not suggested
end
```

FIG. 3.30

Counting the number of `for`-type loops in a program (three ways of supporting conditionals).

```
1.  aspectdef reportNumFORloops
2.    Call A:countFORloops();
3.    println("Number of loops: "+A.num_for_loops);
4.  end
5.
6.  aspectdef countFORloops
7.    output num_for_loops = 0; end   // the no. of loops will be output as a parameter
8.    select loop{type=="loop"} end
9.    apply
10.      num_for_loops = num_for_loops + 1; // count number of loops FOR
11.   end
12. end
```

FIG. 3.31

Counting the number of `for`-type loops in a program and reporting its value (use of two aspects).

the aspect statements in the right order. As can be observed in the `aspect` example in Fig. 3.30, this sequential evaluation leads to the correct reporting of the number of loops (*println* statement in the end of the aspects). An alternative `aspect` specification (yielding the same outcome) would use a second `aspect` to invoke the `aspect` that counts the number of loops and to print its value at the end of its execution (see Fig. 3.31). Note that the code within each `apply` section is strictly imperative.

In the presence of multiple `aspect` definitions in the same file, the first `aspect` definition is considered the main `aspect` and will be automatically executed first. Other `aspects` are only executed if they are explicitly invoked either directly or indirectly by the main `aspect`'s execution.

The list of attributes, actions, and join point children associated to a specific join point can be queried with the following attributes: `attributes`, `actions`, and `selects`, respectively. For instance, `$loop.attributes` outputs the list of attributes (their names to be more precise) for the join point `loop`, `$loop.actions` reports the weaver actions related to the join point `$loop`, and `Weaver.actions` outputs the weaver actions available to LARA.

3.5.2 INSERT ACTION

LARA provides an `insert` action to inject code in the application's source code. This action can be mixed with other statements in the `apply` section. The code to be inserted is identified by the delimiters `%{` and `}%` or ' and ', where the former captures multilined code, and the latter captures single-lined code (similar to a string). The insertion of the code can be performed `before`, `after`, or `replace` the associated join point. Fig. 3.32 shows a simple example that inserts a `printf` statement before each loop in the source code. By default, the `insert` is associated to the join point of the last element of the `select` expression (in a chain), but one can explicitly identify the associated join point by prefixing the `insert` with join point followed by ".". For instance, `$loop.insert` would be equivalent to the `insert` in Fig. 3.32.

```
select function.loop end
apply
  …
    insert before %{printf("Found a loop!\n");}%;
  …
end
```

FIG. 3.32

A simple example of the insert action.

```
select function.loop end
apply
  …
    insert before %{printf("Found a loop at line %d!\n", "+[[$loop.line]]);}%;
  …
end
```

FIG. 3.33

A simple example of the insert action passing values to the code to be inserted.

It is possible to pass data of the aspect and/or join points to the code to be inserted. Fig. 3.33 presents an extension of the previous example to indicate the number of the source-code line of each loop found. In this case, the line attribute of the join point loop ($loop.line) is passed to the inserted code as a parameter between [[]]. The weaving process will substitute, for each execution of the insert statement, [[$loop.line]] by its actual value. In a similar way one can use LARA variables in the sections of code to be inserted.

Insert actions provide a powerful mechanism to add/replace code in an application. The possibility to specify strategies for the insertion of the code is one of the most useful LARA concepts. Fig. 3.34 shows an example of a LARA aspect which specifies the insertion of calls to function QueryPerformanceCounter[6] for measuring the time execution of applications, written in the C programming language, when running in the Windows operating system. Note that the aspect needs to insert the #include (line 5), the declaration of the variables to be used (lines 10 and 11), and the insertion of the code to initialize and start the measurements (select-apply in line 14) and to end the measurements and to output the result (select-apply in line 24). This aspect provides an automatic scheme to modify an application with a timing concern similar to the one presented in Fig. 3.7 and using calls to the clock() function.[7] The code presented in Fig. 3.34 can be easily modified to provide a timing strategy using clock().

---

[6]A function which retrieves the current value of the performance counter and is included in "windows.h."
[7]A C library function which returns the number of clock ticks elapsed since the program was launched and is included in "time.h."

```
1. aspectdef InsertTiming
2.
3.    select file.first_header end
4.    apply
5.        insert after '#include <windows.h>';
6.    end
7.
8.    select function{name=="main"}.first_stmt end
9.    apply
10.       insert before %{__int64 freq, start, end, diff;
11.                        long elapsedTime;}%;
12.   end
13.
14.   select function{name=="main"}.first_stmt end
15.   apply
16.       insert before %{
17.           // get ticks per second
18.           QueryPerformanceFrequency((LARGE_INTEGER*)&freq);
19.           // start timer
20.             QueryPerformanceCounter((LARGE_INTEGER*)&start);
21.       }%;
22.   end
23.
24.   select function{name=="main"}.last_stmt end
25.   apply
26.       insert after %{
27.           // stop timer
28.           QueryPerformanceCounter((LARGE_INTEGER*)&end);
29.
30.           //printf("It took %d ticks\n", (end - start));
31.           printf("Freq %d\n", freq);
32.           elapsedTime = ((end - start) * 1000) / freq;
33.           printf("It took %d ms\n", elapsedTime);
34.       }%;
35.     end
36. end
```

FIG. 3.34

An example using the LARA `insert` action for including code to measure the execution time (in ms) of an application in Windows using the `QueryPerformanceCounter`.

3.5.3 EXEC AND DEF ACTIONS

In the previous section, we presented the `insert` action and showed how to program strategies for instrumenting code in the source code of an application. LARA provides other types of actions. Two actions used to modify the application by using specific code transformations supported by the compiler used are `exec` and `def`. The `exec` action is used to execute weaver-defined actions, such as specific compiler passes (e.g., loop unrolling). The `def` action is used to modify certain application artifacts such as data types of variables.

Fig. 3.35 presents the use of the `exec` action (line 6) to unroll loops. In this case, the `aspect` specifies to unroll by a factor, denoted by variable "factor," loops that are innermost and of type `for`. When applied to the source code of an application, this `aspect` will unroll all the loops respecting these conditions. Fig. 3.36 presents a more elaborated `aspect` which prevents the full unrolling of innermost loops when the

```
1.  aspectdef LoopUnrollInnermost
2.    input factor end
3.
4.    select function.loop end
5.    apply
6.        $loop.exec Unroll(factor);
7.    end
8.    condition
9.        $loop.is_innermost && $loop.type=="for"
10.   end
11. end
```

FIG. 3.35

An example using the LARA exec action to unroll loops.

```
1. aspectdef LoopUnrollInnermost
2.    input factor end
3.
4.    select function.loop end
5.    apply
6.      if(factor == 0) {
7.          if($loop.num_iter <= 8) { // limit fully loop unrolling
8.              $loop.exec Unroll(factor);
9.          } else {
10.             println($loop.id+"no unroll");
11.         }
12.       } else {
13.             $loop.exec Unroll(factor);
14.       }
15.   end
16.   condition
17.       $loop.is_innermost && $loop.type=="for"
18.   end
19. end
```

FIG. 3.36

An example using the LARA exec action to unroll loops and using a rule to decide about the unrolling.

unrolling factor is zero and the selected loop has a large number of iterations, in this case more than eight iterations.

Fig. 3.37 presents an example where the variable z is assigned to type float. This example uses the *def* action and implies changes in the Intermediate Representation (IR) of the compiler.

```
1.  select var{name=="z"} end
2.  apply
3.    def type = "float";
4.  end
```

FIG. 3.37

An example using the LARA def action to change the type of a variable.

```
call LoopUnrollInnermost(2);
```

FIG. 3.38

An example of a call statement.

3.5.4 INVOKING ASPECTS

LARA provides a mechanism for invoking an `aspect` from an `aspect` definition and optionally share data between them through its input and output parameters. This enhances modularity and reuse. Fig. 3.38 shows a simple example where one of the `LoopUnrollInnermost` `aspects` presented before is invoked with 2 as its argument.

When calling an `aspect` with output parameters, the only way to access the output values is through the assignment of an identifier to the call and then to use a syntax similar to a field access. For instance, in `call A:countFORloops();` in line 2 of Fig. 3.31, the identifier `A` is used to represent that specific call of `aspect countFORloops`. The use of `A.num_for_loops` in line 3 allows the value of `num_for_loops` to be accessed in that specific call.

The current semantics related to calls varies in terms of `insert` and `exec/def` actions. The result of the `insert` actions is not made available to subsequent weaving statements until the output code is generated and input to the compiler. That is, the code modifications using `insert` actions are not immediately visible during the weaving process responsible for those insertions.

On the other hand, the changes that result from the `exec/def` actions are available once execution enters a new `aspect`. We show here an example of what the semantic of the `exec/def` actions implies. The `aspect` presented before in Fig. 3.35 unrolls the innermost `for` loops. If we apply the `aspect` with a factor $= 0$, we will fully unroll all the loops that fit a specific condition. This `aspect` does not fully unroll the loops *recursively* because it only considers the original innermost loops found in the application. The recursive invocation of this `aspect` would lead to the full unrolling of all the loops regardless of their original position in the nested loop structure. Fig. 3.39 presents a possible `aspect` that recursively unrolls all loops in the program. Note the use of the `break` instruction in line 23 to prevent the unrolling of loops that no longer exist as a result of having been fully unrolled. Fig. 3.40 illustrates an `aspect` with the same goal but using iteration instead of recursion.

3.5.5 EXECUTING EXTERNAL TOOLS

LARA also allows to explicitly invoke external tools from aspects and to import data output from the execution of such tools, providing a transparent way to use the feedback information to make decisions at the LARA level and iterations over a specific tool flow.

Fig. 3.41 presents an example which invokes Xilinx backend tools having as input a VHDL or Verilog description of the hardware to be synthesized, mapped, placed, and routed to a specific target FPGA. The LARA aspect also provides support for the execution of one or more tools based on the value of the `opt` input parameter.

```
1. aspectdef  mainloopunroll
2.    var loopsDone = {};
3.    call loopunroll(loopsDone);
4. end
5.
6. aspectdef  loopunroll
7.   input loopsDone end
8.
9.   select loop{type=="for"} end
10.  apply
11.       println("-> CONSIDERING ACTION TO LOOP ID: "+$loop.ID);
12.       if(!loopsDone[$loop.ID]) {
13.            println("ACTION TO BE PERFORMED TO LOOP ID: "+$loop.ID);
14.            println("ITER: "+$loop.num_iterations);
15.
16.            loopsDone[$loop.ID] = true;
17.
18.            exec Unroll(0);  // do loop unrolling
19.
20.            call A:loopunroll(loopsDone); // recursive
21.            loopsDone = A.loopsDone; // update loopsDone
22.
23.            break;
24.       }
25.   end
26.   condition $loop.is_innermost && ($loop.num_iterations != -1) end
27. end
28.
```

FIG. 3.39

An example using the LARA exec action to unroll loops recursively.

```
1. aspectdef Strategy
2.    do { call A:loopunroll(); } while(A.changed);
3. end
4.
5. aspectdef  loopunroll
6.    output changed = false end
7.    select loop{type=="for"}  end
8.    apply
9.         exec Unroll(0);
10.        changed = true;
11.   end
12.   condition $loop.is_innermost && ($loop.num_iterations != -1) end
13. end
```

FIG. 3.40

An example using the LARA exec action to unroll loops iteratively.

The @function used in the println statements in lines 6, 11, 15, and 19 is the data output from the execution tool represented as a JSON object.

The execution of the *xst* tool (line 3 of the LARA aspect) will provide the following attributes and the correspondent values according to the input VHDL/Verilog code and target FPGA:

```
1. aspectdef xilinx
2.      input opt=1, name = "myIP", folder = "myPrj" end
3.      run(tool: "xst", args: {ModuleName: name,
4.              pathFolder: folder, pathISETools: ""});
5.      println("--- FUNCTION ATTRIBUTES AFTER XST EXECUTION:");
6.      printObject(@function);
7.      if(opt > 1) {
8.          run(tool: "ngdbuild", args: {ModuleName: name});
9.          run(tool: "map", args: {ModuleName: name});
10.         println("--- REPORTING RESULTS AFTER MAP EXECUTION:");
11.         printObject(@function);
12.         if(opt > 2) {
13.             run(tool: "par", args: {ModuleName: name});
14.             println("--- REPORTING RESULTS AFTER MAP EXECUTION:");
15.             printObject(@function);
16.             if(opt > 3) {
17.                 run(tool: "xpr", args: {ModuleName: name});
18.                 println("--- REPORTING RESULTS AFTER XPR EXECUTION:");
19.                 printObject(@function);
20.             }
21.         }
22.     }
23. end
```

FIG. 3.41

An example using the LARA run action to invoke Xilinx backend tools (xst, ngbuild, par, and xpr).

```
--- FUNCTION ATTRIBUTES AFTER XST EXECUTION:
myIP:
  numSliceRegisters: 881
  maxFreq: 324.528
  msgWarnings: 477
  device: 5vlx50tff1136
  minPeriod: 3.081
  msgInfos: 16
  delay: 1.097
  numSliceLUTs: 660
  msgErrors: 0
  numLUTasSRLs: 5
```

Fig. 3.42 presents another LARA `aspect` that includes a call to the aspect shown in Fig. 3.41, to a High-Level Synthesis (HLS) tool to generate the VHDL description from an input C function and to a VHDL simulator. The `aspect` is responsible for reporting the results regarding clock cycles and execution time considering the maximum clock frequency reported by the tools.

This support provided by LARA to execute tools (including ones aided with LARA) conveys developers with artifacts and with a unified view which diminishes the efforts to program and evaluate DSE schemes. Fig. 3.43 shows a simple example of a DSE scheme. In this case, four different loop unrolling factors and no loop unrolling are explored with the goal of achieving a hardware design with the lowest possible latency.

```
1. import xilinx;
2. aspectdef C2Gates
3.     call A:hls("filter_subband", "vhdl");
4.     call B:simul("filter_subband");
5.     println("RESULT:");
6.     printObject(@design, "\t");
7.     var lat = @design.filter_subband_kernel.Latency;
8.     println("###### Number of clock cycles: "+lat);
9.     call C:xilinx(1,"filter_subband");
10.    println("Execution time: "+(lat/C.MaxFreq)+" us");
11. end
```

FIG. 3.42

An example using the LARA run action to invoke different tools and reporting the results considering performance.

```
1. import xilinx;
2. aspectdef ol_UnrollKInnerLoops1_modular
3.     var confs = {}; var best_lat = Number.MAX_VALUE;
4.     var best_conf; var exploreParam = ["1", "2", "4", "8", "0"];
5.     for(var i = 0; i < exploreParam.length; i++) {
6.         call A:compile("filter_subband", "vhdl", "UnrollKInnerLoops1_inner",
7.                              "-argv=(" + exploreParam[i] + ")");
8.         call B:simul("filter_subband");
9.         println("RESULT:");
10.        printObject(@design, "\t");
11.        var lat = @design.filter_subband_kernel.Latency;
12.        confs[exploreParam[i]] = lat;
13.        if(lat < best_lat) {
14.            best_lat=lat;
15.            best_conf=exploreParam[i];
16.        }
17.        println("###### Number of clock cycles: "+lat);
18.    }
19.    println("best_lat: " + best_lat + " | best_conf: " + best_conf );
20.    println("Design points and correspondent no. of clock cycles:");
21.    printObject(confs);
22. end
```

FIG. 3.43

An example using the LARA run action iteratively.

3.5.6 COMPILATION AND SYNTHESIS STRATEGIES IN LARA

The compilation and synthesis strategies in LARA include code transformations, exploration of parameters, and specification of complementary program knowledge that can be conveyed to other compilation tools in producing better quality code. As mentioned in Chapter 1, the use of LARA in this book intends to fulfill two goals: (1) to provide a specification of code transformations and optimization strategies and (2) as a DSL to be used in experiments regarding learning activities. Goal (2) has focused on using specific tools with LARA support, namely, the following tools:

- MANET, a source-to-source C compiler based on Cetus: http://specs.fe.up.pt/tools/manet/
- KADABRA, a source-to-source Java compiler based on Spoon: http://specs.fe.up.pt/tools/kadabra/
- MATISSE, a MATLAB to C/OpenCL compiler: http://specs.fe.up.pt/tools/matisse/

The LARA strategies used in the context of goal (2) have been developed partially based on the support that third-party tools provide to implement the semantics of the LARA actions. It is conceivable that LARA strategies, while well defined, cannot be used in cooperation with tools that do not export a "control interface" that allows the LARA aspects to carry out the corresponding actions.

3.6 SUMMARY

This chapter presented the main concepts regarding the first stages of an application's design cycle such as its specification, prototyping and development with the main emphasis on the abstraction levels, and on how to deal with different concerns; the specializations required when dealing with generic code and with high-level models, and on how to deal with multiple targets. This chapter also introduced the concepts of translation, compilation, and synthesis design flows, and hardware/software partitioning (including the mapping of computations to heterogeneous architectures). Lastly, we have described an AOP language, LARA, specially designed to allow developers to describe sophisticated code instrumentation schemes and advanced mapping and compilation strategies.

3.7 FURTHER READING

Design flows operating on heterogeneous platforms with hardware accelerators have been the focus of recent research (see, e.g., the hArtes design flow in [24]). One of the main tasks of a design flow involves the decision to map computations into software and/or hardware components. This task is traditionally known as hardware/software partitioning (see, e.g., [25]), especially when the target system considers software components implemented in CPUs and hardware components synthesized from the input computations. More complete forms of hardware/software partitioning also consider hardware accelerators being then synthesized and/or existent as coprocessors. Recently, the migration of computations from the CPU to hardware accelerators (including GPUs and FPGAs) is referred as offloading computations to these devices.

Hardware/software partitioning started with static approaches, i.e., with partitioning performed at design/compile time [26, 40]. At compile time there have been approaches starting with the computations described in high-level code (such as from

C/C++ code) or with the binaries and/or traces of executed instructions [41]. Approaches addressing dynamic hardware/software partitioning have been focused more recently (see, e.g., [27,42]). Other approaches consider the static preparation of hardware/software components, but delegate to runtime the decision to execute computations in hardware or software. For instance, Beisel et al. [28] present a system for deciding at runtime between hardware/software partitions at library function level. The system intercepts library calls and for each call it decides to offload the call to a hardware accelerator. The decision is based on tables storing information about the execution time for each supported function and for different data sizes. Additional decisions can also consider other information, such as the number of iterations (calculated at runtime) each loop will execute for each execution point, to decide offloading computations to hardware accelerators. Vaz et al. [29] propose to move the decision point within the application to possibly hide some overheads, such as the preparation of the coprocessor execution.

Current heterogeneous multicore architectures support GPUs and/or reconfigurable hardware (e.g., provided by FPGAs) with the possibility to provide different execution models and architectures, thus increasing the complexity of mapping computations to the target components. Systems may have to consider not only code transformations that might be suitable for a particular target, but also decide where to execute the computations, which is not trivial. For instance, when considering a target architecture consisting of a CPU+GPU, a system may need to decide about the execution of OpenCL kernels in a multicore CPU or in a GPU [30]. The complexity of the problem and the variable parameters involved to make a decision are being addressed by sophisticated solutions, such as the ones using machine learning techniques to estimate execution time based on static and dynamic code features [31]. Other authors address the data migration problem when targeting GPU acceleration [32]. As these are hot research topics, it is expected that further solutions will be proposed especially considering the interplay between code transformations, workloads, runtime adaptivity, and the specificities of the target architecture.

REFERENCES

[1] Mathworks Inc., MATLAB—the language of technical computing. http://www.mathworks.com/products/matlab [Accessed May 2016].
[2] Simulink—simulation and model-based design—MathWorks, © 1994–2016 The MathWorks, Inc., www.mathworks.com/products/simulink/ [Accessed May 2016].
[3] Corre Y, Hoang V-T, Diguet J-P, Heller D, Lagadec L. HLS-based fast design space exploration of ad hoc hardware accelerators: a key tool for MPSoC synthesis on FPGA. In: International conf. on design and architectures for signal and image processing (DASIP' 2012), Oct. 23–25; 2012. 8 p.
[4] Kernighan BW. The C programming language. 2nd ed. Piscataway, NJ: Prentice Hall; 1988.
[5] The Octave Home Page. http://www.gnu.org/software/octave/ [Accessed May 2016].
[6] Scilab: Home, © Scilab Enterprises S.A.S 2015. http://www.scilab.org/ [Accessed January 2016].
[7] UTDSP Benchmark Suite. http://www.eecg.toronto.edu/~corinna/DSP/infrastructure/UTDSP.html [Accessed March 2016].

[8] Fowler M. Domain specific languages. 1st ed. Boston, USA: Addison-Wesley Professional; 2010.

[9] Welcome To UML Web Site! Copyright © 1997–2016 Object Management Group®, Inc. http://www.uml.org/ [Accessed May 2016].

[10] Ptolemy Project Home Page, Copyright © 1999–2016 UC Regents, ptolemy.eecs.berkeley.edu/ [Accessed May 2016].

[11] What Is Hardware-in-the-Loop Simulation? © 1994–2016 The MathWorks, Inc. http://www.mathworks.com/help/physmod/simscape/ug/what-is-hardware-in-the-loop-simulation.html [Accessed May 2016].

[12] Kiczales G, Lamping J, Mendhekar A, Maeda C, Lopes CV, Jean-Marc L, et al. Aspect-oriented programming. In: 11th European conference on object-oriented programming (ECOOP'97), Jyväskylä, Finland, June 9–13, 1997, Lecture Notes in Computer Science (LNCS), vol. 1241. Heidelberg: Springer-Verlag; 1997. p. 220–42.

[13] Elrad T, Filman RE, Bader A. Aspect-oriented programming: introduction. Commun ACM 2001;44(10):29–32.

[14] Corner detection. https://en.wikipedia.org/wiki/Corner_detection [Accessed May 2016].

[15] Fingeroff M. High-level synthesis blue book. Bloomington, IN: Xlibris Corporation; 2010.

[16] Vivado high level synthesis. http://www.xilinx.com/products/designtools/vivado/integration/esl-design.html [Accessed January 2016].

[17] Arató P, Mann ZÁ, Orbán A. Algorithmic aspects of hardware/software partitioning. ACM Trans Des Autom Electron Syst (TODAES) 2005;10(1):136–56.

[18] Duran A, Ayguadé E, Badia RM, Labarta J, Martinell L, Martorell X, et al. Ompss: a proposal for programming heterogeneous multi-core architectures. Parallel Process Lett 2011;21(02):173–93.

[19] Wernsing JR, Stit G. Elastic computing: a framework for transparent, portable, and adaptive multi-core heterogeneous computing. In: Proc. of the ACM SIGPLAN/SIGBED conference on languages, compilers, and tools for embedded systems; 2010. p. 115–24.

[20] Cardoso JMP, Carvalho T, Coutinho JGF, Nobre R, Nane R, Diniz PC, et al. Controlling a complete hardware synthesis toolchain with LARA aspects. Microprocess Microsyst 2013;37(8):1073–89.

[21] Cardoso JMP, Coutinho JGF, Carvalho T, Diniz PC, Petrov Z, Luk W, et al. Performance driven instrumentation and mapping strategies using the lara aspect oriented programming approach. In: Software: practice and experience (SPE). New York, NY, USA: John Wiley & Sons Ltd; 2014. December.

[22] Fabry J, Dinkelaker T, Noyé J, Tanter É. A taxonomy of domain-specific aspect languages. ACM Comput Surv 2015;47(3). Article 40, 44 pages.

[23] Cardoso JMP, Diniz P, Coutinho JG, Petrov Z, editors. Compilation and synthesis for embedded reconfigurable systems: an aspect-oriented approach. 1st ed. New York, Dordrecht, Heidelberg, London: Springer; 2013. May.

[24] Bertels K, Sima VM, Yankova Y, Kuzmanov G, Luk W, Coutinho JGF, et al. HArtes: hardware-software codesign for heterogeneous multicore platforms. IEEE Micro 2010;30(5):88–97.

[25] López-Vallejo M, López JC. On the hardware-software partitioning problem: system modeling and partitioning techniques. ACM Trans Des Autom Electron Syst 2003; 8(3):269–97.

[26] Ernst R, Henkel J, Benne T. Hardware-software cosynthesis for microcontrollers. IEEE Des Test 1993;10(4):64–75.

[27] Stitt G, Lysecky R, Vahid F. Dynamic hardware/software partitioning: a first approach. In: Proceedings of the 40th annual design automation conference (DAC'03). New York, NY: ACM; 2003. p. 250–5.

[28] Beisel T, Niekamp M, Plessl C. Using shared library interposing for transparent acceleration in systems with heterogeneous hardware accelerators. In: Proc. int. conf. on application-specific systems, architectures, and processors (ASAP'10). IEEE Computer Society. July; 2010. p. 65–72.

[29] Vaz G, Riebler H, Kenter T, Plessl C. Potential and methods for embedding dynamic offloading decisions into application code. Comput Electr Eng 2016;55(C):91–111.

[30] Wang Z, Grewe D, O'Boyle MFP. Automatic and portable mapping of data parallel programs to OpenCL for GPU-based heterogeneous systems. ACM Trans Archit Code Optim 2014;11(4):26.

[31] Wen Y, Wang Z, O'Boyle M. Smart multi-task scheduling for OpenCL programs on CPU/GPU heterogeneous platforms. In: Proc. 21st annual IEEE intl. conf. on high performance computing (HiPC'14), Goa, India, IEEE, Dec. 17–20; 2014. 10 p.

[32] Wang B, Wu B, Li D, Shen X, Yu W, Jiao Y, et al. Exploring hybrid memory for GPU energy efficiency through software-hardware co-design. In: Proc. of the 22nd international conf. on parallel architectures and compilation techniques (PACT'13), IEEE Press, Piscataway, NJ; 2013. p. 93–102.

[33] Hickey PC, Pike L, Elliott T, Bielman J, Launchbury J. Building embedded systems with embedded DSLs, In: Proceedings of the 19th ACM SIGPLAN international conference on Functional programming (ICFP '14). New York, NY, USA: ACM; 2014. p. 3–9.

[34] Graepel T, Candela JQ, Borchert T, Herbrich R. Web-scale Bayesian click-through rate prediction for sponsored search advertising in Microsoft's Bing search engine, In: Proc. of the 27th Intl. Conf. on Machine Learning (ICML-10); 2010. p. 13–20.

[35] Augonnet C, Thibault S, Namyst R, Wacrenier P-A. StarPU: a unified platform for task scheduling on heterogeneous multicore architectures. Concurr Comput Pract Exper 2011;23(2):187–98.

[36] Linderman MD, Collins JD, Wang H, Meng TH. Merge: a programming model for heterogeneous multi-core systems. ACM SIGOPS Oper Sys Rev 2008;42(2).

[37] O'Neill E, McGlone J, Coutinho JGF, Doole A, Ragusa C, Pell O, Sanders P. Cross resource optimisation of database functionality across heterogeneous processors, In: Parallel and distributed processing with applications (ISPA); 26–28 Aug.; 2014. p. 150–7.

[38] Cardoso JMP, Carvalho T, de F. Coutinho JG, Luk W, Nobre R, Diniz PC, et al. LARA: an aspect-oriented programming language for embedded systems. In: Proc. of the intl conf. on aspect-oriented software development (AOSD'12), Potsdam, Germany, March 25–30. ACM; 2012. p. 179–90.

[39] Kiczales G, Lamping J, Mendhekar A, Maeda C, Videira Lopes C, Loingtier J-M, Irwin J. Aspect-Oriented Programming, In: 11th European conference on object-oriented programming (ECOOP'97), Jyväskylä, Finland, June 9–13, 1997, Lecture Notes in Computer Science (LNCS), vol. 1241, Springer; 1997. p. 220–42.

[40] Gupta RK, De Micheli G. Hardware-software cosynthesis for digital systems. IEEE Des Test Comput 1993;10(3):29–41.

[41] Bispo J, Paulino N, Cardoso JMP, Ferreira JC. Transparent trace-based binary acceleration for reconfigurable HW/SW systems. IEEE Trans Ind Inform 2013;9(3):1625–34.

[42] Lysecky R, Vahid F. Design and implementation of a microblaze-based warp processor. ACM Trans Embed Comput Syst 2009;8(3):22:1–22:22.

Source code analysis and instrumentation

4

4.1 INTRODUCTION

Source code analysis and instrumentation are fundamental aspects in the software development process for understanding application behavior and potential code transformations. Understanding the structure of the code both at a high granularity level (global program scope) as well as at a lower granularity level (procedure/function scope level) is very important for debugging and validation. At a high level, understanding the structure of the code by examining which procedures invoke other procedures or which procedures allocate storage enables the use of sophisticated source code transformations or performance-oriented transformations (or "optimizations"). Understanding storage allocation and its use is a key analysis for embedded systems given their often limited memory capacity. Last, but not least, understanding where the execution spends the bulk of its time (execution time profiling) is a key information to help developers select a set of transformations that have impact on performance.

Programmers might be interested in many aspects of code analysis. An extensive number of software metrics have been proposed by the software engineering community (see, e.g., [1–3]). These include simple metrics such as the number of lines of code (LOCs), cyclomatic complexity, and cohesion. If the developer's goal is to assess the potential for migration to a CPU with high floating-point computation capability, then an analysis of floating-point computation versus integer arithmetic computation is desirable. Yet, in the context of concurrent execution, there is a need to know the data communication volume to assess the benefits of porting the application code to a system with more suitable internode communication bandwidth.

In general, source code analysis can be viewed in two perspectives. The first perspective looks at code analysis as the means to an end. That is, a particular goal must be defined in order to identify the techniques that can achieve it. For instance, one commonly used technique to help optimize an application's execution time (the "goal") is *code profiling* to find hotspots, also known as *critical sections*. Hotspots are regions of the code where program execution spends a high portion of the overall execution time, and thus are prime candidates for optimization. By reducing the execution time of hotspots, higher global reductions are achieved

Embedded Computing for High Performance. http://dx.doi.org/10.1016/B978-0-12-804189-5.00004-1

than by reducing the execution of code regions with lower contribution to the overall execution time.[1]

Still, code analyses are not exclusively geared toward performance and other optimization goals. In a second perspective, the goal of discovering information about an application through an exploratory experimental process aims at uncovering unforeseen properties of an application—related to functional and nonfunctional concerns—and to allow the development of new code analysis techniques that can handle the growing complexity of software applications. Code analyses can provide insights, e.g., into assertion discovery, clone detection, debugging, empirical software engineering research, fault localization, optimization techniques, performance modeling, program evolution, quality assessment, reverse engineering, safety criticality, software maintenance, software reliability engineering, software versioning, symbolic execution, testing, validation (conformity checking), and verification.

In many scenarios, tools that can automatically analyze code are increasingly desirable. These tools are invariably diverse as the type of information they capture. For simple analysis, such as the calling structure, a simple source code analyzer will suffice and code execution is not required. On the other end of the spectrum, dynamic measures such as the amount of storage used or data transferred, tools must examine a running executable under representative input datasets. In order to address the dynamic behavior of applications and their main characteristics in terms of the input data, operating environment, and target system, profiling is becoming an essential stage when developing an application.

In this book, we focus on code analysis and instrumentation to help developers (and in some contexts, automated tools) to better decide about how to transform a given section of code and/or to better map an application to a target computer architecture, possibly consisting of multiple cores and hardware accelerators. Of paramount importance to these goals is the extraction of data- and task-level parallelism, data communication demands, and program execution distribution at function and code section levels. Here, we assume the existence of the source code of the application and a process consisting of code transformations, compiler optimizations, and code translation and/or extensions to different programming models.

4.2 ANALYSIS AND METRICS

The output of a source code analysis can take many forms. It can provide high-level information about the application, such as metrics identifying program properties, and annotated internal representations such as call graphs, capturing the number

---

[1]Amdahl's Law [4].

of times a function has been invoked. Unlike other transformations that modify the source code, code instrumentation[2] is often meant to be executed in order to uncover dynamic properties of the application and discarded afterwards. A classic example of instrumentation consists of inserting timing calls in strategic regions of code to identify hotspots.

We can thus classify code analyses as either *static* or *dynamic*. *Static* code analysis is applied without running the application and requires the inspection and analysis of the source code. It focuses mainly on the structure of the application code itself and is, in general, intended for application code understanding. Programmers need to understand which sections of the code invoke which routines (or procedures) and what form of concurrent constructs are used. These analyses thus inspect the source code and do not require the knowledge of the program input to extract metrics of "performance" as the application is never executed. The scope of the derived information is thus limited.

TOOLS FOR PROFILING

Typical tools used for profiling an application include GNU *Gprof*[a] [5], *Valgrind*[b] [6], VTune,[c] and Vampir.[d] Note, however, that according to the target system there might be specific APIs and libraries to acquire certain system information such as power consumption.

[a]GNU gprof: http://www.cs.utah.edu/dept/old/texinfo/as/gprof.html.
Gprof man page: http://www.gnu.org/software/binutils/manual/gprof-2.9.1/html_mono/gprof.html.
[b]Valgrind Home: http://www.valgrind.org/ [Accessed June 2014].
[c]Intel VTune Amplifier XE 2013: http://www.intel.com/software/products/vtune/ [Accessed June 2014].
[d]Vampir: https://www.vampir.eu [Accessed October 2015].

In contrast, a *dynamic* analysis aims at uncovering metrics of "performance" that are inherently tied to the execution of the code. There is a wide variety of metrics that are of interest, and analyses such as code *profiling* are supported by *instrumentation* of either the source code and/or of its binary executable form.

Given the diversity and possibly the huge volume of the data uncovered by dynamic analyses (as these can vary widely given the characteristics of the input datasets) it is not uncommon for tools to generate aggregate summary data or to simply focus on selected metrics of performance. A specific example includes metrics such as number and size of messages exchanged between concurrently executing threads in MPI (Message Passing Interface) programs. Depending on the number of threads, the size of the generated dataset using such analysis (instrumenting the MPI send/receive calls) can be extremely large.

Complementary to the type of analysis, we can also classify them as *safe* if they can provide assurance of a particular outcome (for instance, if function A is executed, then function B is executed as well). In addition, an analysis is said to be *sound* if

---

[2]Note that the instrumentation can be applied at compiler intermediate representations and/or at assembly and binary levels.

it provides correctness guarantees with respect to the program semantics. One example of an *unsound* analysis is word length optimization, which assigns custom word lengths to variables and expressions of the program (as opposed to fixed 32- or 64-bit widths) to derive a more efficient implementation (e.g., using fewer hardware resources, saving memory) based on the expected input ranges and the desired output precision.

We can also classify the outcomes of static analyses as code properties and/or source code metrics, and the outcome of dynamic properties as execution metrics. Code properties capture structural, syntactic, and semantic information about the source code. They can identify, for instance, whether a specific variable is of integer type, whether a function is only declared within the context of a file, or if a variable's value can be reached in a particular region of code. On the other hand, source code metrics provide a quantitative measure that allows assertions to be made about the application's code, for instance, about its complexity, computational requirements, and even design quality. A simple commonly used measure for code complexity is the number of lines of code (LOC) (Table 4.1).

Table 4.1 Examples of common code metrics

Metric	Description	Method	Scope
Lines of code	Number of lines of code in all files	Code inspection	Complexity
# operators	Number of operators in a module	Code inspection	Complexity
Cyclomatic complexity	Complexity of the module structure	Code inspection	Complexity
Coupling	Degree of interdependence between software modules	Code inspection	Complexity
Cohesion	Degree in which elements of a module belong together	Code inspection	Complexity
Code coverage	Degree in which the source is tested by unit and integration tests	Code instrumentation and execution	Testing
Profiling	Execution time for modules in the program	Code instrumentation and execution	Optimization
Power consumption	Dynamic power consumed when executing the program	Code instrumentation and execution	Optimization
Performance model	Provides an estimation of how much profitable a module can be on a particular device based on the input data (size, data type, etc)	Code inspection, instrumentation and execution	Optimization

4.3 STATIC SOURCE CODE ANALYSIS

We now focus on tools and analysis techniques geared toward static code analysis. These tools begin by parsing the source code to generate one or more internal representations, abstracting away lexical details, while supporting a representation that preserves program semantics and is more adequate for automated code analysis. Typical examples of internal representations include abstract syntax trees (ASTs), control flow graphs (CFGs), call graphs (CGs), dataflow graphs (DFGs), representations based on the static single assignment (SSA) form [7], and Data Dependence Graphs (DDGs). While internal representations can be derived directly from the code during the parsing process (e.g., ASTs), other representations require prior analysis. For instance, the question of whether a function F directly (or indirectly) calls G, or whether a variable x uses a value defined in a prior statement, requires analysis of calls (and the generation of call graphs) and dataflow analysis, respectively.

An important static analysis task is the identification of data dependences. This identification is fundamental to decide about the parallelization of the code and about the application of many code transformations described in Chapter 5. The following subsection describes data dependences and some of the representations used to identify those dependences.

4.3.1 DATA DEPENDENCES

A substantial amount of a modern compiler's effort is dedicated to program analysis and transformations often incorrectly described as "optimizations."[3] These transformations take advantage of the characteristics of the target architecture such as its pipelined execution units, cache memories, and/or multiple execution units in the form of multiple homogeneous or heterogeneous cores as is the case of systems with multiple CPU cores and additional GPU devices.

Often, to exploit these features, compilers change the execution order of the operations as specified by programmers. For example, operations that manipulate the same data items should be "bundled" together in the same processing unit. Furthermore, operations that manipulate the same data items should also be executed adjacent in time. In other words, operations that operate on the same items should be colocated in space and in time to expose the benefits of concurrency and locality, respectively.

At the cornerstone of the compiler transformations, which expose these notions of concurrency and locality, is the notion of *data dependence* that ensures the fundamental property of every compiler—*correctness*. Two sequential operations, op1 and op2 (or instructions, i1 and i2) are data dependent if they manipulate (either

---

[3]The dependence on input values precludes a compiler to generate optimal code for any nontrivial code in what is referred to as "undecidability."

by reading or by writing) the same data item d. This dependence can thus be classified as four types of dependences, namely:

- True-data dependence: op1 writes d; op2 reads d, i.e., the first instruction possibly modifies the value of the data item *d*; which op2 will read.
- Anti-data dependence: op1 reads d; op2 writes d, i.e., the second instruction possibly modifies the value of the data item *d*; which op1 has read.
- Output-data dependence: both op1 and op2 modify the value of the data item d. The value written by op2 is the value of *d* after both operations execute.
- Input-data dependence: both op1 and op2 read the value of the data item d. Neither operation modifies the value of *d*, which remains unchanged after their execution.

With the exception of input data dependences, all the other forms of dependences force the compiler to preserve the original execution order of the two operations as otherwise there is no guarantee that the final value of the data item d is the same.

Fig. 4.1A depicts an example with three operations (specified as simple C program statements) manipulating scalar variables, a, b, and c. In Fig. 4.1B we

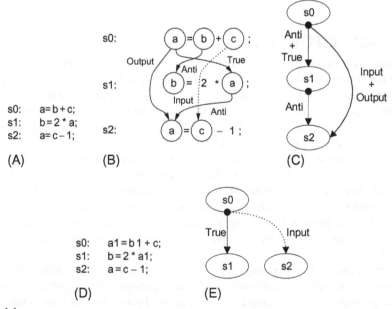

FIG. 4.1

Example of a sequence of statements on scalar variables, the corresponding types of data dependences between the statements, and the data dependence graph (DDG). (A) Sequence of statements, (B) types of data dependences, (C) DDG, (D) sequence of statements after variable renaming, and (E) DDG after variable renaming.

present graphically the various types of dependences between these operations. For example, there is a *true* data dependence between the operations in statement s1 and s0 as the value of the variable a used (or read) in s1 is defined (or written) by the operation in s0. Conversely, there is an *anti*-data dependence between s1 and s0 as the value of the variable b defined (or written) in s1 is used (or read) in the operation s0. The other types of dependences are also shown being apparent that the same operation can have more than one type of data dependence with other operations. For example, the operation in statement s0 has both *output* and *input* dependence with the operation in statement s2.

Fig. 4.1C shows the representation of the data dependences in the example as a data dependence graph (DDG). The output- and the antidependences can be eliminated by applying variable renaming as shown in Fig. 4.1D, which results in the DDG of Fig. 4.1E. The data dependence graph can be seen as a specific case of a dataflow graph (DFG) where nodes can be, e.g., statements, tasks, functions, and the edges represent the dependences (which of course are associated to the flow of data in the case of the true dependences).

As the example illustrates, any compiler must be conservative and perform precise data dependence analysis so as to guarantee the correctness of the transformation it applies to the code. Data-independent operations (or instructions) can be freely interchanged in terms of their execution order to improve their locality of reference or simply executed in distinct execution units for concurrency. Data-dependent operations, however, must be executed in the same relative order (either in the same processing unit or in distinct units) although other operations unrelated to them can be executed in between them. For this reason, we rename variables "a" and "b" from the code example in Fig. 4.1A to remove output and antidependences, respectively, thus allowing a compiler to change the relative order of any of the operations (Fig. 4.1D and 4.1E), as otherwise any execution order (other than the one present in the original code) would yield different results.

While for scalar variables is rather simple for a compiler to uncover all types of data dependences,[4] for other constructs such as loops and arrays, accurate data dependence requires a more sophisticated analysis. A particular context where accurate data dependence analysis is feasible is the case of loop constructs whose body does not include control flow statements and manipulate exclusively scalar variable or array variables where the array indexing functions are defined as integer affine functions[5] of the enclosed loop control (or index) variables.

When faced with loop constructs, the compiler data dependence analysis needs to understand the data access pattern of the various array elements (the data items) with respect to each other and with respect to the loop iterations. A key question is then to

---

[4]We are assuming here that there exists no alias between variable names, that is, a distinct scalar variable name refers to a distinct memory location at runtime. Languages such as C that allow pointers usually hamper the compiler's ability to distinguish between them.

[5]An integer affine function of variables $i_0, i_1, \ldots, i_k$ is defined as $a_0 \times i_0 + a_1 \times i_1 + \ldots a_k \times i_k + c$ where the values a_0 through a_k are known integer constants.

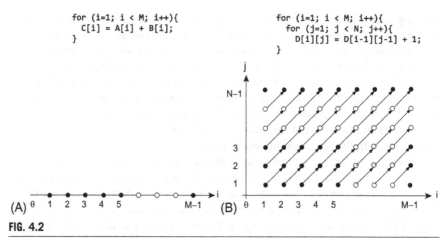

FIG. 4.2

C source code examples of loops that manipulate array variables using affine index functions: (A) a single dimensional example; (B) a two-dimensional example. The iteration spaces (one- and two-dimensional) are depicted below each example source code.

determine which, if any, iteration of the loops is data dependent on which other iterations of the same loop.

To support the data dependence analysis in the context of loop nests and arrays with affine index functions, researchers developed the notion of iteration space and dependence vectors. The iteration space and the corresponding iteration vector define the space of iterations of the loops as an integer (or discrete) Cartesian space with as many dimensions as there are nested loops in the code section under analysis. The dependence vector determines which iterations of this space depend on which iterations of the same space, i.e., in which iterations of the loop the statements of the body of the loop have data dependences with the same statements of the same loop but in distinct iterations. Fig. 4.2 depicts two simple examples of loops that manipulate array variable using affine index functions. In the lower section of Fig. 4.2 we depict the corresponding iteration spaces, respectively, a single dimensional space and a two dimensional space.

Given the iteration space, formally represented by a vector space $I=(i_1, ..., i_k)$ where i_1 and i_k represent the base vectors of this space, and correspond to each of the loop index control variables, the data dependence analysis for the loop must determine if there exist two distinct iterations, say I_1 and I_2 such that the array elements accessed by the operations in these iterations are nondisjoint. In other words, the compiler must determine if for every pair of array references (to the same array) there exists I_1 and $I_2 \in I$, such that $F_1(I_1)=F_2(I_2)$ where the F function denotes the affine indexing function for each of the array references, say reference 1 and 2. Once data

```
for(i=0; i < M; i++)                parfor(i=0; i < M; i++)
  for(j=1; j < N; j++)                for(j=1; j < N; j++)
    A[i][j] = A[i][j-1] + 1;            A[i][j] = A[i][j-1] + 1;
```

FIG. 4.3

Parallelization of the outermost loop i in a doubly loop nest. Dependence vector $D=(0,1)$.

dependence is ascertained, a further refinement is required to determine the type of dependence as that can influence the range of program transformations a compiler can legally apply. For the example on the left in Fig. 4.2, there is no data dependence between any of the iterations of the loop as every iteration accesses a distinct data element for all the arrays. We represent this lack of data dependence by the dependence vector $D=(0)$. For the example on the right, however, there is a data dependence between distinct iterations of the loop denoted by the dependence vector $D=(1,1)$. In this particular case, this dependence vector is very precise, as it indicates that there is a dependence between iterations (i_1,j_1) and (i_2,j_2) of the loop where $i_2=i_1+1$ and $j_2=j_1+1$. Fig. 4.3 shows another example of a loop with a dependence distance vector (for the code example on the right) $D=(0,1)$ clearly showing which iterations are dependent on which other.

Given the importance of this data dependence formalization in the context of scientific computing and compiler transformations for concurrency and memory locality, researchers have developed, over the years, numerous numerical methods to efficiently determine the set of solutions to the data dependence problem. Solutions include integer-linear programming (ILP), greatest-common divisor (GCD) tests [8] and the Fourier-Motzkin methods [9]. As with any other NP-complete decision problem, data dependence testing algorithms for the affine domain range from solutions that are quick to evaluate but yield imprecise answers or more computational expensive resulting in more precise results. Invariably, compilers have to opt for conservative solutions. As such, and in the presence of inclusive results, where the method yields a result that indicates a possible data dependence, compilers have to assume the existence of this dependence and hence restrict some program transformations. In these scenarios, the data dependence resolution can be delayed until runtime by a technique named "inspector-execution" (see, e.g., [10,11]). Here, the compiler generates code that checks for data dependences at runtime during a first iteration of a loop nest. If at runtime no dependences are detected during this first run, assuming that the dependences do not change during the execution of the loop (a fact that can be derived at compile time), the remainder of the iterations can be executed concurrently.

Unlike the examples depicted in Fig. 4.2, where the dependence vectors uncovered are very precise and the dependence distances are constant, there are other cases where the data dependence analysis algorithms cannot determine with precision the dependence distances. In some cases, the algorithms can only determine that the dependence distances have some "shape," meaning that there is a precise dependence in some loops, but for other loops the dependence is less precise. For instance, a dependence vector can have the form $D = (0, >)$ which indicates that there is no dependence along the iterations of the first loop of the nest, but there are positive dependence distances[6] between the iterations of the second loop still for the same iteration of the first loop. While less precise, this dependence distance is still useful as the iterations of the first loop can be executed concurrently as long as the iterations of the second loop execute sequentially, thus following their original execution order. In this example, the compiler can transform the outer **for** loop into a **parfor** construct to indicate that iterations of the specific loop can be executed concurrently and hence in arbitrary order with respect to each other, possibly even on distinct execution units.

Given a loop nest, the compiler can determine which loop of the nest does carry a dependence, meaning which loop does require all of its iterations to be executed in the original sequential order. To determine this information, a compiler can make use of the notion of a *lexicographically positive* dependence vector. We define a dependence vector $D = (d_1, ..., d_n)$ to be lexicographically positive, if and only if its first nonzero component (starting from d_1 towards d_n) is positive. In addition, we say that the loop corresponding to this first nonzero component is the loop that carries the (data) dependence of the loop nest. A compiler can thus build a simple concurrency test by examining all the dependence vectors uncovered and check which one has the first loop in the nest that carries a data dependence. All loops inward of this loop including itself must execute sequentially. All outward loops in the nest can execute concurrently. The example in Fig. 4.3, albeit simple, shows how the compiler can determine that the first loop of the nest, the i-loop, can be executed concurrently whereas the inner loop, the j-loop, must execute sequentially.

While in many cases it is not possible to directly uncover parallelizable loops in a given loop nest, it is still possible to apply transformations that expose parallel loops. In Fig. 4.4A we present a loop nest that has a dependence distance vector of $D = (1, 0)$. The outermost loop, the i-loop, carries the dependence thus making it impossible to parallelize this loop. However, it is possible to permute the two loops in the nest, i.e., exchange the order in which the two loops are executed thus exposing the concurrency at the outermost loop.

One can formalize this loop permutation transformation by using what is referred in the literature as *unimodular* loop transformations as captured by a transformation matrix T [12]. Given an input loop nest with a set of dependence vectors $d \in D$, T is a legal loop transformation if and only if, for all $d \in D$, $T \cdot d \geq 0$. In other words, for every dependence distance vector the transformed dependence distance vectors need to be lexicographically positive.

---

[6]A dependence distance is positive if its first nonzero element (with the lower index) is positive irrespective of the values of the subsequent vector values.

```
for (i=1; i < N; i++){          for (j=1; j < N; j++){
  for (j=1; j < N; j++){          for (i=1; i < N; i++){
    C[i][j] = C[i-1][j] + 1;        C[i][j] = C[i-1][j] + 1;
  }                               }
}                               }
```

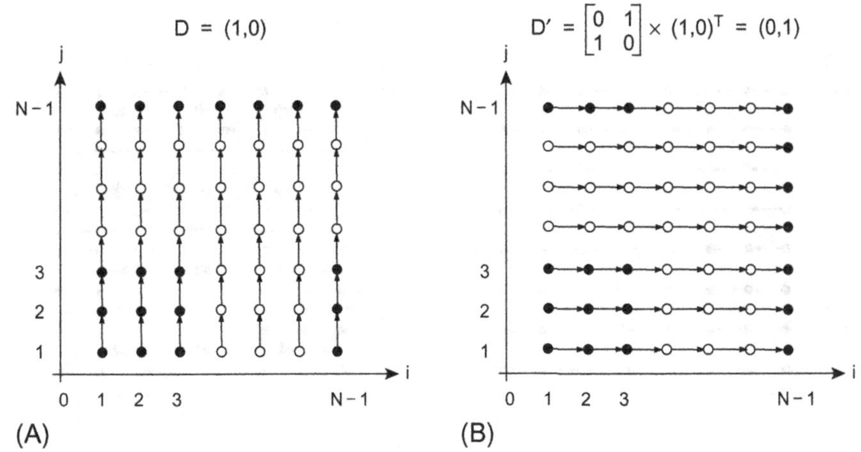

FIG. 4.4

Use of loop permutation (interchange) to expose loop-level concurrency. (A) Original loop nest and (B) interchanged loop nest.

The loop nest example in Fig. 4.4A has a dependence distance vector $D = (1, 0)$. When permuted using the unimodular transformations $T = \begin{bmatrix} 0 & 1 \\ 1 & 0 \end{bmatrix}$, the resulting transformed dependence distance vector is $D' = (0, 1)$ yielding the transformed loop nest in Fig. 4.4B. In this transformed loop nest the outer loop (the j-loop) can now be executed concurrently.

In other contexts, it is simply not possible to apply loop transformations that expose concurrent loops. Still, it is possible to apply other loop transformations (non-unimodular loop transformations) that improve specific aspects of the code execution. Such an example is loop tiling often referred as loop blocking (see Chapter 5). In this transformation, a loop of the original loop nest is "blocked" or "tiled" resulting in the creation of two loops, an outermost "control" loop that controls the execution of each tile of the iterations of the original loop, and a second innermost loop that controls the execution of the iterations inside each tile. Fig. 4.5 depicts an example of loop tiling on a two-dimensional loop nest. The original loop in Fig. 4.5A is recast as a two-dimensional tiling loop nest in Fig. 4.5B where the order of the execution of each tile (in this illustrative example a 2-by-2 tile) is controlled by the two outermost loops in the transformed loop nest.

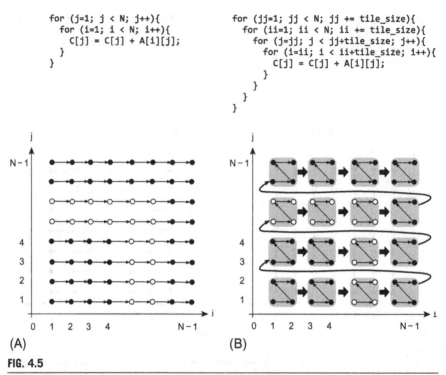

```
for (j=1; j < N; j++){
    for (i=1; i < N; i++){
        C[j] = C[j] + A[i][j];
    }
}
```

```
for (jj=1; jj < N; jj += tile_size){
    for (ii=1; ii < N; ii += tile_size){
        for (j=jj; j < jj+tile_size; j++){
            for (i=ii; i < ii+tile_size; i++){
                C[j] = C[j] + A[i][j];
            }
        }
    }
}
```

FIG. 4.5

Use of loop tiling (also known as loop blocking) for data locality. (A) Original loop nest and (B) tiled loop nest.

Depending on the data layout of the manipulated arrays, the tilled version of the code in Fig. 4.5B can exhibit a substantial performance advantage over the original version. While in the original loop nest the accesses to the array a have a substantial stride (assuming a row-major organization as in C), in the transformed code these accesses are more localized resulting in better cache reuse.

An even better loop organization would result from using loop interchange on two control loops of the tiled loop nest as depicted in Fig. 4.6. Here, the order in which the tiles are traversed enhance the locality of both the accesses to the c and a arrays.

These examples illustrate the use of precise data dependence analysis in the presence of loop nests that manipulate multidimensional arrays using affine index functions. The formalization of loop transformations as a linear algebra framework allows the compiler to reason about the legality of the transformations and the opportunities to exploit concurrency and data locality.

While in the context of scientific and high-performance computing the use of data dependence analysis frameworks such as the one outlined here has been very

```
for (ii=1; ii < N; ii += tile_size){
    for (jj=1; jj < N; jj += tile_size){
        for (j=jj; j < jj+tile_size; j++){
            for (i=ii; i < ii+tile_size; i++){
                C[j] = C[j] + A[i][j];
            }
        }
    }
}
```

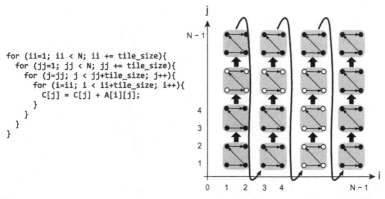

FIG. 4.6

Application of loop permutation after loop tiling for improved cache locality.

successful, for other application domains, the presence of programming language features such as aliasing and pointer references (as is the case of the C language) hampers the use of these sophisticated analyses. In many practical cases, the compiler cannot simply know (at compile time) if there is a dependence. This fundamental inability thus prevents the use of advanced transformations. The classical example is the use of indirection indexing in sparse matrix operations.

Other compiler transformations (see Chapter 5 for a collection of code transformations and optimizations) require different analysis abstractions than the ones described earlier for data concurrency and locality of loop nests. When applying optimizations, such as software pipelining, it is common for compilers to represent the data dependences of a loop nest in a Data Dependence Graph (DDG), which identifies the intra- and inter-iteration dependences by also annotating the loop-carried delays and distances. In this DDG, a loop-carried delay $<d,p>$ from instruction i to instruction j implies that j depends on a value computed by instruction i, p iterations earlier, and j can start at least d cycles (denote pipelining delays) after the appropriate instance of i has executed. A distance $d=0$ means an intra-iteration dependence. The hardware resources available to execute the operations in the DDG, the distances and cycles present in the edges impose the constraints responsible for the minimum achievable software pipelining initiation interval (II).

Depending on the use of this information, the DDG might be formed by low-level intermediate representations (close to target assembly code), at the operation level, or at the statement level. In cases involving the scheduling of operations, as with software pipelining, it is common to have DDG nodes representing single operations instead of statements. Fig. 4.7 illustrates an example of a DDG with the information regarding cycles and distances. In this example, we consider that the load, multiplication, and division operations require 2, 2, and 3 clock cycles,

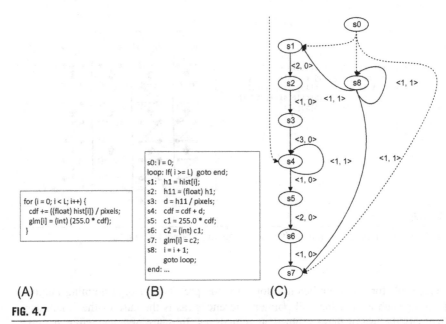

FIG. 4.7

Cycles and distances: (A) code example with a loop (based on code from the UTDSP benchmark repository [13]), (B) intermediate three-address representation, and (C) DDG example.

respectively, while all other operations require 1 clock cycle to execute. The loops in this DDG show the loop-carried dependences with a distance of 1.

In the presence of sequences of loops (each one consisting of a nested loop or a single loop) as in the example in Fig. 4.8A, it might be important to identify if there are data dependences between them. This information can be represented in a graph known as Loop Dependence Graph (LDG) as the one presented in Fig. 4.8B. The edges of the LDG represent information regarding the dependences. The LDG of Fig. 4.8B illustrates as edge labels the array variables responsible for the true dependences between the loop nests (represented as nodes).

In the example presented in Fig. 4.8, all the loops in sequence impose data dependences between every two loops. For instance, the two loops in sequence have a data dependence as the first nested loop writes the hist array and the second loop reads elements of the hist array. The indirect indexing in the first nested loops prevents the compiler from determining if the elements written at this point are used in the subsequent loop. The LDG can be seen as a special case of the Task Graph (see Section 4.4), where nodes are always loops and edges represent the data dependences between loops.

```
L1: for (i = 0; i < L; i++)
      hist[i] = 0;

L2:  for (i = 0; i < N; i++) {
       for (j = 0; j < N; ++j) {
         hist[img[i][j]] += 1;
       }
     }

L3:  for (i = 0; i < L; i++) {
       cdf += ((float) hist[i]) / pixels;
       glm[i] = (int) (255.0 * cdf);
     }

L4:  for (i = 0; i < N; i++) {
       for (j = 0; j < N; ++j) {
         img[i][j] = glm[img[i][j]];
       }
     }
```

(A)   (B)

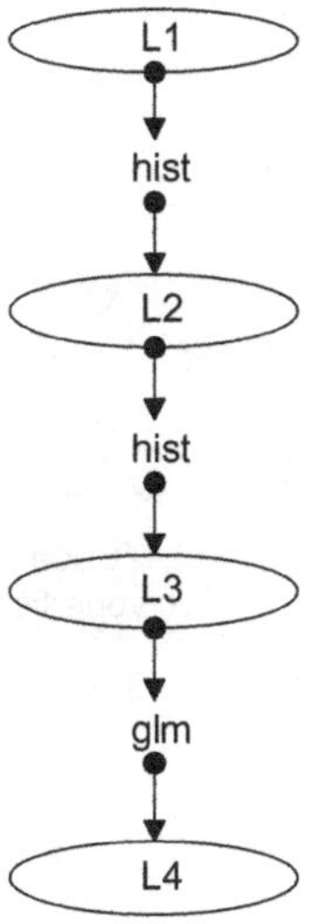

FIG. 4.8

Sequence of loops: (A) code example with a sequence of loops (based on code from the UTDSP benchmark repository [13]) and (B) a resultant loop dependence graph (LDG).

4.3.2 CODE METRICS

In general, and as illustrated in Fig. 4.9, code analysis relies on code metrics and on code properties to derive increasingly more complex metrics and/or properties. In Table 4.2, we depict examples of representative code properties. The examples include data types, loop type, loop rank, use-def chains, AST, CFG, and Call Graphs (static only).

As is readily observed, none of these metrics are target dependent as they depend exclusively on the structure of the source code and are aimed at program comprehension as opposed to application performance tuning. One such metric that captures the inherent "complexity" of the source code is the cyclomatic complexity. This specific metric relies on the Control Flow Graph (CFG) of the source code where nodes represent basic blocks (or instructions) and edges correspond to the flow of the execution between basic blocks (or instructions).[7] Given a CFG, the cyclomatic complexity metric is computed as $E - N + 2 \times P$, where E is number of edges of the CFG, N is the number of nodes, and P is the number of modules in the program. This cyclomatic complexity metric (see, e.g., [2]) is used to measure the complexity of a program by taking into account the number of linearly independent paths of a program.

---

[7] A basic block captures straight-line pieces of code where the execution flow always starts with the first instruction and only leaves in the last instruction (i.e., if the first instruction executes, then all subsequent instructions are executed).

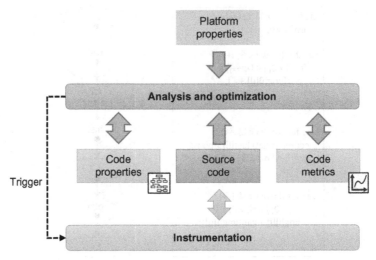

FIG. 4.9

Code analysis and instrumentation workflow.

Table 4.2 Examples of code properties

Property	Context	Description	Method
Data type	Variables	Type of a variable (e.g., integer, float, or string) identifying possible values and operations performed on those values	Code inspection
Loop type	Loop	Type of loop construct: count controlled (e.g., for), condition controlled (e.g., while), or collection controlled (e.g., foreach)	Code inspection
Loop rank	Loop	Relative position of a loop in relation to other loops in the same module. For instance, the following nested loop has the following rank values: loop i: rank 1 loop j: rank 1.1 loop k: rank 1.2	Code inspection
Use-def chain	Variables	Data structure that for each use of a variable, provides	Code inspection
Abstract syntax tree (AST)	Program	Tree representation of the syntactic structure of the source code	Code inspection
Control flow graph (CFG)	Program	Graph representation of all paths that may be traversed during program execution	Code inspection
Static call graph	Program	Graph representation of all possible invocation relationships between program modules (functions, tasks)	Code inspection

The intuition behind this metric is that the more independent paths a program has, the larger the impact in terms of maintainability and testability, including the probability of errors when updating the code. High values of cyclomatic complexity thus characterize a control-dominated code (e.g., with many if-then-else constructs) whereas low values of cyclomatic complexity characterize code with very regular loop-dominated and sequential constructs.

Let us consider the program fragment to compute the mass distribution of an N-body simulation problem depicted in Fig. 4.10. The CFG of this code, shown in Fig. 4.11, has 8 edges, 7 nodes, and 1 module, and a cyclomatic complexity of 3.

4.4 DYNAMIC ANALYSIS: THE NEED FOR INSTRUMENTATION

Many metrics of interest can only be collected dynamically and at various levels. One can profile the code's execution to collect metrics about the frequency of execution of specific sections of the code or collect the values of specific variables, as well as execution metrics (e.g., the number of instructions of a specific kind in a given section of executed code). A common and important metric is execution time,

```
function computeMassDistribution(Node node) {
    if (number of particles in this node equals 1) {
        centerOfMass = particle.position;
      mass = particle.mass;
    } else {
        for (all child quadrants that have particles in them) {
            quad.computeMassDistribution();
            mass += quad.mass();
            centerOfMass += quad.mass() * quadrant.centerOfMass();
        }
        centerOfMass = centerOfMass / mass;
    }
}
```

FIG. 4.10

Code example for calculating the mass distribution of an N-body simulation problem.

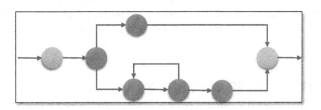

FIG. 4.11

Control flow graph (CFG) example.

and as such it becomes imperative to determine which sections of the code are responsible for the vast majority of the execution time in what is named a "hotspot." To find such hotspots, the typical approach consists in instrumenting the code by inserting timing primitives that measure the execution time of specific regions of code, such as function calls and loops. Once the instrumented application is executed, the timing data can be collected and used for subsequent analysis. This is the typical approach of the *profiling* tools that instrument the code to collect a wide range of metrics related to the execution of the program which in many cases, and unlike intrinsic code metrics or properties, are intimately tied to the architecture of the target system.

Profiling outputs a report about the characteristics of the application and of its behavior in one or more executions as it is usually possible to aggregate in a single report the results of different execution runs. The information in the report can be output in a human readable way or to be used by other tools or compilers. Due to the complexity of the information output, more advanced profiling tools use visualization schemes such as graphs (e.g., annotated call graphs, data dependence graphs), and charts (data distribution). The output reports usually have explicit cross-references to the application source code in order to guide users and/or tools and compilers. Still, and in order to be helpful, profiling must be performed using representative input data.

The information reported by the profiling process can be passed on to toolchains with annotations using directive-driven programming model approaches, attributes, compiler options, and/or more sophisticated strategies, such as the ones supported by LARA [14,15] (see the "LARA and Instrumentation" sidebox and Chapter 3).

Most profiling approaches use instrumentation schemes, i.e., code is inserted at key points of the application code to log/monitor dynamic behavior. They usually use a library for instrumentation and the code inserted usually consists of calls to library functions. The application is then compiled and linked against the instrumentation library. The information is reported after and/or during the executing of the instrumented application. One of the problems of this approach is the impact of the inserted code in the applicability of compiler optimizations and thus the corresponding code generation effectiveness and subsequently its impact on the execution time. It is sometimes required to profile the same application multiple times with the same input data distributing the instrumentation among the different runs and/or to instrument only regions of code. In fact, this can be a multistage process as in a first run critical functions (paths and/or regions) are identified and then the profiling is focused on those critical functions, possibly to report additional and more refined information.

4.4.1 INFORMATION FROM PROFILING

At compile time, profiling can uncover some properties of the application, such as the number of load/store instructions, the number of branch instructions, number of iterations for well-structured loops, etc. Other properties can be usually estimated.

At runtime, one can derive the exact number of occurrences for a specific execution scenario, e.g., not only the number of load/store instructions but also the number of times each one was executed, as the edges of the CFG can be annotated with its execution frequencies. One important representation is the Call Graph (CG). It can be created by a static analysis or by a dynamic analysis and it is thus referred to as a Static CG or Dynamic CG, respectively. The Dynamic CG can capture the same information as the Static CG, or it can represent part of the Static CG by considering only the function calls executed in a specific execution scenario. The power of the Dynamic CG derives not only the identification of the actual calls executed at runtime, but also from the possibility to be annotated with dynamic information such as the size of data flowing between calls and the number of times each function was called.

LARA AND INSTRUMENTATION

LARA [14,15] is an aspect-oriented programming (AOP) language specially designed for allowing developers to program code instrumentation strategies, to control the application of code transformations and compiler optimizations, and to effectively control different tools in a toolchain. Besides many other features, LARA aspects allow the description of sophisticated code instrumentation schemes (e.g., for profiling customization). The unified view provided by LARA also contributes to the development of strategies that use as input information output from profiling.

The LARA technology is currently being used in four compiler tools: MATISSE[a] (a MATLAB to C compiler), Harmonic[b] (a source-to-source compiler), MANET[c] (a source-to-source compiler), and ReflectC[d] (a CoSy-based C compiler).

[a]MATISSE: http://specs.fe.up.pt/tools/matisse/.
[b]Harmonic: http://specs.fe.up.pt/tools/harmonic/.
[c]MANET: http://specs.fe.up.pt/tools/manet/.
[d]ReflectC: http://specs.fe.up.pt/tools/reflectc/.

Another useful representation is the Task Graph (TG), also similar to a graph representing a workflow. A TG represents the application as a collection of tasks along with the control and data dependences between them, and thus can be used to identify task-level parallelism opportunities, including task-level pipelining. The TG can also be seen as a Data Dependence Graph (DDG) at the task level.

At a lower level, one can view the creation of a Dynamic DDG at the statement/ instruction/operation level. Using traces of the accessed memory addresses one can determine memory access distances and guide code transformations to promote data reuse, regions of memory accessed (which can be used to guide data partitioning), memory access patterns, producer/consumer tasks, their communication access patterns (which can be used to guide task-level pipelining), etc.

The information one can acquire from the execution of an application is diverse and very dependent on the specific analysis and/or transformation goal. Table 4.3 shows a representative set of features in the context of high-performance embedded computing. The monitoring is grouped according to three types: control, data, and operations. We consider here that the information acquired is used to guide code transformations, compiler optimizations, and partitioning and mapping. The acquired features or metrics include range values, data sizes, loop trip counts, memory alias, and execution frequency of paths and basic blocks (considering branches).

Table 4.3 Example of representative features to extract from applications

Type of monitoring	Feature	Static/dynamic feature	Representation	Example of goals
Data	Data values	Dynamic	Distribution frequencies Ranges	Code specialization Reduction of word lengths
Data	Data sizes	Dynamic	Annotations in graphs Report about variables	Acquire data communication requirements Memory storage requirements
Data	Memory addresses	Dynamic	Dynamic data dependence graphs (DDGs)	Variables are privatizable Parallelism Reduction operations overlapping of computation and communication Determine locations for setup, initialization of the hardware acceleration Identify distances between accesses Identify memory regions being accessed
Data	Miss rates for data and instruction caches	Dynamic	Annotations or text report	Guide code transformations and compiler optimizations
Operations	Memory accesses (load/stores)	Static/dynamic		Guide partitioning and mapping
Operations	Operations executed	Dynamic	Execution frequencies for each operation Dynamic execution graphs	Guide partitioning and mapping
Control	Branches taken and frequencies	Dynamic	Dynamic execution graphs Annotations in CFGs	Guide compiler optimizations Guide scheduling, partitioning, mapping Deciding about branch prediction scheme
Control	Branch misprediction rate	Dynamic	Annotations or text report	Guide code transformations and compiler optimizations
Control	Calls	Static/dynamic	Static call graph Dynamic call graph	Leaf procedure inlining and procedure specialization using common argument values
Control	Loop iterations	Static/dynamic	Annotations in graph representations	Focus the optimizer in the loops with large number of iterations

All of them can be important in different stages of the mapping of applications to an embedded system when considering the use of multiple cores and hardware accelerators.

Instrumentation can also be important to support critical path analysis (CPA) and to highlight regions of code or execution paths where one should focus on optimizations and/or acceleration. By properly instrumenting the application code, the execution of the application can generate an execution trace which can then be analyzed to build a dynamic dependence graph (DDG). In this DDG, each instruction executed is a node and edges represent the dataflow (dependences between instructions). It is also possible to construct a dynamic Control/Data Flow Graph (CDFG) and explicitly expose control and data flow. Note that all the graphs built from traces and profiling can be enriched with information associated to nodes and/or edges regarding the runtime properties. The inspection of the graphs can determine important properties. For instance, inspecting the incoming and outgoing data dependence edges can be helpful to determine if variables are privatizable. Other useful schemes can find reduction operations, streaming-based data accesses, etc.

Value profiling extracts information such as range values, enumeration of values for a certain variable, which can also be used to identify variables as invariant or constant, and perform more aggressive constant folding, code specialization, and partial evaluation. This information can be used to guide function inlining, code partitioning for CPUs and accelerators, etc. For instance, after acquiring dynamic data dependences and memory access patterns one can determine contiguous memory accesses and, for instance, identify opportunities to apply vectorization for SIMD parallelism. Also, important for guiding vectorization are features such as loop trip counts, access strides for the arrays, alignment of the arrays and, finally, the outcomes of the branches inside a loop.

Identifying memory allocation and free operations, system calls, calls to functions of a specific library (e.g., Math.h), can also be of paramount importance to guide code transformations, partitioning, and mapping. For instance, this information can restrict the mapping of certain functions to hardware accelerators, and can trigger a set of transformations on a specific code region to make it ready for migration to the hardware accelerator.

As it is apparent, some code metrics, such as execution time and power consumption, can be platform dependent, i.e., the measurements may vary depending on the hardware used. In this case, the code analysis process may require platform properties (in addition to code properties) to identify, for instance, whether a particular task can (or should) be mapped to a hardware accelerator such as a GPGPU. Useful platform properties include memory and cache size, storage volume size, number of processing cores, and core clock frequency.

While many of these metrics are very architecture oriented, such as the number of clocks per instructions, there are other metrics of great interest in the context of transformations and which relate to the structure of the application code. For example, in various contexts it is important to know the range of the values specific loop bounds assume as they dictate the number of executed iterations or the sizes of the allocated

Table 4.4 Example of metrics acquired from code analysis and profiling

Metric	Goal	Description
Operation intensity Ratio of arithmetic operations per byte of data moved from/to memory	Estimate performance upper bounds	Used in the Roofline Model
Self-parallelism [16]	Parallelization	It represents the parallelism potential for a single region
Ratio of the number of nodes on the DDG and the critical path length [17]	Parallelization	An estimate of parallelism potential (of how many instructions can be executed in parallel)
Instructions per cycle (IPC)	Estimate performance and acquire uncovering parallelism	A metric representing the ILP (Instruction-Level Parallelism) degree
Frames per second (FPS) and energy per frame		Metrics used in the context of image/video processing applications
Application cost [24] (product of CPU utilization and CPU frequency)	Highlight performance and/or memory bound	With low memory accesses, the CPU utilization is approximately linear to the frequency thus application cost is flat with the core frequency

arrays. To uncover this information, instrumentation of the code (and not necessarily execution or performance profiling) is required. The instrumented code simply collects the specific values as the code executes and compiles a list of relevant statistics.

With the information acquired using profiling it is possible to calculate some metrics of interest. For instance, the ratio between the amount of work performed and the critical path length gives an estimate of how many instructions can be executed concurrently. Table 4.4 presents a number of metrics developers use to assess the performance of their applications and possibly identify bottlenecks, parallelism potential, etc.

4.4.2 PROFILING EXAMPLE

Fig. 4.12 presents part of the core source code of the Edge Detection algorithm included in the UTDSP benchmark repository [13]. The algorithm consists of a smooth filter, horizontal and vertical gradients, gradient combining, and a threshold task. The code in Fig. 4.12 illustrates the benchmark with modifications regarding the encapsulation of the initialization and the gradient combining and threshold regions of code in two functions (`initialize` and `combthreshold`).

The application was compiled with GNU *gcc* –O2 and executed in an Intel i5-2467M CPU, @ 1.60 GHz, 4 GB of RAM, and 64-bit Windows 7 as operating system. Fig. 4.13 shows part of the profiling report (the flat profile information in

```
…
  /* Initialize to zero image_buffer2 and image_buffer3 */
  initialize(image_buffer2, image_buffer3);

/* Set the values of the filter matrix to a Gaussian kernel.    */
  filter[0][0] = 1;
  …
  filter[2][2] = 1;

  /* Perform the Gaussian convolution. */
  convolve2d(image_buffer1, filter, image_buffer3);

  /* Set the values of the filter matrix to the vert. Sobel operator. */
  filter[0][0] =  1;
  …
  filter[2][2] = -1;

  /* Convolve the smoothed matrix with the vertical Sobel kernel. */
  convolve2d(image_buffer3, filter, image_buffer1);

  /* Set the values of the filter matrix to the horiz. Sobel operator. */
  filter[0][0] =  1;
  …
  filter[2][2] = -1;

  /* Convolve the smoothed matrix with the horiz. Sobel kernel. */
  convolve2d(image_buffer3, filter, image_buffer2);

  /* Combine and form a new image based on threshold. */
  combthreshold(image_buffer1, image_buffer2, image_buffer3);
…
```

FIG. 4.12

Code based on the Edge Detection UTDSP benchmark.

this case) output by GNU *gprof* [5] and considering code modifications for repeating
1000 × the execution of the algorithm. From the profiling information one can see
that the algorithm spends 93.23% of the execution time executing the *convolve2d*
function (invoked 3 times in a single run) and 3.76% and 3.01% executing *combthreshold* and *initialize* functions, respectively. Fig. 4.14 shows the Call Graph
(CG) obtained and representing the number of times each function is invoked. Other
information that might be represented in the CG is, e.g., the execution time and the
percentage of the global execution time for each function.

```
Flat profile:

Each sample counts as 0.01 seconds.
  %   cumulative   self              self     total
 time   seconds   seconds    calls  us/call  us/call  name
93.23     1.24      1.24      3000   413.33   413.33  convolve2d
 3.76     1.29      0.05      1000    50.00    50.00  combthreshold
 3.01     1.33      0.04      1000    40.00    40.00  initialize
```

FIG. 4.13

Gprof flat profile for the Edge Detection UTDSP benchmark.

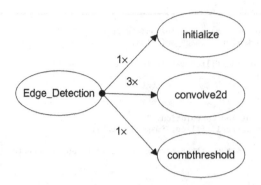

FIG. 4.14

Call-Graph for the Edge Detection UTDSP benchmark (labels in the edges identify the number of times each callee function is called from a caller function).

A task graph (TG) obtained by instrumenting the code is presented in Fig. 4.15. We however do not include dynamic information obtained that characterizes the flow of information between tasks and within each task. As can be seen, the TG explicitly shows the data communication requirements between tasks and the tasks that can be executed in parallel. In this case, the TG shows that two *convolve2d* executions can be performed in parallel and this can guide developers, e.g., to map two instances of the *convolve2d* function in two cores.

Other information that can be extracted is the access patterns from producer/consumer tasks which can be an important information to guide task-level pipelining and the hardware structure to support data communication between tasks (e.g., according to the access patterns it can be possible to communicate data using FIFOs).

4.5 CUSTOM PROFILING EXAMPLES

This section presents a number of custom profiling examples for code analysis commonly used in the context of embedded platforms. All the examples require the instrumentation of the applications in order to derive specific dynamic metrics. Although the instrumentation of the applications can be done manually, we emphasize here the use of the LARA language [14,15] to specify strategies for code instrumentation and the use of source-to-source compilers that produce the code modifications based on those strategies.

4.5.1 FINDING HOTSPOTS

One important step to accelerate the execution of an application is to identify its *hotspots*, i.e., regions of code where most of the execution time is spent, and which are

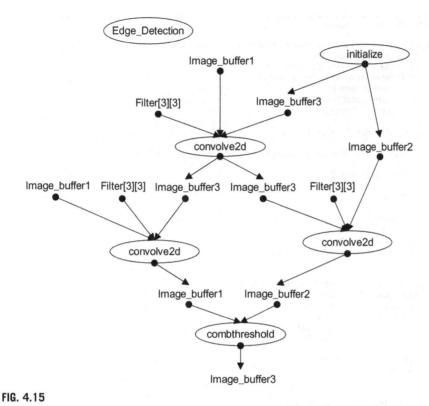

FIG. 4.15

Task graph (TG) for the Edge Detection UTDSP benchmark.

therefore prime candidates for optimization. To identify hotspots, most developers rely on freely available tools such as GNU *gprof*, which provides information about the amount of execution of time spent on each module of the program. GNU *gcov* is another utility, which can be useful in this case to present code coverage results. Such tools exhibit limited capabilities as they do not provide a general mechanism for selecting which regions of code to profile and which regions to ignore. Without relying on profiling tools, one simple strategy to find hotspots is to manually instrument the code as follows:

1. *Profiling API header*. Include the profiling API header at the beginning of each source file to access timing and reporting functions.
2. *Candidate code statements*. Insert timing calls at the beginning and at the end of each function definition to compute the corresponding elapsed time. We only time functions that either have calls or loops.
3. *Timing report*. Before the application terminates, a timing report must be generated and output.

```
#include <profiling.h>

Boolean_T crc32file(char *name, DWORD *crc, long *charcnt) {
   timer_begin("crc32file");
   oldcrc32 = 0xFFFFFFFF; *charcnt = 0;
   if ((fin=fopen(name, "r"))==NULL) {
        perror(name);
        timer_end("crc32file");
        return Error_;
   }
   while ((c=getc(fin))!=EOF) {
      ++*charcnt;
      oldcrc32 = UPDC32(c, oldcrc32);
   }
   if (ferror(fin)) {
       perror(name);
      *charcnt = -1;
   }
   fclose(fin);
   *crc = oldcrc32 = ~oldcrc32;
   timer_end("crc32file");
   return Success_;
}

DWORD crc32buf(char *buf, size_t len) {
   timer_begin("crc32buf");
   register DWORD oldcrc32;
   oldcrc32 = 0xFFFFFFFF;
   for ( ; len; --len, ++buf) {
      oldcrc32 = UPDC32(*buf, oldcrc32);
   }
   timer_end("crc32buf");
   return ~oldcrc32;
}

int main(int argc, char *argv[]) {
   timer_begin("main");
   while(--argc > 0) {
      errors |= crc32file(*++argv, &crc, &charcnt);
      printf("%08lX %7ld %s\n", crc, charcnt, *argv);
   }
   timer_end("main");
   timer_report();
   return(errors != 0);
}
```

FIG. 4.16

Code based on the CRC32 benchmark.

As an example, consider the code in Fig. 4.16, based on the CRC32 benchmark [18,19], where we highlight in bold the statements that have been instrumented. The timer_begin, timer_end and timer_report primitives are part of a specialized API developed to monitor the execution time and number of times a function is invoked and to provide a timing report. While our profiling strategy is relatively simple, it can be challenging to instrument the code manually if the code is very large and spans through many source files. Our strategy requires identifying functions that have loops and function calls and also all exit points (e.g., return statements) to insert the timer_end primitive.

```
1. aspectdef MyProfiler
2.     // select the first (global) statement of the file
3.     select file.first end
4.     apply
5.        $first.insert before  %{ #include <profiling.h> }%;
6.     end
7.
8.     // select all function calls
9.     select function end
10.    apply
11.        var loops = $function.pointcut("loop");
12.        var calls = $function.pointcut("call");
13.        if (loops.length > 0 || calls.length > 0) {
14.
15.           var entries = $function.pointcut("entry");
16.           for (var i in entries)
17.              entries[i].insert after %{
18.                 timer_begin("[[$function.name]]"); }%;
19.
20.           var exits = $function.pointcut("exit");
21.           for (var i in exits)
22.              exits[i].insert before %{
23.                 timer_end("[[$function.name]]"); }%;
24.        }
25.
26.    end
27.
28.    // select last statement of the main function
29.    select function.exit end
30.    apply
31.        $exit.insert before  %{ timer_report(); }%;
32.    end
33.    condition $function.name == "main" end
34.
35. end
```

FIG. 4.17

Example of a LARA strategy for profiling.

The LARA aspect presented in Fig. 4.17 automates this profiling process by instrumenting a C application with an arbitrary number of sources based on our profiling strategy, in particular:

1. Lines 3–6: Select the first statement of every source file, and insert the header file of the profiling API.
2. Lines 9–26: For each function in the application, we identify whether it contains loops or function calls. In this case, we select all entry and exit statements for that function, and insert the corresponding `timer_begin` and `timer_end` primitives, respectively.
3. Lines 29–33: Select all exit points of the main function, and insert a call to `timer_report()`.

4.5.2 LOOP METRICS

Loop metrics can help determine which loops are candidates for optimization: in the context of hardware execution, they are prime candidates for offloading computation to reconfigurable hardware. In this analysis, we wish to identify for every loop in the program the average number of iterations and the number of times each loop is executed (number of instances). As in the previous section, this code analysis requires instrumenting the code to collect information about loops during execution.

Our strategy to extract both loop metrics is to instrument every loop in the program as follows:

1. *Profiling API header.* Include the profiling API header in the beginning of each source file to access timing and reporting functions.
2. *Loop statements.* Insert a monitoring API call (`monitor_count`) before each loop statement to count the number of times it is executed. Furthermore, we insert a counter inside the loop body to monitor the number of iterations of each loop execution, and use the `monitor_avg` API call to track the average.

```
#include <profiling.h>

void BF_set_key(BF_KEY *key, int len, unsigned char *data) {
    ...
    d = data;
    end = (data + len);
    monitor_count("loop-instances","BF_set_key_1");
    int COUNT_BF_set_key_1 = 0;
    for (i = 0; i < 16 + 2; i++) {
        COUNT_BF_set_key_1++;
        ri = ( *(d++));
        ...
    }
    monitor_avg("loop-iterations","BF_set_key_1", COUNT_BF_set_key_1 );
    in[0] = 0L;
    in[1] = 0L;
    monitor_count("loop-instances","BF_set_key_2");
    int COUNT_BF_set_key_2 = 0;
    for (i = 0; i < 16 + 2; i += 2) {
        COUNT_BF_set_key_2++;
        BF_encrypt(in,key,1);
        p[i] = in[0];
        p[i + 1] = in[1];
    }
    monitor_avg("loop-iterations","BF_set_key_2", COUNT_BF_set_key_2);

    p = (key -> S);
    monitor_count("loop-instances","BF_set_key_3");
    int COUNT_BF_set_key_3 = 0;
    for (i = 0; i < 4 * 256; i += 2) {
        COUNT_BF_set_key_3++;
        BF_encrypt(in,key,1);
        p[i] = in[0];
        p[i + 1] = in[1];
    }
    monitor_avg("loop-iterations","BF_set_key_3", COUNT_BF_set_key_3);
}
```

FIG. 4.18

Code example from the *blowfish* benchmark (statements in bold identify code inserted for instrumentation).

3. *Loop report.* Just before the application terminates, a loop report is generated and output.

The code in Fig. 4.18, based on the *blowfish* benchmark [18,19], shows the instrumented code based on the above strategy.

While the monitoring API tracks the number of iterations and instances, instrumenting the code manually is labour intensive and error prone. We can automate this process using the LARA `aspect` presented in Fig. 4.19 as follows:

1. Lines 2–8: Select the first statement of every source file, and insert the header file of the profiling API.
2. Lines 10–21: Select all loops of the application and the corresponding entry points. Before each loop statement, insert a `monitor_count` call to track the number of instances and an initialization statement for the iterations counter. Insert a loop count increment inside the loop body, and after the loop statement insert the `monitor_avg` API call to compute the average number of iterations (taking into account previous executions of the loop).
3. Lines 23–30: Select all exit points of the main function, and insert a call to `monitor_report()` to output the number of loop iterations and instances metrics.

```
1. aspectdef LCount
2.     select file.first end
3.     // add profile header
4.     apply
5.         $first.insert before %{
6.             #include <profiling.h>
7.         }%;
8.     end
9.
10.    select function.loop.entry end
11.    apply
12.        var key = $loop.key.replace(/:|\./g, "_");
13.        $loop.insert before
14.        %{ monitor_count("loop-instances", "[[key]]"); }%;
15.
16.        $loop.insert before %{ int COUNT_[[key]] = 0; }%;
17.
18.        $entry.insert after %{ COUNT_[[key]]++; }%;
19.        $loop.insert after
20.           %{monitor_avg("loop-iterations", "[[key]]", COUNT_[[key]]);}%;
21.    end
22.
23.    select function{name=="main"}.exit end
24.    // report monitor
25.    apply
26.        $exit.insert before
27.           %{ monitor_report("loop-iterations"); }%;
28.        $exit.insert before
29.           %{ monitor_report("loop-instances"); }%;
30.    end
31. end
```

FIG. 4.19

Example of a LARA strategy for profiling loops.

4.5.3 DYNAMIC CALL GRAPHS

Call graphs provide a window into program behavior by representing the relationship between different program modules (functions, subroutines). In particular, each node in the call graph represents a module, and an edge represents one or more calls to a module. The call graph can be built at compile time (statically) by identifying the statements with function calls. It represents the structure of all the invocations that can happen during program executions. In the case of a dynamic call graph, we are able to trace all modules invoked for a particular execution. In particular, which modules were invoked and which module triggered them. Dynamic call graphs can be annotated with additional information such as its execution time or other metrics. In this section, we focus on the generation of a dynamic call graph by instrumenting the code. The instrumentation strategy is as follows:

1. *Profiling API header.* Include the profiling API header in the beginning of each source file to access call graph monitoring functions.
2. *Call statements.* Insert a monitoring API call (`cgraph_task`) before each function call. In this example, we ignore all system calls.
3. *Generate call graph.* Before the application terminates, we generate the call graph with `cgraph_report`.

Let us consider the code in Fig. 4.20 based on the SHA benchmark [18,19]. It shows the instrumented code highlighted in bold based on the earlier strategy.

We can automate this process using the LARA `aspect` presented in Fig. 4.21 as follows:

1. Lines 3–8: Select the first statement of every source file, and insert the header file of the profiling API.
2. Lines 10–18: Insert the `cgraph_task` API call before each call. The `cgraph_task` API call receives two arguments: the name of the function that triggers the call and the function called. We add a condition that we only track the call if it is not a system call.
3. Lines 20–25: Select all exit points of the main function, and insert a call to `cgraph_report()` to generate the call graph.

4.5.4 BRANCH FREQUENCIES

Branch frequencies is another metric that can be important to determine hotspots, in particular knowing which branches are mostly executed, thus guiding the process of determining which region of the code is more profitable for optimization. As in previous examples, we must instrument the code, in this case focusing on conditional constructs, with counters and run the application with representative datasets. Our instrumentation strategy is as follows:

```
#include <profiling.h>

void sha_final(SHA_INFO *sha_info) {
    ...
    if (count > 56) {
        memset((((BYTE *)(&sha_info -> data)) + count),0,(64 - count));
        cgraph_task("sha_final","sha_transform");
        sha_transform(sha_info);
        memset((&sha_info -> data),0,56);
    }
    else {
        memset((((BYTE *)(&sha_info -> data)) + count),0,(56 - count));
    }
    (sha_info -> data)[14] = hi_bit_count;
    (sha_info -> data)[15] = lo_bit_count;
    cgraph_task("sha_final","sha_transform");
    sha_transform(sha_info);
}

void sha_stream(SHA_INFO *sha_info,FILE *fin) {
    int i;
    BYTE data[8192UL];
    cgraph_task("sha_stream","sha_init");
    sha_init(sha_info);
    while((i = (fread(data,1,8192,fin))) > 0) {
        profile_cgraph_monitor("sha_stream","sha_update");
        sha_update(sha_info,data,i);
    }
    cgraph_task("sha_stream","sha_final");
    sha_final(sha_info);
}

void sha_print(SHA_INFO *sha_info) {
    printf("%08lx %08lx %08lx %08lx %08lx\n",
        (sha_info -> digest)[0],
        (sha_info -> digest)[1],(sha_info -> digest)[2],
        (sha_info -> digest)[3],(sha_info -> digest)[4]);
}
```

FIG. 4.20

Code example based on the SHA benchmark.

1. *Profiling API header*. Include the profiling API header in the beginning of each source file to access branch frequency monitoring functions;
2. *Conditional statements*. Insert a monitoring API call (monitor_bfreq) for each branch in the application.
3. *Branch frequency report*. Just before the application terminates, we generate the branch frequency report with the report_breq API call.

We now consider the code in Fig. 4.22, based on the Dijkstra benchmark [18,19], which shows the instrumented code highlighted in bold based on the earlier strategy.

We can automate this process using the LARA aspect presented in Fig. 4.23 as follows:

1. Lines 3–8: Select the first statement of every source file, and insert the header file of the profiling API.

```
1. aspectdef CostCGraph
2.
3.      // select the first (global) statement of the file
4.      select file.first end
5.      // add profile header
6.      apply
7.          $first.insert before  %{ #include <profiling.h> }%;
8.      end
9.
10.     // select all function calls
11.     select function.call end
12.     // add a monitor before each call
13.     apply
14.
15.         $call.parent_stmt.insert before %{
16.             cgraph_task("[[$function.name]]", "[[$call.name]]"); }%;
17.     end
18.     condition ! $call.is_sys end
19.
20.     // select last statement of the main function
21.     select function.exit end
22.     // display call graph
23.     apply
24.         $exit.insert before  %{ cgraph_report(); }%;
25.     end
26.     condition $function.name == "main" end
27. end
```

FIG. 4.21

Example of a LARA strategy for dynamic Call Graphs.

2. Lines 10–25: For each conditional, select the "then" and "else" branches and insert inside each branch the `monitor_bfreq` API. The `monitor_bfreq` API has two arguments: the first is a key that identifies the conditional, and the second parameter identifies the conditional branch (then or else).
3. Lines 27–32: Select all exit points of the main function, and insert a call to `report_bfreq()` to output the total number of times a conditional is executed, and the frequency of each of its paths.

4.5.5 HEAP MEMORY

One of the sources of errors when developing a program without automatic garbage collection is heap memory management. While sophisticated tools such as *valgrind* [6] can help debug potential problems, we can also use custom instrumentation to intercept calls to heap memory management functions, and monitor their use. Our instrumentation strategy for tracking heap memory usage is as follows:

1. *Profiling API header*. Include the profiling API header in the beginning of each source file to access heap monitoring functions.
2. *Heap memory functions*. Intercept every call to `malloc`, `free`, and `realloc` and replace them with wrapper functions `profile_heap_malloc`, `profile_heap_free`, and `profile_heap_realloc`, respectively.

```
#include <profiling.h>
void enqueue(int iNode,int iDist,int iPrev) {
    QITEM *qNew = (QITEM *)(malloc((sizeof(QITEM ))));
    QITEM *qLast = qHead;
    if (!(qNew != 0)) {
        monitor_bfreq("enqueue_1", 1);
        fprintf(stderr,"Out of memory.\n");
        exit(1);
    } else {
        monitor_bfreq("enqueue_1", 0);
    }
    qNew -> iNode = iNode;
    qNew -> iDist = iDist;
    qNew -> iPrev = iPrev;
    qNew -> qNext = ((struct _QITEM *)((void *)0));
    if (!(qLast != 0)) {
        monitor_bfreq("enqueue_2", 1);
        qHead = qNew;
    }
    else {
        monitor_bfreq("enqueue_2", 0);
        while((qLast -> qNext) != 0) {
            qLast = (qLast -> qNext);
        }
        qLast -> qNext = qNew;
    }
    g_qCount++;
}


void dequeue(int *piNode,int *piDist,int *piPrev) {
    QITEM *qKill = qHead;
    if (qHead != 0) {
        monitor_bfreq("dequeue_1", 1);
        piNode = (qHead -> iNode);
        *piDist = (qHead -> iDist);
        *piPrev = (qHead -> iPrev);
        qHead = (qHead -> qNext);
        free(qKill);
        g_qCount--;
    } else {
        monitor_bfreq("dequeue_1", 0);
    }
}
```

FIG. 4.22

Code example based on the SHA benchmark.

3. *Heap usage report.* Just before the application terminates, we generate the branch frequency report with the `heap_report` API function.

The code in Fig. 4.24, based on the *patricia* benchmark [18,19], shows the instrumented code after applying the earlier strategy.

We can automate this process using the LARA `aspect` presented in Fig. 4.25 as follows:

1. Lines 3–7: Select the first statement of every source file, and insert the header file of the profiling API.

```
1. aspectdef BFreq
2.
3.      // select the first (global) statement of the file
4.      select file.first end
5.      // add profile header
6.      apply
7.          $first.insert before  %{ #include <profiling.h> }%;
8.      end
9.
10.     // select all function calls
11.     select function.if.then.entry end
12.     apply
13.         $entry.insert after %{
14.             monitor_breq("[[$if.key]]", 1);
15.         }%;
16.     end
17.
18.     // select all function calls
19.     select function.if.else.entry end
20.     // add a monitor before each call
21.     apply
22.         $entry.insert after %{
23.             monitor_bfreq("[[$if.key]]", 0);
24.         }%;
25.     end
26.
27.     // select last statement of the main function
28.     select function.exit end
29.     apply
30.         $exit.insert before  %{ report_bfreq(); }%;
31.     end
32.     condition $function.name == "main" end
33.
34. end
```

FIG. 4.23

LARA aspect for instrumenting branches and compute branch frequencies.

```
#include <profiling.h>
int pat_remove(struct ptree *n,struct ptree *head) {
    ...
    if (( *(t -> p_m)).pm_data != 0) {
        profile_heap_free(( *(t -> p_m)).pm_data);
    } else {
    }
    profile_heap_free((t -> p_m));
    if (t != p) {
        t -> p_key = (p -> p_key);
        t -> p_m = (p -> p_m);
        t -> p_mlen = (p -> p_mlen);
    } else {
    }
    profile_heap_free(p);
    return 1;
}
    ...
    /* Allocate space for a new set of masks. */
    buf = ((struct ptree_mask *)
      (profile_heap_malloc((sizeof(struct ptree_mask ) *
            ((t -> p_mlen) - 1)))));
    ...
    /* Free old masks and point to new ones. */
    t -> p_mlen--;
    profile_heap_free((t -> p_m));
    t -> p_m = buf;
    return 1;
}
```

FIG. 4.24

Code example based on the *patricia* benchmark.

```
1. aspectdef MemoryCheck
2.
3.      select file.first end
4.      // add profile header
5.      apply
6.        $first.insert before  %{ #include <profiling.h> }%;
7.      end
8.
9.      select function.call end
10.     apply
11.       if (($call.name == "malloc") || ($call.name == "free") ||
12.         ($call.name == "realloc"))
13.       {
14.         var call_code = $call.parent_stmt.unparse;
15.         var new_code = call_code.replace($call.name + "(",
16.           "profile_heap_" + $call.name + "(");
17.         $call.parent_stmt.insert around %{
18.           [[new_code]]
19.         }%;
20.       }
21.     end
22.
23.     select function.exit end
24.     // report monitor
25.     apply
26.        insert before %{ heap_report("dynamic heap report"); }%;
27.     end
28.     condition $function.name=="main" end
29.
30. end
```

FIG. 4.25

LARA aspect for memory check.

2. Lines 9–21: Select all function calls that perform heap management (malloc, free, and relloc) and replace them with the corresponding wrapper functions. This is accomplished by unparsing the function call in a string and do a text replacement. We then replace the old call with the new call.
3. Lines 23–28: Select all exit points of the main function, and insert a call to `heap_report()` to output heap management report. The current implementation of this API supports detecting memory leaks, invalid memory deallocation, as well as reporting the maximum heap memory allocated during the life cycle of the application.

4.6 SUMMARY

This chapter addressed the importance of code analysis and profiling in the context of high-performance embedded applications. We described key application features to guide developers to efficiently map computations to contemporary heterogeneous multicore-based embedded systems. We presented the main concepts of code analysis that are commonly used in the context of embedded platforms to extract information about the application in order to optimize it according to its requirements. The use of features acquired by code analysis and profiling are highlighted in Chapter 6 when considering code transformations and compiler optimizations.

4.7 FURTHER READING

In this chapter, we focused on the analysis of the application source code and on properties and metrics that can be used in order to help developers to understand the code of, e.g., the application hotspots. We have also introduced custom profiling techniques and the use of monitoring which have been extensively researched in the scholarly literature. Complementary to the profiling examples presented in the chapter, there are other profiling techniques such as path profiling [20] and vertical profiling [21] that enable developers to better understand runtime behavior. Profiling can provide important information to developers and tools by, e.-g., capturing: (1) the branch frequency of executed paths in `if-then-else` constructs, (2) invariant argument values in specific function calls which enable distinct specializations for the same function, and (3) data ranges and numerical accuracies of variables to guide word length optimizations. Moreover, code instrumentation is becoming increasingly important not only to detect faults/bugs, but also to acquire runtime information to guide tools to compile to hardware [22], to GPUs [17], and to multicore-based systems [23]. One example is the instrumentation-based data dependence profiling approach used to guide speculative optimizations. Another example is the use of instrumentation to help identify and/or suggest regions of code to parallelize [16,23]. Although the instrumentation strategies employed are commonly dependent on specific tools and are limited in terms of scope and flexibility, these approaches provide mechanisms for extracting relevant runtime information.

REFERENCES

[1] Chidamber S, Kemerer C. A metrics suite for object oriented design. IEEE Trans Softw Eng 1994;20(6):476–93.

[2] Fenton NE. Software metrics: a rigorous approach. London: Chapman & Hall, Ltd; 1991.

[3] Fenton NE, Pfleeger SL. Software metrics: a rigorous and practical approach. 2nd ed. Boston, MA: PWS Pub. Co.; 1998.

[4] Amdahl GM. Validity of the single processor approach to achieving large scale computing capabilities. In: Proceedings AFIPS spring joint computer conference; 1967. p. 483–5.

[5] Graham SL, Kessler PB, Mckusick MK. Gprof: a call graph execution profiler. In: SIGPLAN Not. vol. 17, no. 6, June; 1982. p. 120–6.

[6] Nethercote N, Seward J. Valgrind: a framework for heavyweight dynamic binary instrumentation. In: Proceedings ACM SIGPLAN conference on programming language design and implementation (PLDI'07). New York, NY: ACM; 2007. p. 89–100.

[7] Torczon L, Cooper K. Engineering a compiler. 2nd ed. San Francisco, CA: Morgan Kaufmann Publishers Inc; 2007.

[8] Wolfe M, Banerjee U. Data dependence and its application to parallel processing. Int J Parallel Progr 1987;16(2):137–78.

[9] Dantzig G, Curtis Eaves B. Fourier-Motzkin elimination and its dual. J Comb Theory A 1973;14:288–97.

[10] Rauchwerger L, Padua D. The LRPD test: speculative run-time parallelization of loops with privatization and reduction parallelization. In: Proceedings of the ACM SIGPLAN 1995 conference on programming language design and implementation (PLDI'95). New York, NY: ACM; 1995. p. 218–32.

[11] Salz J, Mirchandaney R, Crowley K. Run-time parallelization and scheduling of loops. IEEE Trans Comput 1991;40(5):603–12.

[12] Wolf ME, Lam MS. A data locality optimizing algorithm. In: Proc. of the ACM SIG-PLAN 1991 conf. on programming language design and implementation (PLDI'91). New York, NY: ACM Press; 1991. p. 30–44.

[13] UTDSP Benchmark Suite. http://www.eecg.toronto.edu/~corinna/DSP/infrastructure/UTDSP.html [Accessed December 2015].

[14] Cardoso JMP, Carvalho T, Coutinho JGF, Luk W, Nobre R, Diniz PC, et al. LARA: an aspect-oriented programming language for embedded systems. In: International conference on aspect-oriented software development (AOSD'12), Potsdam, Germany, March 25–30; 2012. p. 179–90.

[15] Cardoso JMP, Coutinho JGF, Carvalho T, Diniz PC, Petrov Z, Luk W, et al. Performance driven instrumentation and mapping strategies using the LARA aspect-oriented programming approach. Software: practice and experience (SPE), vol. 46, no. 2. Hoboken, NJ: John Wiley & Sons Ltd; 2016. p. 251–287.

[16] Garcia S, Jeon D, Louie CM, Taylor MB. Kremlin: rethinking and rebooting Gprof for the multicore age. In: 32nd ACM ACM/SIGPLAN conf. on programming language design and implementation (PLDI'11). New York, NY: ACM; 2011. p. 458–69.

[17] Holewinski J, Ramamurthi R, Ravishankar M, Fauzia N, Pouchet L-N, Rountev A, et al. Dynamic trace-based analysis of vectorization potential of applications. In: Proc. 33rd ACM SIGPLAN conf. on programming language design and implementation (PLDI'12), SIGPLAN Not. vol. 47, no. 6, June. New York, NY: ACM; 2012. p. 371–82.

[18] Guthaus MR, Ringenberg JS, Ernst D, Austin TM, Mudge T, Brown RB. MiBench: a free, commercially representative embedded benchmark suite. In: Proceedings of the IEEE international workshop on workload characterization, (WWC'01). Washington, DC: IEEE Computer Society; 2001. p. 3–14.

[19] MiBench version 1. http://www.eecs.umich.edu/mibench/ [Accessed November 2015].

[20] Ball T, Larus JR. Efficient path profiling. In: Proceedings of the 29th annual ACM/IEEE international symp. on microarchitecture (MICRO 29). Washington, DC: IEEE Computer Society; 1996. p. 46–57.

[21] Hauswirth M, Sweeney P, Diwan A, Hind M. Vertical profiling: understanding the behavior of object-oriented applications. In: SIGPLAN Not. vol. 39, no. 10, October; 2004. p. 251–69.

[22] Ben-Asher Y, Rotem N. Using memory profile analysis for automatic synthesis of pointers code. ACM Trans Embed Comput Syst 2013;12(3). Article 68, 21 pages.

[23] Lazarescu MT, Lavagno L. Dynamic trace-based data dependency analysis for parallelization of C programs. In: Proc. 12th IEEE int'l working conference on source code analysis and manipulation, September; 2012. p. 126–31.

[24] Bai Y, Vaidya P. Memory characterization to analyze and predict multimedia performance and power in embedded systems. In: Proceedings of the IEEE international conf. on acoustics, speech and signal processing (ICASSP'09). Washington, DC: IEEE Computer Society; 2009. p. 1321–4.

Source code transformations and optimizations

5

5.1 INTRODUCTION

In the presence of strict requirements, involving, e.g., performance, energy, or power consumption, it may not be enough to delegate to compilers the task of automatically satisfying these requirements through the use of standard compiler optimizations (such as using –O2 or –O3 command-line options with compilers such as GCC or ICC). While code transformations have an important role in improving performance, save energy, reduce power consumption, etc., many code transformations are not included in the portfolio of optimizations in mainstream compilers. Especially because most code transformations are not general enough to justify the effort to include them. Thus, code transformations may need to be manually applied by developers. This, however, imposes an additional burden on developers, as in order to apply a specific code transformation one needs to understand if it is legal and if it is profitable. Usually, to understand if it is legal, one needs to perform a specific type of static analysis that depends on the transformation at hand. An analysis of profitability also needs to be conducted, and it is usually not easy for inexperienced developers to understand the impact of a transformation unless they manually apply it and measure its impact directly. In addition, the analysis might need experiments with this code transformation, e.g., to tune its parameters.

In practice, profiling is also used to decide whether to apply a specific code transformation. There are cases, however, where the improvements achieved by a code transformation depend on the dataset and execution environment. In this case, developers may need to consider multiple versions of the code, each of them resulting from applying different code transformations and compiler optimizations, and to include code to decide at runtime which one to be executed in each execution pass. More advanced mechanisms delegate the tuning of the code transformations and their application to the runtime system and are usually part of adaptive compilation and online autotuning systems (briefly described in Chapter 8).

This chapter describes the most relevant code transformations. First, it covers basic code transformations and then it follows with more advanced code and loop transformations.

Embedded Computing for High Performance. http://dx.doi.org/10.1016/B978-0-12-804189-5.00005-3

5.2 BASIC TRANSFORMATIONS

Most basic code transformations are internally applied by compilers on a high-level intermediate representation (IR). Examples of these code transformations include constant propagation, strength reduction, constant folding, common subexpression elimination, dead-code elimination, scalar replacement, if-conversion, function inlining, and call specialization.

We now consider a few examples of strength reduction. A trivial case of strength reduction is when integer multiplications and divisions by a power of two integer constants are substituted by left and right shifts, respectively. For example, being x an integer variable, $8 \times x$ can be substituted by $x \ll 3$. More complex cases involve constants that are not power-of-two where the multiplication and division might be converted to expressions using shifts, additions, and subtractions. For instance, in the following expression, the constant 105 is transformed to $15 \times 7 = (16-1) \times (8-1)$, and thus:

```
B = 105 * A;
```

can be substituted by:

```
A1 = (A<<4)-A;
B = (A1<<3)-A1
```

The choice of whether to apply this transformation depends on the cost of performing two shifts and two subtractions instead of one multiplication on the target architecture.

The following strength reduction example uses different approaches to substitute the expression 113*A. More specifically, (1) uses directly the binary representation of $113 = 1110001$ $(2^6 + 2^5 + 2^4 + 2^0)$, (2) considers subtractions and in this case 1110001 can be represented as $2^7 - 2^4 + 1$, (3) with a factorization of the expression in (1) but using only additions, and finally (4) with a factorization of the expression in (1) but using additions and subtractions.

```
int B = (A<<6)+(A<<5)+(A<<4)+A;       (1)
int C = (A<<7) - (A<<4)+A;            (2)
int D = (((((A<<1)+A)<<1)+A)<<4)+A;   (3)
int E = (((A<<3)-A)<<4)+A;            (4)
```

Another example of strength reduction is the substitution of a modulo operation:

```
A = n % d
```

with the expression (its application is mainly dependent on the cost of calculating n/d):

```
A = n-d*floor(n/d)
```

While it is highly unlikely that a programmer would manually perform such transformations, compiler transformations such as loop coalescing can include a large number of such expressions at the intermediate level representation of the code, which can then be simplified in later phases of the compiler optimization passes.

There are cases where one can substitute expressions by approximate ones. One example related to strength reduction is the use of $(x \gg 1) + (x \gg 3) - (x \gg 6) - (x \gg 9)$ to substitute $x * 0.607259$. This is a topic that we focus in more detail and in the context of function approximation.

When considering floating-point numbers, there are also opportunities to apply strength reduction. For example, the multiplication of a floating-point value by 2 can be done by adding one to the exponent of the representation. The following code shows how this can be done in the C programming language. We note however that C is not a particularly good example to perform this transformation, as it requires many operations in order to capture the right bits of the exponent, adding one, and placing the new exponent in the right place. In general, any multiplication of a floating-point number by an integer power of two can be substituted by adding a constant to the exponent of the floating-point representation.

```
// get the bit representation of the floating-point as an uint
unsigned int p1 = * (unsigned int *) &a;

// get the exponent
unsigned char exp = (p1 & (0xFF<<23))>>23;

// equivalent to multiply by 2
exp = exp + 1;

// add the new exponent to the representation of the floating-point value
p1 = (p1 & ~(0xFF<<23)) | (exp<<23);

// the resultant floating-point value: 2*a
float ax2 = * (float *) &p1;
```

Another example regarding floating-point values is when we need to negate a value, e.g., as in $-1 * a$. This can be done by modifying the bit signal of the floating-point representation as it is shown in the following C code (for illustrative purposes as an implementation of this in a microprocessor is not profitable).

```
unsigned int p2 = * (unsigned int *) &a;
p2 = p2 ^ (1 << 31);
float neg_a = * (float *) &p2;
```

Strength reduction can be also applied in the context of loops as is illustrated in Fig. 5.1. In this case, the multiplication in Fig. 5.1A can be substituted by an addition (see Fig. 5.1B). Note that we can even go further if we change the loop control to reflect the index computations (see Fig. 5.1C).

This form of strength reduction can be typically applied to induction variables (i.e., to variables whose values are functions of the loop iteration values), and in some cases can lead to the elimination of the induction variable (induction variable elimination) altogether as shown in the example code in Fig. 5.1C.

```
for(i=0; i<N%4; i++) {        int j = 0;                    int j = 0;
    Sum += A[4*i];            for(i=0; i<N%4; i++) {        for(j=0; j<N; j+=4) {
}                                 Sum += A[j];                  Sum += A[j];
                                  j = j + 4;                }
                              }
```

(A)   (B)   (C)

FIG. 5.1

Strength reduction in the context of loops: (A) original loop; (B) applying strength reduction to $4*i$; (C) moving the strength reduction to the loop control (a transformation also known as induction variable elimination).

Another important transformation is scalar replacement where references to array elements are replaced by references to scalar variables. Typically, a computation such as an accumulation of values is first performed on a scalar variable (possibly even mapped to a hardware register by the compiler). When the accumulation is completed, the value of the scalar variable is then transferred to the array location thus resulting in substantial savings in terms of array address calculation and load/store operations. In addition, scalar replacement can achieve data reuse when applied in the context of the reuse of subscripted variables. In this case, redundant array accesses can be eliminated and replaced by scalar accesses.

The use of scalar variables to replace accesses to arrays can be done for some of the elements of the array or for the entire array. A special case of scalar replacement, and usually enabled by loop unrolling, is register blocking. By unrolling loops, it is common to expose blocks of scripted variables (representing array accesses) and to increase the opportunity to apply scalar replacement.

The following example presents an example of scalar replacement (sometimes known as loop scalar replacement). In this case accesses to array y over i are replaced with accesses to scalar y_aux and only one access to y for each i is required. This example shows the elimination of redundant array accesses using scalar replacement.

```
for (i=0;i<64;i++) {          for (i=0;i<64;i++) {
    y[i] = 0.0;                   y_aux = 0.0;
    for (j=0, j<8;j++)            for (j=0, j<8;j++)
        y[i] += z[i+64*j];            y_aux += z[i+64*j];
}                                 y[i] = y_aux;
                              }
```

It is also possible to use scalar replacement on more sophisticated examples, in particular those that result from the application of loop unrolling as depicted in the following example. Here the value written to y[i] is stored in scalar variable yi and is subsequently used to compute y[i+1].

```
for (i=1;i<N;i++) {      for (i=1;i<N;i+=2) {      for (i=1;i<N;i+=2) {
    y[i] = x[i]*y[i-1];      y[i] = x[i]*y[i-1];      yi = x[i]*y[i-1];
}                            y[i+1] = x[i]*y[i];      y[i] = yi;
                         }                            y[i+1] = x[i]*yi;
                                                  }
```

5.3 DATA TYPE CONVERSIONS

Data types impact memory usage and execution time. Depending on the data type, operations may require more or less clock cycles and the number of values that can be simultaneously loaded may also vary, e.g., affecting vectorization. It is common to convert floating-point data from double to single precision (if the resultant accuracy stays at acceptable levels). There are also cases of conversions from floating-point to integers and to fixed-point data types. While the effect of data type conversions may not be noticeable in most CPUs and GPUs, the impact can be very significant when using field-programmable gate array (FPGA)-based accelerators. Hence, an analysis of the impact of data conversions must include not only the resultant accuracy, but also the overhead associated with these conversions and the efficiency of the target architecture to compute operations with these transformed data types.

5.4 CODE REORDERING

In many cases, code reordering may significantly impact performance/energy/power. One example is the reordering of loops in nested loops (described in the section about loop transformations). In terms of instructions, it is common to rely on the reordering performed by the compiler based on data dependences, e.g., when scheduling instructions. There are cases, however, where developers may need to reorder instructions manually. One example is the reordering of `cases` in `switch` statements. The most frequent `case` (the common case) can be moved to the top as the top case needs less test and jump operations.

5.5 DATA REUSE

There are code transformations with the aim of maximizing data reuse. Data reuse is very important as it reduces the number of accesses to slow memory by using instead faster storage. Data reuse techniques eliminate repeated accesses to the same data, saving such data in internal registers and/or in faster access memories than where the data is originally stored. Frequently accessed data is saved in registers when it is first used and then reused in subsequent accesses. This increases data availability and avoids accesses to main memories. However, in the case of microprocessors, data reuse techniques may increase register pressure (as we may add additional scalar variables to the code), and it is not easy to apply them automatically due to compiler difficulties to identify data reuse opportunities for some data access patterns. There are cases of data reuse where the optimization benefits from hardware support, such as rotating registers.

Consider the code example in Fig. 5.2. For each iteration of the loop, we load one new position of x and two x positions already loaded in previous iterations (as shown in Fig. 5.3). We can transform the loop to store in scalar variables data that is reused

```
for (int i = 2; i< N; i++) {
    y[i] = x[i] + x[i-1] + x[i-2];
}
```

FIG. 5.2

Simple code example with data reuse opportunities.

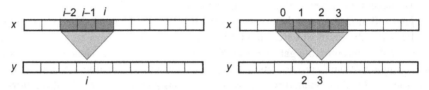

FIG. 5.3

Accesses in each iteration of the loop in Fig. 5.2. Left image shows the use of three values of x (indexed by $i-2$, $i-1$, and i) to calculate a value of y (indexed by i). Right image shows the first two loop iterations and the use of the x elements 1 and 2 twice.

between successive iterations, and thus for each iteration of the loop only one access to array x is needed, as illustrated in Fig. 5.4. This allows a reduction from $3 \times (N-2)$ accesses to array x to N accesses.

In some cases, code transformations can be performed and possibly leverage fast access memory components, which can provide considerably larger storage size than the internal registers provided by microprocessors (e.g., on-chip distributed memories and block RAMs in FPGAs).

Consider the "smooth" image processing operator presented in Fig. 5.5. At each iteration of the outermost loop, the data of 9 pixels (a 3×3 window) is loaded from memory. Across consecutive iterations, only the data of three new pixels is needed as six data items can be reused (see Fig. 5.6A). After traversing ("horizontally") all the columns of the image, the 3×3 window moves to the next three rows and in this case, it only needs to load three new values in the beginning and only one new value thereafter (see Fig. 5.6B). This combined "horizontal" and "vertical" data reuse requires the use of storage for three rows of the image in a storage component with faster access than the memory where the image is stored.

As this example shows, we can transform some codes to reduce the number of loads from memory at the expense of additional storage to save (or cache) data that has been previously loaded from memory. The degree of data reuse, thus changes with the amount of storage required resulting in various degrees of data reuse. Table 5.1 lists the number of memory loads and the corresponding reductions for the various reuses resulting from this scalar replacement transformation for a two-dimensional image of 350 by 350 pixels. As can be seen, for the more aggressive "horizontal" and "vertical" reuse transformation, the number of loads per pixel is "optimal" (just 1 load per pixel) as the image has exactly 122,500 pixels. The reduction over the naïve implementation, without any data reuse, is in this case 88.76% at the expense of 3×350 data registers (possibly realized using a scratchpad memory).

```
int x_2 = x[0]
int x_1 = x[1];
int x_0;
for (int i = 2; i< N; i++) {
    x_0 = x[i];
    y[i] = x_0 + x_1 + x_2;
    x_2 = x_1;
    x_1 = x_0;
}
```

FIG. 5.4

Code modified for data reuse.

```
int sizeX = 350;
int sizeY = 350;

void smooth(short[][] IN, short[][] OUT) {
    short[][] K =  {{1, 2, 1}, {2, 4, 2}, {1, 2, 1}};
    for (int j=0; j < sizeY-2; j++)
        for (int i= 0; i < sizeX-2; i++) {
            int sum = 0;
            for (int r=0; r < 3; r++)
                for (int c = 0; c<3; c++)
                    sum += IN[j+r][i+c]*K[r][c];
            sum= sum / 16;
            OUT[j+1][i+1] =  (short) sum;
        }
}
```

FIG. 5.5

Smooth image operator example.

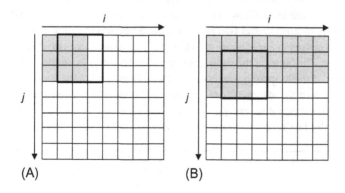

(A)   (B)

FIG. 5.6

The 3×3 window accesses in the smooth image operator example: (A) first three image rows
and the reuse of 6 pixels after the first column of pixels; (B) after the first three image rows and
the reuse of 8 pixels after the first column.

Table 5.1 Versions of the smooth example and the number of accesses to array IN

Code version	#Loads to array IN $(Y \times X)$	#Loads to array IN (350×350)	Reduction
Original smooth	$3*3*(X-2)*(Y-2)$	1,089,936	
Smooth w/horizontal data reuse	$(3*3+3*(X-3))*(Y-2)$	365,400	66.48%
Smooth w/horizontal and vertical data reuse	$(3*3+3*(X-3))+(3+1* (X-3))*(Y-3)$	122,500	88.76%

X and Y identify the horizontal and the vertical size of the images (variables sizeX and sizeY in the code), respectively.

5.6 LOOP-BASED TRANSFORMATIONS

Applications tend to spend a significant amount of their execution time in a few critical sections dominated by loops and/or nested loops. Therefore, loops are usually the hotspots in an application, i.e., important code regions that have the highest impact in performance/energy/power. The list of loop transformations a compiler (or a programmer) can apply is very extensive and most compilers (even commercial ones) only support a few (e.g., *loop unrolling* and *loop tiling*).

The following subsections present loop transformations that are mostly used in practice. At the end of this section we present an overview of these techniques, including their feasibility and suitability.

5.6.1 LOOP ALIGNMENT

The *loop alignment* transformation aims at promoting the reuse of array references in each iteration of the loop. Consider the following example. The code on the left has two references to array *b* and two references to array *a*. However, both arrays have misaligned accesses in each iteration of the loop, since we have two distinct accesses for each array. The code on the right, however, has both arrays aligned. Here we have "peeled" one of the loop assignments and placed them before the loop, and "shifted" the occurrences of the statements of the loop by "one." Now, in each iteration of the loop the references to either array b or array a are identical. Also, note that we need to take care of the last loop iteration, which needs to be partially backpeeled.

```
for(i=1; i<=N; i++) {
    b[i]=a[i];
    d[i]=b[i-1];
    c[i]=a[i+1];
}
```

```
d[1]=b[0];
for(i=2; i<=N; i++) {
    b[i-1]=a[i-1];
    d[i]=b[i-1];
    c[i-1]=a[i-1];
}
b[N]=a[N];
c[N]=a[N+1];
```

As can be seen, this transformation preserves the order of the execution of the operations and is therefore always legal to apply. Furthermore, its utilization promotes the use of scalar replacement since identical references in the same loop iteration can make use of a scalar variable.

5.6.2 LOOP COALESCING

Loop coalescing [1] can be used to transform two or more nested loops in a single loop. This technique can reduce the loop control overhead and improve instruction scheduling (given the potential increase in Instruction-Level Parallelism in the loop body), but typically adds some instruction complexity by introducing modulo and division operations used to compute array indexing functions. Next, we show a simple example of loop coalescing. The two loops j and i (left) are coalesced in loop t (right), and the i, j indices are calculated based on the value of t and on the trip count of the innermost loop. This technique can be applied even when the trip count of the outermost loop is not statically known.

```
for(j=0; j<N; j++)
  for(i=0; i<M; i++)
    sum += A[j][i];
```

```
for(t=0; t<N*M; t++) {
  j = t/M;
  i = t%M;
  sum += A[j][i];
}
```

The profitability of using loop coalescing depends on the performance and cost of the modulo operation. In some cases, one can use strength reduction over the modulo operation. For example, the modulo of powers of 2 can be expressed as a bitwise AND operation as $x \% 2^n = x \& (2^n - 1)$. In other cases, it might be better to use $x - y * \lfloor x/y \rfloor$ (i.e., $x - y*$floor(x/y)) instead of $x\%y$ (a transformation already mentioned in the beginning of this chapter).

Another alternative to the use of modulo and division operations is the use of conditional code. The following example shows the application of loop coalescing to the previous example, but considering conditional code to calculate the indexing values.

```
i=0;
j=0;
for(t=0; t<N*M; t++) {
    sum += A[j][i];
    if(i==M-1) {i=0;j++;}
    else i++;
}
```

The following example shows loop coalescing applied to a triple nested loop. In general, loop coalescing requires one division and one modulo operation per loop coalesced. This example introduces two divisions and two modulo operations.

```
for(i=0; i<=X; i++) {
    for (j=0; j<=Y; j++) {
        for (k=0; k<=Z; k++) {
            val = A[i][j][k];
            ...
        }
    }
}
```

```
for(m=0; m<(X*Y*Z); m++) {
    i = m / (Y*Z) + 1;
    j = m % (Y*Z) / Z+1;
    k = m % Z + 1;
    val = A[i][j][k];
}
```

Unlike many loop transformations, loop coalescing does not require loops to be perfectly nested. For imperfectly nested loops, additional code needs to be included to ensure the right execution.

A special case of loop coalescing is loop *collapsing* [2], which can be applied when loop iteration bounds match array bounds, and arrays are accessed once per element. This is the case of the previous example. The following codes show the result after applying loop collapsing.

```
int *p = &A[0][0];
for(t=0; t<N*M; t++) {
    sum += *p;
    p++;
}
```

```
int *p = &A[0][0];
for(t=0; t<N*M; t++) {
    sum += p[t];
}
```

As with loop alignment, loop coalescing and loop collapsing are always legal since they preserve the execution order of the original loop.

5.6.3 LOOP FLATTENING

Loop flattening [3] consists of replacing two or more nested loops in a single loop. Some authors refer to loop coalescing as *loop flattening*. However, we prefer to use the term *loop flattening* to refer to a more generic scheme to transform nested loops and sequenced loops in a single loop. In this categorization, *loop coalescing* and *loop collapsing* can be seen as special cases of *loop flattening*.

The following example is based on [3] and presents the result of applying loop flattening on a matrix-vector multiplication code for compressed sparse row (CSR).

```
for (i=0; i<N; i++) {
    y[i] = 0.0f;
    for (k=pntr[i]; k<pntr[i+1]-1; k++) {
        y[i] = y[i] + val[k]*vec[indx[k]];
    }
}
```

```
k=pntr[0]; i=-1;
for (j=0; j<flatlength; j++) {
    if(k > pntr[i+1]-1) {
        i++;
        y[i] = 0.0f;
        k = pntr[i];
    }
    y[i] = y[i] + val[k]*vec[indx[k]];
    k++;
}
```

Generally, loop flattening can be based on the code template presented below. The idea is to ensure that the innermost loop bodies execute in all iterations of the new flattened loop and to limit the execution of the blocks at the level of the outermost loop according to the original loop definition. Also, loop flattening is always a legal loop transformation since the original execution order is not modified.

```
LOOP Outer                 Loop FlatLoop: FlatIndex = Outer x max(Inner)
    Body_1;                    If(Last iteration of Inner (FlatIndex))
    LOOP Inner                     Body_1
        Body_2;                Body_2;
    End Inner                  If(Last iteration of Inner (FlatIndex))
    Body_3;                        Body_3
End Outer                  End FlatLoop
```

5.6.4 LOOP FUSION AND LOOP FISSION

Loop fusion (also known as loop merge) and *loop fission* (also known as loop distribution) merge a sequence of loops into one loop and split one loop into a sequence of loops, respectively.

Unlike other loop transformations previously mentioned, these two loop transformations change the order in which operations are executed, and therefore are only legal if the original data dependences are preserved. With respect to data dependences, loop fusion is legal if it does not introduce antidependences. Flow dependences are supported if they exist between the original loops before performing loop fusion. If the trip count of the loops being merged is not the same, the fusion of the loops needs additional code to enable the execution of the original iteration space for each loop's block of code. With respect to data dependences, loop fission is illegal when there are lexically backward loop-carried data dependences.

Despite these restrictions, both transformations present various potential benefits (see, e.g., [4]). Loop fusion may increase the level of parallelism, data locality, and decrease the loop control overhead (by reducing the number of loops), but may also increase the pressure on register allocation. Loop fission, on the other hand, might be used to distribute computations and memory accesses in a way that may increase the potential for loop pipelining and loop vectorization, may reduce cache misses, and may decrease the pressure on register allocation. There are also cases where loop fusion allows the use of scalar replacement to array variables (also known as array contraction) as data may not need to be fully stored and can be communicated using scalars. Conversely, the use of loop fission may require that some scalars be stored in arrays (known as scalar expansion) to be available to other loop(s). Loop fission can also enable other transformations such as loop interchange.

5.6.5 LOOP INTERCHANGE AND LOOP PERMUTATION (LOOP REORDERING)

Loop interchange (also known as iteration interleaving) changes the order of execution between two loops in a loop nest (see, e.g., [5]). The technique is useful to improve the data memory access patterns and thus increase the overall code spatial locality. Also, it can enable other important code transformations. Loop permutation (or loop reordering) is a generalization of this loop interchange transformation when more than two loops are reordered.

The following code shows a simple example of applying loop interchange. In this case, this transformation provides stride 1 accesses to array A (code on the right) instead of stride M accesses (code on the left). Note, however, that the changes in the stride accesses are dependent on the programming language. For instance, the memory layout in C/C++ is different from Fortran/MATLAB. In particular, in Fortran/MATLAB, the corresponding codes on the left would yield stride 1 accesses to array A.

```
for(j=0; j<M; j++)
   for(i=0; i<N; i++)
      A[i][j] += C;
```

```
for(i=0; i<N; i++)
   for(j=0; j<M; j++)
      A[i][j] += C;
```

The legality of loop interchange depends on the type of dependences of the nested loops. When the direction of the dependences of the two loops to interchange are positive and negative, the interchange results in an illegal distance vector. The following code shows an example of an illegal distance vector. Consider the code on the left. The distance vector for i is -1, while the distance vector for j is $+1$, resulting in $<-1, +1>$. If we apply loop interchange (code on the right) the distance vector changes to $<+1, -1>$ producing illegal code as antidependences change to true dependences (as shown with the following arrows).

```
for(i=0; i<M-1; i++)
   for(j=1; j<N; j++)
      A[i][j] = A[i+1][j-1] + C;
```

```
A[0][1] = A[1][0] + C
A[0][2] = A[1][1] + C
...
A[0][N-1] = A[1][N-2] + C
A[1][1] = A[2][0] + C
A[1][2] = A[2][1] + C
...
A[1][N-1] = A[2][N-2] + C
A[2][1] = A[3][0] + C
...
```

```
for(j=1; j<N; j++)
   for(i=0; i<M-1; i++)
      A[i][j] = A[i+1][j-1] + C;
```

```
A[0][1] = A[1][0] + C
A[1][1] = A[2][0] + C
...
A[M-2][1] = A[M-1][0] + C
A[0][2] = A[1][1] + C
A[1][2] = A[2][1] + C
...
A[M-2][2] = A[M-1][1] + C
A[0][3] = A[1][2] + C
...
```

5.6.6 LOOP PEELING

Loop peeling consists on separating (or peeling off) iterations from the beginning and/or the end of the loop (see a simple example below). Loop peeling is always legal and can be used as the basis for better code generation in the context of scalar replacement and software pipelining. It is sometimes required to generate vector code with aligned vector loads/stores and to peel off some loop iterations to prologue and/or epilogue in loop unrolling and/or software pipelining.

```
for(i=0; i<N; i++)
  sum += A[i];
```

```
sum += A[0];
for(i=1; i<N; i++)
  sum += A[i];
```

5.6.7 LOOP SHIFTING

Loop shifting (see, e.g., [6]) consists of moving some of the statements from their original iteration to another loop iteration. This technique can be used to enable loop fusion and to identify when to move a loop inside a loop nest. In the following example, the original loop (left) is transformed to a loop (right) where in the first iteration only S2 is executed and in the last iteration only S1 is executed, i.e., as if one of these statements was shifted one iteration to the left or one iteration to the right.

```
for(i=1; i<N; i++) {
  a[i]=b[i];     //S1
  d[i]=a[i-1];   //S2
}
```

```
for(i=0; i<N;i++) {
  if(i>0) a[i]=b[i];
  if(i<N-1) d[i+1]=a[i];
}
```

5.6.8 LOOP SKEWING

Loop skewing [7] is a transformation that changes the indexing and the corresponding loop control. For instance, in the following example the column accesses to array A are now given by a subtraction between the two induction variables i and j.

```
for(j=0; j<M; j++)
  for(i=0; i<N; i++)
    sum += A[j][i];
```

```
for(j=0; j<M; j++)
  for(i=j; i<N+j; i++)
    sum += A[j][i-j];
```

5.6.9 LOOP SPLITTING

Loop splitting partitions a loop or loop nest in various loops, each one traversing a different iteration space (see a simple example below). This technique can be performed when considering data parallelism where the iteration space of the loop is split and each section is now executed as a thread, for example.

```
//float A, float B
for(i = 0; i < N; i++)
  A[i] = B[i] + C;
```

```
//float A, float B
for(i = 0; i < N/2; i++)
  A[i] = B[i] + C;
for(i = N/2; i < N; i++)
  A[i] = B[i] + C;
```

Loop splitting can be also used to create prologues and or epilogues of a loop (in this case it is similar to *loop peeling*) as in the case of loop vectorization when the iteration space is not a multiple of the vector length, or in the case of loop unrolling when the iteration space is not multiple of the unrolling factor. This can be seen in the following loop vectorization example where the remainder $N\%4$ of the iterations of the loop is moved to a second loop.

```
//float *restrict A, float *restrict B

for(i = 0; i < N; i++)
  A[i] = B[i] + C;
```

```
//float *restrict A, float *restrict B

// w/o assuming N%4==0
for(i = 0; i < (N-N%4); i+=4)
  A[i:i+3] = B[i:i+3] + C;
for(; i < N; i++) //epilogue
  A[i] = B[i] + C;
```

5.6.10 LOOP STRIPMINING

Loop stripmining (also known as loop sectioning) transforms a loop in a double-nested loop and can be seen as a special case of loop tiling (see next subsection) in which only one of the loops is tiled (blocked). The following is an example of loop *stripmining* and as we can see, the loop on the left is transformed into two loops on the right: an outer loop responsible to iterate through the blocks and an inner loop to iterate over each block.

```
for(i=0; i<N; i++) {
  sum += A[i];
}
```

```
for(is=0; is<N; is+=S) { // S is the size of the 1-
dimension block
  for(i=is; i<min(N,is+S-1); i++) {
    sum += A[i];
  }
}
```

5.6.11 LOOP TILING (LOOP BLOCKING)

Loop tiling, also known as *loop blocking*, is a loop transformation that exploits spatial and temporal locality of data accesses in loop nests. This transformation allows data to be accessed in blocks (tiles), with the block size defined as a parameter of this transformation. Each loop is transformed in two loops: one iterating inside each block (intratile) and the other one iterating over the blocks (intertile). Fig. 5.7 shows a simple example considering the use of loop tiling on two of the three nested "for" loops.

```
for(i=0; i<N; i++)
  for(j=0; j<N; j++)
    for(k=0; k<N; k++)
      C[i][j] = C[i][j] +
               A[i][k]*B[k][j];
```

```
for(jj=0; jj<N; jj+=Bj)
  for(kk=0; kk<N; kk+=Bk)
    for(i=0; i<N; i++)
      for(j=jj; j<min(jj+Bj,N); j++)
        for(kk=0; kk<min(kk+Bk,N); kk++)
          C[i][j] = C[i][j] + A[i][k]*B[k][j];
```

(A)   (B)

FIG. 5.7

Loop tiling example: (A) original code; (B) code after loop tiling to loops *j* and *k*.

Loop tiling can target the different levels of memory (including the cache levels) and can be tuned to maximize the reuse of data at a specific level of the memory hierarchy. The transformation involves the use of specific block sizes and they can be fixed at compile time, and are calculated based on data sizes and memory (e.g., cache) size, and/or tuned at runtime.

5.6.12 LOOP UNROLLING

Loop unrolling is a well-known loop transformation. When unrolling a loop by a factor of K, the loop body is repeated K number of times and the loop iteration space is reduced (or eliminated when the loop is fully unrolled). Loop unrolling enables other optimizations and/or increases the parallelism degree in the loop body given the increase of its operations. As the number of iterations of a loop is not always known, there is a need to include a "clean-up" code as part of the prologue and/or epilogue of the loop when unrolled. However, when the number of iterations of the loop is known at compile time and it is a multiple of the unrolling factor no prologue or epilogue code is needed.

In the following example, the loop on the left is fully unrolled, which results in the code in the right.

```
for(i=0; i<4;i++) {
   c[i] = a[i] + b[i];
}
```
```
c[0] = a[0] + b[0];
c[1] = a[1] + b[1];
c[2] = a[2] + b[2];
c[3] = a[3] + b[3];
```

The following example shows the loop unrolled by a factor of 2. In this case, the loop is not eliminated.

```
for(i=0; i<4;i+=2) {
    c[i] = a[i] + b[i];
    c[i+1] = a[i+1] + b[i+1];
}
```

When the number of iterations is not known at compile time and the intention is to unroll a loop by a factor, there is the need to include code to test if the number of iterations is greater or equal than the unrolling factor, and to include an epilogue (example on the left) or a prologue (example on the right).

```
if(N >= 2) {
   for(i=0; i<N-N%2;i+=2) {  // K=2
      c[i] = a[i] + b[i];
      c[i+1] = a[i+1] + b[i+1];
   }
} else i=0;
for(; i<N; i++)  // epilogue
   c[i] = a[i] + b[i];
```
```
for(i=0; i<N%2; i++)  // prologue
   c[i] = a[i] + b[i];
if(N >= 2) {
   for(; i<N;i+=2) {  // K=2
      c[i] = a[i] + b[i];
      c[i+1] = a[i+1] + b[i+1];
   }
} else
   for(; i<N; i++)
      c[i] = a[i] + b[i];
```

Loop unrolling is always a legal transformation as the order in which the operations are executed remains unchanged (special care must be taken in the presence of `continue` instructions). Yet, and as with other transformations that replicate code instructions, the compiler needs to evaluate the impact of code expansion that can result from the use of loop unrolling, in particular when the iteration space or the number of body statements is very large.

5.6.13 UNROLL AND JAM

Unroll and jam is a loop transformation that unrolls an outer loop by a factor and then fuse/merge (jam) the inner loops resultant from the outer loop unrolling. The following example shows an unrolling of $2 \times$ and a jam which results in two stores of the y array per iteration of the outermost loop, maintaining a single innermost loop (this one with two loads of array z).

```
for(i=0;i<64;i++) {
  y_aux = 0.0;
  for(j=0, j<8;j++)
    y_aux += z[i+64*j];
  y[i] = y_aux;
}
```

```
// unroll 2x outermost loop and jam
for(i=0;i<64; i+=2) {
  y_aux1 = 0.0;
  y_aux2 = 0.0;
  for(j=0, j<8;j++){
    y_aux1 += z[i+64*j];
    y_aux2 += z[i+1+64*j];
  }
  y[i] = y_aux1;
  y[i+1] = y_aux2;
}
```

5.6.14 LOOP UNSWITCHING

Loop unswitching consists of moving loop invariant conditionals (conditions without side effects and whose logical values are independent of the loop iterations) outward. This transformation involves having as many loops as there are branch conditions, and each loop body executing the corresponding branch statements. The following example shows on the left a loop where there is a condition (op $==1$) which is not dependent on the loop iterations (i.e., during the execution of the loop it is always true or false). In this case, the condition can be moved to outside the loop and each branch of the if-statement has now a loop responsible for each of the original branch statements (see the following example on the right).

```
for(i=0;i<M;i++) {
  if(op==1)
    sum += A[i];
  else
    sum *= A[i];
}
```

```
if(op==1)
  for(i=0;i<M;i++) {
    sum+=A[i];
  }
else
  for(i=0;i<M;i++) {
    sum *= A[i];
  }
```

The legality of this transformation hinges on the compiler's ability to determine if a given predicate is a loop invariant, and thus enables the use of this transformation.

5.6.15 LOOP VERSIONING

Loop versioning consists of generating multiple versions of a loop, in which each version's execution is predicated and selected at runtime. This transformation is always legal and is commonly used in conjunction with partial loop unrolling to test if the number of iterations of the loop evenly divides the selected unrolling factor.

This transformation can also be used to ensure the legality of other transformations. For example, the following code shows how a compiler can generate transformed code and use a predicate to ensure that a loop can be vectorized. In this case, it emits code that checks at runtime the absence of data dependences between the array variables (i.e., if arrays *A* and *B* are not fully or partially overlapped) and thus can be vectorized. If this predicate does not hold at runtime, then the loop is not vectorizable and the code will execute an alternative version of the loop (possibly the original loop version).

```
//float *A, float *B
for(i = 0; i < N; i++)
    A[i] = B[i] + C;
```

```
//float *A, float *B
// USE ORIGINAL VERSION:
if ((&A[N-1] >= &B[0]) && (&B[N-1] >= &A[0]))
    for(i = 0; i < N; i++)
        A[i] = B[i] + C;
// USE A VECTORIZED VERSION:
else // assuming N%4==0
    for(i = 0; i < N; i+=4)
        A[i:i+3] = B[i:i+3] + C;
```

Typically, multiple versions corresponding to different optimizations of the same loop can coexist at runtime and selected depending on certain runtime properties. This transformation can be even extended when considering the use of hardware accelerators and/or computation offloading. In this case, multiple implementations of the same loop can be provided, and the decision to execute one of them is postponed to runtime.

5.6.16 SOFTWARE PIPELINING

Software pipelining [8] (also known as loop pipelining and loop folding) is a technique that overlaps loop iterations (i.e., subsequent iterations start before previous finished). This technique is suitable to increase performance but may also increase register pressure (not a main problem in reconfigurable array architectures with pipeline stages). One of the most used software pipelining techniques is the iterative modulo scheduling [9].

All efficient compilers include software pipelining as part of their set of optimizations. This technique is mostly applied at the intermediate representation (IR) level of a program, but can also be applied at the source code level (and in this case, it is considered a code transformation technique), as the following example shows.

Software pipelining requires a prologue, a kernel, and an epilogue (see Fig. 5.8). They can be explicit as shown in the following example (middle) or implicit during execution as is the case of code on the right. In the latter, predicated execution is used. The kernel is the section of code that iterates capturing all loop instructions. The prologue and the epilogue execute a subset of instructions (ramp-up and ramp-down).

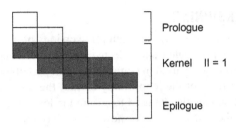

FIG. 5.8

Software pipelining stages: prologue, kernel, and epilogue.

An important parameter used in software pipelining is the Initiation Interval (II) [9], which identifies the number of cycles between the start of successive iterations. The ultimate goal of software pipelining to maximize performance is to achieve an II of one clock cycle, which means that the kernel is executed at one iteration per cycle. However, this may impose too many hardware resources that are not available or impose significant overhead from register pressure. The minimum possible II depends on the hardware resources that are simultaneously available, of their latency and pipelining stages, and of the latencies imposed by cycles in the data dependence graph (DDG).

```
for(i=0; i<10; i++) {
  C[i] = A[i] * B[i];
}
```

```
a_tmp = A[0];
b_tmp = B[0];
for(i=0; i<9; i++) {
  C[i] = a_tmp * b_tmp;
  a_tmp = A[i+1];
  b_tmp = B[i+1];
}
C[9] = a_tmp * b_tmp;
```

```
for(i=0; i<11; i++) {
  C[i-1] = a_tmp * b_tmp:if i!=0
  a_tmp = A[i]: if i!=10;
  b_tmp = B[i]: if i!=10;
}
```

5.6.17 EVALUATOR-EXECUTOR TRANSFORMATION

The evaluator-executor loop transformation was proposed in Ref. [10] and allows the pipelined execution of loops with conditional constructs whose values cannot be ascertained at compile time. The technique splits the loop into an evaluator loop and an executor loop (see the following example). The main idea is to reduce computations inside a loop with conditions, which avoids predicated execution when applying loop pipelining.

```
for(i=0; i<N; i++) {
  ai = A[i];
  if(ai > 0) {
    B[i] = sqrt(ai);
  }
}
```

```
int ExecLC = 0;
for(i=0; i<N; i++) { // evaluator loop
  ai = A[i];
  if(ai > 0) {
    ExecIter[ExecLC] = i;
    ExecLC++;
  }
}
for(j=0; j<ExecLC; j++) { // executor loop
  i = ExecIter[j];
  ai = A[i];
  B[j] = sqrt(ai);
}
```

5.6.18 LOOP PERFORATION

Some loop transformations may not preserve the original results, since they change the order of the floating-point operations. This is however not intentional and is the result of the limited precision used to represent real numbers. There are other cases where code transformations lead to approximate computing as is the case of *loop perforation* [11]. This loop transformation considers only part of the iteration space by skipping some of the iterations. The following example shows (on the right) the result of loop perforation applied to the code on the left. In this example, the loop iterations skip $k-1$ iterations of the original loop between every two consecutive iterations of the new loop.

Loop perforation can be used to improve performance, reduce energy/power consumption, as long as the QoS (Quality-of-Service) or the QoE (Quality-of-Experience) are acceptable.

```
for(i=0; i<N; i++) {          for(i=0; i<N; i+=k) {
   sum += A[i];                  sum += A[i];
}                             }
```

5.6.19 OTHER LOOP TRANSFORMATIONS

In addition to the loop transformations briefly described in the previous subsections, there are other transformations that enable the use of other transformations or perform an intermediate transformation.

One example of such transformation is the conversion between loop types, e.g., transforming *while do* and *do while* into *for* type loops. A useful technique is *loop inversion* which consists in replacing a *while* loop by a repeat-until (*do while*) loop. The following example illustrates this conversion. Note that the if-statement may not be needed when the original loop always executes at least one iteration.

```
while (e) {                   if(e)
   s;                            do {
}                                  s;
                              } while (e);
```

Loop normalization is a common transformation performed to make data dependence testing easier. It modifies the loop bounds so that the lower bound of all *do* loops is one (or zero) and the increment is one. This simplifies data dependence tests because two out of three loop bound expressions will be a simple known constant.

Loop reversal consists of changing the order in which the iteration space is traversed. Loop reversal is illegal when the loop has loop-carried data dependences.

Hoisting of loop invariant (also known as *loop invariant code motion*) computations consists of moving computations that do not change with the iterations of the loop and thus can be moved to before the loop.

Node splitting consists of copying data to remove data dependence cycles.

Loop scaling consists of increasing the step traversing the iteration space and can be useful in the context of other loop transformations such as loop tiling.

Loop reindexing (also known as loop alignment or index set shifting) consists of changing the indexing of array variables by, e.g., considering a different loop iteration control.

Two interprocedural code motion techniques related to loops are *loop embedding* and *loop extraction* [12]. Loop embedding pushes a loop header into a procedure called within the loop, and loop extraction extracts an outermost loop from a procedure body into the calling procedure.

Memory access coalescing is an optimization performed on some computation architectures where multiple data elements can be loaded or stored at the same time (e.g., coalesced by GPU hardware [13]). Loop transformations can be used to allow coalescing by aligning memory accesses and by transforming code to achieve stride 1 accesses to memory.

5.6.20 OVERVIEW

This section provides a global picture of the loop transformations briefly described in the previous subsections. Even though there are many loop transformations, compilers support a very limited subset, and thus much of the burden to optimize code—especially when targeting heterogeneous multicore platforms—is placed on developers.

It is recognized that there are some loop transformations that have a wider applicability, such as loop unrolling and loop tiling, but even very simple techniques such as loop reversal can be very important. For example, changing the order for traversing the iteration space may allow other transformations (e.g., loop fusion) that were impossible to apply due to data dependences.

Table 5.2 summarizes the loop transformations described in this chapter and provides simple illustrative examples for each of them. The aim of this list is to provide a quick guide to these loop transformations.

A key aspect in a compiler organization is how to leverage these transformations and combine them in a coherent and effective sequence of program transformations that can be guided by a set of well-defined and qualitative performance metrics. In general, choosing the set and order in which these loop transformations are executed is very challenging as there are inherent undecidability limitations a compiler cannot possibly overcome. Still, researchers have developed very sophisticated algorithms that are guided by specific metrics such as data locality which can suggest a sequence of transformation that, in many practical cases, result in high-performance code [12]. In other contexts, and in the absence of effective compile time guiding metrics, researchers have resorted to the use of autotuning exploration techniques in optimization frameworks, such that a compiler can experiment with different parameters and sets of transformation in search of a transformation combination that leads to good performance results [14].

Table 5.3 indicates the usefulness of a number of loop transformation techniques in terms of main goals and context. We note that many of the loop transformations are not useful if isolated but they can permit the applicability of other loop transformations and/or compiler optimizations.

Table 5.2 Loop transformations and illustrative examples

Loop transformation	Illustrative examples	
	Original source code	**Transformed code**
Loop alignment	```for(i=1; i<=N; i++) { b[i]=a[i]; d[i]=b[i-1]; c[i]=a[i+1]; }```	```d[1]=b[0]; for(i=2; i<=N; i++) { b[i-1]=a[i-1]; d[i]=b[i-1]; c[i-1]=a[i-1]; } b[N]=a[N]; c[N]=a[N+1];```
Loop coalescing	```for(j=0; j<N; j++) for(i=0; i<N; i++) sum += A[j][i];```	```for(t=0; t<N*N; t++) { j = t/N; i = t%N;; sum += A[j][i]; }```
Loop collapsing (a special form of loop coalescing)	```for(j=0; j<M; j++) for(i=0; i<N; i++) sum += A[j][i];```	```// p is a pointer to &A[0][0] for(i=0; i<N*N; i++) sum += p[i];```
Loop flattening	```for(i=0; i<N; i++) { ai = A[i]; sum = 0; for(j=0; j<M; j++) sum += B[j]+ai; A[i] = sum/A[i]; }```	```j = M; i=-1; for(k=0; k<N*M; k++) { if(j>M-1) { i++; ai = A[i]; sum = 0; } sum+= B[j]+ai; if(j>M-1) { A[i] = sum/A[i]; } j++; }```

Continued

Table 5.2 Loop transformations and illustrative examples—*cont'd*

	Illustrative examples	
Loop transformation	Original source code	Transformed code

Loop fission/distribution	`for(i=0; i<N; i++) {`
	`  sum += A[i];`
	`  prod += B[i]*B[i];`
	`}`
		`for(i=0; i<N; i++) sum += A[i];`
		`for(i=0; i<N; i++) prod += B[i]*B[i];`

Loop fusion/merging	`for(i=0; i<N; i++) sum += A[i];`
	`for(i=0; i<N; i++)`
	`  prod += B[i]*B[i];`
		`for(i=0; i<N; i++) {`
		`  sum += A[i];`
		`  prod += B[i]*B[i];`
		`}`

Loop interchange/reordering	`for(j=0; j<M; j++)` `  for(i=0; i<N; i++) sum += A[j][i];`	`for(i=0; i<N; i++)` `  for(j=0; j<M; j++) sum += A[j][i];`
Loop normalization	`for(i=2; i<N; i++) sum += A[i-2];`	`for(i=0; i<N-2; i++) sum += A[i];`

Loop peeling	`for(i=0; i<N; i++)`
	`  sum += A[i];`
		`sum += A[0];`
		`for(i=1; i<N; i++)`
		`  sum += A[i];`

Loop reversal	`for(i=0; i<N; i++) sum += A[i];`	`for(i=N-1; i>=0; i--) sum += A[i];`

Loop shifting	`for(i=1; i<=N;i++) {`
	`  a[i]=b[i];`
	`  d[i]=a[i-1];`
	`}`
		`for(i=0; i<=N;i++) {`
		`  if(i>0) a[i]=b[i];`
		`  if(i<N) d[i+1]=a[i];`
		`}`

Loop skewing	`for(j=0; j<M; j++)`
	`  for(i=0; i<N; i++)`
	`    sum += A[j][i];`
		`for(j=0; j<M; j++)`
		`  for(i=j; i<N+j; i++)`
		`    sum += A[j][i-j];`

Loop splitting	`for(i=0; i<N; i++) sum += A[i];`	`for(i=0; i<N/2; i++) sum += A[i];` `for(i=N/2; i<N; i++) sum += A[i];`

| Loop stripmining (single nested loops) | `for(i=0; i<N; i++) sum += A[i];` | ```for(is=0; is<N; is+=S)
  for(i=S; i<min(N,is+S-1); i++)
    sum += A[i];``` |
| Loop tiling/blocking (generic nested loops) | ```for(j=0; j<M; j++)
  for(i=0; i<N; i++)
    sum += A[j][i];``` | ```for(jc=0;jc<M; jc+=B)
  for(ic=0;ic<N; ic+=B)
    for(j=jc;j<min(M,jc+B-1); j++)
      for(i=ic;i<min(N,ic+B-1);i++)
        sum += A[j][i];``` |
| Unroll and jam | ```for(j=0; j<M; j++)
  for(i=0; i<N; i++)
    sum += A[j][i];``` | ```for(j=0; j<M; j+=2)
  for(i=0; i<N; i++) {
    sum += A[j][i];
    sum += A[j+1][i];
  }``` |
| Loop unrolling (fully or by a factor k) | ```for(i = 0; i < N; i++) {
  sum += A[i];
}``` | ```for(i = 0; i < N; i+=2) {
  sum += A[i];
  sum += A[i+1];
}``` |
| Loop unswitching | ```for(i=0; i<N; i++) {
  sum += A[i];
  if(b) A[i] = 0;
}``` | ```if(b)
  for(i=0; i<N; i++) {
    sum += A[i];
    A[i] = 0;
  }
else for(i=0; i<N; i++) sum += A[i];``` |
| Loop versioning | ```for (i = 0; i < N; i++)
  A[i] = B[i] + C;``` | ```If(N%2==0)
  for (i = 0; i < N; i+=2) {
    A[i] = B[i] + C;
    A[i+1] = B[i+1] + C;
  }
else
  for (i = 0; i < N; i++)
    A[i] = B[i] + C;``` |

Continued

Table 5.2 Loop transformations and illustrative examples—*cont'd*

Illustrative examples

Loop transformation	Original source code	Transformed code
| Loop evaluator–executor | ```
for(i=0; i<N; i++) {
  ai = A[i];
  if(ai > 0) {
    B[i] = sqrt(ai);
  }
}
``` | ```
int ExecLC = 0;
for(i=0; i<N; i++) { // evaluator loop
  ai = A[i];
  if(ai > 0) {
    ExecIter[ExecLC] = i;
    ExecLC++;
  }
}
for(j=0; j<ExecLC; j++) { // executor loop
  i = ExecIter[j];
  ai = A[i];
  B[j] = sqrt(ai);
}
``` |
| Loop perforation | ```
for(i=0; i<N; i++) {
  sum += A[i];
}
``` | ```
for(i=0; i<N; i+=k) {
  sum += A[i];
}
``` |
| Loop hoisting | ```
for(i=0; i<N; i++) {
  A[i] = f(x)*B[i];
}
``` | ```
y = f(x);
for(i=0; i<N; i++) {
  A[i] = y*B[i];
}
``` |
| Node splitting | ```
for(i=0; i<N; i++) {
  A[i] = t*B[i];
  C[i] = A[i+1] + D[i];
}
``` | ```
for(i=0; i<N; i++) {
  temp[i] = A[i+1];
  A[i] = t*B[i];
  C[i] = temp[i] + D[i];
}
``` |
| Loop scaling | ```
for(i=0; i<N; i++) {
  sum += A[i];
}
``` | ```
for(i=0; i<2*N; i+=2) {
  sum += A[i/2];
}
``` |

Table 5.3 Indication of the usefulness of a number of loop transformations

Goals/context	Loop transformations
Increase data locality (reduce cache misses)	Loop fusion, loop fission Loop tiling, loop stripmining, and loop interchanging
Increase ILP and to potentiate other optimizations	Loop unrolling, loop fusion, array replication, unroll and jam, loop unswitching
Increase ILP	Software pipelining
Use SIMD units	Loop vectorization, loop alignment
Make possible the postponing to runtime	Loop versioning
Skip iterations in the context of approximate computing	Loop perforation
Reduce loop overhead and expose more work to a single loop	Loop coalescing, loop flattening, and loop collapsing
Improve compiler analysis	Loop normalization, loop reversal
Eliminate dependences, improve coarsening memory accesses	Loop shifting, loop skewing
Eliminate dependences	Node splitting
Increase the application of other loop transformations	Loop peeling, loop splitting, and loop scaling
Increase the applicability of software pipelining and loop vectorization	Loop evaluator-executor
Reduce loop work	Loop hoisting

5.7 FUNCTION-BASED TRANSFORMATIONS

At the function level there are important code transformations that can impact the performance and resource utilization. In this section we describe a representative set of these transformations.

5.7.1 FUNCTION INLINING/OUTLINING

Function or procedure inlining is a transformation technique that consists of substituting a function/procedure call with the body of the called function/procedure. This transformation helps reduce the call overhead and exposes more opportunities for further code analysis and transformations, such as constant folding and constant propagation, as well as other code optimizations that can now be applied at the call site. For instance, partial evaluation (see Section 5.7.2) can be applied, which allows function arguments that have a specific value to propagate to the body of the function. Conversely, this technique may increase register pressure and result in code bloating, in particular when the entire call chain is inlined. Clearly, recursive regions of the call graph cannot be inlined unless previously transformed to iterative versions.

To avoid these problems, it is common to apply "partial inlining" which requires the selection of candidate call sites where function inlining must be applied. This selection hinges on which call sites are deemed more profitable taking into account, for instance, constraints about code size.

Function outlining (also known as function exlining) performs the opposite of inlining, promoting code reuse at the expense of the call/return overhead. More specifically, in this transformation a section of code is extracted to a function/procedure and substituted by a call to that function/procedure. The technique may reduce code size when the function substitutes more than one code section (which happens with code cloning sections). It is usually applied as a step to enable multiple versions of a code section.

5.7.2 PARTIAL EVALUATION AND CODE SPECIALIZATION

Partial evaluation, which is also known as "currying" [15], is a technique where the computation is evaluated with respect to a given operand's value. That is, rather than treating an operand as a variable, its value becomes "fixed." Given a specific value of an argument, the code is specialized by replacing the occurrences of the variable with the corresponding value. Clearly, and in the absence of any information about runtime values of the program inputs, a compiler can create multiple code variants of a procedure/function for specific values of its arguments. The choice of which value to specialize can be guided either by runtime profiling or by static analysis of the procedure/function call sites. Code specialization is particularly beneficial when combined with transformations such as constant propagation, strength reduction, and in general control-flow optimization.

Code specialization can be performed statically or dynamically. Dynamic code specialization is used in JIT compilers [16], while static code specialization is performed based on information collected by a static analysis (e.g., the compiler is able to determine that at least one of the arguments in a call site is a statically known constant value) or using profiling data.

Code specialization can be categorized as control-flow specialization and data specialization. Control specialization leverages the execution paths to furnish specialized version of the code. Data specialization, on the other hand, takes advantage of the data values (or their properties) to provide specialized versions. Both techniques can be fully identified by static analysis or using profiling data, runtime data, or a mix between them.

The specialization of functions is a type of optimization that can be used to improve performance and/or energy/power consumption. This specialization is usually applied based on the runtime values of the arguments in call sites. For instance, one of the arguments of a function might be at all times a constant value or some of the times have a specific value. This translates into one specialized version or multiple versions of that function, respectively.

Code specialization can enable a wide range of program transformations. At a very low level, a compiler can use the information about a specific operand value to apply instruction-level optimizations such as strength reduction and algebraic simplification. For example, if for the following statement on the left it is known that the value of b is 2, then it can be transformed to the statement on the right:

```
c=pow(a, b);
```

```
c = a*a;
```

In case b has multiple values, including 1 and 2, one can adopt a multiple versioning strategy such as the one presented in the following example:

```
if (b == 1) c = a;
else if (b == 2) c =a*a;
else c = pow(a, b);
```

The specialization of functions with at least one known constant argument is usually conducted by cloning the function and then providing the correspondent specialized version. The following code example implements a 4-point stencil computation for two stencil patterns controlled by the "sel" input parameter that is set to either "0" or "1" (or any other nonzero) value at the function "funcRelax" call site to define the traversal pattern over the array *A* here assumed to be globally defined:

```
void funcRelax(int N, int sel){
  int i, j;
  for (i=1; i < (N-1); i++){
    for (j=1; j < (N-1); j++){
      if (sel == 0){
        A[i][j] = (A[i-1][j]+A[i+1][j]+A[i][j-1]+A[i][j+1])/4;
      } else {
        A[i][j] = (A[i-1][j-1]+A[i-1][j+1]+A[i+1][j-1]+A[i+1][j+1])/4;
      }
    }
  }
}
```

Based on this code, the compiler can generate two code variants of this function as shown below and replace them at the corresponding call sites. Each function variant now has a single argument *N* rather than two arguments.

```
void funcRelaxSel0(int N){
  int i, j;
  for (i=1; i < (N-1); i++){
    for (j=1; j < (N-1); j++){
      A[i][j] = (A[i-1][j]+A[i+1][j]+A[i][j-1]+A[i][j+1])/4;
  }
}
```

```
...
funcRelax(16,0);
...
```

```
...
funcRelaxSel0(16);
...
```

It is also possible to further specialize this function if for some call sites the remaining arguments (or the already partially evaluated function) have specific values. For the example in the previous figure (right), we could further propagate the value of *N* and create another data specialization version of this function as shown as follows:

```
void funcRelaxSel0N16(){
  int i, j;
  for (i=1; i < 15; i++){
    for (j=1; j < 15; j++){
      A[i][j] = (A[i-1][j]+A[i+1][j]+A[i][j-1]+A[i][j+1])/4;
  }
}
```

Given now the knowledge of the loop bounds the compiler can apply other transformations such as loop unrolling or scalar replacement to further improve the performance of this specific variant of the `funcRelax` function.

5.7.3 FUNCTION APPROXIMATION

If the resultant accuracy is adequate, the use of approximate functions instead of exact functions may increase performance, reduce power and/or energy consumption. The methods used for approximate computing of functions include:

- Lookup tables;
- Lookup tables and interpolation, e.g., generating the table by using the Ramer-Douglas-Peucker algorithm[1];
- Lower cost functions;
- Iterative methods such as Taylor's series [17] and the Newton-Raphson method [18].

Lookup tables can be an efficient scheme to substitute functions such as the trigonometric functions. A function can be substituted by a table with values for a number of input values and the values not present in the table for a given number of inputs can be obtained by approximating to the closest ones or by interpolating between the two closest points. This is an effective and efficient method, especially in the context of custom hardware, but does not scale for nontrivial functions as this table can become quite large and infeasible for applications that target embedded systems.

An option to generate an approximation of a given function is to use the Ramer-Douglas-Peucker algorithm. This algorithm reduces the number of points in a curve by considering for each pair of points a line between them, and then identify a point between the two with the largest vertical distance to that line (this process is repeated a number of times while considering the addition of points under a certain maximum distance).

---

[1]https://en.wikipedia.org/wiki/Ramer%E2%80%93Douglas%E2%80%93Peucker_algorithm.

The concept behind lower cost functions is a generalization of strength reduction extended to functions. The basic idea is to replace the intended function with a simpler implementation performing algebraic simplifications or taking advantage of symmetry properties. In some contexts, and for regions of the function's domain one can approximate the function by a linear function, thus substantially simplifying its evaluation. Truncation of the function's Taylor series, as described next, is a popular implementation of this technique.

Approximation using Taylor's series is one of the methods used to implement many of the computationally expensive trigonometric functions such as "sin," "cos," "tan," and "arctan." The "sin" function can be implemented with:

$$\sin(x) = x - \frac{x^3}{3!} + \frac{x^5}{5!} - \frac{x^7}{7!} + \ldots$$

The more terms are used, the more accurate the "sin" function evaluation is. If acceptable, one might only use a small number of terms, thus resulting in a lower cost approximation function.

One of the most used methods to calculate the square root of a number is the Newton-Raphson method (also known as Newton's method). Using the Newton-Raphson method, the square root of x, $\sqrt{x}$, can be calculated iteratively using:

$$y_{n+1} = \frac{1}{2}\left(y_n + \frac{x}{y_n}\right)$$

The method starts with y_0, a first approximation to $\sqrt{x}$. Increasing the number of iterations increases the accuracy of the result.

Another example of the use of the Newton's method is the calculation of the inverse square root: $1/\sqrt{x}$. The iterative calculation is managed by the following equation:

$$y_{n+1} = \frac{1}{2}y_n\left(3 - x \times y_n^2\right)$$

An implementation of the inverse square root using the Newton's method is presented in Fig. 5.9,[2] which only needs a single iteration to produce acceptable accuracy for many problems (this version considers single precision input/output, but a double precision version mainly differs on the data types and on the constant value used to calculate the first estimation). The main improvement of this implementation in comparison to a typical one using the Newton's method is the efficiency of the scheme to calculate a first estimation close enough to the solution (it uses a number usually referred in this context as the "magic number").

With the inverse square root one can obtain the square root: sqrt(x)=x*invsqrt (x). This approach was mostly used in computer games, but it is less prevalent in

---

[2]This method was used in the Quake 3 game (www.gamedev.net/community/forums/topic.asp?top icid=139956) and later in other applications. Although its roots seem to predate the use in Quake 3, its authorship is not fully confirmed. The values of the magic numbers" used here were suggested by Chris Lomont and Matthew Robertson.

```
float invsqrt(float x) {
    float x2 = x * 0.5f;
    int i  = *(int *) &x;        // get floating-point bits
    i = 0x5f375a86 - ( i >> 1 ); // calculate a first estimation
    float y  = * (float *) &i;       // the first estimation in float
    y  = y * ( 1.5f - x2 * y * y ); // 1st iteration
//  y  = y * ( 1.5f - x2 * y * y ); // 2nd iteration, if needed
    return y;
}
```

FIG. 5.9

Possible single precision approximate implementation of a fast inverse of the square root. For double precision, 0x5fe6eb50c7b537a9 is the suggested "magic number."

Modified from Wikipedia. https://en.wikipedia.org/wiki/Fast_inverse_square_root [Accessed September 2015].

contemporary processors that include native hardware for calculating the inverse square root or the square root.

5.8 DATA STRUCTURE-BASED TRANSFORMATIONS

In many cases a program may be optimized in terms of performance, energy, or power if the data structures are modified and/or translated to change the way they are stored. One example is the use of an array instead of a linked list. There are cases where software developers may not have made the most appropriate decision about the data structure to use, and/or the decision was suitable in terms of code quality (regarding other metrics), but may result in lower performance, higher energy, or power consumption.

The data structure selected results in different memory requirements, in different costs to access its elements and to add or remove elements. These data structure operations have different costs and depending on the their frequency of use, one may opt for a more profitable data structure.

5.8.1 SCALAR EXPANSION, ARRAY CONTRACTION, AND ARRAY SCALARIZATION

Scalar expansion consists of substituting scalar variables by array variables and it can eliminate output- and antidependences. Scalar expansion is always legal/safe and can enable autovectorization and/or help parallelization. The transformation is often required when applying loop fission as scalars shared between statements of the original loop, and that are now distributed in both loops after loop fission, need now to be stored in arrays in the first loop so that they can be available in the second loop.

Array contraction [19,20] is a code transformation technique to reduce memory requirements and consists of transforming an array to one or more lower size/dimensional arrays. The transformation can also be used when intermediate data hold in arrays is now communicated via buffers (e.g., FIFOs). In this case, arrays are substituted with data structures with lower storage requirements.

Although some authors (see, e.g., [20]) refer to array contraction in the case when an array variable is converted into a scalar variable or into a buffer containing a small number of scalar variables, we prefer to consider the former as a special case of array contraction known as array scalarization. Array scalarization can be seen as a form of scalar replacement where arrays are substituted by scalars. The feasibility of this transformation depends on the size of the array, the existence of loop-carried dependences, the use of indirect indexing, and the number of array elements needed to be stored at the same time. This transformation is the dual of scalar expansion (in which scalar variables are substituted by array variables).

Below, we depict a simple example of array contraction (code in the middle). The two-dimensional array T is transformed to one-dimensional array. In this example, however, we can apply array scalarization (scalar replacement or loop scalar replacement) and substitute the entire T array to a scalar variable T (code in the right).

```
int A[N], B[N][M], T[N][M];       int A[N], B[N][M], T[N];        int A[N], B[N][M], T;
...                               ...                             ...
for(i=0;i<N;i++) {                for(i=0;i<N;i++) {              for(i=0;i<N;i++) {
    T[i][j] = 0;                      T[i] = 0;                       T = 0;
    for(j=0;i<M;j++) {                for(j=0;i<M;j++) {              for(j=0;i<M;j++) {
        T[i][j] += B[i][j]*c;             T[i] += B[i][j]*c;              T += B[i][j]*c;
    }                                 }                              }
    A[i] = T[i][j]*d;                 A[i] = T[i]*d;                  A[i] = T*d;
}                                 }                               }
```

5.8.2 SCALAR AND ARRAY RENAMING

Often, it is useful to rename scalar and/or array variables. The aim of scalar and array renaming is to partition the definitions and uses, and break recurrences. The following two examples show simple cases of scalar renaming and array renaming, respectively.

```
T = A[i] * B[i];          T1 = A[i] * B[i];
C[i] = T*C[i];            C[i] = T1*C[i];
T = A[i] / B[i];          T2 = A[i] / B[i];
D[i] = T*D[i];            D[i] = T2*D[i];

A[i] = A[i-1] * B[i];     A1[i] = A[i-1] * B[i];
C[i] = A[i] / B[i];       C[i] = A1[i] / B[i];
A[i] = t*B[i];            A[i] = t*B[i];
```

5.8.3 ARRAYS AND RECORDS

In order to save memory, the fields of record structures might need to be reordered. This happens when the fields are of different size, and the ordering used might reduce its storage requirements due to packing. Another optimization of records is the alignment of their fields. This can be achieved by reordering the fields and/or adding padding fields. The following example shows an example of adding 3 bytes after the field a in order to align field x.

```
char a;   // 1 byte
int x;    // 4 bytes
```

```
char a;        // 1 byte
char pad[3];   // 3 bytes
int x;         // 4 bytes
```

Transforming an array of structs (arrays of records) to a struct of arrays (or sometimes to arrays of primitive types one for each record field) may in some contexts contribute to performance improvements. Following we show an example where an array of complex values is translated to two arrays, one with the imaginary values and the other with the real values. This transformation places consecutive imaginary and real values in contiguous memory positions. This can be important for enabling loop vectorization.

```
// phi: array of complex numbers

typedef struct {
   float real;
   float imag;
} complex;

float phiMag[N];
complex phi[N];

void CompPhiMag(int M, complex* phi,
float* phiMag) {
  for (int i = 0; i < M; i++) {
    float real = phi[i].real;
    float imag = phi[i].imag;
    phiMag[i] = real*real + imag*imag;
  }
}
```

```
// phiI: array of imaginary part of
complex numbers
// phiR: array of real part of complex
numbers

float phiR[N];
float phiI[N];
float phiMag[N];

void CompPhiMag(int M, float* phiR,
float* phiI, float* phiMag) {
  for (int i = 0; i < M; i++) {
    float real = phiR[i];
    float imag = phiI[i];
    phiMag[i] = real*real + imag*imag;
  }
}
```

5.8.4 REDUCING THE NUMBER OF DIMENSIONS OF ARRAYS

It is sometimes profitable to transform multidimension arrays into lower dimension arrays. This might be needed, e.g., because of the nonsupport of multidimension arrays by some hardware compilers. The following is an example where two-dimension arrays are converted into one-dimension arrays.

```
int A[N][M], B[N][M];
...
for(i=0;i<N;i++) {
  A[i][j] = 0;
  for(j=0;i<M;j++) {
    A[i][j] += B[i][j]*c;
  }
}
```

```
int A[N*M], B[N][M];

for(i=0;i<N;i++) {
  A[i*M+j] = 0;
  for(j=0;i<M;j++) {
    A[i*M+j] += B[i*M+j]*c;
  }
}
```

5.8.5 FROM ARRAYS TO POINTERS AND ARRAY RECOVERY

In some cases, it might be useful to modify code such that array variables are accessed as pointers. In this case, array elements are not accessed through indexing but through pointer arithmetic. The following is an example of transforming arrays to pointers and then using pointer arithmetic to access the data.

```
int A[N*M], B[N][M];          int *A, *B;

...                           ...
for(i=0;i<N;i++) {            for(i=0;i<N;i++) {
  A[i*M+j] = 0;                 *A = 0;
  for(j=0;i<M;j++) {            for(j=0;i<M;j++) {
    A[i*M+j] += B[i*M+j]*c;       *A += *B*c;
  }                              A++; B++;
}                              }
                              }
```

Array recovery [21] is the opposite of the previous transformation and consists of transforming pointer-based code to array-based code. This transformation can help compilers perform further compiler optimizations and loop transformations, which otherwise would not be considered.

5.8.6 ARRAY PADDING

As the sizes of caches are usually a power of 2, large arrays that have sizes that are powers of 2 may cause conflicts. Array padding consists of increasing the size of one of the array dimensions by one (known as interarray padding) to reduce such conflicts or to "force" the base address of subsequent arrays by introducing pad arrays between successive array declarations (known as interarray padding). The following example shows the use of interarray (code on the middle) and intraarray padding (code on the right) techniques.

```
double A[1024];        double A[1024];        double A[1024+1];
double B[1024];        double pad[M];         double B[1024];
                       double B[1024];
...                                           ...
double sum=0.0;        ...                    double sum=0.0;
for(i=0;i<1024; i++)   double sum=0.0;        for(i=0;i<1024; i++)
  sum+=A[i]*B[i];      for(i=0;i<1024; i++)     sum+=A[i]*B[i];
                         sum+=A[i]*B[i];
```

5.8.7 REPRESENTATION OF MATRICES AND GRAPHS

Matrices can be represented by different data structures depending on the number of elements equal to zero they store (known as sparsity). The common way is to represent them with two-dimensional (2D) arrays, but in case of sparse matrices one may opt to represent them as Compressed Sparse Row (CSR) or Compressed Sparse Column (CSC).

The following is an example of a 3×7 sparse matrix and its CSR and CSC representations. The use of compressed representations may significantly reduce the memory requirements to represent sparse matrices, and the benefits to use CSR or CSC depend on how values are located (e.g., high frequency of values in columns or in rows.)

$$\begin{bmatrix} 0 & 0 & 5 & 0 & 0 & 0 \\ 9 & 0 & 0 & 7 & 0 & 0 & 15 \\ 0 & 0 & 0 & 0 & 0 & 0 \end{bmatrix}$$

A CSR representation:
Val: [5 9 7 15]
Indx: [2 7 10 13]
Pntr: [5 9 16]
A CSC representation:
Val: [9 5 7 15]
Indx: [1 6 10 19]
Pntr: [9 5 7 15 16]

Graphs can be represented as data structures consisting of the nodes (structs in C), edges, and the connection between them using pointers or as adjacency matrices. The decision about a particular data-structure to use depends, e.g., on the graph size and algorithms to be used, and may lead to performance improvements and/or energy savings.

5.8.8 OBJECT INLINING

Object inlining [22,23] is a code transformation technique that can be applied in the context of object-oriented programming languages and consists of fusing classes in the class hierarchy and/or removing classes by inlining their fields and moving their methods. Thus, object inlining can be applied to remove class hierarchies and/or to remove classes. Its benefits are related to the reduction of the overhead associated to the support at runtime of object-oriented features, including inheritance and virtual methods, and may have a significant performance impact.

The following is a simple example showing object inlining. The code in the middle only considers the inlining of the class hierarchy formed by Point1D and Point2D classes, while the code on the right shows the use of inlining on all of the three original classes (on the left) which results in one class. In this example, we omit code transformations related to the methods of these classes.

```
class Point1D {
   public int X;
}
class Point2D, extends Point1D {
   public int Y;
}
class Rectangle {
   public Point2D left;
   public Point2D right;
}
```

```
class Point2D {
   public int X;
   public int Y;
}
Class Rectangle {
   public Point2D left;
   public Point2D right;
}
```

```
Class Rectangle {
   public int leftX;
   public int leftY;
   public int rightX;
   public int rightY;
}
```

5.8.9 DATA LAYOUT TRANSFORMATIONS

Data layout transformations, in particular when combined with loop transformations such as loop interchange, can lead to significant performance improvements as the data reference locality can be substantially improved.

The classic example of this transformation consists of using matrix transposition so that the data layout of an array in memory (using either column-major or row-major) organizations matches the data access pattern. When the code traverses the column or row of the matrix, consecutive accesses would translate into accesses to consecutive data items in the address space, and thus into consecutive cache lines (possibly even within the same line for short sequences). This promotes cache line reuse and increases the effectiveness of execution techniques such as prefetching.

The following example depicts a code in which matrix A is transposed to improve data reference locality. Alternatively, loops can be interchanged (not always legal) to achieve the same effect (as illustrated in the loop interchange section). In many cases, we do not need additional overhead (in this case of copying and transpose the values of array A to Anew) since the way data is stored can be changed in a way that suits the computations accessing that data.

```
for(j=0; j<M; j++)
  for(i=0; i<N; i++)
    A[i][j] += C;
```

```
for(j=0; j<M; j++)
  for(i=0; i<N; i++)
    Anew[j][i] = A[i][j];
for(j=0; j<M; j++)
  for(i=0; i<N; i++)
    Anew[i][j] += C;
```

However, this layout organization is not exclusive for multidimensional arrays. In the context of more discrete data structures, it is possible to layout the fields of structures as discussed earlier or convert arrays of structs (AoS) to structs of arrays (SoA) to promote multithreading execution in the context of GPU execution.

5.8.10 DATA REPLICATION AND DATA DISTRIBUTION

Replicating data can be an important code transformation to increase the level of parallelism, especially in the presence of distributed memories. However, data replication may impose a high overhead in terms of memory usage, and thus the trade-off between performance improvements and memory requirements need to be evaluated.

A simple example of data replication is the replication of arrays. By creating more than one array storing the same data and by distributing them over multiple memories, we allow concurrent accesses to these arrays.

The best scenario is to trigger the replication process when data is created (i.e., in the source), as opposed to make an additional copy which may reduce or eliminate data replication benefits. When data also needs to be stored in a replicated scheme, the update might be done only at the end of the computations over that data, especially when not in the presence of negative distances in data dependences. In the presence of negative distances in data dependences, the replication of data may not be feasible and/or efficient. Overall, data replication can be suitable when computations consume input data and produce output data using distinct input/output arrays.

When there is no need to replicate all the data structures, the replication method becomes similar to data distribution in which chunks or sections of a data structure are split and distributed across different memories and computation devices. Data distribution may require code transformations to split data, in the case of multiple memories, or it might be only based on sending the information needed to identify the chunk or section to each of the concurrent computations. The latter occurs in the presence of a global memory with multiple ports where each port is responsible to access the respective data chunk or section.

The following code shows an example of array replication which allows two statements of the loop body (on the left) to be simultaneously executed by storing the arrays in distributed memories.

```
double A[N];
double B[N];
...
double sum=0.0;
for(i=0;i<N; i+=2) {
   sum+=A[i]*B[i];
   sum+=A[i+1]*B[i+1];
}
```

```
double A1[N];
double A2[N];
double B1[N];
double B2[N];
...
double sum=0.0;
for(i=0;i<N; i+=2) {
   sum+=A1[i]*B1[i];
   sum+=A2[i+1]*B2[i+1];
}
```

5.9 FROM RECURSION TO ITERATIONS

When targeting some architectures, it is sometimes suitable and/or required to transform recursive algorithms into functionally equivalent iterative implementations. In some cases, such as embedded systems (especially in critical systems), it is a requirement to implement the code without recursion.

The simplest conversion is when in the presence of tail recursive functions and without needing the use of stacks. Following is an example of the elimination of a tail recursive function for a simple computation that finds the maximum value of a vector A.

```
int funcMax(int n){
  if(n == 0)
    return A[0];
  else
    return max(A[n],funcMax(n-1));
}
```

```
int funcMaxIterative(int n){
  int i, res;
  res = A[0];
  i = n;
  while(i != 0){
    res = max(A[i],res);
    i = i - 1;
  }
}
```

5.10 FROM NONSTREAMING TO STREAMING

The use of a load/store model is by nature nonstreaming and most programming languages do not natively support streaming (e.g., with structures for data streaming and operations to access them). Often, developers use specific APIs for data streaming or data structures such as FIFOs. Fig. 5.10 shows the conceptual differences between a

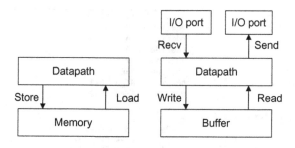

FIG. 5.10

Load/store (left) vs streaming (right).

load/store model and a streaming model. While the load/store model assumes data stored in memory, the streaming model assumes that data arrives in sequence and operations such as get and put (receive and send, or push/pop/peek as in the StreamIt language [24]) access the data according to the order in which data arrives. The streaming model also includes memory (identified as "Buffer" in Fig. 5.10) where intermediate results or even parts of the input/output data can be stored.

The conversion between code using the load/store model to a streaming scheme can be difficult and very hard to perform automatically. Fig. 5.11A shows a simple example of a code using the load/store model and in Fig. 5.11B it is shown a streaming version of the code.

5.11 DATA AND COMPUTATION PARTITIONING

Partitioning is an important code transformation that can be applied to data structures and/or code regions with computations. These transformations have been extensively used in the context of parallelizing compilers for scientific computations as in this domain there has been a strong desire to automatically translate legacy applications onto distributed memory multiprocessors [25]. Typically, large array data structures have to be partitioned and distributed across the various memories of each computing node in a multiprocessor, and along with it the corresponding computation also needs to be partitioned.

5.11.1 DATA PARTITIONING

In many cases and especially in the presence of data parallelism one may partition data structures in order to store them in distributed memories. Often, although not necessarily, this data partitioning is also accompanied by a computation partition so that computations that manipulate the partitioned data structures can be executed by distinct processors.

In the context of compilation for distributed memory machines, e.g., considering automatically parallelizing compilers such as the FORTRAN-D compiler [25],

```
#define c0 2
#define c1 4
#define c2 4
#define c3 2
#define M 256
#define N  4
int  c[N] = {c0, c1, c2, c3};

...

  for(int j=N-1; j<M; j++) {
    int output=0;
    for(int i=0; i<N; i++) {
      output+=c[i]*x[j-i];
    }
    y[j] = output;
  }
...
```

(A)

```
#include "io_ports.h"
#define c0 2
#define c1 4
#define c2 4
#define c3 2
#define M 256
#define PORT_A  0x1
#define PORT_B  0x2

...

  int x_0, x_1, x_2, x_3, y;
  x_2= receive(PORT_A);
  x_1= receive(PORT_A);
  x_0= receive(PORT_A);
  for(int j=0; j<M-N+1; j++)  // while(1) {
    x_3=x_2;
    x_2=x_1;
    x_1=x_0;
    x_0= receive(PORT_A);
    y = c0*x_0 + c1*x_1 + c2*x_2 + c3*x_3;
    send(PORT_B, y);
  }
...
```

(B)

FIG. 5.11

From load/store to streaming: (A) load/store example; (B) example converted to streaming.

sequential codes (most notably loops) are partitioned according to the so-called owner-computes rule. Here, arrays are partitioned into various arrays and distributed by a notional multidimension organization of the target parallel machine using distribution schemes such as Block (either row, column, or tile), Cyclic, or both (see also Section 5.11.2).

In general, data partitioning can be performed on data structures such as Arrays-of-Structures (AoS), Structures-of-Arrays (SoA), trees, or graph representations. For simplicity, we illustrate here a simple example of data partitioning for arrays, with its dual transformation named array coalescing.

Fig. 5.12 depicts a simple example where we have partitioned the A array into two arrays so that they can be mapped to distinct memories and hence improve the corresponding data availability. Here, we have assumed the value of N to be even and that prior to the execution of the loop, arrays A1 and A2 contain the values corresponding to the odd and even indexed location of the original array A possibly by a distribution of the data of this array from the onset of the execution. Notice also, that it is possible to partition the computation by partitioning the loop into disjoint loops as discussed in the next section.

5.11.2 PARTITIONING COMPUTATIONS

When multiple devices are available, computations can be distributed across them using a suitable mapping. When the multiple devices are instances of the same processing element, such as in homogeneous multicore architectures, the partitioning is

```
double A[N]; // Assume N is even          double A1[N/2];
double B;                                 double A2[N/2];
...                                       ...
double sum=0.0;                           double sum=0.0;
for(i=0; i<N; i++) {                      for(i=0; i<N/2; i++) {
   sum+=A[i]*B;                              sum+=A1[i]*B;
}                                            sum+=A2[i]*B;
                                          }
```

FIG. 5.12

Data partitioning example.

usually guided by the level of parallelism that can be attained, the balancing of computations, and data communication and synchronization costs. In terms of parallelism, one may transform a serial program into a parallel program and use threads or use a directive-driven programming model (such as OpenMP [26]). Additionally, one may reprogram parts of the program or the entire program in a parallel programming language, or rely on the capability of the compiler to automatically parallelize the application. While the translation to other programming languages, the use of threads and directive-driven programming models are described in Chapter 7, in this subsection we focus on the manual partitioning of computations.

In this style of parallel execution, often called SPMD (Single Program, Multiple Data), the compiler generates code that creates multiple threads, each of them with a unique identifier, that execute the same code. Each thread is mapped to a distinct processor and manages its own address space. The following example on the left illustrates a simple computation where a single vector is assigned a linear combination of two other vectors of the same length.

```
int  j, k1, k2, N=128;               int  j, k1, k2, N=128;
double A[N], B[N], C[N];             double A[N], B[N], C[N];
                                     $DISTRIBUTE A(BLOCK), B(BLOCK), C(BLOCK)
...                                  ...
for(j=0; j < N; j++){                $PARALLEL FOR SCHEDULE(4)
  A[j] = k1 * B[j] + k2 * C[j];      for(j=0; j < N; j++){
}                                      A[j] = k1 * B[j] + k2 * C[j];
                                     }
```

The code on the right includes a distribution directive ($DISTRIBUTE) which indicates that the corresponding arrays are to be distributed using a BLOCK distribution strategy (i.e., evenly divided consecutive elements per each computing node). The code also includes a computation distribution directive that directs the compiler to partition the iteration space of the loop into four equal chunks. When the arrays A, B, and C are distributed across four processors they access the corresponding array sections of the original declared arrays. Each section is locally addressed starting from index 0. Processors will concurrently operate on their local array sections for each of the distributed arrays. Processor 0 will execute the first 32 iterations of the original loop writing to the locations 0 through 31 of its local section of A, B, and C. Processor 1 will execute also iterations 0 through 31, but will operate on its local section of A, B, and C. The two remaining processors will execute in a similar way. Note that in this SPMD paradigm, the address spaces are disjoint. This situation is remarkably different from the compilation scenario for shared-memory multiprocessors where there is no need to physically distribute the array data, but instead there is a single globally addressed array and individual threads act upon disjoint sections of the same array storage.

In other contexts, in particular in hybrid computing systems, it might be desirable for a computation not to be partitioned homogeneously across multiple computing nodes, but between a traditional compute node (e.g., a CPU) and another computing device (e.g., either a GPU or an FPGA). While this partitioning is often viewed exclusively as a computation partition, it often involves data partitioning as well since data offloaded to the accelerator can be kept private to that computing device.

5.11.3 COMPUTATION OFFLOADING

To accelerate applications, one possibility is to migrate the most computationally intensive parts (e.g., also known as hotspots or critical regions) to more powerful computing devices, such as hardware accelerators (e.g., GPUs, FPGAs), servers, supercomputing resources, or cloud computing infrastructures. This migration of computations is known as computation offloading and has become of particular relevance in the context of mobile computing [27] where devices may not provide the hardware acceleration capabilities for increasing the performance of the critical regions of computations.

In terms of code generation, the compiler needs to replace the code that is to be offloaded from the main thread of execution (e.g., on a CPU) to the accelerator with a sequence of operations that transfer data to the accelerator, initiate the execution of the accelerator (possibly invoking a previously compiled binary image for that accelerator), synchronize the termination of the execution, and transfer the results of the execution back to the main thread. Although simplified here, these steps make use of variants of library functions such as memory allocation and synchronization. As the overhead of data transfer is often nonnegligible, it is desirable to minimize the volume of data transferred per invocation of the offloaded computation by prompting the use of accelerator private data or data that can be reused and accessed in multiple accelerator invocations.

The offloading of computations requires the availability of implementations in the target architecture where the code regions will be offloaded and the transformation of the host code of the application to offload the computations. The offloading of computations needs to identify a specific implementation and target device and/or request a service, to communicate input/output data between the host computing system and the target computing device, and the synchronization between both.

Computation offloading can be statically defined or decided at runtime. In the former case, the host code is prepared to deal with the execution of the critical region in the target computing system and the offloading does not depend on the runtime information and data used. In the latter case, specific code can be added to dynamically manage the offloading of the computations or not. In this case, multiple versions of the same code region (e.g., function) can be used and one is selected according to runtime information. For example, according to the number of iterations, only known at runtime, of a loop, it may be offloaded or not. As the offloading process may incur in a setup, communication, and synchronization overheads, a runtime decision about the offloading of the computations can provide more efficient implementations.

Recent versions of directive-driven programming models, such as OpenMP 4.0 [28], already include accelerator directives, delegating to the compiler the task of processing these directives, generating the necessary setup code for the host and the code for the accelerator.

5.12 LARA STRATEGIES

In this section, we show some examples (inspired by the ones available on the MANET online demo[3]) of definitions of loop transformations using LARA in the context of a source-to-source compiler with C code as input and output.

Fig. 5.13 illustrates a LARA aspect that applies loop unrolling by a specific factor (4 by default) to the innermost loops of a function identified by a name ("fun1" by default) provided as an input parameter of the aspect. In addition to the innermost

```
1. aspectdef SimpleLoopUnroll
2.
3. input
4.    funcName = 'fun1',
5.    factor = 4
6. end
7.
8. /* Call the Unroll action using the exec keyword */
9. select function{funcName}.loop end
10. apply
11.    exec Unroll(factor);
12. end
13. condition
14.    $loop.is_innermost
15. end
16.
17. println('\nSimpleLoopUnroll done!');
18. end
```

FIG. 5.13

Loop unrolling in LARA.

---

[3]MANET online demo: http://specs.fe.up.pt/tools/manet/.

```
1. aspectdef SimpleLoopTiling
2.    var size = 8;
3.    select function.loop end
4.    apply
5.       exec Tiling(size);
6.    end
7. end
```

FIG. 5.14

Loop tiling in LARA.

```
1. aspectdef SimpleUnrollAndJam
2.    select function.($l1=loop).($l2=loop) end
3.    apply
4.       exec UnrollAndJam($l1, $l2, 2);
5.    end
6.    condition $l2.is_innermost end
7. end
```

FIG. 5.15

Loop unroll and jam in LARA.

property of the loops, we can also restrict the use of loop unrolling to loops that have a number of iterations statically known ($loop.bound), a number of iterations less than a certain number N ($loop.num_iter < N), a number of iterations multiple of the unrolling factor ($loop.num_iter % factor == 0), etc.

Fig. 5.14 shows an example for applying loop tilling based on a size of the block/tile specified by the *size* variable, while Fig. 5.15 illustrates a LARA aspect to apply unroll and jam.

Fig. 5.16 illustrates a LARA aspect to apply function multiversioning by first cloning a function, then applying loop tiling to a loop in the function, and then substituting the call to the cloned function with a switch statement which selects the actual function to call (i.e., the original or the cloned version with loop tiling).

One important specification capability is the possibility to describe sequences of loop transformations. Fig. 5.17 presents a LARA example specifying the use of loop coalescing on the two innermost loops (line 3 to line 7), and of loop unrolling by 2 on the innermost loop (line 9 to line 13) obtained by coalescing.

Fig. 5.18 shows another example of a sequence of loop transformations, this time defining unroll and jam with the use of loop unrolling and then loop merge (fusion). The first apply statement unrolls the second innermost loop by a factor of 2. The second apply statement gets the innermost loops, which are now the two loops resultant from the previous loop unrolling using an unrolling factor of 2. The third aspect applies loop merge to the loops stored in the LoopsToMerge array variable.

```
1.  aspectdef CloningAndTransformations
2.
3.     input
4.        funcName = 'fun1'
5.     end
6.
7.     /* The names of the new functions */
8.     var newName = funcName + '_new';
9.
10.    /* Clone functions */
11.    select function{funcName} end
12.    apply
13.       exec Clone(newName);
14.    end
15.
16.    /* Perform optimizations */
17.    select function{newName}.loop end
18.    apply
19.       exec Tiling(32);
20.    end
21.    condition $loop.is_outermost end
22.
23.    /* Change calls to the function */
24.    select file.call{newName} end
25.    apply
26.       var originalCode = $call.code + ';';
27.       var tiledCode = originalCode.split(funcName).join(tiled);
28.
29.       insert before '/*';
30.       insert after '*/';
31.
32.       insert after %{
33.          switch (get_best_version(/*...*/)) {
34.             case 0: [[originalCode]] break;
35.             case 1: [[tiledCode]] break;
36.             default: [[originalCode]] break;
37.          }
38.       }%;
39.    end
40. end
```

FIG. 5.16

Function cloning and optimizations in LARA.

```
1.  aspectdef CompoundLoopTrans
2.
3.     select function{}.($l1=loop).($l2=loop) end
4.     apply
5.        exec Coalescing($l1, $l2);
6.     end
7.     condition $l2.is_innermost end
8.
9.     select function{}.loop end
10.    apply
11.       exec Unroll(2);
12.    end
13.    condition $loop.is_innermost end
14. end
```

FIG. 5.17

Composing sequences of loop transformations in LARA.

```
1.  aspectdef SimpleUnrollAndJam
2.
3.      var LoopsToMerge = [];
4.
5.      select function.($l1=loop).($l2=loop) end
6.      apply
7.          exec Unroll($l1, 2);
8.      end
9.      condition $l2.is_innermost end
10.
11.     select function.loop end
12.     apply
13.         LoopsToMerge.push($loop);
14.     end
15.     condition $l1.is_innermost end
16.
17.     select function end
18.     apply
19.         exec Merge(LoopsToMerge);
20.     end
21. end
```

FIG. 5.18

Loop unroll and jam in LARA specified by using loop unrolling and loop merge.

5.13 SUMMARY

This chapter presented several code transformations that are usually considered to improve performance, reduce power or energy consumption. The portfolio of code transformations is diverse and large, and to the best of our knowledge there is no compiler or source-to-source compiler that automatically performs all of them. In fact, most compilers (including GCC) only support a limited set of the code transformations introduced in this chapter. This makes the user knowledge about them even more important. However, the decision to apply most of these transformations is not easy and requires specific expertise and/or an apply-and-evaluate approach. In most cases, it is difficult to understand the implications in terms of performance/ energy/power without real measurements and any further optimization opportunities that could arise by applying a specific code transformation. Still, information given by code analysis tools, the manual analysis of the code, or by runtime profiling is usually helpful in guiding developers in their choice of which code transformations to use.

5.14 FURTHER READING

The literature regarding code transformations is vast due to their use in many application domains. An important aspect of code transformations is the underlying techniques used for code analysis, not only to determine their legality but also their potential profitability. Code analysis techniques are part of any compiler as described extensively in the literature (see, e.g., [29,30,31,32].

Most loop transformations that have been proposed are commonly associated with a specific publication, such is the example of loop versioning [33]. However, we suggest interested readers to refer to the survey of code transformations with an emphasis on loop transformations presented in Ref. [34]. Relevant bibliography exists for readers interested in knowing more about specific topics. For example, the work presented in Ref. [16] about JIT specialization in the context of JavaScript code includes a very general and comprehensible overview of specialization.

Other code transformations, such as code specialization, are part of advanced JIT compilers such as the ones used for executing Java bytecodes or JavaScript code (see, e.g., [16,35,36]). While JIT compilers do not have the benefit of expensive compile time static analyses, they have the advantage of using runtime data knowledge (see, e.g., [37]) and thus better gage the impact of the specialization on metrics such as performance or power. Folding, even limited static compile time information in the generated code, allows them to dynamically adapt the code's execution.

Code transformations might also be important to satisfy other nonfunctional requirements that were not addressed in this book. For example, safety requirements may profit from software techniques and thus amenable for code transformations (see, e.g., [38,39]). One example is to increase resilience through triple-module redundancy (TMR) techniques applied at the software code level.

REFERENCES

[1] Polychronopoulos CD. Loop coalescing: a compiler transformation for parallel machines. In: Proceedings of the international conference on parallel processing; 1987. p. 235–42.

[2] Kuck DJ, Kuhn RH, Leasure B, Wolfe M. The structure of an advanced vectorizer for pipelined processors. In: Proc. IEEE Computer Society fourth international computer software and applications conf., October; 1980. p. 709–15.

[3] Ghuloum AM, Fisher AL. Flattening and parallelizing irregular, recurrent loop nests. ACM SIGPLAN Not 1995;30(8):58–67.

[4] Kennedy K, McKinley KS. Maximizing loop parallelism and improving data locality via loop fusion and distribution. In: Proceedings of the 6th international workshop on languages and compilers for parallel computing. London: Springer-Verlag; 1994. p. 301–20.

[5] Yi Q, Kennedy K, Adve V. Transforming complex loop nests for locality. J Supercomput 2004;27(3):219–64.

[6] Darte A, Huard G. Loop shifting for loop compaction. Int J Parallel Prog 2000; 28(5):499–534.

[7] Wolfe M. Loop skewing: the wavefront method revisited. Int J Parallel Prog 1986; 15(4):279–93.

[8] Lam M. Software pipelining: an effective scheduling technique for VLIW machines. In: Wexelblat RL, editor. Proceedings of the ACM SIGPLAN conference on programming language design and implementation (PLDI'88). New York, NY: ACM; 1988. p. 318–28.

[9] Ramakrishna Rau B. Iterative modulo scheduling: an algorithm for software pipelining loops. In: Proceedings of the 27th annual international symposium on microarchitecture (MICRO 27) New York, NY: ACM; 1994. p. 63–74.

[10] Jeong Y, Seo S, Lee J. Evaluator-executor transformation for efficient pipelining of loops with conditionals. ACM Trans Archit Code Optim 2013;10(4). Article 62, 23 pages.

[11] Misailovic S, Sidiroglou S, Hoffmann H, Rinard M. Quality of service profiling. In: Proceedings of the 32nd ACM/IEEE international conference on software engineering (ICSE'10), vol. 1. New York, NY: ACM; 2010. p. 25–34.

[12] McKinley KS. A compiler optimization algorithm for shared-memory multiprocessors. IEEE Trans Parallel Distrib Syst 1998;9(8):769–87.

[13] Davidson JW, Jinturkar S. Memory access coalescing: a technique for eliminating redundant memory accesses. In: Proc. ACM SIGPLAN conference on programming language design and implementation (PLDI'94). New York, NY: ACM; 1994. p. 186–95.

[14] Rudy G, Khan MM, Hall M, Chen C, Chame J. A programming language interface to describe transformations and code generation. In: Cooper K, Mellor-Crummey J, Sarkar V, editors. Proceedings of the 23rd international conference on languages and compilers for parallel computing (LCPC'10). Berlin/Heidelberg: Springer-Verlag; 2010. p. 136–50.

[15] Jones ND, Gomard CK, Sestoft P. Partial evaluation and automatic program generation. 1st ed. Upper Saddle River, NJ: Prentice-Hall; 1993.

[16] Costa IRdA, Santos HN, Alves PRO, Pereira FMQ. Just-in-time value specialization. Comput Lang Syst Struct 2014;40(2):37–52.

[17] Weisstein EW. Taylor series, From MathWorld—a Wolfram web resource. http://mathworld.wolfram.com/TaylorSeries.html [Accessed November 2016].

[18] Weisstein EW. Newton's method, from MathWorld—a Wolfram web resource. http://mathworld.wolfram.com/NewtonsMethod.html [Accessed November 2016].

[19] Lim AW, Liao S-W, Lam MS. Blocking and array contraction across arbitrarily nested loops using affine partitioning. In: Proceedings of the eight ACM SIGPLAN symposium on principles and practices of parallel programming (PPoPP'01). New York, NY: ACM; 2001. p. 103–12.

[20] Sarkar V, Gao GR. Optimization of array accesses by collective loop transformations. In: Davidson ES, Hossfield F, editors. Proceedings of the 5th international conference on supercomputing (ICS '91). New York, NY: ACM; 1991. p. 194–205.

[21] Franke B, O'Boyle MFP. Array recovery and high-level transformations for DSP applications. ACM Trans Embed Comput Syst 2003;2(2):132–62.

[22] Dolby J, Chien A. An automatic object inlining optimization and its evaluation. In: Proceedings of the ACM SIGPLAN conference on programming language design and implementation (PLDI'00). New York, NY: ACM; 2000. p. 345–57.

[23] Dolby J. Automatic inline allocation of objects. In: Michael Berman A, editor. Proceedings of the ACM SIGPLAN conference on programming language design and implementation (PLDI'97). New York, NY: ACM; 1997. p. 7–17.

[24] Thies W, Karczmarek M, Amarasinghe SP. StreamIt: a language for streaming applications. In: Nigel Horspool R, editor. Proceedings of the 11th international conference on compiler construction (CC'02). London: Springer-Verlag; 2002. p. 179–96.

[25] Hiranandani S, Kennedy K, Tseng C-W. Compiling Fortran D for MIMD distributed memory machines. Commun ACM 1992;35(8):66–80.

[26] Chapman B, Jost G, van der Pas R. Using OpenMP: portable shared memory parallel programming (scientific and engineering computation). Cambridge, MA: The MIT Press; 2007.

[27] Kumar K, Liu J, Lu Y-H, Bhargava B. A survey of computation offloading for mobile systems. Mob Netw Appl 2013;18(1):129–40.

[28] OpenMP application program interface, version 4.0; July 2013. http://www.openmp.org/mp-documents/OpenMP4.0.0.pdf.

[29] Aho AV, Lam MS, Sethi R, Ullman JD. Compilers: principles, techniques, and tools. 2nd ed. Boston, MA: Addison-Wesley Longman; 2006.

[30] Banerjee UK. Dependence analysis. New York, NY: Springer; 1997.

[31] Kennedy K, Allen JR. Optimizing compilers for modern architectures: a dependence-based approach. San Francisco, CA: Morgan Kaufmann; 2001.

[32] Muchnick SS. Advanced compiler design and implementation. San Francisco, CA: Morgan Kaufmann; 1998.

[33] Byler M, Davies JRB, Huson C, Leasure B, Wolfe M. Multiple version loops. In: Proceedings of the 1987 international conference on parallel processing, August 17–21; 1987. p. 312–8.

[34] Bacon DF, Graham SL, Sharp OJ. Compiler transformations for high-performance computing. ACM Comput Surv 1994;26(4):345–420.

[35] Cramer T, Friedman R, Miller T, Seberger D, Wilson R, Wolczko M. Compiling Java just in time. IEEE Micro 1997;17(3):36–43.

[36] Santos HN, Alves P, Costa I, Pereira FMQ. Just-in-time value specialization. In: Proceedings of the IEEE/ACM international symposium on code generation and optimization (CGO'13). Washington, DC: IEEE Computer Society; 2013. p. 1–11.

[37] Gal A, Eich B, Shaver M, Anderson D, Mandelin D, Haghighat MR, et al. Trace-based just-in-time type specialization for dynamic languages. ACM SIGPLAN Not 2009;44(6):465–78.

[38] Cheynet P, Nicolescu B, Velazco R, Rebaudengo M, Sonza Reorda M, Violante M. System safety through automatic high-level code transformations: an experimental evaluation. In: Nebel W, Jerraya A, editors. Proceedings of the conference on design, automation and test in Europe (DATE'01). Piscataway, NJ: IEEE Press; 2001. p. 297–301.

[39] Reis GA, Chang J, Vachharajani N, Rangan R, August DI, Mukherjee SS. Software-controlled fault tolerance. ACM Trans Archit Code Optim 2005;2(4):366–96.

Code retargeting for CPU-based platforms

6

6.1 INTRODUCTION

In this chapter, we focus exclusively on code retargeting issues in the context of CPU-based architectures and where the application source code is optimized to execute more efficiently on a given platform. In Chapter 7, we extend the topic of code retargeting to cover heterogeneous platforms, such as GPUs and FPGAs.

Here, we assume as input the application's source code, written in a high-level language such as C/C++, possibly even translated from higher levels of abstraction as described in Chapter 3. This source code captures the algorithmic behavior of the application while being independent of the target platform. As a first step, this code version is compiled and executed on a CPU platform, allowing developers to test the correctness of the application with respect to its specification.

However, as computer architectures are becoming increasingly complex, with more processing cores, more heterogeneous and more distributed, applications compiled for existing machines will not fully utilize the target platform resources, even when binary compatibility is guaranteed, and thus do not run as efficiently as they could. In particular, modern-day computing platforms (see Chapter 2 for a brief overview) support many independent computational units to allow parallel computations, contain specialized architectural features to improve concurrency and computational efficiency, support hierarchical memories to increase data locality and reduce memory latency, and include fast interconnects and buses to reduce data movement overhead. Hence, to maximize performance and efficiency it is imperative to leverage all the underlying features of a computing platform.

While imperative languages, such as C and C++, allow developers to write portable applications using high-level abstractions, the complexity of modern computing platforms makes it hard for compilers to derive optimized[1] and efficient code for each platform architecture. Retargetable compilers do exist, but they typically limit themselves to generate code for different CPU instruction set architectures. This limitation forces developers to manually optimize and refine their applications to support the target computation platform. This process requires considerable expertise to port the application, including applying code optimization strategies based on

---

[1] In this chapter, as with most of the literature, we use the term "optimization" loosely as a synonym for "performance improvement" as in general (and excluding trivial computations) program optimization is an undecidable problem at compile time (or design time).

Embedded Computing for High Performance. http://dx.doi.org/10.1016/B978-0-12-804189-5.00006-5

best practices, understanding available retargeting mechanisms, and deploying and testing the application. The resulting code, while being more efficient, often becomes difficult to maintain since it becomes polluted with artifacts used for optimization (e.g., with new API calls and data structures, code transformations). For this reason, developers often keep two versions of their source code: a functional version used to verify correctness and an optimized version which runs more efficiently on a specific platform.

This chapter is organized as follows. In Section 6.2, we provide a brief overview of common retargeting mechanisms. Section 6.3 briefly describes parallelism opportunities in CPU-based platforms and compiler options, including phase selection and ordering. Section 6.4 focuses on loop vectorization to maximize single-threaded execution. Section 6.5 covers multithreading on shared memory multicore architectures, and Section 6.6 describes how to leverage platforms with multiprocessors using distributed memory. Section 6.7 explains CPU cache optimizations. Section 6.8 presents examples of LARA strategies related to code retargeting. The remaining sections provide further reading on the topics presented in this chapter.

To illustrate the various retargeting mechanisms described in the following sections, we consider the multiplication of two matrices A (nX rows and nY columns) and B (nY rows and nZ columns) producing a matrix C (nX rows and nZ columns), generically described as follows:

$$C = AB,$$

$$s.t.\ C_{ij} = (AB)_{ij} = \sum_{k=0}^{nY-1} A_{ik} B_{kj} \ \wedge\ 0 \le i < nX \ \wedge\ 0 \le j < nZ$$

This matrix product computation is a key operation in many algorithms and can be potentially time consuming for very large matrix size inputs. Although several optimized algorithms have been proposed for the general matrix multiplication operation, we focus, as a starting point, on a simple implementation in C, described as follows:

```
void matrix_mult(float *A, float *B, float *C) {
   for (int i = 0; i < nX; i++) {
      for (int j = 0; j < nZ; j++) {
         C[i*nZ+j] = 0;
         for (int k = 0; k < nY; k++) {
            C[i*nZ+j] += A[i*nY+k] * B[k*nZ+j];
         }
      }
   }
}
```

To compute each element of matrix C (see Fig. 6.1), the algorithm iterates over row i of matrix A and column j of matrix B, multiplying in a pair-wise fashion the elements from both matrices, and then adding the resulting products to obtain C_{ij}.

Although this is a simple example, it provides a rich set of retargeting and optimization opportunities (clearly not exhaustively) on different platforms. Yet, its use

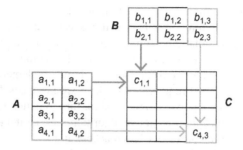

FIG. 6.1

Matrix multiplication kernel.

is not meant to provide the most effective implementation for each target system. In practice, we recommend using domain-specific libraries, such as BLAS [1], whenever highly optimized implementations are sought.

6.2 RETARGETING MECHANISMS

Developers have at their disposal different mechanisms to optimize and fine-tune their applications for a given computing platform. Given the complexity of today's platforms and the lack of design tools to fully automate the optimization process, there is often a trade-off between how much effort an expert developer spends optimizing their application and how portable the optimized code becomes. In this context we can identify the following retargeting mechanisms:

1. *Compiler control options*. This mechanism controls the code optimization process by configuring the platform's toolchain options. For instance, some options select the target processor architecture (e.g., 32- or 64-bit), others select the use of a specific set of instructions (e.g., SSE, SSE2, AVX, AVX2), or to set the level of optimization (favoring, for instance, faster generated code over code size). Additional options enable language features and language standards (including libraries). In general, this mechanism requires the least amount of developer effort, but it is also the least effective in fully exploiting the capabilities of modern-day computation platforms given the inherent limitations of today's compilers.

2. *Code transformations*. Programmers often need to manually rewrite their code to adopt practices and code styles specific to the platform's toolchain and runtime system. This is the case, for instance, with the use of hardware compilation tools for application-specific architectures on FPGAs. These tools typically impose restrictions on the use of certain programming language constructs and styles (e.g., arrays instead of pointers), as otherwise they can generate inefficient hardware designs. There are also transformations (see Chapter 5) one can apply

systematically to optimize the application on a hardware platform while guaranteeing compilation correctness with respect to the original code. Even when performing automatic code transformations by a compiler, developers might need to identify a sequence of code transformations with the correct parametrization (e.g., loop unroll factors) to derive implementations complying with given nonfunctional requirements. There are instances, however, when developers must completely change the algorithm to better adapt to a platform, for example, by replacing a recursive algorithm with an iterative stream-based version when targeting an FPGA-based accelerator.

3. *Code annotations.* Developers can annotate their programs using comments or directives (e.g., pragmas in C/C++) to support a programming model or to guide a compiler optimization process. Code annotations are not invasive and usually do not require changing the code logic. Nonetheless, this method has been successfully used by developers to parallelize their sequential applications by identifying all the concurrent regions of their code. Such approaches include directive-driven programming models as is the example of OpenMP [21]. The code annotation mechanism has the advantage to allow programs to preserve a high degree of portability since code annotations can be easily removed or ignored if not activated or even supported.

4. *Domain-specific libraries.* Libraries are often employed to extend the compiler capabilities and generate efficient code. In contrast with code annotations, integrating a library into an application often requires considerable changes in the application source code, including introducing new data structures and replacing existing code with library calls. Hence, portability can become an issue if the library is not widely supported on different platforms. Still, libraries can provide an abstraction layer for an application domain, allowing developers to write applications using the library interface without having to provide implementation details. This way, applications can be ported with little effort to a different platform as long as an optimized library implementation is available for that platform, thus also providing some degree of performance portability. An example of a portable application domain library is ATLAS [2] for linear algebra, which is available for many platforms. In addition, libraries can support a programming model for a specific computation platform, allowing the generation of efficient code. The MPI library [22], for instance, supports platforms with distributed memory.

5. *Domain-specific languages.* Another mechanism for retargeting applications involves rewriting parts of the source code using a domain-specific language (DSL) [3] to support an application domain or a specific type of platform. DSLs can be embedded within the host language (e.g., C++, Scala), often leading to "cleaner" code when compared to code that results from the use of domain-specific libraries. Alternatively, DSLs can be realized using a separate language and/or programming model (e.g., OpenCL) than the one employed by the host. In this case, the DSL requires its own toolchain support.

Other widely used approaches to assist code retargeting include: compiler auto-vectorization (in the context of CPU SIMD units), OpenMP (in the context of parallelization using shared memory architectures), OpenCL (in the context of CPUs, GPUs, and FPGAs), MPI (in the context of distributed memory architectures), and High-Level Synthesis (HLS) tools to translate C programs to reconfigurable hardware provided by FPGAs.

Table 6.1 summarizes these approaches and the retargeting mechanisms used by each of them: the auto-vectorization process is mainly driven by code transformations—manual or automatic—to infer CPU vector instructions; OpenMP requires code annotations and library calls to parallelize code targeting multicore/processor platforms with shared memory, and with the latest OpenMP specification the support for vectorization; MPI requires library calls to query the environment and trigger communication between nodes, and code must be restructured to support the MPI model; OpenCL requires modifying the host code to query the platform and configure the devices for execution and translating hotspots into OpenCL kernels; HLS requires the use of directives and code transformations to make the source code more amenable to FPGA acceleration by the HLS tool, and the host code must be modified to interface to the hardware accelerator.

Table 6.1 Retargeting mechanisms and approaches

	Auto-vectorization	OpenMP	MPI	OpenCL	HLS
Compiler options	Yes	Yes	No	No	Yes
Code transformations	**Yes**	Yes	**Yes**	Yes	Yes
Code annotations	Yes	**Yes**	No	No	Yes
Libraries	No	**Yes**	**Yes**	**Yes**	Yes
DSL	No	No	No	**Yes**	No
Targets	CPU with vector instructions	• CPU with multiple cores (shared mem) • CPU with vector instructions (OpenMP 4.0)	• CPU with multiple cores/ processors (distributed mem) • large-scale distributed systems	• CPU • GPU • FPGA	FPGA
Ref. section	6.4	6.5	6.6	7.4	7.5

6.3 PARALLELISM AND COMPILER OPTIONS

While there have been considerable advances in compiler technology targeting CPU platforms, many of the optimizations performed automatically are limited to single-threaded execution, thus missing out vast amounts of computational capacity one can attain from multicore and distributed computing. As such, developers must manually exploit the architectural features of CPUs to attain the maximum possible performance to satisfy stringent application requirements, such as handling very large workloads.

6.3.1 PARALLEL EXECUTION OPPORTUNITIES

Fig. 6.2 illustrates the different parallelization opportunities for commodity CPU platforms. At the bottom of this figure, we have SIMD processing units available in each CPU core which simultaneously execute the same operation on multiple data elements, thus exploiting data-level parallelism. To enable this level of parallelism, compilers automatically convert scalar instructions into vector instructions in a process called auto-vectorization (Section 6.4). Data-level parallelism can also be enabled in the context of multicore architectures where multiple instances of a region of computations, each one processing a distinct set of data elements, can be executed in parallel using thread-level approaches such as OpenMP (Section 6.5). Next, we have task-level parallelism, which requires developers to explicitly define multiple concurrent regions of their application also using approaches such as OpenMP.

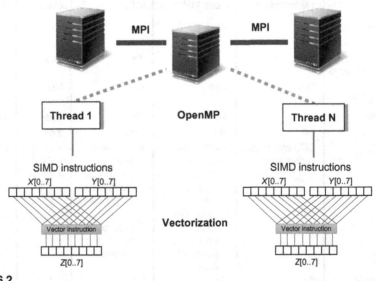

FIG. 6.2

Different levels of parallelism in CPU-based platforms: multiprocessor, multicore and SIMD processor units.

These concurrent regions of an application, implemented in OpenMP as *threads*, share the same address space and are scheduled by the operating system to the available CPU cores. Large workloads can be further partitioned to a multiprocessor platform with distributed memory, where each processor has its own private memory and address space, and communicate with each other using message-passing, such as MPI (Section 6.6). Finally, data movement is an important consideration to ensure data arrives at high enough rates to sustain a high computational throughput. For CPU platforms, one important source of optimization at this level is to leverage their hierarchical cache memory system (Section 6.7).

OTHER USEFUL GCC OPTIONS

The GCC compiler supports many compilation options[a] controlled by specific flags at the command line. The "–E" option outputs the code after the preprocessing stage (i.e., after applying and expanding macros, such as #define, #ifdef, preprocessor directives). The "-S" option outputs, as ".s" files, the generated assembly code. The "-fverbose-asm" flag outputs the assembly code with additional information.

When dealing with optimizations of math operations (and without being conservative as to preserve original precision/accuracy), one can exercise the flag "-funsafe-math-optimizations" (or "-Ofast"). When available, one can take advantage of FMA (fused multiply-add) instructions using the flag "-ffp-contract=fast" (or "-Ofast").

When targeting native CPU instructions one can use "-march=native," or to explicitly define a particular target such as "-march=corei7-avx" or a specific unit such as one of the SIMD units: -msse4.2, -mavx, -mavx2, -msse -msse2 -msse3 -msse4 -msse4.1, -mssse3, etc.

In terms of reporting developers can use flags such as "-fopt-info-optimized" which output information about the applied optimizations.

In terms of specific loop and code optimizations, there are several flags to enable them. For example, "-floop-interchange" applies loop interchange, "-fivopts" performs induction variable optimizations (strength reduction, induction variable merging, and induction variable elimination) on trees.

[a]https://gcc.gnu.org/onlinedocs/gcc/Optimize-Options.html.

6.3.2 COMPILER OPTIONS

The most popular CPU compilers and tools supporting high-level descriptions (e.g., in C, C++) include GCC, LLVM, and ICC (Intel C/C++ compiler). These compilers support command-line options to control and guide the code generation process, for instance, by selecting a predefined sequence of compiler optimizations aimed at maximizing the performance of the application or alternatively reducing its size. As an example, the widely popular GNU GCC compiler includes 44 optimizations enabled using the flag –O1, an additional 43 if –O2 is used, and an additional 12 if –O3 is used (see Ref. [4]). Moreover, the programmer may explicitly invoke other transformations at the command-line compiler invocation. Examples of compilation options include:

- Compiling for reduced program size (e.g., gcc –Os). Here the compiler tries to generate code with the fewest number of instructions as possible and without considering performance improvements. This might be important when targeting computing systems with strict storage requirements;

- Compiling with a minimal set of optimizations, i.e., using only simple compiler passes (e.g., gcc –O0), which can assist debugging;
- Compiling with optimizations that do not substantially affect the code size but in general improve performance (e.g., gcc –O1);
- Compiling with a selected few optimizations, such that do not lead to numerical accuracy issues (e.g., gcc –O2);
- Compiling with more aggressive optimizations, e.g., considering loop unrolling, function inlining, and loop vectorization (e.g., gcc –O3);
- Compiling with more advanced optimizations, possibly with a significant impact on accuracy for certain codes where the sequence of arithmetic instructions may be reordered (e.g., gcc –Ofast);

COMPILER OPTIONS FOR LOOP TRANSFORMATIONS

The GCC compiler includes a number of loop transformations[a] such as "-floop-interchange," "-floop-strip-mine," "-floop-block," "-ftree-loop-distribution," and "-floop-unroll-and-jam" (supported via the Graphite framework[b]).

For some of the compiler flags, it is possible to define the value of parameters that may control internal loop transformation heuristics. For example, the parameter "max-unroll-times=n" (that can be used when invoking gcc and following the "—param" option) asserts the maximum number (n) of unrolling operations on a single loop. To force loop unrolling, one can use the flag "-funroll-loops" and use parameters such as "max-unroll-times," "max-unrolled-insns," and "max-average-unrolled-insns" to control this process.

[a]https://gcc.gnu.org/onlinedocs/gcc/Optimize-Options.html.
[b]https://gcc.gnu.org/wiki/Graphite.

GCC REPORTING

It is important that compilers report information about the effectiveness of their transformations so that developers can decide which transformations to use and to tune each of them via the parameters they support.

To this effect, GCC[a] supports reporting flags. To output the intermediate representation (IR) for each function after applying loop vectorization one can use the flag "-fdump-tree-vect-blocks=foo.dump."

The "-fdump" flag has other useful options such as "-fdump-tree-pre" and "-fdump-tree-pre-blocks," whereas the "-fopt-info" flag with its various options such as "-fopt-info-vec-all" which reports detailed information after applying vectorization optimizations. With respect to loop vectorization information, one can use the flag "-ftree-vectorizer-verbose=n" where n (ranging from 1 to 7) represents the level of information to be reported (a higher value of n means that more details are reported).

[a]https://gcc.gnu.org/onlinedocs/gcc/Developer-Options.html.

Overall, these compilation options offer developers a simple mechanism to find suitable trade-offs between code size and performance. However, such mechanisms are not extended to support compiler options aiming at minimizing power and/or energy consumption. Still, optimizations aimed at reducing the total amount of work tend to minimize both energy consumption and execution time.

Compilers also allow users to select specific compilation options from a vast repertory of flags, often controlled using their command-line interface. The order in which the transformations associated with these flags are applied is not, however, typically controlled by the user (i.e., users may select some of the compilation phases but not their ordering). Common compiler flags control the following compiler functionality:

- Function inlining and heuristics to control function inlining (e.g., maximum number of statements and maximum number of instructions of the function to be inlined)—in gcc, passed as arguments using the "-param" command-line option.
- Loop unrolling and heuristics to control loop unrolling, such as the unrolling factor.
- Loop vectorization and the SIMD unit to be targeted (this depends on backward compatibility and is mostly used when targeting ×86 architectures).
- Math options which may result in accuracy loss. The associated compiler flags may also be needed to enable the use of FMA units.
- Target a specific machine which may improve results but may lead to code incompatible with other machines.

We note that it is common for these compiler flags to also require the internal execution of specific compiler analyses and preparation phases, as well as their corresponding phase orderings.

The number of available compiler flags is typically in the order of hundreds, and there are several options to report analysis information on the use of compiler optimizations (e.g., report on attempts to auto-vectorize loops in the application code). Usually, most of these flags can also be activated with the use of source code directives (e.g., using pragmas in the case of the C programming language). Note that each compiler supports its own set of pragmas for controlling the compiler options.

6.3.3 COMPILER PHASE SELECTION AND ORDERING

The problem of selecting a set of optimizations and a sequence of such optimizations is known as phase selection and phase ordering, respectively, and has been a long-standing research problem in the compiler community.

While some combinations of transformations are clearly synergistic (such as constant propagation followed by algebraic simplification and strength reduction), the feasibility and profitability of other transformation sequences are far less obvious since many transformations adversely interact.

Not surprisingly, there has been an extensive body of research in this area with the use of optimization techniques, ranging from generalized optimization [5] to machine learning [6,7] and genetic algorithms [8,9], as well as random-based search. Mainly, the specialization of phase ordering, taking into account specific function properties and/or application domain, may provide significant improvements in performance, power, and energy, when compared to the best achievements using general predefined optimization sequences provided by −Ox options and compiler flags.

Very few compilers allow developers to define a specific ordering of its phases. An example of a compiler without user's support for specifying a specific phase ordering is the GCC compiler. The ordering can be, however, specified by modifying the compiler itself, but this requires general expertize about the inner works of a compiler, the compiler source code, and deep knowledge about target compiler architecture. In contrast, the LLVM compiler infrastructure [10] allows developers to specify the ordering of the compiler optimizations in addition to the predefined optimization sequence options.

PHASE SELECTION AND ORDERING IN LLVM

The LLVM compiler infrastructure [10][a] provides a tool named opt[b] that receives as input a sequence of optimizations[c] and applies that sequence to the LLVM IR (e.g., stored in a file using the bitcode[d] format, which is the binary format used by LLVM to store the IR and that can be generated by the clang frontend). This IR can then be translated to assembly code using the llc tool.[e]

An example of a compiler sequence (phase order) that can be applied with opt is presented below. In this example, we consider a C program named x.c. The clang tool translates this program to the LLVM representation which is then passed to the opt tool. The opt tool then applies a sequence of compiler optimizations specified through the command line to generate an LLVM IR file. Finally, llc translates this LLVM IR file to assembly code, which is subsequently translated to an executable by gcc.

```
clang -emit-llvm x.c -c -o x.bc
opt -loop-simplify -loop-rotate -inline -
simplify-libcalls -basicaa -licm -constmerge,
-indvars -unroll-allow-partial -loop-unroll -
reassociate -gvn x.bc -o y.bc
llc y.bc -o y.s // translate to assembly code
gcc y.s -o y // create executable "y"
```

[a]The LLVM compiler infrastructure, http://llvm.org/.
[b]opt—LLVM optimize, http://llvm.org/docs/CommandGuide/opt.html.
[c]LLVM's analysis and transform passes, http://llvm.org/docs/Passes.html.
[d]LLVM bitcode file format, http://llvm.org/docs/BitCodeFormat.html.
[e]llc - LLVM static compiler, http://llvm.org/docs/CommandGuide/llc.html.

6.4 LOOP VECTORIZATION

Loop vectorization is the process of translating scalar operations inside a loop body into vector (SIMD) instructions (see Chapter 2). Since a vector instruction can simultaneously operate on multiple pairs of operands, this technique can be used to speedup applications if data parallelism can be exploited. Most modern CPUs feature vector processing instructions, including Intel x86's MMX, SSE and AVX instructions, MIPS' MSA, SPARC's VIS, and ARM NEON extensions.

To understand why vectorization can improve performance, consider the following code:

```
for (i = 0; i < 100; i++) {
    z[i] = x[i] * y[i]
}
```

Assume arrays x, y, and z are 32-bit single precision arrays, and the CPU supports 128-bit SIMD registers. Without vectorization, the scalar multiplication instruction is executed 100 times, using only 1/4 of each SIMD register:

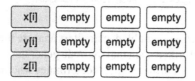

With vectorization, all SIMD registers are used to perform four multiplications at once in a single vector instruction:

Hence, in our earlier example, we only need to execute 25 multiply instructions instead of the original 100 instructions, thus increasing the performance of this loop.

In C/C++, developers can manually perform the vectorization process by translating the selected code into a sequence of assembly vector instructions, or using intrinsic functions (e.g., for SSE) provided by some compilers. These intrinsic functions include a set of C functions and associated data types providing direct access to vector instructions. Unfortunately, vectorizing by hand requires considerable effort and results in unreadable, unportable, and unmaintainable code. For this reason, it is far more convenient to allow compilers to perform the vectorization process automatically.

ASSEMBLY AND INTRINSIC FUNCTIONS

The C programming language allows to embed assembly code using asm (or "__asm") statements as in the following example:

```
asm("ADD x, x, #1\n" "MOV y, x\n");
```

or

```
asm {
    ADD x, x, #1
    MOV y, x
}
```

Another way is the use of intrinsic functions (also known as *intrinsics*). An intrinsic function is a function that is handled by the compiler in a special fashion, e.g., substituting it by a sequence of assembly instructions. Following are examples of intrinsics in C code targeting an ARM CPU.[a]

```
si = vld1_s16(s+i+j);
ci = vld1_s16(c+j);
o = vmlal_s16(o, si, ci);
```

[a]https://gcc.gnu.org/onlinedocs/gcc-4.6.1/gcc/ARM-NEON-Intrinsics.html.

When auto-vectorization is enabled, compilers analyze the code to verify whether vectorization can be performed such that the code generated is correct with respect to the original scalar version. Further analysis determines whether vectorization is profitable. For instance, if the computation performs noncontiguous memory accesses, then vectorization may not be beneficial. To support vectorization, the compiler may need to apply a set of transformations, such as loop peeling and loop unrolling (see Chapter 5).

Although the auto-vectorization process has improved considerably over the years, the level of support and efficiency is not consistent across different C/C++ compilers. Some compilers are still not able to vectorize code if it does not conform to specific idioms or style, thus requiring manual effort to make the code more amenable to auto-vectorization.

The compiler options presented in Table 6.2 control the auto-vectorization process for popular C compilers, namely, GNU C Compiler (GCC) [11], Intel C Compiler (ICC) [12], and CLANG/LLVM [13]. As can be seen, each compiler has its own set of options to control auto-vectorization. For instance, auto-vectorization can be enabled implicitly when specifying a high optimization level (-O2 or -O3) or can be enabled explicitly (e.g., -ftree-vectorize). There are also options to disable auto-vectorization and to report how auto-vectorization was applied to each loop.

Table 6.2 Options to control auto-vectorization for three C compilers (assuming x86 targets)

Option	GCC	ICC	CLANG/LLVM
Version	4.9.4	17.0	3.9
Enabling vectorization	-O3 *or* -ftree-vectorize	-O2 *or* -vec	*(enabled by default)*
Disabling vectorization	-fno-tree-vectorize	-no-vec	-fno-vectorize
Vectorization report	-fopt-info *and* -fdump-tree-vect-details	-vec-report=[n]	`-Rpass-missed=loop-vectorize` and `-Rpass-analysis=loop-vectorize`

Depending on the verbose level used, if the loop was not vectorized, developers are informed what prevented the loop from being vectorized so that they can revise the code accordingly. In addition to compiler options, developers can also provide hints to the auto-vectorization process using code annotations.

The following are general guidelines applicable to all the aforementioned compilers to improve the chances of a loop being auto-vectorized:

1. *Loop count.* The number of loop iterations should be constant and preferably known at compile time.
2. *Control flow.* The loop body should have one entry point and one exit point. Furthermore, it is advisable to not include control statements, such as conditionals (e.g., `if` statements). However, some conditionals may be removed automatically by the compiler using *predication*, where control statements (e.g., `if (c) { y=f(x); } else { y=g(x); }`) are converted to predicated expressions (e.g., `y = (c? f(x) : g(x))`).
3. *Function calls.* Function calls also prevent vectorization unless the compiler supports vectorized versions of these functions. These usually include math functions, supporting single and double precision, such as `sin()`, `pow()`, and `round()`.
4. *Data dependences.* Since each SIMD instruction operates on data elements from multiple iterations at once, the vectorization process must ensure this order change maintains the result of the original scalar version. For this purpose, the compiler must compute the dependences between loop iterations and ensure there are no read-after-write and write-after-write loop-carried dependences that prevent vectorization. Note that compilers can vectorize code with dependences when reduction idioms can be detected, e.g., `sum = sum + A[i]`.
5. *Memory accesses.* Vectorizing can be more efficient if memory load instructions access contiguous memory addresses, allowing a single SIMD instruction to load them directly, rather than using multiple load instructions.

Overall, these guidelines aim at ensuring that each data lane associated with a loop iteration executes the same set of operations, thus allowing them to be executed in parallel. Let us consider the following loop, which infringes the earlier guidelines, thus preventing auto-vectorization:

```
void no_vec(float a[]) {
   for (int i = 1; i < 100; i++)  {
     a[i] = a[i-1]*2;
     if (a[i] < 100.0) {
        a[i] = f(a[i]);
        break;
     }
   }
}
```

First, the loop has a read-after-write dependence between consecutive iterations (`a[i]` and `a[i-1]`). Second, the `break` statement inside the `if` statement implies the loop count is unknown and there is more than one loop exit point. Finally, there is a call to a function f.

There are other techniques which can be applied manually to enhance the applicability of the auto-vectorization of loops (see, e.g., Refs. [11–13]), including: (a) using loop indices in array accesses instead of pointers or pointer arithmetic, (b) minimizing indirect addressing in array accesses, (c) aligning data structures to 16 byte boundaries (SSE instructions) or 32 byte boundaries (AVX instructions), (d) favoring the use of structures of arrays (SoA) over arrays of structures (AoS).

While the auto-vectorization process is performed at compile time, not all information may be available when compiling. For instance, the compiler might not know whether two pointers reference the same memory position inside a loop, thus creating a dependence and preventing vectorization. In this case, the compiler may generate a vectorized and a nonvectorized version, and invoke one of them at runtime depending on the addresses of the pointers (see Chapter 5).

MEMORY ALIGNMENT

Memory alignment is important as it allows the concurrent execution of load/store operations from/ to successive memory positions.

Alignment support[a] for dynamically allocated memory is provided by specific functions (see the following examples), such as aligned_alloc and _alligned_malloc for Linux and Windows, respectively.

```
float *c = (TYPE *) aligned_alloc(16,sizeof(float)* N);
float *c = (TYPE *) _aligned_malloc(16,sizeof(float)* N);
```

In case of a static memory allocation of array variables, it is common to provide support via attributes as depicted in the following example.

```
float c[LEN] __attribute__(( aligned(16) ));
```

Additional alignment information can be conveyed via the use of special built-in functions to instruct the compiler to assume aligned data as in the following example.

```
TYPE_OF_ARG *c1 = __builtin_assume_aligned (arg, 16);
```

[a]http://www.gnu.org/software/libc/manual/html_node/Aligned-Memory-Blocks.html.

Regarding the implementation of auto-vectorization, we can distinguish two general techniques, namely, loop level and block level. Consider the following code:

```
for (i = 0; i < 512; i++)
    D[i] = A[i]+B[i]*C[i];
```

With the loop-level vectorization technique, the compiler first determines whether the loop can be vectorized. Then, it performs loop stripmining by a factor corresponding to the number of scalars that can fit into a SIMD register. This step is followed by loop distribution, which generates a sequence of loops replaced with the vector instructions, as follows:

```
// intermediate step after stripmining and loop distribution
for (i = 0; i < 512; i=i+4) {
    for (j = 0; j < 4; j++) vA[j] = A[i+j];
    for (j = 0; j < 4; j++) vB[j] = B[i+j];
    for (j = 0; j < 4; j++) vC[j] = C[i+j];
    for (j = 0; j < 4; j++) vt[j] = vB[j]*vC[j];
    for (j = 0; j < 4; j++) vtD[j] = vA[j]+vt[j];
    for (j = 0; j < 4; j++) D[i+j] = vtD[j];
}
```

The block-level technique, on the other hand, is a more general technique focused on vectorizing basic block statements. As such, it relies on unrolling the innermost loop body by a factor corresponding to the vector register size (the same factor used in strip-mining with the loop-level technique), packing all scalar instructions performing the same operation into vector instructions if dependences are not violated.

```
// intermediate step after unrolling and before packing
for (i = 0; i < 512; i=i+4) {
    vA0 = vld(&A[i+0]);
    vB0 = vld(&B[i+0]);
    vC0 = vld(&C[i+0]);
    vt0 = vmul(vB0, vC0);
    vtD0 = vadd(vA0, vt0);
    vst(&D[i+0], vtD0);
    ...
    vA3 = vld(&A[i+3]);
    vB3 = vld(&B[i+3]);
    vC3 = vld(&C[i+3]);
    vt3 = vmul(vB3, vC3);
    vtD3 = vadd(vA3, vt3);
    vst(&D[i+3], vtD3);
}
```

The use of both techniques generates the following vectorized code:

```
for (i = 0; i < 512; i=i+4) {
    vA = vld(&A[i]);     // vector load
    vB = vld(&B[i]);
    vC = vld(&C[i]);
    vt = vmul(vB, vC);   // vector mult
    vtD = vadd(vA, vt);  // vector add
    vst(&D[i], vtD);     // vector store
}
```

RESTRICT KEYWORD

The restrict keyword is part of the C programming language introduced in the C99 standard. This keyword is used when declaring pointers to convey to compilers that these pointers do not address memory regions that overlap with regions addressed by other pointers and are therefore un-aliased by other pointers. Note that C++ does not support the restrict keyword. Hence, compilers such as GCC and CLANG/LLVM support the __restrict__ directive that works on both C and C++ codes.

```
void addv(TYPE * restrict c, TYPE *
restrict d, TYPE * restrict e, int N)
{
    for(int i=0 ; i < N; i++) {
        e[i] = d[i] + c[i];
    }
}
```

We now revisit the matrix multiplication example presented in Section 6.1. When using the GCC compiler (4.8) and enabling auto-vectorization with the report generation option, GCC will report that none of the three loops are vectorized as shown below:

```
matrix_vec.cpp:10:22: note: not vectorized: multiple nested loops.
matrix_vec.cpp:11:25: note: not vectorized: complicated access pattern.
matrix_vec.cpp:12:28: note: not vectorized: complicated access pattern.
```

A close inspection of the code reveals two problems. First, matrices A, B, and C are passed to the matrix_mult function as pointers. Without additional information about the relative location of the corresponding storage addresses they point to, the compiler is unable to determine whether or not they point to the same memory location, e.g., if pointer to C is an alias of A. For instance, if these pointers were aliased, the loop would carry a dependence, thus preventing vectorization. In the previous example, the pointers are unaliased, i.e., A, B, and C point to disjoint memory locations, hence programmers must include the __restrict__ directive in their declaration to indicate that there are no dependencies between them. The second problem is that in the original code the loop bounds were not defined as constants, even though they were initialized in the global scope. The compiler decided not to vectorize the loops as it cannot identify the exact number of iterations. Programmers can address this issue by specifying the bounds as const in the corresponding variable declaration. The final code is as follows:

```
const int nX = 1024; // bounds have been specified as constant
const int nY = 1024;
const int nZ = 1024;

// the restrict directive has been added
void matrix_mult(float *__restrict__ A,
                 float *__restrict__ B,
                 float *__restrict__ C) {
  for (int i = 0; i < nX; i++) {
    for (int j = 0; j < nZ; j++) {
      C[i*nZ+j] = 0;
      for (int k = 0; k < nY; k++) {
        C[i*nZ+j] += A[i*nY+k] * B[k*nZ+j];
      }
    }
  }
}
```

With these two changes, the compiler is now able to automatically generate vector instructions to multiply and add the elements of A and B.

Note that directives to support and guide the auto-vectorization process are not standardized across compilers. Furthermore, support for auto-vectorization keeps improving with new compiler version releases, both in terms of analysis and transformations performed. It is therefore important to read the latest guidelines for auto-vectorization for each compiler used.

6.5 SHARED MEMORY (MULTICORE)

OpenMP [21] is an API that allows programmers to exploit data- and task-level parallelism on multicore platforms with *shared memory* (see Chapter 2). One of the key features of OpenMP is that programs can be parallelized incrementally from an initial sequential version. Once developers identify the regions of code that can benefit from parallel execution (e.g., hotspots), the code can be annotated with OpenMP directives to define how computations can be distributed across different cores and what data are accessed within each core.

OpenMP provides a set of compiler directives, a routine library, and a runtime to implement its execution model (Fig. 6.3). The OpenMP runtime supports parallelism using threads. A thread is an autonomous subroutine that *can* be executed in parallel within the context of a process and is transparently scheduled by the operating system taking into account available resources and resource utilization. Unlike processes, multiple threads share the same address space. One of the design goals of OpenMP has been portability: a well-constructed OpenMP program outputs the same result whether it uses one thread or multiple threads, affecting only the performance according to the level of parallelism attained. To maximize performance, the number of threads is usually set as a function of the number of cores available in the platform and the workload size. Hence, an OpenMP application can be developed such that its workload is efficiently distributed across the available compute resources without having to be recompiled.

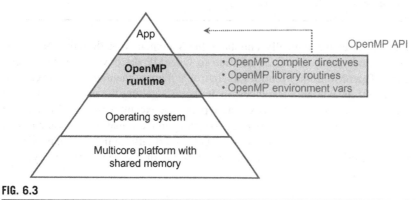

FIG. 6.3

The OpenMP API components.

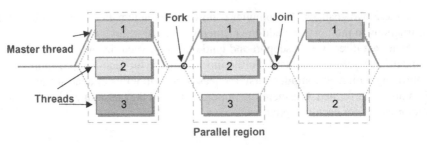

FIG. 6.4

The OpenMP *fork-join* execution model.

To allow applications to adjust to available resources, OpenMP uses the *fork-join* execution model [14] (see Fig. 6.4). All OpenMP programs start execution within the master thread which runs the code sequentially. When a parallel region is found, the master thread creates a team of threads of a given number, with the master thread also part of this team of threads. The operating system will then schedule these threads, assigning them to available processor cores. As thread management incurs an overhead, developers must adjust the number of threads so that the workload distribution is properly balanced and each thread maximizes core utilization. When a thread in the parallel region completes execution, it waits for all other threads to complete. At this point, sequential execution resumes within the master thread. In OpenMP, developers are required to specify the parallel regions of their programs explicitly and may control the number of threads associated in each parallel region. The OpenMP runtime and the operating system coordinate the parallel execution.

Developers identify parallel regions with OpenMP code directives. In C/C++, compiler directives are controlled by source code #pragma annotations to identify: (i) concurrency, (ii) how work can be distributed between threads, and (iii) synchronization points. An OpenMP directive has the following syntax format in C/C++:

```
#pragma omp <omp-directive-name> [clause, ...]
<statement>
```

An OpenMP directive typically annotates the statement that directly follows it, including a code bock {...}. In addition to OpenMP directives, developers can use a set of OpenMP library routines to control and query the underlying execution platform about its available resources, including: (i) getting the number of threads operating on a particular program execution point, the executing thread *id* and nested level; (ii) setting the number of threads; (iii) setting and terminating locks and nested locks. Note that if the platform is not configured explicitly in the program, such as setting the number of threads, then the default behavior can be overridden by environment variables.

We now consider a simple OpenMP program:

```
#include <omp.h>
...
void main() {
    int X[500];
    omp_set_num_threads(omp_get_num_procs())
    #pragma omp parallel
    {
        int ID = omp_get_thread_num();
        f(ID, X);
    }
    print("done!");
}
```

All OpenMP programs must be compiled with the -fopenmp option when using the GCC compiler or /Qopenmp with the ICC compiler. When these options are used, the compiler processes the OpenMP directives and links the program against the OpenMP library. The first source code line of this example inserts the OpenMP header to allow access to its library routines. Inside the main function, the program sets the number of threads of any subsequent parallel region to match the number of available processors (cores). Next, the program defines a code block as a parallel region using the *parallel* directive. When running this program, an instance of this code block is executed by each thread in the parallel region as illustrated in Fig. 6.5.

In this example, four threads execute the same code in parallel. Each thread waits until all of them complete. At this point, the parallel region completes execution, and the main thread prints the word "done." Note that OpenMP places an implicit barrier at the end of any parallel region, in which all threads are joined. Another noteworthy aspect is the use of two arguments in function f: the first, ID, is a private variable visible only to the assigned thread as it was defined locally, the second, X, is a shared

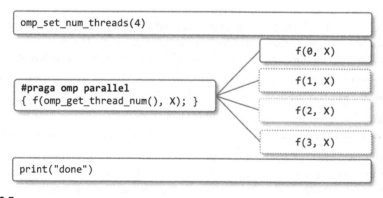

FIG. 6.5

OpenMP execution of a simple code block using four threads.

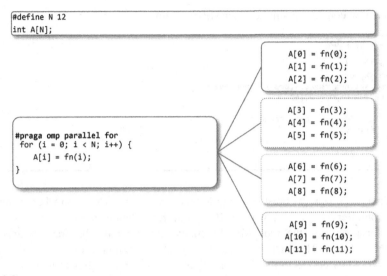

```
#define N 12
int A[N];
```

```
A[0] = fn(0);
A[1] = fn(1);
A[2] = fn(2);
```

```
A[3] = fn(3);
A[4] = fn(4);
A[5] = fn(5);
```

```
#praga omp parallel for
  for (i = 0; i < N; i++) {
    A[i] = fn(i);
}
```

```
A[6] = fn(6);
A[7] = fn(7);
A[8] = fn(8);
```

```
A[9] = fn(9);
A[10] = fn(10);
A[11] = fn(11);
```

FIG. 6.6

OpenMP loop worksharing execution.

variable as it was defined outside the parallel block. Shared variables can be accessed by all threads in the team and can be used for interthread communication, however special care is required to avoid data races. In this example, the parallel directive creates a SPMD (single program, multiple data) computation where each thread executes the same code on different data items.

In addition to providing an interface to expose concurrency, OpenMP also supports directives for workload distribution between threads within a team. Specifically, OpenMP supports different forms of *worksharing*: (1) loop, (2) sections, and (3) tasks, which we explain next.

Loops are often the hotspots in a program, and are therefore prime candidates for optimization and parallelization. The *loop* worksharing directive `omp parallel for` distributes loop iterations across all threads in a team (Fig. 6.6) as follows:

```
int A[N];
#pragma omp parallel for
for (i = 0; i < N; i++) {
  A[i] = fn(i);
}
```

With the `omp parallel for` directive, the loop iteration space is divided by the number of threads available in the parallel region, and therefore iterations cannot have dependences between them. In many cases, output- and anti-dependences can be removed with techniques such as variable renaming, scalar expansion, node splitting, and induction variable substitution. Other techniques to remove dependences require complex data dependence analysis and code restructuring, e.g., reordering statements, to parallelize loops. OpenMP, however, supports parallelization of loops exhibiting true loop-carried dependences that stem from reduction operations. In particular, the `reduction(op:list)` clause is used to specify a reduction operation, where `op` is a reduction operator (e.g., +, *, −) and `list` is a sequence of variables separated by commas.

As an example of reduction support in OpenMP, consider the following code which computes the average of a list of floating-point numbers:

```
float A[N]; float avg = 0.0; int i;
#pragma omp parallel for reduction(+:avg)
for (i = 0; i < N; i++) {
   avg += A[i];
}
avg = avg/N;
```

In this example, the loop exhibits a true loop-carried dependency caused by the variable `avg`, where the result of the accumulation is used in the subsequent iteration. With the reduction clause, a local copy of each list variable (`avg`) is assigned to each thread in the team and initialized depending on the operation (`op`) used (e.g., for the *sum* operation, the initial value is 0). Each thread then performs the reduction over their local copy. At the end, the result of every local copy is reduced to a single value (using the operator specified as a parameter in the OpenMP directive) and assigned to the original global variable (`avg`).

One important aspect of loop worksharing is the distribution of loop iterations among threads. In OpenMP, this distribution is controlled by developers using the `schedule([type][,chunk_size])` clause. There are three main `schedule` types, namely: (1) the `static` schedule type divides the loop iterations into equal-sized chunks at compile time. By default, the chunk size is the ratio between the loop count and the number of threads. (2) The `dynamic` schedule type uses an internal work queue in which each thread retrieves a block of iterations of chunk size (by default it is 1). When a thread terminates, it retrieves the next block at the top of the queue. (3) The `guided` schedule type is similar to the dynamic type, however it starts with a large chunk size and then decreases it to balance the load. The choice of type of schedule and chunk size is aimed at maximizing load balancing while limiting its runtime overhead. In general, the `static` schedule type has the lowest overhead but is more vulnerable to load imbalances, while the `dynamic` schedule type has the highest runtime overhead but provides better load balancing. Additionally, OpenMP supports the `auto` schedule type, in which an OpenMP runtime implementation automatically determines the scheduling policy.

We now focus on the remaining two OpenMP workshare constructs, namely, `sections` and `tasks`. OpenMP `sections` allows regions of code to run in parallel by assigning each section to a thread and are identified using the `omp parallel sections` directive.

We illustrate the use of the `sections` construct with the following code example:

```
a = alice();
b = bob();
c = charles(a, b);
```

Assuming that `alice()` and `bob()` perform independent computations, the code can be structured into sections as follows:

```
#pragma omp parallel sections
{
    #pragma omp section
    a = alice();

    #pragma omp section
    b = bob();
}
c = charles(a, b);
```

In this case, each section is assigned to an available thread.

For more complex scenarios involving, for instance, unbounded loops, recursive algorithms, and producer/consumer interactions, it is more appropriate to use task *worksharing*, which is specified using the `omp task` directive. An OpenMP task defines an independent unit of work executed by a thread. The OpenMP runtime decides whether a task might be executed immediately or be deferred.

We illustrate the use of the `task` construct with the following code example, which iterates over a linked list to process each of its nodes:

```
#pragma omp parallel
{
    #pragma omp single private(p) shared(lst)
    { /* block A */
        node *p = lst;
        while (p) {
            #pragma omp task
            process(p);
            p = p->next;
        }
    }
}
```

The first directive, `omp parallel`, creates a team of threads. The second directive, `omp single`, assigns a single thread to execute block *A*. This thread is responsible for iterating the list and instantiating the tasks that process each element independently. The call to function `process()` is annotated with the `omp task` directive, which implies that each invocation of this function instantiates a task. As a result, each task instantiation is executed by a thread in the parallel region.

As previously mentioned, it is important in this programming model to distinguish between which variables are shared by all threads in a team, and which variables are private within the scope of a thread. By default, all variables defined outside a parallel region, including static and global variables, are shared. Loop index variables and stack variables in subroutines called from within parallel regions are private. The scope of variables can be defined explicitly through data scope attribute clauses in conjunction with parallel and worksharing constructs. For instance, in the previous example, variable p was defined as a private variable. The general format of the data scope attribute is `data_scope(var1<, var2, ...>)`. Data scope attributes include `shared`, `private`, `firstprivate`, and `lastprivate`. The latter three attribute types create an instance of a variable for each thread. However, a private variable is not initialized and its result is not exposed outside the parallel or *workshare* region. A `firstprivate` variable will have its value initialized with the value of the variable defined before the parallel construct, while the value of the `lastprivate` variable is set by the thread that executed the last section or the last loop iteration. In the previous example, p was explicitly declared as a private variable, and lst as a shared variable.

OpenMP also provides directives to synchronize thread execution to ensure threads wait until their dependences are met. Constructs like `for` loops and statements annotated with the `omp single` directive have implicit barriers at the end of their execution. Unnecessary barriers, however, lead to performance loss and can be removed with the `nowait` clause. As the following example illustrates, without the `nowait` clause, there would be an implicit barrier at the end of the first loop. This barrier would have prevented any idle threads (having completed the first loop) to start executing the second loop.

```
#pragma omp parallel
{
#pragma omp for schedule(dynamic,1) nowait
for(int i=0; i<n; i++) a[i] = bigFunc1(i);

#pragma omp for schedule(dynamic,1)
for(int j=0; j<m; j++) b[j] = bigFunc2(j)
}
```

There are cases, however, when programmers need to enforce a barrier, so that execution waits until all threads arrive at the barrier. This is achieved with the `omp barrier` directive. For instance, in the following code, `g()` is only invoked after `f()` so that the dependence from B is correctly handled:

```
#pragma omp parallel shared(A, B, C)
{
    f(A,B); // Processed A into B
    #pragma omp barrier
    g(B,C); // Processed B into C
    ...
}
```

With the use of OpenMP concurrency constructs, programmers are responsible for ensuring that their programs do not exhibit data races if they wish to guarantee deterministic execution. Race conditions arise when two or more threads simultaneously access a shared variable possibly leading to nondeterministic behavior. To protect shared data against race conditions, programmers can define critical regions using the `omp critical` directive.

To illustrate the use of the `critical` directive, consider the following code where a loop has been annotated with a `parallel for loop` directive. Each iteration of this loop updates the value of the variable sum. With the `critical` directive, only one of the concurrent threads can enter the critical region at a given time ensuring that the updates to the sum variable are thus performed atomically and are race free.

```
float dot_prod(float* a, float* b, int N) {
   float sum = 0.0;
   #pragma omp parallel for shared(sum)
   for (int i=0; i<N; i++) {
      #pragma omp critical
      sum += a[i] * b[i];
   }
   return sum;
}
```

Note that while `omp critical` can serialize any region of code, it exhibits an overhead. As an alternative, when the critical region is an expression statement updating a single memory location, the `omp atomic` clause may be used to provide lightweight locks. In OpenMP there are four atomic mode clauses: `read`, `write`, `update`, and `capture`. The `read` clause guarantees an atomic read operation, while the `write` clause ensures an atomic write operation. As an example, x is read atomically in the case of $y = x + 5$. The `update` clause guarantees an atomic update of a variable, e.g., y in the case of $y = y + 1$. Finally, the `capture` clause ensures an atomic update of a variable as well and the final value of the variables. For instance, if the `capture` clause is used with $y = x++$, then x is atomically updated and the value of y is captured.

Although shared variables can be accessed by all threads in a parallel region, OpenMP supports a relaxed consistency memory model, where at any point in time threads may not have the same view of the state of shared variables. This is because write operations performed in each thread may not immediately store data in main memory, opting instead to buffer the results to hide memory latency. To enforce a consistent view of shared variables at specific points in the thread execution, programmers need to use the `omp flush [(a,b,c)]` directive with the list of variables to be committed to main memory. If the list of variables is not specified, then all variables are flushed. As an example, consider the following code with two threads sharing two variables, x and y.

thread 1	thread 2
int x = 0, y = 0; // shared variables	

`x = 1;`
`#pragma omp flush(x, y)`
`if (y == 0) { /* critical`
`            section */ }`
	`y = 1;`
	`#pragma omp flush(x,y)`
	`if (x == 0) { /* critical`
	`            section */ }`

To ensure that only one thread has access to the "critical section," the program must flush both variables to ensure the values observed by one thread are also observed by the other thread. While only one of the threads accesses the critical section, there is also a chance that neither will access the critical section. Memory flushes are thus not meant to synchronize different threads, but to ensure thread state is consistent with other threads. In general, a `flush` directive is required whenever shared data is accessed between multiple threads: after a write and before a read. Assuming a program with two threads T1 and T2 that share variable x, then the following sequence of operations must occur to ensure that both threads share a consistent view of that variable:

```
T1 [write X] → T1 [flush X] → T2 [flush X] → T2 [read X]
```

Since data sharing between threads can lead to an inconsistent view of state upon termination, OpenMP implicitly executes a flush operation in barriers, and when entering and exiting the following regions: `parallel`, worksharing (unless `nowait` is invoked), `omp critical`, and `omp atomic`.

In addition to the basic fork-join model described at the beginning of this section, the more recent release of OpenMP 3.0 supports *nested parallelism*. This nested parallelism can be enabled in two ways, namely, by invoking the library routine `omp_set_nested(1)` (as shown in the following code example) or by setting the OMP_NESTED environment variable. If nested parallelism is enabled, when a thread within a parallel region encounters a new `omp parallel` pragma statement, an additional team of threads is spawned, and the original thread becomes their master. If nested parallelism is disabled, then a thread inside a parallel region ignores any parallel pragma construct it encounters. It is important to understand the impact of nesting parallel regions, since they can quickly spawn a large number of threads. In general, nested parallelism incurs a larger overhead than using a single parallel region. Yet, they can be useful in execution scenarios with load unbalanced problems, and where one code region can be further parallelized.

```
...
omp_set_nested(1);
...
#pragma omp parallel sections
{
    #pragma omp parallel section
    {
        #pragma parallel for
        for (i = 0; i < n; i++) { x[i] = 1.0; }
    }

    #pragma omp parallel section
    {
        #pragma parallel for
        for (i = 0; i < n; i++) { y[i] = 2.0; }
    }
}
```

We now focus on how to accelerate the matrix multiplication example presented in Section 6.1 using OpenMP. One possible solution to parallelize this example with OpenMP is as shown below:

```
void matrix_mult(float *A, float *B, float *C) {
    {
        omp_set_num_threads(OMP_NUM_THREADS);

        #pragma omp parallel for schedule(static)
        for (int i = 0; i < nX; i++) {
            for (int j = 0; j < nZ; j++) {
                float sum = 0.0;
                for (int k = 0; k < nY; k++) {
                    sum += A[i*nY+k] * B[k*nZ+j];
                }
                C[i*nZ+j] = sum;
            }
        }
    }
}
```

Here, we simply annotate the outermost loop body with a `parallel omp for` **pragma**. Because the iteration space size is known at compile time, we use the static schedule, which will partition the outermost loop iterations according to the specified number of threads. Specifying a parallel pragma in any of the inner loops would reduce the work done by each thread, and unnecessarily serialize the computation, since we can compute each element of the matrix in parallel. One further change in the original code includes the use of a temporary variable (`sum`) to store the inner product of a row of the matrix *A* and a column of the matrix *B*. This precludes having multiple threads writing to memory at every iteration of the innermost loop. We invite the reader to experiment combining vectorization (discussed in the previous section) with OpenMP directives to further speedup this matrix multiplication code on multiple cores and using larger matrix sizes.

6.6 DISTRIBUTED MEMORY (MULTIPROCESSOR)

In the previous section, we covered the OpenMP programming model which allows the development of multithreaded applications. The OpenMP model is used within the context of a process, allowing multiple threads to execute on available processor cores and share the same memory space (*intraprocess parallelization*).

In this section, we cover the MPI (Message Passing Interface) model, which is suitable for parallelizing computations distributed across a set of processes, where each process has its own memory space and execution environment (*interprocess parallelization*). These processes can run on the same computing platform or across different computing platforms. As processes do not share the same memory space, MPI offers an interprocess communication API supporting synchronization and data movement from one process memory space to another. With this API, interaction between processes is made via explicit message exchanges. MPI is therefore suitable for harnessing the computation capacity of multiple (and potentially heterogeneous) processing elements connected via fast interconnects, from many-core architectures to distributed system platforms.

To use MPI, developers must adapt their applications to conform to the MPI communication model with supplied library routines. The MPI library is based on a well-established standard, making MPI programs portable across a wide range of parallel computing platforms with support for C/C++ and Fortran. This portability feature means that MPI code are designed to preserve functional behavior when they are recompiled to different parallel architecture platforms. However, to maximize performance on a given platform, MPI applications must be designed to be scalable and match workload requirements to available resources.

We now illustrate the use of MPI with the problem of adding the elements of a vector of *N* integers. One way to parallelize this computation is to have a *master* process to partition a vector of *N* integer elements to available *worker* processes. Each worker then adds the values within its partition and sends the result back to the master process. The master process then adds all the workers' results to produce the final result. This example uses a common distributed computing pattern called map-reduce or scather-gather, which decomposes a big problem into smaller parts (shards) that are computed independently and then reduced to a single result. The following code shows an MPI implementation of this program using the scather-gather pattern:

```
#include <stdio.h>
#include <stdlib.h>
#include <mpi.h>

#define N 200 /* vector size */
#define TAG 540

int main(int argc, char *argv[])
{
    int rank, num_procs;

    /* 1. initialization stage */
    MPI_Init(&argc, &argv); //initialize MPI operations
    MPI_Comm_rank(MPI_COMM_WORLD, &rank); //get the rank
    MPI_Comm_size(MPI_COMM_WORLD, &num_procs); //get number of processes

    int A[N]; int i, n;
    int sum = 0;

    /* 2. map stage */
    if (rank == 0) { // master
        MPI_Request req;
        set_vector(A); // sets vector values
        int offset = 0;
        int partition = N / (num_procs - 1);

        for (i = 1; i < num_procs; i++) {
            n = (i < num_procs - 1)? partition : N - ((num_procs-2) * partition);
            MPI_Isend(&n, 1, MPI_INT, i, TAG, MPI_COMM_WORLD, &req);
            MPI_Isend(&A[offset], n, MPI_INT, i, TAG+1, MPI_COMM_WORLD, &req);
            offset += n;
        }
    } else { // workers
        MPI_Status status;
        MPI_Recv(&n, 1, MPI_INT, 0, TAG, MPI_COMM_WORLD, &status);
        MPI_Recv(A, n, MPI_INT, 0, TAG+1, MPI_COMM_WORLD, &status);

        for (i = 0; i < n; i++) {
            sum += A[i];
        }
    }

    /* 3. reduce stage */
    int total_sum;
    MPI_Reduce(&sum, &total_sum, 1, MPI_INT, MPI_SUM, 0, MPI_COMM_WORLD);
    if (rank == 0) {
        printf(":::> sum: %d\n", total_sum);
    }

    /* 4. finalize stage */
    MPI_Finalize();

    return 0;
}
```

In the previous example, we divided the `main` function into four stages (Fig. 6.7):

- *Stage 1* initializes the MPI environment (`MPI_Init`), gets the process rank (`MPI_Comm_rank`), and the number of processes spawned (`MPI_Comm_size`) within the *communicator* `MPI_COMM_WORLD`. A communicator defines a group of processes that can communicate with each other. Each process in a communicator is assigned a unique rank. Processes communicate with each other explicitly using their ranks. The `MPI_COMM_WORLD` communicator corresponds to all processes within an MPI job. Unless a more complex communication pattern is required, an MPI program typically begins with these three lines of code, as they offer a full view of all processes in an MPI job and their associated ranks.
- In *stage 2*, the master process (identified by rank 0) partitions the vector among the workers (remaining processes). The master process sends a partition (part of the vector) to each available worker using the `MPI_Isend` function. This function sends data without waiting until it is received. The process of sending the partition to each worker is performed in two steps: first, the size of the partition is sent, followed by the partition itself. If the vector cannot be evenly divided by the number of workers, then the last worker is assigned a larger partition. Conversely, the workers receive the partition from the master worker with the `MPI_Recv` function, which blocks execution until data is received. This process mirrors the protocol used by the master in this stage: first the worker receives the size of the partition, and then the partition. Each worker will then add the values in their assigned partition.
- In *stage 3*, the results from all workers are sent back to the master using the *reduction* collective communication primitive, `MPI_Reduce`, which automatically adds the results into a single value for the master process. The reduction operation, in this case `MPI_SUM`, must be supplied in the `MPI_Reduce` call.
- Finally, in *stage 4*, the `MPI_Finalize` routine is invoked to clean up all MPI states, and free all used resources. After this call, no other MPI routine can be invoked.

There are many available implementations of MPI, including Open MPI, Intel MPI, and MS-MPI. However, the most popular MPI implementation is MPICH, which is available for both Linux and Windows distributions. To verify if MPI has been properly installed on a specific system, programmers can use the following command:

```
% mpiexec --version
```

To compile MPI applications, the MPI framework includes the `mpicc` and `mpicxx` tools which wrap the default C and C++ compilers, respectively. These tools automatically configure the location of the MPI framework (headers and libraries) and automatically link the application with the MPI-specific libraries. The parameters to these tools are the same as the ones used for the underlying C/C++ compilers:

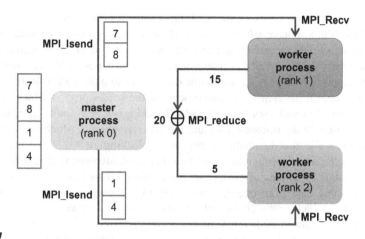

FIG. 6.7

An example of an MPI program which adds the elements of a vector using two workers to improve workload performance.

```
% mpicc -o sum_vec sum_vec.c
```

Once built, multiple processes can be launched on the same machine invoking the `mpiexec` tool as follows (using the MPICH implementation):

```
% mpiexec -n <num of processes> ./sum_vec [args]
```

The $-n$ parameter allows the user to specify the number of processes for the MPI job, which is then supplied to the application through the `MPI_Comm_size` routine. Note that in our example, it is expected the MPI job executes with at least two processes, since one of the processes acts as the master, and the remaining processes act as the workers. We can spawn processes across multiple machine nodes by supplying a file capturing information about all available hosts:

```
% mpiexec -n <num of processes> -f machines ./sum_vec [args]
```

The *machines* file has the following format:

```
host1
host2:2 # comment
```

In this file, "host1" and "host2" are the hostnames of the machine nodes we want to deploy the MPI job. The ":2" specifies the maximum number of processes that can be spawned in a specific machine, usually taking into account the number of available cores. If the number of processes is not specified, then ":1" is assumed. Note that the master node (machine) is where the MPI job is launched (i.e., where mpiexec is executed), and it should have *ssh* access to all slave nodes, typically not requiring password (though SSH key authentication). In cases where an MPI job requires slave nodes to store data, then the NFS distributed file system can be used on cluster nodes.

MPI supports two types of communication: point to point and collective. Point-to-point communication involves two processes: the *sender* process which packs all the necessary data and uses the MPI_Send (blocking) or MPI_Isend (nonblocking) routines to initiate the transmission; and the *receiver* process which acknowledges that it is to receive this data with the MPI_Recv (blocking) or MPI_Irecv (nonblocking). The collective communication, on the other hand, involves all the processes in a communicator. Examples of collective communication include MPI_Bcast which sends the same data from one process to all other processes in a communicator, MPI_Scatter which sends chunks of an array to different processes, MPI_Gather which receives data from different processes and gathers them to a single process, and MPI_Reduce, which, as we have seen in our example, performs an operation on data received from different processes.

Both types of communication routines, point to point and collective, allow the implementation of a diverse set of well-known distributed computing patterns, such as master-slave, scatter-gather, stencil, pipeline, and ring, as illustrated in Fig. 6.8. The master-slave pattern employs a coordinator process which is responsible for distributing workload to the remaining processes. The *scatter-gather* pattern, as previously mentioned, is a variant of the master-slave pattern in which a process (e.g., the master) performs the reduce phase. The stencil pattern allows processes to communicate with their neighbors, while the pipeline pattern decomposes computations

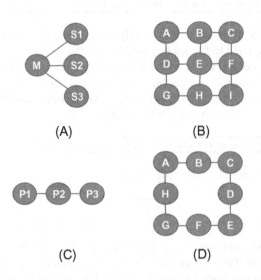

(A)   (B)

(C)   (D)

FIG. 6.8

Distributed computation patterns: (A) master-slave; (B) stencil; (C) pipeline; (C) ring.

into a set of stages that performs in parallel. The ring pattern distributes the workload similarly to the pipeline pattern; however, the last process (stage) communicates with the first.

In MPI, the selection of which distributed pattern to use depends largely on two factors, namely, the level of concurrency inherent in the application and which pattern can maximize workload distribution. The level of concurrency can be derived by using dataflow analyses and/or other techniques (such as polyhedral analysis) to uncover potential concurrency. If the algorithm is embarrassingly parallel, meaning that it exhibits no data dependences, then patterns such as master-slave or scatter-gather are often used. Other forms of concurrency patterns, such as the stencil pattern, occur in algorithms that update all array elements at regular time steps, such as in image processing. Nonparallel loops may still be optimized using the pipeline or ring execution patterns, which preserve the order of execution of the iterations, but execute parts of the loop body in parallel in a sequence of stages (P1, P2, P3...).

A fundamental issue of any form of parallel execution consists in maximizing performance. To achieve it, programmers must ensure that computational resources are adjusted to support a given workload and not the converse. In other words, the workload size and type should dictate what and which (of the available) resources should be used. In addition, when parallelizing a program and distributing its workload, programmers need to ensure that all resources operate as close to their peak performance as possible. A common issue when decomposing a problem into work chunks and mapping them to available processors is the potential reduction in arithmetic intensity, as each processor performs less work and thus becomes more prone to be bound by memory or I/O operations. Hence, the number of processors used in an MPI job must be adjusted to the given workload. This is not the case with the example provided at the beginning of this section, which is designed to use all processing elements available regardless of the vector size, and where the partition size is computed as a function of the number of processing elements available. This simple partition strategy leads to nonoptimal performance when the number of processing elements is comparably larger than the size of the vector.

To address the issue of adjusting resources to workload, programmers can use performance models to estimate how the application performs for a given workload size and number (and type) of resources. These performance models are derived by profiling the application on a set of representative workloads and then applying statistical analysis (such as regression). More details about workload distribution are provided in Chapter 7 in the context of heterogeneous platforms.

Regarding the running example described in Section 6.1—matrix multiplication $(C = AB)$, an obvious way to parallelize this problem consists in using the master-slave pattern: each worker computes a set of rows of matrix C independently, provided it has the necessary rows from matrix A and a copy of matrix B. The master therefore needs to partition matrix A and send the corresponding partition to each worker:

```
if (rank == 0) { // master
  for (i = 1; i < nprocs; i++) { // for each worker other than the master
    partition_size = (nX / (nprocs - 1)); // calculate partition without master
    lower_bound = (i - 1) * partition_size;
    if (((i + 1) == nprocs) && ((nX % (nprocs - 1)) != 0)) {
      upper_bound = nX; //last worker gets all the remaining rows
    } else {
      upper_bound = lower_bound + partition_size; // rows are equally divisable
    }
    // send the lower bound first to the intended worker
    MPI_Isend(&lower_bound, 1, MPI_INT, i, MTAG, MPI_COMM_WORLD, &request);
    // send the upper bound without blocking to the intended worker
    MPI_Isend(&upper_bound, 1, MPI_INT, i, MTAG + 1, MPI_COMM_WORLD, &request);
    // send the row partition [A] to the intended worker
    MPI_Isend(&A[lower_bound*nY], (upper_bound - lower_bound) * nY, MPI_DOUBLE, i,
              MTAG + 2, MPI_COMM_WORLD, &request);
  }
}
```

Next, matrix B is broadcasted from the master to all the workers. This requires a single routine call which must be performed by all participants (workers and master):

```
//broadcast [B] to all the slaves
MPI_Bcast(B, nY*nZ, MPI_DOUBLE, 0, MPI_COMM_WORLD);
```

Once the workers receive their corresponding portion of matrix **A**, they can compute the sections of the matrix C independently:

```
if (rank > 0) {
  //receive lower bound from the master
  MPI_Recv(&lower_bound, 1, MPI_INT, 0, MTAG, MPI_COMM_WORLD, &status);
  // receive upper bound from the master
  MPI_Recv(&upper_bound, 1, MPI_INT, 0, MTAG + 1, MPI_COMM_WORLD, &status);
  // receive [A] row partition from the master
  MPI_Recv(&A[low_bound*nY], (upper_bound - lower_bound) * nY, MPI_DOUBLE, 0,
           MTAG + 2, MPI_COMM_WORLD, &status);

  // iterate through the given set of rows of [A]
  for (i=lower_bound; i<upper_bound; i++)
    for (j = 0; j < nZ; j++)
      for (k = 0; k < nY; k++)
        C[i*nZ+j] += (A[i*nY+k] * B[k*nZ+j]);

  //send back the lower bound first to the master
  MPI_Isend(&lower_bound, 1, MPI_INT, 0, STAG, MPI_COMM_WORLD, &request);
  //send the upper bound to the master
  MPI_Isend(&upper_bound, 1, MPI_INT, 0, STAG + 1, MPI_COMM_WORLD, &request);
  // send the processed rows of C to the master
  MPI_Isend(&C[lower_bound*nZ], (upper_bound - lower_bound) * nZ, MPI_DOUBLE, 0,
            STAG + 2, MPI_COMM_WORLD, &request);
}
```

The master now gathers different sections of the computed C matrix to assemble or produce the final result:

```
/* master gathers processed work*/
if (rank == 0) {
    for (i = 1; i < nprocs; i++) {
        //receive lower bound from the worker
        MPI_Recv(&lower_bound, 1, MPI_INT, i, STAG, MPI_COMM_WORLD, &status);
        //receive upper bound from a slave
        MPI_Recv(&upper_bound, 1, MPI_INT, i, STAG + 1, MPI_COMM_WORLD, &status);
        //receive processed data from worker
        MPI_Recv(&C[low_bound*nZ], (upper_bound - lower_bound) * nZ, MPI_DOUBLE, i,
                STAG + 2, MPI_COMM_WORLD, &status);
    }
}
```

This implementation is not optimal, as it requires sending matrix **B** over the network for every worker. Given its importance, there has been considerable research on how to reduce communication bandwidth and increase parallelism for this problem, including using stencil distributed patterns and performing block matrix decompositions [15].

6.7 CACHE-BASED PROGRAM OPTIMIZATIONS

Despite considerable advances in computer architectures and in compilation techniques aimed at accelerating computations, often the bottleneck in performance lies in the relatively long latencies of memory and I/O, with data not arriving fast enough to the CPU to be processed at full computational rate. In this context, it is important to leverage the different types of memories available in the system, in particular to use as much as possible faster memories or caches. Because data is transferred transparently (without manual intervention) between slower and faster memories, it is important to understand how they operate to make effective use of them.

Caches exploit the principle of locality. This principle takes into consideration two aspects. The first, *temporal locality*, states that individual memory locations once referenced are likely to be referenced again. The second, *spatial locality*, states that if a location is referenced, then it is likely that nearby locations will be referenced as well. Hence, whenever a data element or an instruction is sought, the system first verifies if it is in the cache, otherwise the system loads it automatically from the slower memories (e.g., RAM) to the faster memories (e.g., cache L3, L2, and L1), including data or instructions from nearby locations. The goal is to maximize the use of the cache (minimizing the number of cache misses), thus increasing the performance of the application.

CACHE-OBLIVIOUS ALGORITHMS

Cache-oblivious algorithms are designed to make effective use of CPU cache systems. However, unlike explicit blocking algorithms and other cache-aware algorithms, these algorithms do not depend on explicit hardware parameters, such as cache size or cache-line length. Such algorithms can thus perform well without modification on machines with different cache sizes and levels.

A cache-oblivious algorithm often employs a *recursive* divide-and-conquer approach,[a] where a problem is divided into increasingly smaller subproblems until reaching a base case. The key idea behind these algorithms is that eventually one reaches a subproblem size that fits into the available cache. This approach works regardless of the cache size and the number of levels it supports.

[a]Kumar P. "Cache-Oblivious Algorithms". Algorithms for Memory Hierarchies. Lecture Notes on Computer Science (LNCS) 2625. Springer Verlag., 2003, p. 193–212.

In the example described in Section 6.1, the matrix multiplication algorithm accesses all columns of matrix B to compute each row of matrix C. This leads to nonoptimal use of the cache if the number of columns of B is considerably larger than the cache size. In this case, every access of matrix B will lead to a cache miss and thus never use the fast memory. One way to solve this problem is to ensure that matrix B is accessed *row-wise*, and this can be achieved by performing loop interchange between the two inner loops. This is a legal operation since it does not violate the dependences of the original program:

```
void matrix_mult(float *A, float *B, float *C) {
  for (int i = 0; i < nX; i++) {
    for (int j = 0; j < nZ; j++) {
      C[i*nZ+j] = 0;
    }
  }

  for (int i = 0; i < nX; i++) {
    for (int k = 0; k < nY; k++) {
      for (int j = 0; j < nZ; j++) {
        C[i*nZ+j] += A[i*nY+k] * B[k*nZ+j];
      }
    }
  }
}
```

Optimized libraries, however, often rely on a technique called *blocking*, which involves fitting data structures in the cache. The key idea behind blocking is to completely fill the cache with a subset of a larger dataset and maximize its reuse to reduce unnecessary loads from slower memories. This blocking technique can often be performed on 1D, 2D, or 3D data structures, typically involving the *loop tiling* code transformation (see Chapter 5). A key factor in this optimization is determining the block (tile) size, which should match the cache size of the target machine.

For our matrix multiplication example, if n corresponds to both the number of rows and columns of the input matrices, we can see our algorithm employs $2n^3$ arithmetic operations (adders and multipliers) and refers to $3n^2$ data values. While this shows that the computation exhibits considerable data reuse, it may not entirely fit the cache. The following code uses loop tiling to partition the iteration space into smaller blocks of size `blk`:

```
for (int i0 = 0; i0 < nX; i0 += blk)
  for (int j0 = 0; j0 < nZ; j0 += blk)
    for (int k0 = 0; k0 < nY; k0 += blk)
      for (int i = i0; i < min(i0+ blk, nX); i++)
        for (int j = j0; j < min(j0+ blk, nZ); j++)
          for (int k = k0; k < min(k0+ blk, nY); k++)
            C[i*nZ+j] += A[i*nY+k] * B[k*nZ+j];
```

Although this code executes using the same operations as the unblocked version, the sequence of independent operations is performed differently. In this case, each iteration (`i0`, `j0`, `k0`) performs $3 \times blk^2$ memory accesses. We can now choose a `blk` value small enough such that $3 \times blk^2$ data fit in the target machine cache. Note that optimized libraries are likely to further partition the loop iteration space into more levels to make a more effective use of the cache hierarchy.

6.8 LARA STRATEGIES

In this section, we consider three problems based on topics covered in this chapter: controlling code optimizations (Section 6.8.1), leveraging a multicore CPU architecture with OpenMP (Section 6.8.2), and monitoring the execution of MPI applications (Section 6.8.3). We use LARA `aspects` to capture strategies that address these problems, allowing them to be applied automatically and systematically to different application codes with the appropriate weaver infrastructure.

6.8.1 CAPTURING HEURISTICS TO CONTROL CODE TRANSFORMATIONS

As discussed in Section 6.3.2, compilers have their own internal heuristics for applying a specific set of optimizations. With LARA, developers can describe their own strategies without changing the compiler's internal logic or manually applying them.

In the following `aspect` definition, we present a simple LARA example that inlines all calls of a function when specific criteria are satisfied. The target function name is specified through the `aspect` input parameter. In this example, we only wish to inline invoked functions if the target function (the caller) does not contain loops. It is easy to modify this strategy to include other criteria, such as based on function properties and/or to consider all the functions in the input program instead of only targeting a specific function passed as argument to the `aspect`.

```
1. aspectdef FunctionInlining
2.
3.    input
4.       funcName
5.    end
6.
7.    var inline = true;
8.
9.  /* First determines the properties of the given function */
10.   select function{funcName} end
11.   apply
12.      if($function.has_loops) {
13.          inline = false;
14.      }
15.   end
16.
17.   /* Call the function inlining action using the exec keyword */
18.   select function.call{funcName} end
19.   apply
20.      if(inline) {
21.          $call.exec inline();
22.          println("function "+$call.name+" inlined in "+$function.name+"\n");
23.      }
24.   end
25.   println('\n FunctionInlining done!');
26. end
```

In this `aspect`, we use the `inline` variable to identify whether the target function should be inlined or not. This is verified in lines 10–15, which checks whether the function code has loops. If it does not then the `aspect` invokes the inline action for each call in the target function (line 21).

6.8.2 PARALLELIZING CODE WITH OpenMP

As described in Section 6.5, OpenMP offers several mechanisms to parallelize sequential descriptions on multicore CPU architectures. The choice of which mechanism to use depends largely on how the original code is structured and the level of concurrency that can be attained from the code.

In the following example, we target loops using OpenMP's *loop* worksharing directive `omp parallel for` which distributes loop iterations through a specified number of threads. The operating system will then schedule these threads to the available processing cores. There are two considerations to take into account in our optimization strategy. First, we need to decide which loops should be optimized; and second, how many threads should we allocate to each loop selected for optimization. Both considerations are meant to ensure that computations can benefit from parallelization, which can be adversely affected if there is not enough computational workload. The LARA `aspect` definition that captures our strategy is presented as follows:

```
1.  aspectdef AutoOmpLoop
2.      input
3.          numCores
4.      end
5.
6.      select loop end
7.      apply
8.          var nt;
9.          if ($loop.iterCpuShare > 0.80) {
10.             nt = numCores;
11.         } else if ($loop.iterCpuShare > 0.30) {
12.             nt = numCores * 2;
13.         } else {
14.             nt = numCores * 3;
15.         }
16.
17.         var numThreadsSpec = "num_threads(" + nt.toString() + ")";
18.
19.         $loop.insert before "#pragma omp for schedule(guided) " + numThreadsSpec;
20.     end
21.     condition $loop.type == "for" &&
22.               $loop.isOutermost &&
23.               $loop.isParallel &&
24.               $loop.isHotspot end
25. end
```

This `aspect` selects all loops in the program (line 6) and then filters this list according to the criteria defined (lines 21–24). We are interested in outermost "for" loops which are parallel and have been identified as hotspots. The type of loop (e.g., "for") and its nested level are static attributes of the loop that can be determined directly by a weaver at compile time through a simple inspection of the code structure. We can also determine whether a loop is parallel (i.e., all its iterations can execute in any order) by statically analyzing the code, either directly through the weaver, or through an external tool (see Section 3.5.5). This information is then integrated as an attribute (in this case `isParallel`) of each corresponding loop in the context of the weaver. The `isHotspot` attribute must be computed dynamically by profiling the application with a representative input dataset identifying the fraction of execution time over the total execution time threshold in which each part of the code becomes a hotspot. The profiling can be carried out by an external tool using a similar process as described for the parallel attribute or by LARA `aspects` that instrument the application to time its execution as described in Section 4.5.1.

Once loops have been selected for optimization, we still wish to compute the number of threads to assign for its execution (lines 8–17). For this purpose, we parameterize this `aspect` to get the number of available cores in this system (line 3). Our strategy for determining the number of threads is empirical and requires the `iterCpuShare` attribute, which must also be computed dynamically in a similar process as the `isHotspot` attribute and determines the CPU share of running a single iteration sequentially. The `iterCpuShare` attribute indicates whether the iteration is compute bound—say running 80% or more of the CPU share, or memory/IO bound in this case running 20% or less. Intuitively, if the computation is compute bound, we want to match the number of threads to the number of available cores. If it is memory or IO bound, we use more threads to reduce the number of idle cores. The heuristics used to determine the number of threads can be easily changed or adapted in this aspect to capture more complex conditions and metrics. Finally, we instrument selected loops (line 19) with the OpenMP directive #pragma omp for with the identified number of threads.

6.8.3 MONITORING AN MPI APPLICATION

MPI applications can be difficult to monitor and debug since they consist of multiple communicating parallel processes, each of them running in their own memory space. A simple strategy for monitoring and tracing execution, as mentioned in Chapter 4, is to wrap library functions with augmented functionality, which in this case would monitor the behavior of each MPI process.

In our strategy, we develop a new monitoring library, e.g., TrackMPI, for tracking the behavior of each MPI routine used in the program. To ease the integration of TrackMPI on existing MPI programs, we name each monitoring routine after the corresponding MPI routine, prefixing it with "Track." Hence, TrackMPI_Recv tracks calls to MPI_Recv. All that remains is to replace the original MPI calls with the corresponding monitoring calls, which is performed by the following aspect:

```
1. aspectdef TrackMPI
2.
3.    select file end
4.    apply
5.       $file.exec addInclude("mpi_track.h", true);
6.    end
7.
8.    var mpiFn = [ "MPI_Init",
9.                  "MPI_Comm_size",
10.                  "MPI_Comm_rank",
11.                  "MPI_Finalize",
12.                  "MPI_Send",
13.                  "MPI_Isend",
14.                  "MPI_Recv",
15.                  "MPI_IRecv",
16.                  "MPI_Bsend",
17.                  "MPI_Scatter",
18.                  "MPI_Gather" ];
19.
20.    select function.call end
21.    apply
22.       var name = $call.name;
23.
24.       if (mpiFn.indexOf(name) > - 1) {
25.          $call.exec setName("Track" + name);
26.       }
27.    end
28. end
```

In this aspect, we include the TrackMPI header (lines 3–6) containing all the declarations of this library at the beginning of every source file. Next, we declare a list of all MPI functions we wish to track (lines 8–18). Finally, we find all function calls in the source code (line 20) and add the prefix "Track" to its name (line 25).

Note that this simple aspect assumes that each TrackMPI routine has the same prototype declaration as its corresponding MPI routine and that it invokes this MPI routine before or after tracking its activity. One implementation of TrackMPI could involve tracking the name of the routine called, place a timestamp, and add additional information such as the rank of the participant and the size of data received or transferred. Because each MPI process runs independently, information generated by each process needs to be merged when terminating the MPI job. This can be done transparently by TrackMPI_Finalize when invoked by the process with rank 0 (by definition, the master process). A more complex TrackMPI library could generate a graph capturing the skeleton of the MPI job, tracking the total amount of data in and out of each process. Such powerful tracking tool can still use the same aspect presented earlier, regardless of the size and complexity of the application.

6.9 SUMMARY

This chapter described compiler options, optimizations, and the use of developer's knowledge to guide compilers when targeting CPU-based computing platforms. In the topic of compiler options, we restrict our focus on optimizations most compilers provide, as opposed to code transformations and optimizations covered extensively in Chapter 5 and that need to be applied manually or by specialized source-to-source compilers.

This chapter also focused on loop vectorization as an important optimization to support SIMD units in contemporary CPUs (see Chapter 2). Given the multicore and multiple CPU trends, this chapter described the use of OpenMP and MPI to target shared and distributed memory architectures, respectively, and how they address concurrency. Lastly, this chapter introduced cache optimizations, as an important transformation to accelerate applications targeting the hierarchical memory organization of most CPU-based computing platforms.

6.10 FURTHER READING

The selection of compiler flags and compiler sequences that can optimize the performance of specific types of applications has been the focus of many research efforts.

For example, the exploration of compiler sequences (phase ordering) has been recently addressed by many authors, and some research efforts address this problem using machine learning techniques (see, e.g., [6] and [24]). Compiler phase selection and phase ordering has been explored by many authors (see, e.g., [5,9][25]). Purini and Jain [25] proposed a method to generate N-compiler sequences that for a set of applications offer better results than the predefined optimization sequences provided by the – Ox options. The approach in Ref. [5] has mainly the goal of providing a compiler sequence for each function using clustering to reduce the size of the design space.

With respect to the selection of compiler flags, the work in Ref. [26] provides an overview of machine learning techniques for selecting the compiler flags that are more effective in improving performance when compared to the ones used by –Ox options.

Loop auto-vectorization has been focused by many researchers (see, e.g., Ref. [16–18]), including the vectorization of outer loops (see, e.g., Ref. [19]).

For further reading about OpenMP we suggest the book by Chapman et al. [20] and the resources provided at Ref. [21]. For MPI, we suggest the books by Pacheco [22] and Gropp et al. [23].

REFERENCES

[1] BLAS (Basic Linear Algebra Subprograms). http://www.netlib.org/blas/ [Accessed January 2017].

[2] Whaley R, Dongarra JJ. Automatically tuned linear algebra software. In: Proceedings of the ACM/IEEE conference on supercomputing (SC'98), Washington, DC: IEEE Computer Society; 1998. p. 1–27.

[3] Ghosh D. DSLs in action. 1st ed. Greenwich, CT: Manning Publications Co; 2010.

[4] 3.10 Options that control optimization. https://gcc.gnu.org/onlinedocs/gcc/Optimize-Options.html [Accessed May 2016].

[5] Martins LGA, Nobre R, Cardoso JMP, Delbem ACB, Marques E. Clustering-based selection for the exploration of compiler optimization sequences. ACM Trans Archit Code Optim 2016;13(1). Article 8, 28 pages.

[6] Agakov F, Bonilla E, Cavazos J, Franke B, Fursin G, O'Boyle MFP, et al. Using machine learning to focus iterative optimization. In: Proceedings of the international symposium on code generation and optimization (CGO'06), March 26–29; 2006. p. 295–305.

[7] Kulkarni S, Cavazos J. Mitigating the compiler optimization phase-ordering problem using machine learning. In: Proc. of the ACM intl. conf. on object oriented programming systems languages and applications (OOPSLA'12), New York, NY: ACM; 2012. p. 147–62.

[8] Almagor L, Cooper KD, Grosul A, Harvey TJ, Reeves SW, Subramanian D, et al. Finding effective compilation sequences. In: Proceedings of the 2004 ACM SIGPLAN/SIGBED conference on languages, compilers, and tools for embedded systems (LCTES'04), New York, NY: ACM; 2004. p. 231–9.

[9] Cooper KD, Subramanian D, Torczon L. Adaptive optimizing compilers for the 21st century. J Supercomput 2002;23(1):7–22.

[10] Lattner C, Adve V. LLVM: a compilation framework for lifelong program analysis & transformation. In: Proceedings of the international symposium on code generation and optimization: feedback-directed and runtime optimization (CGO'04), March 20–24, San Jose, CA: IEEE Computer Society; 2004. p. 75–88.

[11] Auto-vectorization in GCC. http://gcc.gnu.org/projects/tree-ssa/vectorization.html [Accessed September 2016].

[12] A guide to auto-vectorization with Intel C++ compilers. https://software.intel.com/en-us/articles/a-guide-to-auto-vectorization-with-intel-c-compilers [Accessed July 2016].

[13] Auto-vectorization in LLVM. http://llvm.org/docs/Vectorizers.html [Accessed October 2016].

[14] Dagum L, Menon R. OpenMP: an industry standard API for shared-memory programming. IEEE Comput Sci Eng 1998;5(1):46–55.

[15] Irony D, Toledo S, Tiskin A. Communication lower bounds for distributed-memory matrix multiplication. J Parallel Distrib Comput 2004;64(9):1017–26.

[16] Allen R, Kennedy K. Automatic translation of FORTRAN programs to vector form. ACM Trans Program Lang Syst 1987;9(4):491–542.

[17] Eichenberger AE, Wu P, O'Brien K. Vectorization for SIMD architectures with alignment constraints. In: Proceedings of the ACM SIGPLAN 2004 conference on programming language design and implementation (PLDI'04), New York, NY: ACM; 2014. p. 82–93.

[18] Larsen S, Amarasinghe S. Exploiting superword level parallelism with multimedia instruction sets. In: Proceedings of the ACM SIGPLAN conference on programming language design and implementation (PLDI'00), New York, NY: ACM; 2000. p. 145–56.

[19] Nuzman D, Zaks A. Outer-loop vectorization: revisited for short SIMD architectures. In: Proceedings of the 17th international conference on parallel architectures and compilation techniques (PACT'08), New York, NY: ACM; 2008. p. 2–11.

[20] Chapman B, Jost G, van der Pas R. Using OpenMP: portable shared memory parallel programming. Scientific and engineering computation. Cambridge, MA: The MIT Press; 2007.

[21] The OpenMP API specification for parallel programming. http://www.openmp.org/ [Accessed June 2016].

[22] Pacheco PS. Parallel programming with MPI. San Francisco, CA: Morgan Kaufmann Publishers Inc.; 1996.

[23] Gropp W, Lusk E, Skjellum A. Using MPI: portable parallel programming with the message-passing interface. 3rd ed. Cambridge, MA: MIT Press; 2014.

[24] Fursin G, Kashnikov Y, Memon AW, Chamski Z, Temam O, Namolaru M, et al. Milepost GCC: machine learning enabled self-tuning compiler. Int J Parallel Prog 2011;39(3):296–27.

[25] Purini S, Jain L. Finding good optimization sequences covering program space. In: Proceedings of the ACM Transactions on Architecture and Code Optimization (TACO). vol. 9(4). New York, NY: ACM Press; 2013.

[26] Ashouri AH, Mariani G, Palermo G, Park E, Cavazos J, Silvano C. COBAYN: compiler autotuning framework using Bayesian networks. In: ACM Trans. Archit. Code Optim. vol. 13(2), Article 21. New York, NY: ACM Press; 2016.

Targeting heterogeneous computing platforms

7

7.1 INTRODUCTION

High-level languages, such as C and C++, are designed to allow code to be portable across different types of computation platforms, in contrast to *assembly* language in which the level of abstraction is close to the machine code instruction set. Compilers are responsible for translating such high-level descriptions into efficient instructions, allowing application code to be mostly oblivious to the underlying architecture. This approach worked well during the single-core era, in which CPU-based processors became incrementally more powerful by successive increases in clock frequencies and by the introduction of specialized instruction sets that could be automatically exploited by compilers with little or no effort from developers. However, due to the physical limits concerning heat dissipation and gate delays, CPU speeds ceased to increase. This stagnation gave way to more complex platforms that: (a) embraced native hardware support for parallel execution with more independent processing cores; (b) became more heterogeneous to support specialized and customized computation; and (c) became more distributed to support applications requiring large-scale computations, including Big Data and HPC. However, this considerable increase in computation capacity came at a cost: the burden of optimization shifted from compilers back to developers.

In this chapter, we expand on the topic of code retargeting introduced in Chapter 6, covering techniques geared toward specialized computing devices (GPUs and FPGAs) and heterogeneous platforms in general. Code retargeting is the process of optimizing the application source code to run more efficiently on a particular platform architecture. The most basic computation platform corresponds to a single type of computing device, such as a general-purpose processor (e.g., a multicore CPU) or a hardware accelerator (e.g., FPGAs and GPUs). We can build a more complex and heterogeneous computing platform by combining general-purpose processors with hardware accelerators. Applications targeting these heterogeneous platforms run on general-purpose processors and offload critical parts of their computation to hardware accelerators.

The structure of this chapter is as follows. In Section 7.2, we cover the roofline model and explain how it can guide the code retargeting process. In Section 7.3, we focus on the problem of workload distribution, which deals with how computations can be effectively offloaded to hardware accelerators in a heterogeneous platform. Section 7.4 covers the OpenCL framework for targeting CPU platforms with GPU

227

Embedded Computing for High Performance. http://dx.doi.org/10.1016/B978-0-12-804189-5.00007-7

accelerators, and Section 7.5 focuses on the high-level synthesis (HLS) process for translating C programs into FPGA hardware designs. Section 7.6 presents two LARA strategies assisting HLS. The remaining sections conclude this chapter and provide further reading on the topics presented in this chapter.

7.2 ROOFLINE MODEL REVISITED

When retargeting an application to a complex heterogeneous platform, it is important to understand the main characteristics of the application's workload, as well as the features of the target architecture.

We begin with the workload characterization. The way we characterize workloads depends largely on the type of application we are targeting. For instance, for floating-point applications it is relevant to count the *number* of floating-point operations. We can extend this workload characterization by also counting the number of bytes transferred between the memory and the processor when executing load and store operations. In general, the application workload is proportional to the problem size: a large problem, such as a 1000×1000 matrix multiplication, leads to a larger workload than a 100×100 matrix multiplication since the former computation requires a larger number of operations and bytes transferred.

We now assume a simple platform consisting of one compute node and one memory unit. To estimate the time required to execute a given workload, defined as (#*operations*, #*bytes moved*), we need two pieces of information about the platform: the computational throughput (how many operations the compute node can process per second) and memory bandwidth (the rate at which data is read from or stored to memory).

It is important to note that the computational throughput is often not a constant but rather a function of the size of data processed. This is true, for instance, when computer architectures have deep processing pipelines, requiring them to be filled to attain maximum throughput. However, the most prevalent factor preventing peak performance is that *the rate at which the compute node processes data is dependent on the rate at which it can access data*. In other words, if the data access rate is lower than the computation throughput then bandwidth becomes a performance bottleneck.

This implies that the workload distribution needs to account not only the computation throughput for each of the platform compute nodes, but also data movements, in terms of data size and data access rate, as these factors directly affect performance. For this reason, it is useful to consider another metric to characterize and compare workloads: *operational intensity*, which is the ratio of total number of operations to the total data movement (bytes): $\frac{\#operations}{\#bytes\,moved}$ Flops/byte. For instance, FFTs typically perform at around 2 Flops/byte, while N-body simulation performs in the order of tens of Flops/byte. Intuitively, algorithms requiring more cycles dedicated to data operations (loads and stores) than computation operations will typically exhibit lower computational intensity and be more likely to be memory bound. Conversely, algorithms requiring more computation than data movement will have a higher computational intensity and be more likely to be compute bound.

The roofline performance model [1,2], introduced in Chapter 2, provides a useful visualization of how a given application (or one of its kernels) performs when exploiting various architectural and runtime features of a specific platform (e.g., multicore, hardware accelerators, cache memories). The most basic roofline model can be derived by plotting the computational throughput (y-axis) as a function of operational intensity (x-axis). The resultant curve, as presented in Fig. 7.1, defines *two* performance bounds under which the application performance exists: the memory bandwidth ceiling and the computation performance ceiling, both of which are platform specific. As expected, implementations with high operational intensity will hit the peak computation ceiling as they require more computation than data movement, otherwise they will hit the memory bandwidth ceiling.

When retargeting an application or a kernel to a specific platform, we seek implementations that perform as close as possible to the peak computation performance of the platform. In the example presented in Fig. 7.1, only implementation Z hits this ceiling. While it may not always be possible to achieve peak computation performance, especially in cases where an algorithm has inherently low computational demands, the following techniques can be used to maximize performance:

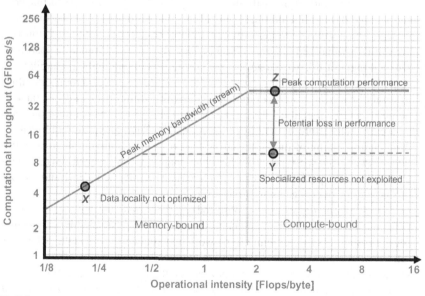

FIG. 7.1

Roofline model showing the attained performance of three application (kernel) implementations (*X, Y, Z*) on a specific platform.

- *Data locality.* Given that modern-day platforms contain several types of memory storage units, with different sizes, speeds, and access models (shared or distributed), it is important to improve data locality, such that compute units can access data as fast as they can process them. This means making effective use of multilevel cache systems (Section 6.7) and using local device memories to store intermediate results for hardware accelerators working as coprocessors. Other techniques to improve data locality include *software data prefetching*, which are used to mitigate the long latency of memory accesses either from main storage or from upper levels of the cache hierarchy and thus reduce the stall cycles in the execution pipeline of modern processors. The basic idea behind prefetching is to load data in advance to hide the latency of memory accesses, hence making data already available when the computation needs it. If the hardware supports prefetching instructions and buffers, compilers can exploit them by judiciously placing prefetching instructions in the code. When data locality is not optimized, there is a risk of increasing the amount of data movement (e.g., due to cache misses or having superfluous transfers between CPU and hardware accelerators), which leads to lower operational intensity and designs becoming memory (or I/O) bound, as is the case of implementation X shown in Fig. 7.1.

- *Heterogeneous computation.* General-purpose processors are flexible enough to execute most workloads. However, this flexibility comes at the price of having a relatively low performance ceiling. Consequently, even implementations with a lower computational intensity may quickly hit the platform's performance ceiling (see dashed line on implementation Y shown in Fig. 7.1). To further increase the height of the performance ceiling, developers need to exploit the platform's specialized features. The key idea is to map a given workload (or selected parts of this workload) to specialized processing units, including: (i) packing scalar instructions into vector instructions to perform more operations in parallel (Section 6.4); (ii) running a kernel in parallel over multiple data points on a GPU (Section 7.4); (iii) streaming data across a customized pipelined data path architecture on an FPGA (Section 7.5). Such mapping requires a deep understanding of the architectural features of the compute devices (CPU, GPU, FPGA) and the type of workload amenable to run on such devices. This effort allows the peak performance to increase, typically between 1 and 2 orders of magnitude, over a general-purpose processor.

- *Multicore and multiprocessors.* With today's platforms consisting of multicore CPU machines with computation capacities that can be extended by connecting several machines together with fast network interconnects, there is the potential to run very large computationally intensive workloads. Such workloads can be partitioned within the cores and processors of each machine (Section 6.5) and across available machines (Section 6.6), such that each compute unit operates at its peak computational throughput. The process of partitioning and mapping workload can be done statically if all parameters (e.g., workload type and size) are known at compile time, or otherwise decided dynamically by the platform's runtime system.

7.3 **WORKLOAD DISTRIBUTION**

As discussed in the previous section, it is important to understand both the nature of the application and the features of the underlying platform to derive an efficient mapping between them. This is particularly critical, as platforms are becoming more heterogeneous, allowing various types of hardware accelerators to assist in speeding up computations running on the host processor. Hence, we need to understand in what conditions should we offload computations to these devices and what factors affect overall performance. This is the subject of this section.

When computations are offloaded to an accelerator, there is a cost overhead that is absent when the entire computation is carried out by the host processor, namely:

1. Data transfer to and from the host to the accelerator's storage or address space.
2. Synchronization to initiate and terminate the computation by the accelerator.

Given the current system-level organization of most computing systems, data needs to be physically copied between storage devices often via a bus. This has been traditionally the major source of overhead when dealing with accelerators. Furthermore, the host needs to actively engage in polling to observe the termination of the computations on the accelerators, thus synchronization also incurs an overhead, which is typically proportional to the number of tasks to be offloaded to the accelerators.

Hence, in cases where the host and the accelerators execute in sequence (i.e., the host blocks until the accelerator terminates execution), it is only profitable to offload kernels to accelerators if they exhibit a very high operational intensity (the ratio of computation to data used—see previous section). Furthermore, for offloading to be profitable, the accelerator needs to execute the computation considerably faster than the host to offset the aforementioned overheads.

To measure the benefits of offloading, we need to first select one or more metrics of performance, such as execution time and energy consumption. Typically, developers compare the execution time of a kernel running on the host for each relevant problem of size n, i.e., $T_{\text{comp}}^{\text{host}}(n)$, against the time it takes to perform the same computation using an accelerator, say $T_{\text{comp}}^{\text{accel}}(n)$.

Note that the execution time (or another metric such as energy) can depend nonlinearly on the problem size. For linear algebra operations, such as matrix-matrix multiplications, simple algorithms can be described as having a computational complexity that increases with the cube of the input matrix dimension size n *(the number of columns or rows for squared matrices)*, i.e., the computation time on the host can be modeled as $T_{\text{comp}}^{\text{host}}(n) = \alpha_0 n^3 + \beta_0$ for a square matrix with dimension size n. For other computations, the complexity might be quadratic as in $T_{\text{comp}}^{\text{host}}(n) = \alpha_0 n^2 + \beta_0$. When the same computation is executed on an accelerator, while the complexity may not change, the values of the coefficients α_0 and β_0 may be different due to other sources of overhead, namely, data transfer cost.

To assess the benefits and hence to aid in deciding whether to offload computations, programmers can build execution models for the host and for the accelerator, capturing both execution time and any additional overheads for a given problem size. As an example, consider the following two execution models:

1. *Blocking coprocessor execution model.* In this execution model, the host processor is responsible for transferring data to and from the accelerator storage space (or simply copying it to a selected region of its own address space) and by initiating and observing the completion of a task's execution by the accelerator. While the host processor can carry on other unrelated computations as the accelerator is computing, it is often the responsibility of the host to check when the accelerator has terminated its execution. The following analytical expression (Eq. 7.1) captures the execution time of this model:

$$T_{\text{comp}}^{\text{accel}}(n) = T_{\text{comm}}^{\text{host2accel}}(n) + T_{\text{exec}}^{\text{accel}}(n) + T_{\text{comm}}^{\text{accel2host}}(n) \tag{7.1}$$

Clearly, for an accelerator operating under this execution model to be effective, the data transfer time needs to be either reduced to a minimum or hidden as is the case of the nonblocking model as explained next.

2. *Nonblocking coprocessor execution model.* In this execution model, and after triggering the execution of the first task on the accelerator, the host can initiate a second task (if is independent from the previous one) by transferring the data for the second task to the accelerator while the accelerator is carrying out the computation corresponding to the first task.

The analytical expression in (Eq. 7.2) captures the execution time of this model for a "steady state" operation mode, where the communication for the first and the last task is ignored, and where the *max* function is used to capture the fact that if the computation takes longer than the communication, the accelerator will delay the communication or if the data transfer from the host to the accelerator takes longer than the computation of the previous task, the accelerator will stall.

$$T_{\text{comp}}^{\text{accel}}(n) = \max\left(T_{\text{comm}}^{\text{host2accel}}(n) + T_{\text{comm}}^{\text{accel2host}}(n), \ T_{\text{exec}}^{\text{accel}}(n)\right) \tag{7.2}$$

This model is only possible if there are no dependences between the two computations and there is enough memory space to save the data for the computation scheduled to be executed next. This execution model reaches its maximum benefit when the communication between the host and the accelerator can be entirely masked by the computation, and excluding the initial and final computations, the execution time is simply dictated by the maximum duration of the communication or the accelerator execution.

Given the execution models described earlier, and under the assumption developers can accurately model the various sources of overhead, it is possible to determine when it is profitable to use an accelerator to execute a set of computational tasks based on the problem (workload) size n. For simplicity, we assume the overall computation is composed of a series of tasks with the same data sizes.

Using the execution models earlier, we can depict in a chart when it becomes profitable to offload the computation's execution to an accelerator with the two execution models. Fig. 7.2 illustrates when it is profitable to offload the computation to an accelerator in both execution models described earlier. In this illustrative

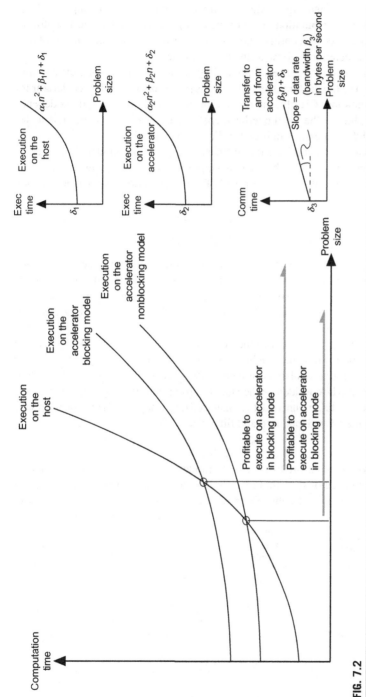

FIG. 7.2

Illustration of computation time with and without accelerator using blocking and nonblocking execution models. This depiction assumes a quadratic computational effort with respect to the input problem size and the linear cost for data transfer to and from the accelerator (shown on the right-hand side of the figure).

example, we have assumed a quadratic cost model with respect to the input problem (or data) size for the computation effort of the host processor and the accelerator for any of the tasks involved. In contrast, the communication costs for the transfer of data to and from the accelerator follow a linear cost model.

This figure depicts two breakeven points beyond which, and despite the communication overhead of the data transfer, it becomes profitable to use the accelerator for offloading computation. Clearly, the relative position of these breakpoints depends on the relative values of the fixed overhead costs, δ, and the α and β coefficients for the various model components outlined in Eqs. (7.1) and (7.2).

The performance speedup for either of these two execution models is thus given by the expression in Eq. (7.3), which can asymptotically reach the raw performance benefit of an accelerator when the overhead of communication and synchronization reaches zero.

$$\text{SpeedUp} = \frac{T_{\text{comp}}^{\text{host}}}{T_{\text{comp}}^{\text{accel}}} = \frac{T_{\text{exec}}^{\text{host}}}{T_{\text{exec}}^{\text{accel}}} \tag{7.3}$$

Note that while it may be profitable to offload the computation to an accelerator, the problem size might become too large to fit the accelerator's internal storage. In this scenario, developers need to restructure computations by resorting to different partitioning strategies so that the data for each task considered for offloading can fit in the accelerator's storage.

The communication cost between the host and the accelerator is modeled using a simple affine function as illustrated in Fig. 7.3, where n corresponds to the problem size (Eq. 7.4), which is proportional to the amount of data transferred. Note that other application parameters can be considered when modeling communication cost. For instance, for image processing, the amount of data transferred might depend not only on the image size, but also on the color depth used and filter size.

$$T_{\text{comm}}^{\text{host2accel}} = \beta n + \delta \tag{7.4}$$

Commonly, developers resort to analytical modeling based on empirical data to model the performance of specific tasks on their accelerators. Often, this approach uses regression models to fit the observed data to an assumed analytical model

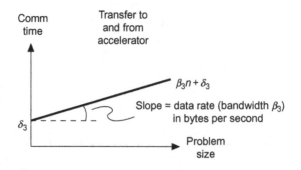

FIG. 7.3

Communication cost model between the host and the accelerator.

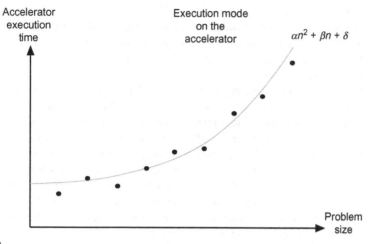

FIG. 7.4

Accelerator execution time model using empirical data and assuming a quadratic model.

(see Fig. 7.4). With these execution models, and knowing the problem size and reasonable estimates of the execution on the accelerators, developers can determine when it becomes profitable to offload computations to the accelerators. The analysis described here, although using a simple sequential execution model, can be extended (arguably not in a trivial fashion) to an execution system with multiple accelerators by adjusting the various coefficients of the communication and synchronization costs.

7.4 GRAPHICS PROCESSING UNITS

A Graphics Processing Unit (GPU)[1] is a specialized type of hardware accelerator originally designed to perform graphics processing tasks. However, with the advent of programmable shaders and floating-point support, GPUs were found to be considerably faster than CPUs for solving specific types of problems, such as scientific applications, that can be formulated as uniform streaming processes. This type of processes exploits data parallelism, applying the same kernel (operation) over a large sequence of data elements.

One popular approach for programming GPUs is OpenCL [3,4], an open standard which is currently maintained by the consortium Khronos Group. Unlike CUDA, OpenCL is vendor independent and supports a wide range of compute devices spanning from multicore CPUs to FPGAs. In this section, we consider the use of OpenCL to program GPUs in the context of a heterogeneous platform where a CPU acts as the

---

[1]It is common to use the term GPGPU (General-Purpose Graphics Processing Unit) to refer GPUs that are programmable and can support different application domains. We use the term GPU and GPGPU interchangeably since most GPUs on the market today belong to the latter category.

host and one or more hardware accelerators (GPU) act as coprocessors. In this type of platform, applications running on the host are sped up by offloading sections of the program to the GPUs. The choice of which parts of the program are offloaded to the GPU, and indeed to any hardware accelerator acting as a coprocessor, is critical to maximize overall performance.

As mentioned in the beginning of this section, data-parallel algorithms are a good fit for GPU acceleration, since the GPU architecture contains hundreds of lightweight processing units able to operate over several data items in parallel. More-over, algorithms must be computationally intensive to maximize the utilization of the GPU compute resources and in this way, hide memory latency. This is because GPUs support fast context switching: when memory accesses are required while processing a subset of data elements, this subset is put on hold, and another subset is activated to keep the GPU compute resources busy at all times. Additionally, problems requiring streaming large sequences of data are also a good fit, as they reduce the data move-ment overhead between the host and the GPU memories.

To express data parallelism in OpenCL, programmers must specify the *global dimensions* of their problem. The global dimensions specify the total problem size, describing an array of data elements processed using the same operation, known as a *kernel*. Global dimensions can be expressed in 1D, 2D, or 3D spaces depending on the algorithm. In this context, a *work-item* is an instance of the kernel that executes on one data element of the array defined in the global dimensions' space, thus being analogous to a CPU thread. Therefore the global dimensions define the number of work-items that will execute on the hardware device. Consider, for instance, the following problems:

1. *1D*: process an 8k audio sample using one thread per sample: $\sim$8 thousand work-items
2. *2D*: process a 4k frame (3840×2160) using one thread per pixel: $\sim$8 million work-items
3. *3D*: perform raytracing using a voxel volume of $256 \times 256 \times 256$: $\sim$16 million work-items

Current GPU devices are not big enough to run 16 million work-items at once, hence these items are scheduled according to available computing resources. Still, the developer is responsible for defining explicitly the total number of work-items and its dimensions according to the problem at hand. For instance, the developer can decide to process a 4k frame by using a work-item that operates on a line instead of a pixel, thus requiring a total of 2160 work-items instead of around 8 million. This affects not only the number of work-items that need to be scheduled but also the gran-ularity of each work-item.

Developers must also specify the *local dimensions* of their problem, which defines the number of work-items executing together in a *work-group*. The size of this work-group must evenly divide the global size in each dimension. Hence, if the global dimensions of a problem are 1024×1024, then 512×512 and 128×128 are valid local dimensions, but 512×100 is not valid as 100 does not evenly divide 1024. The work-groups are, thus, important as they define the set of work-items logically executed together on a physical *compute unit*, and it is only

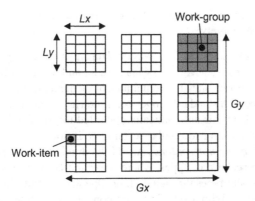

FIG. 7.5

OpenCL workgroups and work-items. The number of work-items, as well as the number and size of work-groups, deployed to an OpenCL device is defined by specifying the global (Gx, Gy) and local dimensions (Lx, Ly). Note that we use two dimensions in this example.

within the context of a work-group that work-items can be synchronized. In other words, if synchronization is required between work-items, then they need to be confined within the same work-group (see Fig. 7.5).

A *kernel* is a unit of code executed in parallel at each point of the problem domain and developers express data-parallel computations by writing OpenCL kernels. OpenCL kernels are described using the C99 language syntax, although they exhibit significant differences with respect to its software (CPU) counterpart. One common way to convert a regular CPU program to OpenCL kernels is to inspect the loops in the program and attempt to convert innermost loop statements as an operation applied at each point of the loop iteration space. We now consider the following C loop which performs element-wise multiplication of two vectors:

```
void mult(const int n, const float *a, const float *b, float *c) {
    for (int i = 0; i < n; i++) {
        c[i] = a[i] * b[i];
    }
}
```

This code can be translated to an OpenCL kernel as follows:

```
__kernel void kmult(__global const float *a,
                    __global const float *b,
                    __global float *c) {
    int id = get_global_id(0);
    c[id] = a[id] * b[id];
}
```

In this example, the kernel corresponds to the innermost loop body, which is executed n times, where n is the specified number of work-items defined by the global dimensions (in this example operating in an 1D space). The `get_global_id` routine returns the identifier of the work-item, so that it knows which data it is meant to work on.

Regarding the kernel description, OpenCL provides a few extensions to the standard C99 language, namely:

- *Vector data types and operations*. Vector data types are defined by the type name (`char`, `uchar`, `ushort`, `int`, `uint`, `float`, `long`, and `ulong`) followed by a literal value *n* which corresponds to the number of elements in the vector. These data types work with standard C operators, such as +, -, and *. The use of vectors in an OpenCL kernel is automatically compiled to exploit SIMD units if the hardware supports it, or to regular scalar code if not.
- *Rounding and conversion routines*. As in C99, implicit conversions are supported for compatible scalar data types, whereas explicit conversions are required for incompatible scalar types through casting. OpenCL extends this support for both scalars and vectors with a set of explicit conversion routines with the form: `convert_<destination_type>(source)`, as shown in the following example:

```
int8 i;
// converts an int8 vector to float8
float8 j = convert_float8(i)
```

In addition, OpenCL supports a set of rounding routines with the syntax `convert_<destination_type>[_sat][_rounding_mode](source)`, where the optional `sat` mode specifies saturation for out-of-range values to the maximum possible value the destination type can support. There is support for four rounding modes, namely: `rte` (round to the nearest even), `rtp` (round toward positive infinity), `rtz` (round toward zero), and `rtn` (round toward negative infinity). If no modifier is specified, it defaults to `rtz` for integer values and `rte` for floating point values.

- *Intrinsic functions*. OpenCL supports a number of math library functions with guaranteed accuracy, e.g., `exp`, `log`, `sin`, `fmax`, and `modf`. OpenCL also supports two additional sets of fast intrinsics versions, which provide a trade-off between precision and performance, in the form of `native_<fn>` (fastest but no accuracy guarantee) and `half_<fn>` (less performant than the corresponding native intrinsic but with higher accuracy), e.g., `native_log` and `half_log`. The use of intrinsics guarantees availability (all OpenCL compliant devices are meant to support them), thus increasing the portability of OpenCL code across heterogeneous devices.

In addition, OpenCL includes utility functions that provide information about each work-item, allowing the kernel to identify which operation to perform and on which data:

- *Global dimensions*: (1) `get_global_id(dim)`: returns a unique global work-item ID for a particular dimension; (2) `get_work_dim()`: returns the number of global dimensions; (3) `get_global_size(dim)`: returns the maximum number of global work-items in a particular dimension.
- *Local dimensions*: (1) `get_local_id(dim)`: returns a unique work-item ID for a particular dimension within its work-group; (2) `get_local_size(dim)`: returns the number of local work-items in particular dimension; (3) `get_num_groups`

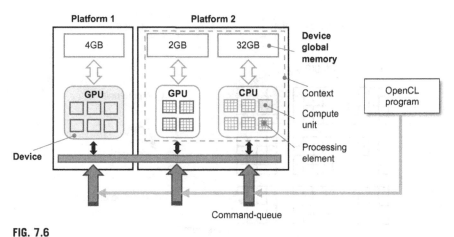

FIG. 7.6

OpenCL platform architecture.

(dim): returns the number of work-groups that will execute a kernel for a particular dimension; (4) get_group_id(dim): returns a unique global work-group ID for a particular dimension.

We now focus on the OpenCL runtime architecture introduced in Chapter 2. At the top level, OpenCL exposes a set of platforms (see Fig. 7.6) each of which is composed by a set of computing devices supplied by the same vendor, such as AMD, Intel, and Nvidia. There are many types of OpenCL devices, including CPUs, GPUs, and FPGAs. Each device has a global memory with a specific size and bandwidth. Typically, GPUs have faster memories than CPUs as they can support higher computational throughputs. Devices can communicate with each other (e.g., via PCIe), but typically devices within the same platform can communicate more efficiently with each other. Each device is composed of a set of compute units which operate independently from each other, and each compute unit has a set of processing elements. All OpenCL devices exhibit this architecture organization, varying in the number of compute units, the number of processing elements, and their computational throughput capacity.

To deploy and execute an OpenCL program into one or more devices, OpenCL supports two important concepts. First, a context which groups a set of devices from the same platform, allowing them to share the same OpenCL objects, such as memory and programs, and thus support the management of multiple devices from a single execution context. Second, a command-queue which must be created on each device (within an execution context) to allow the host to submit work to the device. When using multiple OpenCL devices, developers are responsible for manually partitioning application workload and distributing each part across available devices according to their computational capacities. In addition, and while the OpenCL kernel specification can be deployed to any device without modification, it is often modified, e.g., to take into account that CPUs have lower memory bandwidth but larger cache systems and support far fewer threads when compared to GPUs.

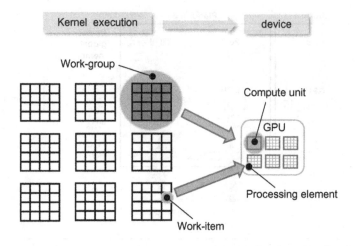

FIG. 7.7

Mapping a kernel onto an OpenCL device.

When the host sends workload to a device, it creates a kernel execution instance as illustrated in Fig. 7.7, where the kernel (along with its global and local dimensions) is deployed to the device. The global dimensions define the total number of work-items (threads) the device must compute. These work-items are combined into work-groups according to the local dimensions specified by the developer. Each work-group is executed by a compute unit, and each work-item is processed by one or more processing elements. The architecture of an OpenCL processing element depends on the type of device and its vendor, but it typically supports SIMD instructions. While the global dimensions are defined by the problem size, the choice of local dimensions can considerably affect overall performance since the number of work-items deployed to each compute unit has to be large enough to hide memory latency. The work-group size must also leverage available parallelism taking into account the number of processing elements within each compute unit and the number of compute units available in the device. For this reason, developers often perform design space exploration, experimenting different local dimensions to find the most performant configuration for a particular OpenCL device.

The OpenCL memory model is illustrated in Fig. 7.8. The OpenCL runtime assumes the existence of a host where an application is originally deployed and executed, and a set of OpenCL devices that handle offloaded computations from the host. The host has a main memory where the application data resides. On the other hand, each OpenCL device has four types of memories: (1) global memory which is the primary conduit for data transfers from the host memory to the device and can be accessed by all work-items, (2) constant memory where content can be accessed by all work-items as read-only, (3) local memory which is only accessed by work-items within a work-group, and (4) private memory which is specific to a work-item and cannot be accessed by any other work-item.

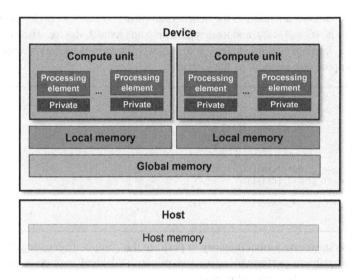

FIG. 7.8

OpenCL memory model.

There is no automatic data movement in OpenCL. Developers are responsible for explicitly allocating global data, transferring data from the host memory to the global memory of the device, allocating local data and copying data from global to local memories and back, and finally transferring the results back to the host. When performing data movements, it is important to take into account both the size of memories and bandwidth. For instance, when the OpenCL device is connected to the host via the PCIe bus, transferring data from the host memory through the global memory can support bandwidths between 5 and 10 GB/s. Work-items can access the global memory with a bandwidth of 50–200 GB/s and the local memory at 1000 GB/s. Hence, caching data on faster memories can result in overall performance speedup. Modern GPUs support the option of automatically cache data to local memories, instead of manually managing it.

OpenCL implements a relaxed consistency memory model. This means work-items may have a different view of memory contents during the execution. Within a work-item, all reads and write operations are consistently ordered, but between work-items it is necessary to synchronize to ensure consistency. OpenCL offers two types of built-in functions to order memory operations and synchronize execution: (a) memory fences wait until all reads/writes to local/global memory made by the work-item prior to the memory fence are visible to all threads in the work-group; (b) barriers wait until all work-items in the work-group have reached the barrier, and issues a memory fence to the local/global memory. Note that synchronization support is limited to work-items within the same work-group. If synchronization between work-groups is required, should they share data in global memory, one solution is to execute the kernel multiple times so that memory is synchronized each time the kernel exits.

We now turn our attention to the matrix multiplication example presented in Section 6.1, that is, $(C = A \times B)$, and its mapping onto an OpenCL device. The most obvious OpenCL implementation strategy is to use two dimensions and allow each work-item to compute one element of the C matrix:

```
__kernel void mmul(const int nX,
                   const int nY,
                   const int nZ,
                   __global float* A,
                   __global float* B,
                   __global float* C)
{
    int i = get_global_id(0);
    int j = get_global_id(1);
    for (int k = 0; k < nY; k++){
        C[i*nZ+j] += A[i*nY+k] * B[k*nZ+j];
    }
}
```

In this version, we use global memory to perform the computation over a 2D space. To further optimize performance, we use private and local memories which are considerably faster than global memory:

```
__kernel void mmul(const int nX,
                   const int nY,
                   const int nZ,
                   __global float *A,
                   __global float *B,
                   __global float *C,
                   __local float *Bw)
{
    int i = get_global_id(0);
    int iloc = get_local_id(0);
    int nloc = get_local_size(0);

    float Aw[DIM_NY];

    // copy A to private memory
    for (int k=0; k<nY; k++) {
        Aw[k] = A[i*nY+k];
    }

    for (int j = 0; j < nZ; j++) {
        // copy B to local memory
        for (int k=iloc; k < nY; k+=nloc) {
            Bw[k] = B[k*nZ+j];
        }

        barrier(CLK_LOCAL_MEM_FENCE);

        float sum = 0.0f;
        for (int k = 0; k < nY; k++){
            sum += Aw[k] * Bw[k];
        }
        C[i*nZ+j] = sum;
    }
}
```

In this improved version, we operate in one dimension, so that each work-item computes one row of matrix C at a time. We note that for each row C, each work-item accesses a row of A exclusively. Hence, we copy the corresponding row from global memory to private memory (Aw) since it offers higher bandwidth than global memory. Note that the size of the private memory must be known at compile-time. In the above example, we specified DIM_NY as a #define constant (not shown), which must correspond to the value of nY supplied by the host.

Furthermore, since each work-item in a work-group also uses the same columns of B, we store them in local memory. Note that in the earlier code each work-item within a group copies part of the B column from global memory to local memory by referencing `iloc` (unique work-item index within work-group) and `nloc` (number of work-items within the current work-group). We then use a barrier to ensure all work-items within the group have a consistent view of B before each work-item computes a row of C.

Regarding the host code, we use the OpenCL C++ wrapper API to deploy and execute the earlier kernels. In the following code, we select a GPU device from the first available OpenCL platform:

```cpp
#include <CL/cl.hpp>
...

    try {
        //get all platforms
        vector<cl::Platform> platforms;
        cl::Platform::get(&platforms);
        if (platforms.empty()){
            throw runtime_error("No platforms found. Check OpenCL installation!");
        }

        cl::Platform platform = platforms[0];
        cout << "Using platform: " << platform.getInfo<CL_PLATFORM_NAME>() << endl;

        vector<cl::Device> devices;
        platform.getDevices(CL_DEVICE_TYPE_GPU, &devices);
        if (devices.empty()) {
            throw runtime_error ("No devices found. Check OpenCL installation!");
        }
        cl::Device device = devices[0];
```

Once a device is selected, we create an execution context and a command-queue to deploy work to the device. Next, we load the OpenCL kernel source file and create an OpenCL program object and associate it to the execution context created earlier. Note that kernel 1 corresponds to the first version presented earlier, and kernel 2 corresponds to the improved version.

```
        // create execution context
        cl::Context context(device);

        // create command-queue
        cl::CommandQueue queue(context, device);

        // load kernel source
#if defined(KERNEL1)
        ifstream fs("kernel1.cl");
#elif defined(KERNEL2)
        ifstream fs("kernel2.cl");
#endif

        if (!fs.is_open()) {
           throw cl::Error(CL_INVALID_VALUE, "cannot open kernel source!");
        }
        stringstream ss;
        ss << fs.rdbuf();
        string code = ss.str();
        cl::Program::Sources sources;
        sources.push_back({code.c_str(), code.length()});

        // build
        cl::Program program(context, sources);
        try {
           program.build({device});
        } catch (cl::Error e) {
           cerr << program.getBuildInfo<CL_PROGRAM_BUILD_LOG>(device) << endl;
           throw e;
        }
```

Next, we create buffers for matrices A and B with their respective sizes and submit a command through the command-queue of the device to copy matrices A and B from the host to the global memory of the device.

```
        cl::Buffer bufA (context, CL_MEM_READ_ONLY, sizeof(float)  * nX * nY);
        cl::Buffer bufB (context, CL_MEM_READ_ONLY, sizeof(float)  * nY * nZ);
        queue.enqueueWriteBuffer(bufA, CL_TRUE, 0, sizeof(float) * nX * nY, A);
        queue.enqueueWriteBuffer(bufB, CL_TRUE, 0, sizeof(float) * nY * nZ, B);
```

We then select the matrix multiplication ("mmul") kernel and set the kernel arguments. Note that in the case of kernel 2, we pass an extra argument, which is the local array:

```
        cl::Kernel kernel = cl::Kernel(program,"mmul");
        kernel.setArg(0, nX); kernel.setArg(1, nY); kernel.setArg(2, nZ);
        kernel.setArg(3, bufA); kernel.setArg(4, bufB); kernel.setArg(5, bufC);

#if defined(KERNEL2)
        kernel.setArg(6, sizeof(float)*nY, NULL);
#endif
```

Finally, we execute the kernel by specifying the global and local dimensions and get the results back from global memory:

```
#if defined(KERNEL1)
    queue.enqueueNDRangeKernel(kernel, cl::NullRange, cl::NDRange(nX,nY),
                                            cl::NDRange(16, 16));
#elif defined(KERNEL2)
    queue.enqueueNDRangeKernel(kernel, cl::NullRange, cl::NDRange(nX),
                                            cl::NDRange(8));
#endif
    queue.enqueueReadBuffer(bufC, CL_TRUE, 0, sizeof(float) * nX * nZ, C);
    queue.finish();
```

We finalize this section with a summary of techniques for exploiting OpenCL devices. First, one of the bottlenecks in performance is the data movement between the host and the devices working as coprocessors since the bus interfacing the devices might be slow. One common technique to minimize data transfers is to organize various kernels in a consumer-producer "chain," in which intermediate results are kept in the device while running a sequence of kernels receiving as input the result of the previous executed kernel. Another important consideration is to use local memory instead of global memory since it allows almost 10 times faster accesses. For some devices, such as AMD GPUs and CPUs, the use of vector operations can have a huge impact in performance. Also, the use of half_ and native_ math intrinsics can help accelerate the computation at the expense of precision. Divergent execution can also reduce performance, which is caused when conditionals are introduced in kernels, and forces work-item branches (then and else parts) to be executed serially. Global memory coalescing also contributes to improve the performance as it combines multiple memory accesses into a single transaction, thus exploiting the fact that consecutive work-items access consecutive words from memory. Still, it is not always possible to coalesce memory accesses when they are not sequential, are sparse, or are misaligned. In this case, one common technique is to move accessed data to local memory.

7.5 HIGH-LEVEL SYNTHESIS

Compiling high-level program descriptions (e.g., C/C++) to reconfigurable devices (e.g., FPGAs), known as High-Level Synthesis or HLS, is a remarkable distinct process than when targeting common processor architectures, such as the x86 architecture. More specifically, software compilation can be seen as a translation process, in which high-level programming constructs are translated into a sequence of instructions natively supported by the processor. High-level synthesis, on the other hand, generates a customized architecture implementing the computations, described by the high-level program, using basic logic elements and their interconnections.

In general, the compilation of high-level programming languages to reconfigurable devices (see, e.g., [5–7]) distinguishes two types of targets: (a) fine-grained reconfigurable devices, and (b) coarse-grained reconfigurable devices or coarse-grained overlay architectures.

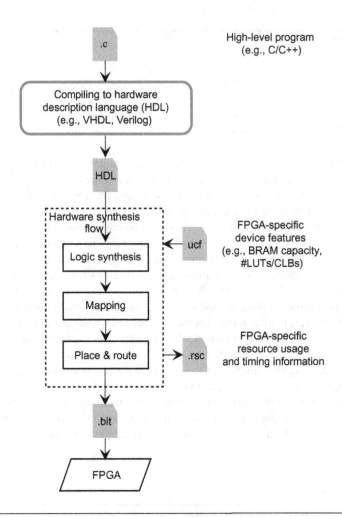

FIG. 7.9

The main stages of a high-level synthesis (HLS) approach.

The HLS compilation flow [8–10] targeting fine-grained reconfigurable devices consists of a number of stages, as illustrated in Fig. 7.9. In the first stage, an RTL description is generated from a high-level program (e.g., a C/C++ program). An RTL model (usually described in a hardware description language such as Verilog or VHDL) represents a hardware design in terms of registers (Flip-Flops), memories, and arithmetic and logical components. In a subsequent stage, this RTL description is synthesized to logic gates (in a process known as *logic synthesis* [11]) and functional units directly supported by the FPGA resources. Next, these logic gates and the functional units are further *mapped* to FPGA elements (LUTs, Slices, BRAMs, DSP blocks, etc.). Finally, the placement and routing (P&R) process assigns these FPGA elements to actual resources on the FPGA and allocates the necessary interconnects between these resources to form a complete hardware circuit.

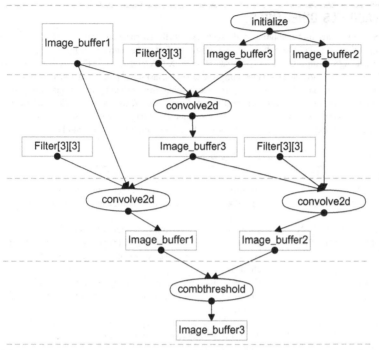

FIG. 7.10

Block diagram of an implementation of edge detection (see task graph presented in Fig. 4.15). Dotted horizontal lines identify the computing stages, rectangular nodes represent data, and elliptical nodes identify computing tasks.

One of the benefits of mapping high-level computations to fine-grained reconfigurable devices, such as FPGAs, is the ability to select the best suited execution model and target custom architecture. As an example, the block diagram presented in Fig. 7.10 captures the structure of the edge detection implementation of the UTDSP benchmark introduced in Chapter 4. This block diagram exposes concurrency between tasks in the same stage (stages are identified in Fig. 7.10 with horizontal dotted lines) of this implementation. For instance, two *convolve2d* task instances can execute in parallel on two distinct implementations of the hardware elements that support their execution. When mapped to an FPGA, the computational nodes (elliptical-shaped nodes) are implemented as logic circuits with discrete elements, such as adders and multipliers, and their own Finite State Machine (FSM) controllers. On the other hand, storage nodes (rectangular-shaped node) can be implemented using on-chip FPGA memory resources (BRAMs), possibly using one memory per array, and in some cases using dual-port memories.

VIVADO HLS DIRECTIVES

HLS tools leverage user annotations and directives (with their associated parameters) to manually guide the optimization tasks. These directives are mostly applied at the source code level, e.g., via pragmas when dealing with input C code as is the example of the Xilinx Vivado HLS [12] directives. Vivado HLS includes directives to guide loop pipelining (the target II), task-level pipelining, function inlining, loop unrolling, loop merging, loop flattening, array partitioning, array reshaping, and resource usage and allocation. There are also directives to inform the tool of certain code/execution properties, such as the maximum and minimum loop trip counts, and information about data dependences.

The following table presents some of the directives supported by Vivado HLS.

Directive	Brief description
INLINE	Inlines functions
PIPELINE	Applies loop pipelining. The target value for II can be specified
LOOP_TRIPCOUNT	Specifies the maximum, minimum, and average number of iterations of a loop
ARRAY_PARTITION	Partitions arrays into multiple smaller arrays
ARRAY_RESHAPE	Reshapes an array in order that instead of one with many elements we have one with fewer elements and larger word length per element
ARRAY_MAP	Combines multiple arrays into a single array
DATAFLOW	Enables task-level pipelining. Loops and functions can execute in parallel
DEPENDENCE	Adds information about loop-carried dependences
EXPRESSION_BALANCE	Turns off automatic balancing of expressions
UNROLL	Unrolls a loop
LOOP_MERGE	Merges consecutive loops
LOOP_FLATTEN	Flattens nested loops
STREAM	Implements a specific array as a FIFO or memory channel

In addition to the task parallelism uncovered in this block diagram (Fig. 7.10), we can also leverage task-level pipelining. In a task-level pipelined execution mode, the computations are structured as a sequence of stages partially overlapped in time. Depending on the data accesses between producer and consumer tasks, the implementation can use FIFOs and/or memory channels to support communication between successive tasks.

There is in fact a substantial number of possible optimizations when using fine-grained reconfigurable devices, including the use of customized resources, code specialization, loop pipelining, and data parallelism. Furthermore, restructuring code (e.g., considering the code transformations presented in Chapter 5) and efficiently using HLS code directives allows the HLS tool to derive efficient hardware implementations when compared to their software counterparts.

Given the potential benefit of energy-efficient computing with reconfigurable devices, there has been a substantial investment in high-level synthesis (HLS) [13] in industry as well as an increased focus on academic research. At this time, and considering FPGAs as target devices and C/C++ code as the main input, there are academic tools such as the LegUp [14], as well as tools provided by FPGA vendors such as the Vivado HLS [12] by Xilinx [15], and tools provided by EDA companies (such as the Catapult C [16] by Mentor Graphics or the Impulse-C by Impulse Accelerated Technologies [17,18]). Recent trends include tools to map OpenCL computations to FPGAs and both Xilinx [19] and Altera [20] (now Intel [21]) provide such tools. Other commercial tools have focused on specific models of computation. This is the case with the MaxJ language and MaxJ compiler provided by Maxeler [22,23] which heavily relies on dataflow models of computation and streaming architectures targeting contemporary FPGAs.

One important aspect about fine-grained compilation to reconfigurable devices is the high computational and memory requirements for some of its compilation stages, in particular placement and routing. Developers used to fast software compilation cycles must contend with long compilation runtimes (several minutes to hours) required to synthesize a hardware design. Hence it is not always feasible to perform an exhaustive search of hardware designs. In this context, developers must understand the implications of source code transformations and compiler options before engaging the hardware compilation design flow.

The compilation flow targeting coarse-grained reconfigurable devices [24] or overlay architectures is fundamentally analogous to the flow described for fine-grained reconfigurable architectures, but often bypasses the hardware synthesis-related stages. In this context, Coarse-Grained Reconfigurable Arrays (CGRAs) [25] are the most used coarse-grained architectures, as they provide computing structures such as Processing Elements (PEs). These PEs provide their own custom instruction set architectures (ISA) which natively support word lengths of 16, 24, or 32-bit, and interconnect resources, between PEs and/or internal memory elements at the same word level. Because of their granularity, CGRAs impose additional constraints on how high-level computations are mapped to PEs, memory elements, as well as how their execution is orchestrated. Although the compilation of most CGRAs still requires a placement and routing (P&R) stage, this process is often less complex than when targeting fine-grained reconfigurable devices.

7.6 LARA STRATEGIES

We now describe two strategies for improving the efficacy of the Xilinx Vivado high-level synthesis (HLS) tool. Both strategies first decide where to apply specific HLS optimizations, and then automatically apply these optimizations by instrumenting the code with HLS directives (see side textbox on Vivado HLS directives in the previous section).

The first LARA strategy (see Fig. 7.11) applies loop pipelining to selected nested loops in a program. As the Vivado HLS tool does not pipeline outer loops without fully unrolling all inner loops, when the PIPELINE directive is associated to a loop, all enclosed loops are fully unrolled. In the beginning of the strategy, all loop nests of a program are analyzed to decide where to include the PIPELINE directive. This is

```
1. aspectdef strategy1_4VivadoHLS
2.
3.    input
4.       funcName = 'smooth',
5.       threshold = 100,  // threshold to decide about fully unrolling
6.       II = 1 //value for the loop pipelining initiation interval
7.    end
8.
9.  /* Select each loop nest and start at the loop nest leaves */
10.    select function{funcName}.loop{isInnermost==true} end
11.    apply
12.       var $currentLoop = $loop;
13.       do {
14.          // calling aspect to determine the cost when fully unroll the loop
15.          // and its inner loops
16.          call A: CostFullyUnrollAll($currentLoop);
17.          if(A.cost > threshold) {
18.             call InsertPragma($currentLoop, '#pragma HLS PIPELINE II=[II]');
19.             continue #loop; //i.e., go to the next join point "loop"
20.          }
21.          $currentLoop = $currentLoop.ancestor('loop');
22.       } while($currentLoop !== undefined);
23.    end
24. end
```

FIG. 7.11

A LARA example to select a loop and to apply loop pipelining.

achieved by traversing all loop nests from the innermost to the outermost. For each traversed loop, the strategy invokes the aspect CostFullyUnrollAll (line 16) to decide about the possible feasibility and profitability of full loop unrolling. The CostFullyUnrollAll aspect (not shown here) estimates the complexity of the loop body (including all enclosed loops) if it were to be mapped to the FPGA. This complexity can be based on the number of iterations of the loops and on their body statements and operations. If the cost of the traversed loop is larger than the given threshold (supplied by the input parameter threshold), then the strategy instruments the code with the PIPELINE directive (see line 18) using the initiation internal (II) supplied by the input parameter II (with a default value of 1).

When this strategy is applied to a C code implementing the smooth image operator we obtain the code in Fig. 7.12, in which the PIPELINE directive is instrumented in the code using C pragmas.

The second LARA strategy (see Fig. 7.13) applies loop flattening (see Chapter 5) to perfectly or semiperfectly nested loops (starting from the outermost loop in the loop nest) while applying full loop unrolling to the remaining inner loops. This strategy mixes two strategies, one for selecting and applying loop flattening and another to apply full loop unrolling. For each traversed loop, the strategy acquires the information required to decide on the feasibility and profitability of full loop unrolling using the aspect used in the first LARA strategy (CostFullyUnrollAll). Also, this strategy can be easily extended to consider loop pipelining, thus making it applicable in a wider set of transformations contexts.

```
#define sizeX  350
#define sizeY  350

void smooth(short IN[sizeX][sizeY], short OUT[sizeX][sizeY]) {
    short K[3][3] = {{1, 2, 1}, {2, 4, 2}, {1, 2, 1}};
    L1: for (int j=0; j < sizeY-2; j++) {
        L2: for (int i= 0; i < sizeX-2; i++) {
#pragma HLS PIPELINE II=1
            int sum = 0;
            L3: for (int r=0; r < 3; r++) {
                L4: for (int c = 0; c<3; c++) {
                    sum += IN[j+r][i+c]*K[r][c];
                }
            }
            sum = sum / 16;
            OUT[j+1][i+1] =  (short) sum;
        }
    }
}
```

FIG. 7.12

Smooth image operator example after applying the strategy to select the loop for the pipeline directive.

```
1. aspectdef strategy2_4VivadoHLS
2.
3.    input
4.       funcName = 'smooth',
5.       threshold = 100  // threshold to decide about fully unrolling
6.    end
7.
8.    /* Select each loop nest starting at the loop nest root */
9.    select function{funcName}.loop{isOutermost==true} end
10.   apply
11.      var look4Perfected = true;
12.      var seqLoops = [];
13.      var $currentLoop = $loop;
14.      do {
15.         if(look4Perfected) {
16.            seqLoops.push($currentLoop);
17.            call B: PerfectedNestedLoops(seqLoops);
18.            if(!B.perfect && (seqLoops.length > 2)) {
19.               call InsertPragma(seqLoops[seqLoops.length-2],
20.                                '#pragma HLS LOOP_FLATTEN');
21.               look4Perfected = false; // at this point the strategy decides about
    full loop unrolling
22.            }
23.         } else {
24.            // calling aspect to determine the cost when fully unroll the loop
25.            call A: CostFullyUnrollAll($currentLoop);
26.            if(A.cost > threshold) {
27.               call InsertPragma($currentLoop, '#pragma HLS UNROLL');
28.            }
29.         }
30.         call child: GetChildLoop($currentLoop);
31.         $currentLoop = child.$loop;
32.      } while($currentLoop !== undefined);
33.   end
34. end
```

FIG. 7.13

A LARA example to select a loop and to apply loop flattening and full loop unrolling.

```
#define sizeX  350
#define sizeY  350

void smooth(short IN[sizeX][sizeY], short OUT[sizeX][sizeY]) {
    short K[3][3] = {{1, 2, 1}, {2, 4, 2}, {1, 2, 1}};
    L1: for (int j=0; j < sizeY-2; j++) {
        L2: for (int i= 0; i < sizeX-2; i++) {
#pragma HLS LOOP_FLATTEN
            int sum = 0;
            L3: for (int r=0; r < 3; r++) {
#pragma HLS UNROLL
                L4: for (int c = 0; c<3; c++) {
#pragma HLS UNROLL
                    sum += IN[j+r][i+c]*K[r][c];
                }
            }
            sum = sum / 16;
            OUT[j+1][i+1] =  (short) sum;
        }
    }
}
```

FIG. 7.14

Smooth image operator example after applying the strategy to select the loop for the loop flattening directive and to consider loop unrolling for the other loops.

When this second strategy is applied to the smooth image operator example we obtain the code in Fig. 7.14, which includes the LOOP_FLATTEN and the UNROLL directives specified using C pragmas.

One of the key aspects of using LARA is that strategies can be extended or combined, thus increasing their transformational power and scope of applicability. This is clearly illustrated in the LARA strategy described earlier, which can be easily extended to consider loop pipelining in addition to the loop unrolling transformation.

7.7 SUMMARY

This chapter expanded the topics on code retargeting for heterogeneous computing platforms, mainly leveraging the use of hardware accelerators such as GPUs and FPGAs. Special attention has been given to OpenCL and high-level synthesis (HLS) which translates C descriptions to hardware designs. The chapter revisited the roofline model and other performance models that aim at helping programmers with issues such as workload distribution and offloading computation to accelerators.

7.8 FURTHER READING

An excellent overview about reconfigurable computing is the book of Hauck and DeHon [5]. With respect to compilation to reconfigurable fabrics (such as FPGAs) the surveys presented in Refs. [6,7] provide a good starting point. A summary of the main high-level synthesis stages is presented in Ref. [8] but for a more in-depth description we suggest the book by Gajski et al. [13]. Readers interested in specific HLS tools can start by learning about LegUp [14], an available academic tool [9]. A recent survey comparing available HLS tools targeting FPGAs can be found in Ref. [26]. The impact of compiler optimizations on the generation of FPGA-based hardware is described in Ref. [27]. Details of the use of the Xilinx Vivado HLS tool are presented in Ref. [12] and the tutorials provided by Xilinx are important material source for beginner users of Vivado HLS.

For an introduction to the OpenCL programming model and its computing platform we suggest the material in Refs. [3,4]. Recent industrial development efforts on using OpenCL as the input programming model and underlying computing platform for FPGAs can be found in Refs. [19,20].

REFERENCES

[1] Williams S, Waterman A, Patterson D. Roofline: an insightful visual performance model for multicore architectures. Commun ACM 2009;52(4):65–76.

[2] Williams S. The roofline model. In: Bailey DH, Lucas RF, Williams S, editors. Performance tuning of scientific applications. Chapman & Hall/CRC Computational Science. Boca Raton, FL, USA: CRC Press; 2010. p. 195–215.

[3] Howes L, editor. The OpenCL specification. Version: 2.1, document revision: 23, Khronos OpenCL Working Group. Last revision date: November 11, 2015. https://www.khronos.org/registry/cl/specs/opencl-2.1.pdf.

[4] Kaeli DR, Mistry P, Schaa D, Ping Zhang D. Heterogeneous computing with OpenCL 2.0. 1st ed. San Francisco, CA: Morgan Kaufmann Publishers Inc.; 2015.

[5] Hauck S, DeHon A. Reconfigurable computing: the theory and practice of FPGA-based computation. San Francisco, CA: Morgan Kaufmann Publishers Inc.; 2007.

[6] Cardoso JMP, Pedro C. D. Compilation techniques for reconfigurable architectures. New York, NY, USA: Springer; Oct. 2008.

[7] Cardoso JMP, Diniz P, Weinhardt M. Compiling for reconfigurable computing: a survey. ACM Comput Surv 2010;42(4):1–65. Article 13.

[8] Cardoso JMP, Weinhardt M. High-level synthesis. In: Koch D, Hannig F, Ziener D, editors. FPGAs for software engineers. New York, NY, USA: Springer; 2016. p. 23–48 [Chapter 2].

[9] Guo Z, Najjar W, Buyukkurt B. Efficient hardware code generation for FPGAs. ACM Trans Archit Code Optim 2008;5(1). Article 6, 26 pages.

[10] Cong J, Liu B, Neuendorffer S, Noguera J, Vissers KA, Zhang Z. High-level synthesis for FPGAs: from prototyping to deployment. IEEE Trans CAD Integr Circuits Syst 2011;30(4):473–91.

[11] De Micheli G. Synthesis and optimization of digital circuits. 1st ed. New York, NY, USA: McGraw-Hill Higher Education; 1994.

[12] Xilinc Inc. Vivado design suite user guide. High-level synthesis. UG902 (v2016.3) October 5, 2016.

[13] Gajski D, Dutt N, Wu A, Lin S. High-level synthesis: introduction to chip and system design. Norwell, MA: Kluwer Academic Publishers; 1992.

[14] Canis A, Choi J, Aldham M, Zhang V, Kammoona A, Czajkowski T, et al. LegUp: an open-source high-level synthesis tool for FPGA-based processor/accelerator systems. ACM Trans Embed Comput Syst 2013;13(2). Article 24, 27 pages.

[15] Xilinc Inc. http://www.xilinx.com [Accessed October 2016].

[16] Fingeroff M. High-level synthesis blue book. Bloomington, IN, USA: Xlibris Corporation; 2010.

[17] Impulse Accelerated Technologies, Inc. http://www.impulseaccelerated.com/ [Accessed in November 2016].

[18] Pellerin D, Thibault S. Practical FPGA programming in C. 1st ed. Upper Saddle River, NJ,: Prentice Hall Press; 2005.

[19] Xilinx Inc. SDAccel environment user guide. UG1023 (v2016.3), November 30, 2016.

[20] Intel Corp. Intel FPGA SDK for OpenCL getting started guide. UG-OCL001, 2016.10.31, Last updated for Quartus Prime Design Suite: 16.1.

[21] Intel Corp., FPGA devices. http://www.intel.com/content/www/us/en/fpga/devices.html.

[22] Pell O, Mencer O. Surviving the end of frequency scaling with reconfigurable dataflow computing. SIGARCH Comput Archit News 2011;39(4):60–5.

[23] Pell O, Averbukh V. Maximum performance computing with dataflow engines. Comput Sci Eng 2012;14(4):98–103.

[24] Mei B, Vernalde S, Verkest D, Lauwereins R. Design methodology for a tightly coupled VLIW/reconfigurable matrix architecture: a case study. In: Proceedings of the conference on design, automation and test in Europe (DATE'04), vol. 2. Washington, DC: IEEE Computer Society; 2004. p. 1224–9.

[25] Hartenstein R. Coarse grain reconfigurable architecture (embedded tutorial). In: Proc. of the 2001 Asia and South Pacific design automation conf. (ASP-DAC'01). New York, NY: ACM; 2001. p. 564–70.

[26] Nane R, Mihai Sima V, Pilato C, Choi J, Fort B, Canis A, et al. A survey and evaluation of FPGA high-level synthesis tools. IEEE Trans CAD Integr Circuits Syst 2016;35(10):1591–604.

[27] Huang Q, Lian R, Canis A, Choi J, Xi R, Calagar N, et al. The effect of compiler optimizations on high-level synthesis-generated hardware. ACM Trans Reconfig Technol Syst 2015;8(3). Article 14, 26 pages.

Additional topics

8

8.1 INTRODUCTION

This chapter focuses on topics that complement the contents of previous chapters. In particular, it covers techniques for design space exploration (DSE), hardware/software codesign, runtime adaptivity, and autotuning. There has been a growing interest and need for these techniques, given the increasing complexity of high-performance embedded architectures and the development of applications with increasingly high computing demands. The challenge of targeting applications to high-performance embedded architectures is further exacerbated by the need to manage different development tools and code versions for each of the target architectures.

The goal of this chapter is to introduce these techniques by exposing the readers to main concepts, hoping that those concepts can assist developers to explore alternative approaches in their own work. In this perspective, we include simulated annealing [1] as a generic optimization approach applicable to many problems and problem domains.

8.2 DESIGN SPACE EXPLORATION

Design Space Exploration (DSE) is the process of finding a design[1] solution, or solutions, that best meet the desired design requirements, from a space of tentative design points. This exploration is naturally complex, as the search may involve tentative designs resultant from applying code transformations and compiler optimizations at various levels of abstraction and/or from the selection of specific values of parameters (e.g., configurations) or even the selection of algorithmic alternatives. As it is common when considering the diversity of embedded systems currently available on the market, the sheer size of this search space makes imperative the automation of the selection of alternative design choices and of the corresponding design generation and evaluation.

---

[1]The term design is often associated with a hardware design, but it is used here in a broader sense to refer to a hardware/software design.

Embedded Computing for High Performance. http://dx.doi.org/10.1016/B978-0-12-804189-5.00008-9

While there are cases where an exhaustive search can be pursued, or where heuristics, dynamic programming, and branch-and-bound approaches are successful in deriving optimal design solutions, in the vast majority of the design cases, an exhaustive exploration of this space, even if automated, is infeasible. DSE approaches must therefore derive designs in useful time while satisfying given requirements (e.g., related to performance). Approaches for DSE use a variety of algorithmic techniques, namely, stochastic optimization methods such as random search, evolutionary algorithms, swarm algorithms, stochastic hill climbing, and even machine learning.

In terms of the evaluation of each design point (tentative solution), developers can typically use one of two approaches (or a combination of both): (1) empirical evaluation using measurements from real execution or from simulation; (2) performance models, possibly analytical, to derive the required information. Regarding the optimization criteria, designs can be categorized as either single objective (possibly with multiple criteria) or multiobjective as described next.

8.2.1 SINGLE-OBJECTIVE OPTIMIZATION AND SINGLE/MULTIPLE CRITERIA

The goal of a single-objective optimization problem is to find the best solution for a specific criterion or metric, such as execution time (or performance) and/or a combination of this metric with energy consumption or power dissipation metrics. We can further combine multiple criteria into a single-objective optimization problem by defining the single-objective cost function as a weighted sum of the normalized costs associated with each of the metrics as given in Eq. (8.1), where $\alpha > 0$ and $\sum_{i=1}^{k} \alpha_i = 1$.

$$\text{Cost} = \alpha_1 \times \text{Cost}_{m1}/\text{Cost}'_{m1} + \alpha_2 \times \text{Cost}_{m2}/\text{Cost}'_{m2} + \cdots + \alpha_k \times \text{Cost}_{mk}/\text{Cost}'_{mk} \qquad (8.1)$$

As a particular case, Eq. (8.2) presents an example of a cost function consisting of a weighted sum of three metrics, namely, execution time, energy consumption, and power dissipation. These three metrics can be normalized using the costs of an initial nonoptimized solution as a reference.

$$\text{Cost} = \alpha_1 \times \text{Cost}_{\text{time}}/\text{Cost}'_{\text{time}} + \alpha_2 \times \text{Cost}_{\text{energy}}/\text{Cost}'_{\text{energy}} + \alpha_3 \times \text{Cost}_{\text{power}}/\text{Cost}'_{\text{power}} \qquad (8.2)$$

In this example, the DSE goal can be defined as finding a design solution with the minimum cost, i.e., all the criteria are now combined in a single cost. However, there are cases where the goal of the DSE consists in minimizing multiple metrics, i.e., as a multiobjective problem. In this case, it is important to consider Pareto optimal solutions, as described next.

8.2.2 MULTIOBJECTIVE OPTIMIZATION, PARETO OPTIMAL SOLUTIONS

A multiobjective optimization problem involves finding a set of optimal solutions for different and often competing (or conflicting) objectives. Fig. 8.1 presents an illustrative plot of various design points based on two criteria: execution time and power dissipation. While it is desirable to reduce both execution time and power dissipation, these tend to conflict. For instance, to reduce execution time we may increase the circuit operating voltage and clock rate, which leads to an increase in dissipated power. As a result, designs with lower power dissipation tend to execute slower, and conversely design points with higher power dissipation tend to run faster. Yet, not all designs plotted in this chart provide a good trade-off between execution time and power dissipation, thus prompting the need to develop a method for comparing all feasible designs so that developers can determine which design is the most profitable.

To this effect, we consider that each design is characterized by a vector $x = (x_1, ..., x_d) \in F$, where each element corresponds to an objective measurement such as speed and power dissipation, d is the number of objectives, and F is a d-dimensional objective space for the design problem. We also assume that each objective $i \in \{1, ..., d\}$ measurement can be compared with orders $<$ (x_i is better than y_i) and $\leq$ (x_i is better or equal than y_i). We say design $x = (x_1, ..., x_d) \in F$ dominates design $y = (y_1, ..., y_d) \in F$ iff:

- x is "better" than y with respect to at least one objective: $\exists i \in \{1, ..., d\} : x_i < y_i$
- x is not "worse" than y with respect to other objectives: $\forall i \in \{1, ..., d\} : x_i \leq y_i$

Using this definition of dominance, design A in our illustrative example (Fig. 8.1) dominates design B as while both exhibit similar execution times, design A dissipates less power. Hence, intuitively, design B is less desirable than design A and can be discarded by the DSE process. In this plot, the designs not dominated

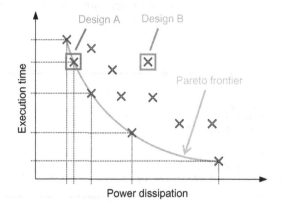

FIG. 8.1

Example of Pareto points and of a Pareto front.

by other designs are named pareto-optimal designs and define the *Pareto frontier*. A Pareto optimal design solution thus exhibits a key property: an improvement in one objective results in worsening at least one other objective.

To solve a multiobjective optimization problem, we identify the set of all Pareto optimal solutions or its most representative points. Assuming a set of designs, we can compute the Pareto frontier by first sorting these designs in descending order of importance by the first objective function, e.g., execution time. Assuming the sorted population of designs as D, we can use the recursive algorithm $frontier(D)$ depicted in Fig. 8.2 to determine the design space Pareto frontier (see Ref. [2] for further reading).

This algorithm works by partitioning the design population D in two halves: T and B. Given the way the initial population is sorted, the top half T is considered to contain dominant designs with respect to the subpopulation considered, and thus we only need to check the bottom half B for designs not dominated by any elements of T. The nondominated designs from B are then merged with T to produce M to compute the Pareto frontier.

Since each computed Pareto frontier design point corresponds to a trade-off between conflicting objectives, we still need to determine which design solution to select. This can be done by manually inspecting the Pareto frontier design points, e.g., using information provided by developers to express some preference or priority possibly based on other nonfunctional requirements.

Given the importance of this problem, researchers have developed various methods to derive the Pareto frontier. Here, we assume a population of designs $x \in X$, where X corresponds to all feasible solutions, and we have k objective functions $f_i(x)$, each one corresponding to a metric of interest. The three major methods described in the literature can be broadly classified as:

- *Linear scalarization.* This method involves recasting a multiobjective optimization problem as a single-objective problem (as previously described), such that the solutions to the latter are Pareto optimal solutions of the former.

```
frontier(D):
  nd = size(D)
  if nd is 1: return D
  T = frontier(D[0:nd/2])
  B = frontier(D[nd/2+1:nd-1]);
  M = T
  for each design t ∈ T:
    for each design b ∈ B:
      if design b is not dominated by design t: M = M ∪ {b}
  return M
```

FIG. 8.2

Algorithm for determining the Pareto Front.

In this context, the decision maker must provide a set of weights $w_i > 0$ to each objective function $f_i(x)$ according to their importance:

$$\min_{x \in X} \sum_{i=1}^{k} w_i f_i(x), \quad s.t. \ x \in X$$

This approach requires normalizing the objective functions since they express incomparable metric values, e.g., execution time and power dissipation. Furthermore, this method cannot identify Pareto points if they are in the nonconvex regions of the Pareto frontier.

- ϵ-*constraint method.* Instead of weights, this method requires selecting one objective function $f_j(x)$ to be minimized, while the remaining objective functions are constrained by an upper-bound limit ϵ_i:

$$\min f_j(x)$$
$$s.t.$$
$$x \in X, f_i(x) \leq \epsilon_i \ \text{ for } i \in \{1, \dots, k\} \setminus \{j\}$$

- *Utility function method.* This is a general method that requires a utility function $u()$ expressing preferences between designs. If $u(f_1(x), \dots, f_k(x)) > u(f_1(y), \dots, f_k(y))$ then design x is preferable over y allowing the best design to be determined by solving:

$$\max u(f(x)), \quad s.t. \ x \in X$$

In practice, finding the population of all feasible designs is a computationally intensive process as the number of possible sequences of optimizations used to generate each individual design is extremely large. Therefore, developers rely on metaheuristic optimization algorithms, such as simulated annealing or evolutionary algorithms [3], to guide the search process. Alternatively, developers can combine the methods described earlier to rank designs and/or identify their neighbors, and find (possibly in an iterative fashion) feasible designs close to the Pareto optimal solutions.

8.2.3 DSE AUTOMATION

The automation of the DSE process is based on three major components: the search space algorithm, the definition (or synthesis) of each design point being explored, and the evaluation of each design point. For each of these components, the DSE process can use several techniques, namely:

- *Search space algorithm* approaches include: 1—combinatorial optimizations, such as Simulated Annealing (SA), Tabu-Search (TS), Genetic Algorithms (GA), Ant Colony optimization algorithms (ACO), Particle Swarm Optimization (PSO); 2—Integer-Linear Programming (ILP) solvers;

3—heuristic-based and domain- or problem-specific search algorithm;
4—general search algorithms such as dynamic programming and branch and bound;

- *Definition of each design point* may involve the use of specific (sequences of) source code transformations (see Chapter 5), as well as assigning specific values to application variables or even substituting a specific function/algorithm with an equivalent and potentially more efficient variant. The automation of the DSE process is thus predicated on the automation of the actions required to "construct" or define each design point. While there are tools, such as compilers, offering interfaces that allow an external DSE process to control its operation (e.g., via the automated insertion of compiler directives to control the sequence of transformations—see Chapter 6), in other cases this automation is not supported and requires developer intervention. For example, developers may need to use source-level directive-driven programming models (e.g., OpenMP—see Chapter 6).
- *Design point evaluation* can be performed by deploying and running the design on the target computing system, or alternatively using simulators and estimators, to produce cost metrics such as execution time, energy, and power consumption. Estimating the cost of a design often involves analyzing the compiler generated IR (Intermediate Representation) or the corresponding assembly code (when targeting computing engines with an ISA as is the case of microprocessors). Depending on the objectives of the DSE, this evaluation can be simplified, for instance, when searching for the minimum program size.[2] In this case, the evaluation simply needs to inspect the size (in bytes) of the code generated for the function/program being optimized.

One of the most popular methods for exploring design spaces is simulated annealing (SA) [1]. SA is a probabilistic iterative method proposed for solving combinatorial optimization problems based on an analogy with the thermodynamics concepts of cooling and heating. The algorithm relies on the abstract notion of temperature (and thus vibration of molecules), where at high temperatures it explores design points in the space "distant" from the current best design points. At higher temperatures, the reach of the search (or *move*) is thus more "global." The algorithm then cools-off narrowing its search reach, confining the search to more "local" designs next to the best design solutions found so far. The algorithm engages in a series of these heating and cooling cycles (or iterations), at each lowering the amplitude of the "temperature swing" until it reaches a stable state where it has identified the best solution or solutions.

Fig. 8.3 presents an example of an SA-based algorithm. The initial temperature (T_0) and the number of iterations (iter) are important parameters of this algorithm. Usually, these parameters are calculated based on search space characteristics. During the

---

[2]Assuming, in this case, that the optimizations applied preserve the functionality of the program. However, this is not always the case, thus requiring functional verification by executing or simulating the transformed program.

```
...
Cost_Old = computeCost(Sol_init); // the cost of the initial solution
Cost_Min = Cost_Old; // for now the minimum cost if the one used by this solution
T_final = 0;      // the minimum temperature considered (e.g., a value near zero)
temp = T_0;       // the initial temperature
α = 0.95;         // the constant factor used to decrease the temperature
iter = ...;       // the number of iterations
β = 1.01;         // the factor used to decrease the number of iterations

do { // Iterate for the number of temperatures requested
    for(int i=0; i<iter;i++) { // Iterate for the prescribed number of moves
        Sol_new = Move();
        Cost_New = computeCost(Sol_new); // compute the cost of tentative best design
        delta = Cost_New - Cost_Old;

        if (delta > 0) {        // If the tentative design is worse...
            if (random.next() >= exp(-1*delta/temp)) { // still considers the move
                Cost_Old = Cost_New; // update the current cost
            }
        } else { // Update the minimum
            if(Cost_New < Cost_Min){
                Cost_Min = Cost_New;
                UpdateBest(Sol_new);
            }
            Cost_Old = Cost_New; // update the current cost
        }
    }
    temp = α * temp; // decrease the temperature.
    iter = β * iter;  // increase the iterations;

} while(temp > T_final); // if temp is zero or approximately zero the search finishes
...
```

FIG. 8.3

A simulated annealing-based exploration scheme.

execution of the algorithm, there are two important aspects to consider, namely, the cooling scheme used (the simplest one gradually reduces the temperature by a constant factor $\alpha: 0 < \alpha < 1$) and the number of iterations (being the two simplest options the use of a constant number or increasing it by a constant factor $\beta \geq 1$ in each step). Possible values for α and β are, respectively, 0.95 and 1.01. For each new design being considered as part of a move, there is a calculation of the cost for the new solution, obtained by actual measurements, simulations, or estimation techniques.

Despite its simplicity, SA is widely used in many domains due to its resilience in the case where the search is "trapped" in local minima (as the SA algorithm can, momentarily, consider worse designs than the best found so far) and the ability to recast many domain problems as SA search problems. In many cases, the use of the "correct" parameters allows SA to find designs close to the optimum solutions.

As an alternative to SA, and depending on the size of the design space and on the importance of finding solutions close to the optimum, DSE implementations may rely on heuristic-based algorithms or even use machine learning-based approaches. Both approaches aim at accelerating the search process by exploring a much smaller number of possible design points, using a set of predefined search directions, or even skipping the evaluation of intermediate design points.

8.3 HARDWARE/SOFTWARE CODESIGN

Hardware/software codesign [24] is the process of designing computing systems consisting of both hardware and software components [4]. It is by nature a cooperative and concurrent design process as decisions to use specific hardware components for selected sections of an application must be taken with a global view of the system (i.e., those decisions are not taken separately and without evaluating the global design impact). Although the main tasks of hardware/software codesign involve describing the system (e.g., using a modeling language) and exploring the best possible architectures to implement such a system as illustrated in Fig. 8.4, often the target architecture is fixed with the possible exception of the reconfigurable hardware component when present.

In this brief introduction to this topic, we focus on the restricted codesign scenario where the goal is to map a software computation to a computing platform that features some degree of hardware architectural flexibility. In this class of architectures, we include SoC-based architectures and other conventional architectures with a limited set of hardware configuration knobs (such as cache memory configurations). This is, we believe, the most common mapping scenario for software developers.

In this context, the two most important hardware/software codesign tasks are hardware/software cosynthesis and hardware/software partitioning [5,6]. Hardware/

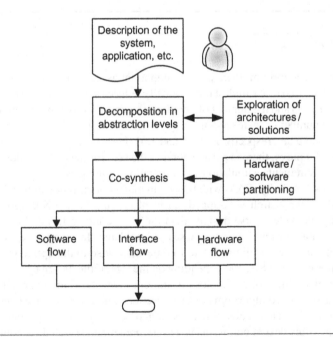

FIG. 8.4

Hardware/software codesign main tasks.

software cosynthesis usually refers to the synthesis of both the software code and the hardware component code, as well as the synthesis of their interfaces (including communication and synchronization). Software code synthesis (referred to as software flow in Fig. 8.4) is also required when the application is described using a high-level description language not directly supported by the toolchain of the target architecture (e.g., when using MATLAB without a suitable cross-compiler). As a result, this synthesis process requires the translation of the application specification to a suitable program description (such as C/C++) subsequently compiled to the target architecture. The flow may also produce parts of the application code, for instance, in C or in OpenCL, amenable to hardware acceleration and optimized for a hardware- and vendor-specific toolchain (referred to as hardware flow in Fig. 8.4), such as high-level synthesis tools when targeting FPGA reconfigurable hardware.

Hardware/software partitioning consists in identifying sections of the software code (in a software centric codesign approach) to be mapped to specialized architectures (such as GPUs and FPGAs) to execute them more efficiently. In the context of FPGAs and other reconfigurable devices, the code selected is synthesized into custom hardware structures, while in the case of GPUs the code is cross-compiled to exploit a specific execution model and its supporting hardware. This code is commonly referred to as being offloaded to the hardware accelerator. In other contexts, as is the case of FPGA-based accelerators, and in addition to the offloading, there is also the need to synthesize hardware structures by typically using a high-level synthesis (HLS) tool, such as Vivado HLS [7].

The selection of which software code section to be offloaded to hardware is often guided by the execution performance ratio between hardware and software, which takes into account the data communication costs between the host processor and the accelerators (see Chapter 6). In other contexts, offloading computations to hardware might be dictated by real-time response requirements. For instance, the hardware/software partitioning problem can be formulated as an optimization problem addressed by a simulated annealing (SA) algorithm as proposed by, e.g., [6]. In this case, the movements in each iteration of the SA algorithm consist of migrating code sections (e.g., instructions, basic blocks, loops, functions) from software to hardware and vice versa. For each new design solution, the cost considers the associated communication costs and the performance of each code section on both the host processor and the hardware accelerator.

8.4 RUNTIME ADAPTABILITY

Runtime adaptivity refers to a system's ability to adapt to runtime changes in its execution environment. As an example, at the application level, runtime adaptivity may focus on switching between algorithms depending on specific parameter values (also known as software knobs), data representation, or on code adaptations with respect to the lack of computing resources. In addition, runtime adaptivity may also involve modifying system-level properties such as the clock frequency or cache memories configurations (also known as hardware knobs).

8.4.1 TUNING APPLICATION PARAMETERS

Depending on the application, there might be various parameters to be tuned (statically or dynamically). An example is the number of taps used for a given digital signal processing filter. The number of taps influences the execution time, power and energy, as well as the effectiveness of the filter (e.g., the signal-to-noise ratio—SNR).

At runtime, parameters might be tuned according to specific objectives. As an example, consider the code in Fig. 8.5, which provides an iterative implementation of the hyperbolic sin or sinh function using its Taylor's expansion series. An adaptive implementation of this computation can tune *the number of iterations* (*N*) parameter at runtime according to a specified execution deadline. A large number N leads to increased precision, but also longer evaluation (computation) times.

8.4.2 ADAPTIVE ALGORITHMS

In addition to algorithm parameters, adaptivity can also take place at the algorithmic level by considering modifications to the baseline algorithm or using alternative algorithms. An example of this type of adaptivity is the implementation of the qsort function in the C standard library "stdlib." It uses insertion sort when the number of elements to sort in each partition is below a certain threshold reverting to quicksort otherwise. A more sophisticated adaptivity case for sorting would make use of additional sorting algorithms (see, e.g., [8] for a presentation of sorting algorithms). For example, one can use a sorting network when the number of elements to sort is small and those elements can be loaded simultaneously as inputs to the network, and/or use a counting sorting algorithm when the elements to be sorted are integers and exhibit small value ranges. In the counting sort algorithm, when the integer values of the array elements range, e.g., between 0 and 255, one can use an array of 256 entries and the input elements can be sorted with $O(n)$ worst-case time complexity by incrementing the entry given by the index corresponding to the element's value. There are

```
int N = 10;
double sinh(double x) {
    int i, j;
    double y = 0.0;
    for (i = 1, j=0; j < N; i+=2, j++) {
        y += pow(x, i)/fact(i);
    }
    return y;
}
```

FIG. 8.5

Example of parameter-based adaptivity.

cases where integer range values are known statically or at compile time (such as when sorting 8-bit data types) and thus the sorting algorithm can be even selected at compile time. If the range of the elements' values is not known at compile time, a runtime calculation of the range values can be done as a preprocessing step, thus imposing a small overhead, to decide, e.g., about the applicability of the counting sort algorithm.

Fig. 8.6A illustrates an example where a preprocessing step is applied to determine the range of values of the elements in the integer array A. The selection of which sorting algorithm to use is performed based on this range. In another version, one can use a minimum size of A which justifies the use of this strategy (see Fig. 8.6B). The minimum size of A can also be statically defined (based on profiling experiments), or in a more advanced approach it can be a software knob tuned at runtime.

8.4.3 RESOURCE ADAPTIVITY

The adaptivity of an application [9] can also be driven by the use of specific resources. For example, in an embedded application using sensors, adaptation can consider the specific number of sensors and their characteristics, or their availability either at runtime or even throughout the life cycle of the application. This adaptation to resources may require changes in the algorithms, for instance, when dealing with changing the number of sensors or just minor algorithmic tuning, for instance, when dealing with different frames-per-second (FPS) rates or image resolutions.

```
...
//BEGIN: preprocessing
int min = MAX_VALUE;
int max = MIN_VALUE;
for(int i=0; i<N; i++) {
    if(A[i] > max) max = A[i];
    if(A[i] < min) min = A[i];
}
int range = max-min;
//END: preprocessing
if(range <= 255) {
    countingsort(A, N, min, max);
} else {
    qsort(A, N);
}
...
```
(A)

```
...
if(N > 1000) {
    //BEGIN: preprocessing
    int min = MAX_VALUE;
    int max = MIN_VALUE;
    for(int i=0; i<N; i++) {
        if(A[i] > max) max = A[i];
        if(A[i] < min) min = A[i];
    }
    int range = max-min;
    //END: preprocessing
    if(range <= 255) {
        countingsort(A, N, min, max);
    } else {
        qsort(A, N);
    }
} else {
    qsort(A, N);
}
...
```
(B)

FIG. 8.6

Example of algorithm-based adaptivity: (A) selection between algorithms based on range of values to sort; (B) selection based on the values' range and number of values to sort.

In addition, this adaptation might take place online (at runtime) through the use of built-in software adaptation, through new software components deployed at runtime, or with the deployment of a new version of the application. More sophisticated systems can even include introspection and self-adaptivity [10].

Some systems are even required to be fully operational with an acceptable quality-of-service (QoS) and/or quality-of-experience (QoE) while adapting to available resources. Systems with these operational requirements are not the focus of this book as this text considers exclusively scenarios of adaptation to existent resources while targeting nonfunctional requirements (NFRs) related to execution time, energy, and power consumption.

8.5 AUTOMATIC TUNING (AUTOTUNING)

In this section, we focus on autotuning systems capable of automatically optimizing their own internal parameters to suit a particular execution environment, e.g., identifying the compiler optimizations that lead to software that exhibits maximum performance on a given architecture. Fig. 8.7 illustrates the use of an autotuner able to observe certain properties during the execution of an application and actuate according to the control units involved and goals addressed. The information required to decide about a particular parameter value, code/algorithmic variants, and/or compiler transformation/optimization might be difficult to acquire or can be unavailable at compile time, thus requiring the use of a runtime approach. In this case, the components presented in Fig. 8.7 perform the whole analysis and decision at runtime. Alternatively, if a lower overhead solution is sought, the analysis process can be performed partly or totally offline.

The goal of software tuning is to derive an efficient configuration via the definition of the appropriate software knobs resulting in an implementation that satisfies a metric or a set of metrics, such as energy consumption or execution time. In this

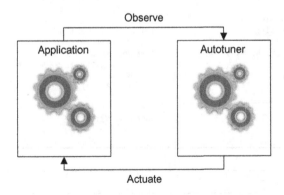

FIG. 8.7

The runtime autotuning seen as a process that observes and actuates.

context, configurations can be defined as tuples consisting of parameter values, code/algorithmic variants, and/or compiler transformation/optimizations. As with other optimization problems in the domain of hardware synthesis or hardware/software codesign alluded to in Section 8.3, software tuning exhibits design spaces that cannot be manually searched, thus requiring automated approaches analogous to the ones described in Section 8.2.

Autotuning can be an important task for runtime adaptivity. For example, to automatically tune the value of N (number of iterations) in the code of Fig. 8.5, or the threshold value 255 used in statement if(range <= 255) in the examples presented in Fig. 8.6.

8.5.1 SEARCH SPACE

Consider, as an example, a program containing a loop (identified as Li) we wish to tune based on the use of three compiler transformations, namely, loop unrolling, loop tilling, and loop parallelization. In this context, a configuration is specified by the tuple <Li, UF, TS, PAR> where Li indicates the loop on which the transformations are applied; UF denotes the unrolling factor (in this illustrative case 1, 2, 4, 8; with an unrolling factor of 1 corresponding to no-unrolling); TS denotes the tile/block sizes used in loop tiling (in this illustrative case 1, 32, 64, 128, 256, 1024; with a tile size of 1 indicating no-tilling); and PAR denotes the presence or absence of loop parallelization. The search space for <Li, UF, TS, PAR> considering the values to be explored consists therefore of $UF \times TS \times PAR = 4 \times 6 \times 2 = 48$ possible parameter configurations.

In a second scenario, and in addition to loop Li, we consider a second loop, Lj, and its configuration denoted by <Lj, UF, PAR> with only three unrolling factors (1, 2, 4) to use when applying loop unrolling and the choice between loop or no loop parallelization. Considering a search space where we assume the tuning of both loops to be independent, one can first search the best configuration for loop Li and then the best configuration for loop Lj. This translates into exploring a space with 48 and 6 possible design points for loops Li and Lj, respectively, and thus a total of $48 + 6 = 54$ design points. If, however, we take into account that the execution of the loops is not independent, we need to consider a search space with $48 \times 6 = 288$ design points.

In general, in a code tuning problem that consists of a sequence of n code sections (considered dependent on each other), the total number of design points to consider is given by $\prod_{i=1}^{n} \prod_{j=1}^{m(i)} \#option_{i,j}$, where $\#options_{i,j}$ identifies the number of options for the optimization i,j, and $m(i)$ represents the total number of optimizations for code section i. When the optimizations and options for each code section (e.g., loop) are identical, the total number of search points is given by $\left(\prod_{j=1}^{m} \#option_j \right)^n$. Both situations may imply large search spaces unfeasible to explore exhaustively, thus prompting the use of search heuristics and/or design space search pruning techniques.

8.5.2 STATIC AND DYNAMIC AUTOTUNING

Autotuning can be performed offline (statically, i.e., at compile time) and/or online (dynamically, i.e., at runtime). In offline autotuning, developers typically use heuristics to guide the parameter settings of applicable compiler optimizations and code transformations, either using compiler analysis and/or profiling (taken from previous executions). The heuristics can lead to the generation of multiversion code implementations akin to the ones described in Section 8.4.1 and tend to produce optimized, but possibly not optimal results, for a wide range of input codes.

In online autotuning, there is usually a mix of static analysis and profiling to build models, typically about performance, leveraging them at runtime to make code execution decisions. Other models are refined according to information collected at runtime. In addition, there are models built entirely at runtime, often incrementally, without requiring an offline analysis and model construction.

As an example, consider a code section with a loop nest to which loop tiling (see Chapter 5) was applied and where the block size is a parameter to be tuned. With static autotuning, developers analyze the execution time of the loop nest considering different datasets and different block sizes. With this profiling information, developers then generate code using the specific block size for each dataset input characteristics (e.g., sizes of the arrays) corresponding to the best observed performance for each combination of dataset input and target architecture.

With dynamic autotuning, developers may defer this block size tuning to runtime. In this context, developers insert additional code in the application in order to dynamically change the block size value based on observed dataset sizes or even on other input dataset characteristics (e.g., specific values of other relevant variables) to implement more sophisticated, albeit with additional overhead, adaptivity schemes.

OFFLINE AUTOTUNING WITH ISAT

One way to generate different code versions and other code required to support offline autotuning is to use specific code annotations to guide source-to-source modifications to output the different versions ready to be compiled and evaluated on the target machine. Some approaches also consider the use of code annotations to select sections of code for tuning and for measurements (e.g., timing) and to provide specific details regarding the search scheme for tuning as well as the software knobs to be explored. One example of a tool that uses this approach is the Intel software autotuning tool (ISAT).[a,b] ISAT is an offline autotuner to tune programs taking into account code parameters (e.g., parameters of OpenMP directives and values of code variables). ISAT is a source-to-source (C language) tool controlled by specific pragmas to create and evaluate multiple code versions based on two types of search (dependent and independent). The values to tune are defined in the pragma directives using a list of values or ranges (with some support for expressions and use of environment parameters).

[a] Intel Corp., Intel Software Autotuning Tool, https://software.intel.com/en-us/articles/intel-software-autotuning-tool/.
[b] Luk C-K, Newton R, Hasenplaugh W, Hampton M, Lowney G. A synergetic approach to throughput computing on x86-based multicore desktops. IEEE Softw 2011;28(1):39–50.

Autotuning is analogous to design space exploration (DSE) as it involves a search space process to find the best (or an acceptable) configuration for the parameters being tuned. For instance, consider the two parameters, TileSize (TS) and Loop-UnrollingFactor (UF), to be tuned according to the following set of values to be explored.

```
TS = {64, 128, 256};
UF = {2, 4}
```

An exhaustive search involves the evaluation of six code versions (design points) when applying loop unrolling and loop tiling with the parameter settings denoted by the tuple (UF, TS) as (2, 64), (2, 128), (2, 256), (4, 64), (4, 128), and (4, 256). This exhaustive design point search is the default search strategy used by the Intel ISAT tool (see the "Offline Autotuning with ISAT").[3]

Alternatively, we can consider a search algorithm in two steps. The first step would evaluate all design points using all possible values related to the UF parameter and an arbitrary value for the TS parameter. The second step would then use the best UF value (UF_{best}) found for all possible values of TS, i.e., (UF_{best}, 64), (UF_{best}, 128), and (UF_{best}, 256). This "dependent" or sequential search reduces the number of points to be evaluated, in general from $\prod_{j=1}^{m(i)} \#option_{i,j}$ to $\sum_{j=1}^{m(i)} \#option_j$, but is not guaranteed to find the optimal design point. Conversely, the exhaustive search does guarantee optimal results at the expense of a potentially much longer search time.

For simplicity, we now consider the implementation of a simple autotuning strategy as depicted in Fig. 8.8. In this case, we consider the use of loop tiling to a matrix multiplication (function matmult) where the size of the block is a parameter (variable blocksize) to be tuned at runtime. The strategy starts with an initial block size. For each block size, it measures the execution time for the matmult function and then increments the block size by a step value. The search terminates when either the execution time increases relative to the previous choice of block size or a maximum value of block size is reached.

8.5.3 MODELS FOR AUTOTUNING

As runtime autotuning selects the code configuration dynamically according to a specific objective function, the current workload, and the target architecture, it is often more efficient if the model capturing the criteria/metric related to the objective function can be built offline. This model must take into account the possible parameter

---

[3]The choice of "independent" and "dependent" naming for these two ISAT tool strategies can be misleading, as it suggests that the best search strategy is for a parameter to be independent from the others, which is seldom the case. A more meaningful naming would be to call "exhaustive search" instead of "independent," and "sequentially decoupled search" instead of "dependent."

```
...
typedef struct {
    int block;
    int maxblock;
} config;
...
int blocksize = 32;  // the initial value of the parameter to tune
int step = 8; // the value to increment/decrement to the parameter to tune
...
config best;
best.maxblock = MAX_BLOCK_SIZE;
best.block = blocksize;
...
while (blocksize <= best.maxblock) {
    t1 = start();
    matmult(A, B, C, N);
    t2 = end();
    delta = t2-t1;
    if(delta < 0) {
        best.block = blocksize;
        blocksize += step;
    } else {
        break;
    }
}
...
```

FIG. 8.8

An example of a simple autotuning algorithm.

choices and their impact on the objective function considering the target architecture. While this model is mainly built to aid runtime decisions, it can also serve as a basis for static autotuning.

We now revisit the example of the tiled loop nest using the block size as the tuning parameter, and consider its execution time as the criteria/metric to be minimized. An offline analysis can be used to build a statistical performance model of the loop nest for different input datasets and block sizes. A model may even be developed for each possible target architecture. A simple approach to develop this model consists in distilling the various best choices of parameter values for each dataset size and architecture, and embed that "decision model" in the generated code using "if-then-else" programming constructs in the scheme described in Fig. 8.6.

In a more systematic and sophisticated approach, one can employ machine learning techniques to incrementally build performance models. In this approach, offline models, based on static analysis and profiling results from previous executions of the loop nest, can be used as part of the learning phase, and later augmented (or refined) using runtime data. Clearly, a concern of this approach is the computational weight of the online learning technique. While traditionally, platforms such as embedded devices have not benefited from these approaches due to the runtime overhead, the advances in computing power are certainly making it increasingly more feasible.

8.5.4 AUTOTUNING WITHOUT DYNAMIC COMPILATION

Without dynamic compilation, autotuning has to resort to the use of code multiversioning so that at runtime the suitable code version is selected according to the observed parameter values or target architecture. Fig. 8.9A presents an example considering three function code versions (f1, f2, and f3) using the option variable to control the invocation of one of these three functions versions via a function pointer. Fig. 8.9B illustrates an alternative code implementation using a switch statement instead.

From an implementation perspective, a dynamic autotuning without dynamic compilation can be realized by generating code consisting of two alternating execution phases, namely, one phase responsible for "sampling," i.e., measuring the performance of the current solution being considered and another phase responsible for "production," i.e., switching to the best solution found so far during sampling [11].[4] Fig. 8.10 illustrates an example of the implementation of this approach considering the existence of multiple versions of a given function and the access to a version using the function pointer multiversioning code method (see Fig. 8.9). The sampling phase is responsible for the measurement of the performance of each version in the current environment by running each version for a fixed time interval. In each production phase, the system uses the function version that yielded the best performance in the previous sampling phase. Obviously, the implementation can even periodically repeat sampling-production phases to adapt to a possible changing execution environment.

```
void f1() {…}

void f2() {…}

void f3() {…}

void (*func_ptr[3]) = {f1, f2, f3};

…
int option;

…
(*func_ptr[option])();
…
```

```
switch(option) {
    case 0: f1(); break; //(*func_ptr[0])();
    case 1: f2(); break; //(*func_ptr[1])();
    case 2: f3(); break; //(*func_ptr[2])();
}
```

(A)   (B)

FIG. 8.9

The use of function multiversioning: (A) the use of a pointer to a function to select the function to execute based on the value of option; (B) a switch that can be used instead of the pointer to functions.

---

[4]It should be clear that this online search strategy is orthogonal to the code generation scheme used, for instance, static code generation using multiversioning, or runtime code generation using a Just-In-Time (JIT) compiler.

```
...
id = 0; // identifies the default version
...
if(sampling) {
   t1 = start();
   (*func_ptr[id])();  // id identifies the current version
   t2 = end();
   delta = t2-t1;
   saveDelta(…)
   id = selectNextVersion() // the search strategy for the next sampling version
} else { // production mode here
   if(firstProductionRun) {
      id = selectBestVersion(); // looks up id of best version in first production run
   }
   (*func_ptr[id])();  // id identifies the current version
}
...
```

FIG. 8.10

An example of dynamic feedback policy considering sampling and production controlled by a given policy.

Despite its elegance, this approach has its drawbacks, which are inherent in any dynamic autotuning approach. First, there is an overhead due to the execution during the sampling phase of code versions that are possibly very suboptimal, when that time could be better spent executing the best code version. This would suggest that the production phase should be much longer than the sampling phase. Second, and in the presence of changing environment conditions, such as varying available resources, an implementation should switch to the sampling mode often to reassess the best code version. This suggests the production phase should be short to improve the reaction response time to such environment changes. Clearly, the best approach to negotiate this trade-off is to make the rates of the "sampling" and "production" stages adaptive parameters in an autotuning adaptive strategy. An initial "sampling" and "production cycle would use default values for the relative lengths of these phases. Subsequent cycles would increase the relative length of the production phase of a cycle while monitoring the performance of the chosen code version. When the performance would degrade to a level inferior to the performance of the "second best" alternative code version (sampled in the previous cycle), the implementation would reengage in a new cycle with a new sampling phase.

8.5.5 AUTOTUNING WITH DYNAMIC COMPILATION

If the compilation system (and the target runtime execution environment) supports dynamic compilation, the autotuning approach does not need to rely on compile time generated code multiversioning. Instead, as is the case of popular Just-In-Time (JIT) compilers, the code generation can rely on low-level templates with parametrization capabilities so that the overhead of runtime code generation is kept to a minimum. In addition, the compilation might even consider to execute some of the static analysis of the code, or just complete this analysis, at runtime. While the use of static analysis

```
void func1_UF0(…){…} // no unrolling        …
void func1_UF2(…){…} // compiled with UF=2    int unroll;
void func1 UF4(…){…} // compiled with UF=4   …
void func1_UF8(…){…} // compiled with UF=8    funcptr=dynGen(func1,unroll);
…                                             (*funcptr)(…);
  int unroll;                                 …
…
if (unroll == 0)
  func1_UF0(…);
else
  if (unroll == 2)
    func1_UF2(…);
  else
    if (unroll == 4)
      func1_UF4(…);
    else
      if (unroll == 8)
        func1_UF8(…);
      else
        func1_UF0(…);   // default version
```

(A)   (B)

FIG. 8.11

Example of autotuning with (A) static compilation vs (B) dynamic compilation.

at runtime undoubtedly imposes an execution overhead, this approach has the benefit of using analysis information, otherwise impossible to acquire.

Fig. 8.11 illustrates a simple example where dynamic compilation is used to dynamically generate code implementations of the `func1` function considering a specific loop unrolling factor at runtime. In Fig. 8.11A, we depict the code structure using autotuning with static compilation, hence relying on multiversioning (with nested "`if-then-else`" statements) whereas in Fig. 8.11B we present the structure code using autotuning but relying on dynamic compilation and code generation.

In the case of the autotuning with static compilation we can see the potential issue of code "expansion" associated with the possible large number of code versions the generated code will have and its possible associated large number of `if-then-else` statements. In addition, testing each `if` statement predicate in turn imposes an overhead, which for large number of versions might not be negligible (and in this case one may opt to use pointers to functions and tables to map parameter values to function indexing values). Conversely, the case of autotuning with dynamic compilation is extremely simple. Once the executable code is generated using the `dynGen` compilation function, the code for the new function is accessed through a function pointer.

8.6 USING LARA FOR EXPLORATION OF CODE TRANSFORMATION STRATEGIES

Among its many uses, the LARA language introduced in Chapter 3 can also be used as a scripting language to control the overall operation of a tool flow and thus support the development of design space exploration strategies.

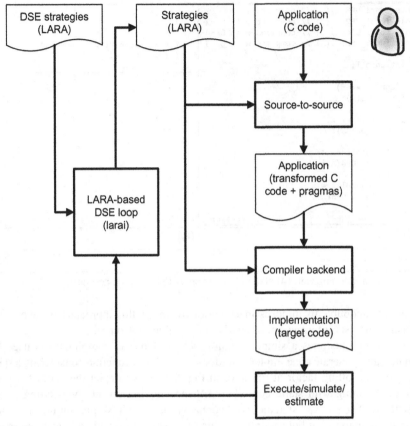

FIG. 8.12

The use of LARA as a scripting control language.

Fig. 8.12 depicts an illustrative example of the use of the LARA language to perform design space exploration using loop transformations. In this design flow, developers can apply loop transformations such as loop unrolling, either explicitly, by controlling a source-to-source compiler to perform the requested transformations, or indirectly via the use of source-level program transformation directives. The tool flow also includes a backend compiler and an execution/simulation environment with which developers can obtain quantitative measures of the impact of the various code transformations.

Fig. 8.13 presents the LARA `aspect` code to carry out the design space exploration for the tool flow illustrated in Fig. 8.12 for a set of predefined loop unrolling factors. This `aspect` considers a loop unrolling strategy also codified using LARA, which is applied by the source-to-source compiler (*manet*,[5] in this case). The result is

---

[5]MANET, a source-to-source C compiler based on Cetus: http://specs.fe.up.pt/tools/manet/.

a C code with innermost loops of the identified function unrolled by the factor considered on line 3 of this LARA `aspect`. The generated C code is then compiled with a C compiler (in the example via a `makefile`) and executed in the target architecture to collect the execution time for the code function of interest.

Fig. 8.14 shows a similar exploration strategy but targeting a high-level synthesis tool, in this case the Vivado HLS tool [7], which for simplicity neither takes into account the execution of the backend FPGA tools (responsible for RTL synthesis,

```
1. aspectdef ExploreLoopUnrollingCPU
2.    input  progname, filename, funcname end
3.    var unrollfactors = [0, 2, 4, 8, 16];  // 0 means full-unrolling
4.
5.    select file{filename} end
6.    apply
7.       // consider the original as the baseline
8.       cmd(progname)> "report.js"; // execution outputs a json structure
9.       var report = importJSON("report.js");
10.      var exec_baseline = report.exec_time;
11.      var exec_best = exec_baseline;
12.      var factor=1;
13.      // iterate
14.      for(i=0; i< unrollfactors.length; i++) {
15.         var manetArgs = [
16.            filename,
17.            "loopunroll.lara",
18.            "-av", {k: unrollfactors[i]; func: funcname}
19.         ];
20.         run manet(manetArgs); // execute manet with the args
21.         cmd(make); // execute Makefile for gcc
22.         cmd(progname)> "report.js";
23.         report = importJSON("report.js");
24.         new_exec = report.exec_time;
25.         if(new_exec < exec_best) {
26.            exec_best = new_exec;
27.            factor = unrollfactors[i];
28.         }
29.      }
30.      println("Program: "+progname);
31.      println("Selected Unroll Factor: "+factor);
32.      println("Speedup obtained: "+(exec_baseline/exec_best));
33.   end
34. end
35.
36. // the loopunroll.lara
37. aspectdef loopunroll
38.    input k, funcname end
39.
40.    select function{funcname}.loop end
41.    apply
42.       $loop.exec Unroll(k);
43.    end
44.    condition
45.       $loop.is_innermost && $loop.type=="for"
46.    end
47. end
```

FIG. 8.13

An example of a search strategy in LARA targeting a CPU.

```
1. aspectdef ExploreLoopUnrollingFPGA
2.    input  progname, filename, funcname, clkfreq=100E6 end
3.    var unrollfactors = [0, 2, 4, 8, 16];  // 0 means full-unrolling
4.
5.    select file{filename} end
6.    apply
7.       // consider the original as the baseline
8.       var vivadoArgs = [
9.           filename, …
10.          ];
11.      run report: vivado_hls(vivadoArgs); // run VivadoHLS (through tcl script)
12.      var new_exec = report.latency/clkfreq;
13.      var exec_baseline = report.exec_time;
14.      var exec_best = exec_baseline;
15.      var factor=1;
16.      // iterate
17.      for(i=0; i< unrollfactors.length; i++) {
18.         var manetArgs = [
19.            filename,
20.            "loopunroll.lara",
21.            "-av", {k: unrollfactors[i]; func: funcname}
22.            ];
23.         run manet(manetArgs); // execute manet with the args
24.         run report: vivado_hls(vivadoArgs); // run VivadoHLS (through tcl script)
25.         new_exec = report.latency/clkfreq;
26.         if(new_exec < exec_best) {
27.            exec_best = new_exec;
28.            factor = unrollfactors[i];
29.         }
30.      }
31.      println("Program: "+progname);
32.      println("Selected Unroll Factor: "+factor);
33.      println("Speedup obtained: "+(exec_baseline/exec_best));
34.   end
35.
36. // the loopunroll.lara
37. aspectdef loopunroll
38.   input k, funcname end
39.
40.   select function{funcname}.loop.header end
41.   apply
42.      insert after '#pragma HLS unroll factor='+k;
43.   end
44.   condition
45.      $loop.is_innermost && $loop.type=="for"
46.   end
47. end
```

FIG. 8.14

An example of a search strategy in LARA targeting an FPGA.

mapping, and placement and routing) nor the execution time of the RTL simulator. In this example, the loop unrolling factor is provided as a directive (#pragma unroll) inserted in the code before the loop of interest and we rely on the estimated number of clock cycles provided by the HLS tool and the target clock frequency to compute an execution time estimate for the generated design. Also note that the report (generated as part of the Vivado HLS execution on line 24) can include metrics such as the target FPGA hardware resources usage.

This example illustrates a common scenario when applying code transformations, in which some (but not necessarily all) of the optimizations are expressed in the context of a high-level synthesis tool via specific source code directives (see Chapter 7) or by the explicit application of the source-code transformations by a source-to-source compiler (see Chapter 5). In cases where only a directive-driven programming model is available, as is the case of OpenMP, LARA strategies can be invaluable as a means to control in an automated fashion the insertion of annotations into source code.

Although, simple, the two examples presented in this section highlight the potential of the LARA language as a DSE scripting language for controlling tool flows to evaluate the outcomes of application transformations and mapping decisions applied at different stages of the flow.

8.7 SUMMARY

This chapter highlighted additional topics complementing the contents of previous chapters, namely, design space exploration (DSE), hardware/software codesign, runtime adaptivity, and autotuning. These topics are increasingly important given the growing complexity of both applications and high-performance embedded architectures.

8.8 FURTHER READING

Design space exploration (DSE) has been the focus of current research in the area of embedded computing and system synthesis (see, e.g., [12,13]). The diversity of possible DSE approaches makes it hard to select an approach or even an algorithm. In most cases, developers use conventional and/or generic approaches based on stochastic algorithms as a way to find near-optimal solutions.

As hardware/software partitioning is one of the main tasks of hardware/software codesign, it has been explored by many authors employing several approaches (see, e.g., [5,14]). Not surprisingly, the hardware/software codesign problem has been the focus of research for many years by the electronic design automation (EDA) community (see, e.g., [5,6,15]) and has recently also attracted the attention of the HPC community (see, e.g., [16]).

The runtime adaptivity topic has received more attention recently due to the availability of computing resources that have rendered its runtime variants increasingly feasible. A representative approach is proposed by PetaBricks (see, e.g., [17]). PetaBricks includes an "implicit parallel language" for program development based on algorithmic choice. Using PetaBricks, the programmer can specify multiple algorithms solving a problem, without the need to specify the one to be used in each particular situation (e.g., according to the dataset size). Instead, based on the set of algorithms to solve the problem and experimental testing, the compiler generates and autotunes an optimized hybrid algorithm. Hybrid algorithms are obtained by combining multiple algorithms and using the best approach for each particular execution environment and dataset. The PetaBricks language consists of rules defining code transformations that its compiler translates to C++ code. Recent work on PetaBricks also considers a two-level input learning algorithm for algorithm autotuning [18].

Much of the research on autotuning, both offline and online, has focused on the selection of compiler optimizations and/or on compiler optimization parameters regarding a specific goal. A representative example is the Automated De-Coupled Adaptive Program Transformation (ADAPT) framework [19–21]. ADAPT consists of the ADAPT language (AL), a DSL for programming runtime iterative compilation processes (including the monitoring points); the ADAPT compiler; and an infrastructure to collect measurements, to execute a policy, and to invoke a remote compiler. The ADAPT approach follows a separation of concerns where the adaptivity is expressed in a specific file (consisting of global variables, one or more "technique" sections and one coordination section), thus not requiring modifications to the original source application. ADAPT overlaps optimization with execution. AL is a C-like language specially dedicated to program optimization policies in the context of runtime exploration of compiler optimizations. Optimization policies are expressed as AL "technique" sections which include optimization phase subsections. A coordination section defines how AL techniques are combined (AL includes linear search, parallel search, and exhaustive search). The language provides mechanisms to constrain the intervals (code regions) where a given ADAPT technique is to be applied (e.g., innermost loops, perfect nested loops, loops where the number of iterations is known at their entry). AL also provides statements to define the interface to the tool to be used to apply the optimization and/or compiler parameters. Examples of interfaces include if the code variant is to be generated by a specific compiler flag. Collect statements define what to measure for each specific interval (e.g., timing). AL policies can use machine information (e.g., clock frequency, cache sizes), iteration counts for innermost and outermost loops, and other information regarding runtime input data through the use of macros. In addition to the phase sections, an AL technique can include default and safe sections. The ADAPT compiler is responsible to process both the application source code and the AL code, and to generate the complete runtime system.

Autotuning can be considered a special case of DSE as it requires searching for the "best" code variants. It can thus leverage the vast number of approaches already proposed for DSE. For instance, iterative compilation, a specific case of autotuning, has also been addressed by iterative algorithms such as batch elimination, iterative elimination, and combined elimination [22]. Finally, other autotuning approaches have also considered approximate computing (see, e.g., [18,23]), providing additional optimization criteria for applications not requiring exact computations. Applications benefiting from this approach include those with requirements that can be defined in terms of QoS (Quality-of-Service) or QoE (Quality-of-Experience), and which exhibit outputs that need neither be deterministic nor exact.

REFERENCES

[1] Kirkpatrick S, Gelatt Jr CD, Vecchi MP. Optimization by simulated annealing. Science 1983;220(13):671–80.

[2] Kung HT, Luccio F, Preparata FP. On finding the maxima of a set of vectors. J ACM 1975;22(4):469–76.

[3] Deb K. Multi-objective optimization using evolutionary algorithms. New York, NY: John Wiley & Sons, Inc.; 2001.

[4] Dick RP, Jha NK. MOGAC: a multiobjective genetic algorithm for hardware-software cosynthesis of distributed embedded systems. IEEE Trans Comput Aided Des Integr Circuits Syst 2006;17(10):920–35.

[5] Arató P, Mann ZÁ, Orbán A. Algorithmic aspects of hardware/software partitioning. ACM Trans Des Autom Electron Syst 2005;10(1):136–56.

[6] Ernst R, Henkel J, Benner T. Hardware-software cosynthesis for microcontrollers. IEEE Des Test 1993;10(4):64–75.

[7] Xilinc Inc. Vivado design suite user guide, high-level synthesis. UG902 (v2016.3) October 5.

[8] Knuth DE. The art of computer programming. 2nd ed. Sorting and searching, vol. 3. Reading, MA: Addison-Wesley; 1998.

[9] Fayad M, Cline MP. Aspects of software adaptability. Commun ACM 1996;39 (10):58–9.

[10] Salehie M, Tahvildari L. Self-adaptive software: landscape and research challenges. ACM Trans Auton Adapt Syst 2009;4(2). Article 14, 42 pages.

[11] Diniz PC, Rinard MC. Dynamic feedback: an effective technique for adaptive computing, In: Michael Berman A, editor. Proceedings of the ACM SIGPLAN 1997 conference on programming language design and implementation (PLDI'97)New York, NY: ACM; 1997. p. 71–84.

[12] Panerati J, Beltrame G. A comparative evaluation of multi-objective exploration algorithms for high-level design. ACM Trans Des Autom Electron Syst 2014;19(2). Article 15, 22 pages.

[13] Palermo G, Silvano C, Zaccaria V. ReSPIR: a response surface-based pareto iterative refinement for application-specific design space exploration. IEEE Trans Comput Aided Des Integr Circuits Syst 2009;28(12):1816–29.

[14] López-Vallejo M, López JC. On the hardware-software partitioning problem: system modeling and partitioning techniques. ACM Trans Des Autom Electron Syst 2003;8(3):269–97.

[15] Teich J. Hardware/software codesign: the past, the present, and predicting the future. Proc IEEE 2012;100(Centennial-Issue):1411–30.

[16] Hu XS, Murphy RC, Dosanjh SS, Olukotun K, Poole S. Hardware/software co-design for high performance computing: challenges and opportunities. In: CODES+ISSS; 2010. p. 63–4.

[17] Ansel J, Chan C, Wong YL, Olszewski M, Zhao Q, Edelman A, et al. PetaBricks: a language and compiler for algorithmic choice. In: Proceedings of the 30th ACM SIGPLAN conf. on programming language design and implementation (PLDI'09)New York, NY: ACM; 2009. p. 38–49.

[18] Ding Y, Ansel J, Veeramachaneni K, Shen X, O'Reilly U-M, Amarasinghe S. Autotuning algorithmic choice for input sensitivity. In: Proceedings of the 36th ACM SIGPLAN

conference on programming language design and implementation (PLDI'15). New York, NY: ACM; 2015. p. 379–90.

[19] Voss MJ, Eigenmann R. ADAPT: automated de-coupled adaptive program transformation, In: Proceedings of the international conference on parallel processing (ICPP'00) Washington, DC: IEEE Computer Society; 2000. p. 163–72.

[20] Voss MJ, Eigemann R. High-level adaptive program optimization with ADAPT. In: Proc. 8th ACM SIGPLAN symposium on principles and practices of parallel programming (PPoPP'01)New York, NY: ACM; 2001. p. 93–102.

[21] Voss MJ. A generic framework for high-level adaptive program optimization (Ph.D. dissertation)West Lafayette, IN: Purdue University; 2001. AAI3075736.

[22] Pan Z, Eigenmann R. Fast and effective orchestration of compiler optimizations for automatic performance tuning, In: Proceedings of the international symposium on code generation and optimization (CGO'06)Washington, DC: IEEE Computer Society; 2006. p. 319–32.

[23] Ansel J, Wong YL, Chan C, Olszewski M, Edelman A, Amarasinghe S. Language and compiler support for auto-tuning variable-accuracy algorithms. In: Proc. of the 9th annual IEEE/ACM intl. symp. on code generation and optimization (CGO'11) Washington, DC: IEEE Computer Society; 2011. p. 85–96.

[24] De Micheli G, Wolf W, Ernst R. Readings in hardware/software co-design. San Francisco, CA: Morgan Kaufmann Publishers; 2002.

Glossary

A

Affine function a function of the form: $f(x_1, x_2, \ldots, x_n) = c_1 x_1 + c_2 x_2 + \ldots + c_n x_n + c_0$, considering $n \geq 1$ variables x_i, and $n+1$ constants c_i (see also affine index functions).

Affine index function used in the context of an array index when the expression that defines is a linear combination of the loop induction variables. For example, the index function $2*i+j$ is an affine index function over the induction variables i and j, but the indexing function $i*j$ is not affine (see also affine functions).

Aspect-oriented programming (AOP) programming paradigm which aims at increasing software code modularity by allowing the separation of cross-cutting concerns from the rest of the application. AOP typically requires extensions to the programming language or a new language to describe cross-cutting concerns (using aspects), and the use of a tool that merges these concerns with the application source code (a process known in the AOP community as weaving and the tool responsible for weaving is known as weaver). Examples of AOP approaches include AspectJ for Java and AspectC++ for C++.

Autotuning the automatic process of deriving an efficient configuration that satisfies a given objective based on one or more performance metrics (e.g., energy consumption or execution time). In this context, configurations are defined as tuples consisting of parameter values, code/algorithmic variants, and/or compiler transformation/optimizations. Autotuning can be performed offline (at compile time), online (at runtime), or both.

Basic block the maximum sequence of instructions (possibly defined at the assembly or intermediate representation level) such that if the first instruction of the sequence is executed, then all the instructions in that sequence are also executed. In other words, it is a sequence of instructions with no "jump" to or from any instructions inside the basic block.

B

big.LITTLE a heterogeneous computing architecture developed by ARM, which couples power-efficient slower processors (LITTLE) with more powerful power-hungry processors (big) in the same device.

Block and cyclic distribution an array can be partitioned on available distributed memories in a multiprocessor platform by specifying for each dimension of the array the mapping between array indices and abstract processors. A dimension of size N is distributed in a block fashion across P if N/P consecutive elements are assigned to a given processor. In a cyclical distribution, every other P element of the N elements is distributed to the same processor. It is possible that an array is distributed using the block scheme along one dimension and cyclical along another dimension.

Built-in functions functions that are specific to a target machine and that take advantage of specific ISA support.

C

Cloud computing the delivery of on-demand computing, storage, and communication resources, as well as computing platforms and software, over the Internet on a pay-for-use basis.

Code specialization the derivation of a customized version of a code section based on specific values of its input parameters, operands, dataset, workload, or environment properties.

Computing in space the execution of different hardware devices or elements. In the context of reconfigurable architectures, space computing refers to the fact that in these architectures all active logic elements operate in parallel in a totally asynchronous fashion. That is, unlike computing in time (see computing in time), there are multiple instances of control threads executing concurrently when computing in space.

Computing in time a sequential execution mode supported by the abstractions of a thread organized around the concept of a program counter and storage. Thread instructions use data from the storage as input and upon completion update or create new data in storage.

Configurable logic blocks (CLBs) a configurable digital logic structure that is a fundamental block of a Field Programmable Gate Array (FPGA). Commonly, composed of logic elements such as Flip-Flops (FFs) and Look-Up tables (LUTs) in addition to other discrete logic elements or gates.

Control step a step of the control unit common in the implementation of high-level hardware synthesis designs. Often in synchronous designs, a control step corresponds to a single clock cycle.

Cycle-accurate simulators a simulator that tracks the number of clock cycles required to execute (and retire) a given code section or application (see instruction-level simulators).

D

Data parallelism, SIMD and SPMD a form of concurrent execution where different processing elements operate on disjoint sections of the same data structure (e.g., an array) and typically, in a very tight synchronization mode (i.e., in locked step). Instruction-level data parallel execution is often referred to as Single Instruction, Multiple Data (SIMD) where the same instruction is executed on different portion or sections of a single data item or data items that are colocated in space (see also SSE and MMX instructions). At a coarse grain level, data parallel execution is also referred to as Single Program, Multiple Data (SPMD) where processing elements operate on disjoint data items with looser execution control.

Dataflow computing a form of execution in which processors are allocated tasks from a task graph (or workflow) and are executed whenever their inputs are available. The task outputs are then propagated to inputs of other tasks (often via the use of FIFO buffers) which will trigger the execution of further tasks. Unlike data-streaming computing, there is no notion of time synchronization between inputs.

Data-streaming computing a form of execution in which processors are allocated tasks from a task graph (or workflow). Tasks are executed when data is streamed (or "pumped") through the inputs (often subject to data rate control) and through the various outputs and inputs of subsequent tasks. Unlike data flow computing (see dataflow computing), data-streaming input items are "time synchronous" in the sense that they are processed as an "item" through the task graph producing the corresponding set of output items (see also task-level pipelining).

Def-use chains a data structure that identifies for a program variable definition (write) all uses (reads) that are reachable from that definition.

Delay the time required for a computation or logic circuit to produce a change in its output (if any), given a change in the inputs.

Dependence direction vector a vector of the iteration space of a given loop that defines the minimum dependence distance between distinct instances of instructions in the referred loop. It is an n-dimensional vector defined over the loop in an n-dimensional Cartesian space. This distance can be a constant vector in which case it is referred to as a dependence distance vector or include approximated distances vector in a summarized form as positive, negative, or unknown distance.

Dependence distance vector an n-dimensional vector representing the iteration space graph of an n-dimensional loop nest, which captures the dependence distance between array accesses. While this vector captures the "shape" of the dependences, it loses where the dependences originates. For example, the array references $A[i]$ and $A[i-1]$ on a single dimensional i-loop have a dependence distance of 1 iteration.

Design space exploration (DSE) a technique for deriving optimized designs by exploring different configurations, such as input parameters, source transformations, and compiler options. Each generated design may exhibit distinct "performance" metrics such as power/energy or wall-clock time performance, and provide different trade-offs between them (see also Pareto points).

Dynamic analysis a program analysis performed at runtime. By exercising the application with one or more input datasets, dynamic analysis can uncover information that cannot be collected statically, such as the number of iterations of a given loop, or the specific values of a procedure's argument.

E

Embedded DSL a Domain-Specific Language (DSL) that inherits the same language constructs as the host language, while adding new domain-specific primitives to allow programmers work at a much higher abstraction. One of the key benefits of Embedded DSLs is that DSL descriptions can often be compiled with the same toolchain as the host language.

H

Hard real-time constraints constraints that must meet all the deadlines prescribed in the requirements to be considered a feasible solution (in contrast to soft real-time constraints). Examples of systems with hard real-time constrains include nuclear facilities, flight control systems, and medical life-support systems.

Hardcore processors a term used when a VLSI design includes a block in the silicon layout that is a copy of the VLSI mask of the processor layout. This is also often referred to as "hard IP."

Hardware design and synthesis the process of capturing the structure and behavior of a digital circuit, including the spatial organization of the hardware as well as its timing control, using a hardware-oriented programming language such as Verilog or VHDL. The process of generating a configuration file targeting a specific reconfigurable device such as an FPGA is called hardware synthesis and requires a specific design-flow toolchain.

Hardware knobs an interface to adjust specific aspects of the hardware operations, such as clock frequency, sharing of caches, and storage capacity allocated to OS (operating system) vs user programs. Unlike software knobs, which are application specific, hardware knobs affect the operation of the system across all applications.

Hardware synthesis the translation from VHDL or Verilog descriptions to a specific Register-Transfer-Level (RTL) description, then used by other tools to synthesize either bit-level specifications for the target hardware or directly targeting a library of predefined IP blocks.

Hardware/software codesign the process of designing computing systems consisting of both hardware and software components. It is by nature a cooperative and concurrent design process as the decision to use specific hardware components targeting selected sections of an application must take into account its global impact (see Hardware/software Cosynthesis and Hardware/software Partitioning).

Hardware/software cosynthesis one of the stages of the hardware/software codesign process, responsible for synthesizing software code and hardware components of the target system, as well as its interface (including communication and synchronization) (see Hardware/software Codesign).

Hardware/software partitioning the process of identifying which sections of the application will execute either on software or on hardware components of the target architecture (see Hardware/software codesign).

Hardware in the loop a term used to identify a computer simulation of a system using real hardware for some of its components.

High-level synthesis (HLS) a software tool that translates computations specified in a high-level programming language such as C to a hardware specification language such as VHDL or Verilog. This is often referred to as a "C-to-gates" high-level synthesis.

Hotspots regions (also known as critical sections) of the program's code that account for a high percentage (or fraction) of the program's execution time, and are thus prime candidates for optimization and/or hardware acceleration.

I

Instruction-level simulators a simulator that can trace the execution of an executable program code one instruction at a time. It provides the user the ability to inspect the various instruction fields and verify the functionality of a given program (see cycle-accurate simulators).

Instruction set architecture the instruction set architecture, or ISA, of a processor defines all the commands that a processor can execute, providing an interface between applications running on the platform and its hardware.

Internet of things (IoT) the synergetic interconnection between embedded devices, appliances, and other physical devices that allows them to share data across the Internet.

Intrinsics sequences of instructions specifically targeted for a given architecture (for instance, taking advantage of the cache line sizes and pipeline depths). These are often called intrinsic functions and are inlined at the corresponding call sites.

Iteration space graphs a representation in which all the iterations of a nested loop are explicitly represented along with the dependences between them. In some representations, each iteration indicates explicitly all the instructions associated to each iteration along with the respective dependences within and across iterations.

Iterative compilation the process where compiler optimizations and/or code transformations are successively applied to a program and then evaluated, for instance, by executing the program. The compiler optimizations that best satisfy a given objective (e.g., performance improvements, energy savings) are selected.

L

Lane segments of elements that are packed into vectors (forming groups of elements) used in the context of SIMD units. For instance, in a 128-bit vector we can consider four lanes of 32-bit elements (i.e., a group of four 32-bit elements), two lanes of 64-bit elements, and so on.

Latency the time needed (usually in terms of the number of clock cycles) for a computation to terminate from the time it started. This specific term is common in the context of pipelined execution of instructions, for instance, when mentioning that a specific instruction has K cycles of latency.

Lexically forward/backward dependence a loop-carried dependence between two statements S1 and S2 is lexically backward if S2 appears before S1 in the loop body, otherwise this dependence is considered lexically forward.

Little-endian and big-endian the order in which bytes in an addressable word are stored in memory. In the big-endian order, the most significant bit (or byte) of a word is stored in the lower physical addresses. For instance, a 4-byte (32-bit) word will have the most significant byte stored at address N and the least signification byte stored at address $N+3$. In the little-endian order, the most significant byte is stored at address $N+3$, whereas the least significant byte is stored at address N.

Logic synthesis the process of translating a hardware design described in register-transfer level (RTL) style into a lower level design representation (circuitry netlist) consisting of gates (e.g., ANDs, ORs) and registers (flip-flops).

Look-up table (LUT) a hardware structure that implements, in the context of FPGAs, a table with N inputs (typically between 3 and 6) and one or two outputs. This table can be reconfigured (i.e., its content can be uploaded postfabrication or in the field) and can be implemented as an SRAM. In FPGAs, each LUT can implement an N-input logic function, a shift register, and/or a distributed memory.

M

Manycore and Multicore Architectures a manycore architecture is composed of a very large number of (homogeneous) cores that are loosely coupled and often used in high-performance applications due to its high degree of parallelism. In contrast, a multicore architecture has comparably less number of cores however each of them is more powerful. Furthermore, these cores are closely coupled, often sharing cache resources, and are thus more amenable to fine grain concurrency management as the synchronization costs are lower than using a message passing style of communication.

Mapping (hardware synthesis) a hardware synthesis stage which assigns all logic and storage elements of the circuit's netlist (output of logic synthesis and consisting of gates and registers) to generic FPGA resources, such as LUTs and registers.

O

Overlay architectures coarse grained architectures with components that are synthesized from a much finer grained set of elements. The common overlay architecture is based on fine grained FPGA configurable blocks to define a "virtual" coarse grained architecture with processing elements, each of which has its own ALU, local storage, and communicate with other processing elements in the overlay architecture via specific interconnect resources or via a network on a chip.

Owner-computes rule a rule used by HPF (High-Performance Fortran) compilers that states that the processor that owns the left-hand side element of an assignment statement performs the calculation. In this context, the processors that own the data used in the right-hand side must communicate the data to the owner, which subsequently performs the computation.

P

Pareto points a set of design points which provide trade-offs between potentially conflicted criteria, whereby improving one criterion invariably worsens another. Often used in the context of multiobjective optimizations.

Performance the numerical inverse of the time to execute a given workload, and is commonly used in the context of evaluating computer architectures and applications. Hence, an increase in performance means a reduction of the execution time. It is, however, common to use performance in a more generic sense to capture other metrics, such as power and/or energy, or the overall efficiency of a given algorithm (including the quality of its results).

Phase detection a term used in the context of application profiling where developers attempt to characterize sections of their applications with remarkably distinct behavior, either in terms of performance, energy or memory access pattern behavior, floating-point intensity, or any other hardware- or software-based metric.

Phase selection and ordering a term used in the context of the optimization (transformation) phase of a compiler. This phase is often structured as a sequence of lower-level phases or "passes." The effectiveness of the compiler's optimization depends largely on which phases (or passes) are selected and in which order they are applied. It is common that a particular ordering of phases (or passes) is applied multiple times.

Placement and routing a hardware synthesis stage which is executed after the mapping stage, and is responsible for assigning the generic logic and storage FPGA resources to available physical FPGA resources and to interconnect them using fabric routing resources.

Predictable memory accesses a type of memory accesses that can be determined or predicted at compile time (statically) by inspecting the source code or even through binary code-level analysis.

R

Reconfigurable fabric a generic term used to describe a computing architecture that contains programmable compute elements (such as in the case of CLBs) and/or interconnections that are also configurable.

Register-transfer level (RTL) a design specification that models synchronous digital circuits in terms of registers (flip-flops) and combinatorial components, e.g., formed by logic elements such as AND, OR, and NOT gates.

Row-major and Column-major two common organizations of multidimensional array variables. In the row-major organization, the array is laid out in memory by rows whereas in a column-major it is laid out by columns. This memory organization is defined in terms of virtual addresses, not physical addresses, as the underlying hardware and operating system might impose a specific mapping for consecutive virtual addresses in terms of the ordering of addresses.

S

Scratchpad memory a storage structure that is typically not a part of the traditional processor address space but instead private to a computation unit or processor, and is used to explicitly save and restore temporary data.

Shader cores a programmable computing core designed to implement in hardware specific vertex geometry shading operations.

Slack a metric used to identify the delay or latency between the completion of a computation and a specific timing mark. For instance, if the objective is to have a computation completed in 100 clock cycles and the implementation is able to accomplish it in 80 clock cycles, then the time slack of this execution is 20 clock cycles. Slack can be negative, which means that the actual completion has extended beyond the preset timing mark.

Slices groups of FPGA logic resources, where each slice contains a small set (typically 2) of configurable logic blocks or CLBs (see look-up table and configurable logic blocks).

Soft real-time constraints constraints that may miss some of the deadlines and still be deemed feasible. A secondary performance metric assesses the utility of the systems as a function of the number and severity of the deadlines missed. Examples of these systems include sound/image systems where missing a deadline may lead to a loss of quality but not to catastrophic results.

Softcore processors term used when a processor component is mapped onto the underlying architecture of the device. This is commonly used in the context of FPGAs, where a processor specification is mapped on configurable logic blocks (CLBs). This is often referred to as a "soft IP" (see also Overlay Architectures).

Software knobs algorithmic parameters that can be tuned for enhanced efficiency or effectiveness to specific inputs. These parameters can be tuned by the programmer using these so-called software knobs, often exposed via a GUI interface or a set of application preferences.

Source-to-source compiler a compiler that receives as input a high-level description using programming languages such as C or FORTRAN, and outputs (transformed) high-level source code, possibly using the same high-level programming language. Source to source is used in the context of analysis, source code-level instrumentation, and source code transformations (e.g., code refactoring).

Static analysis a compile time analysis of a program or part of it. Uses a combination of data- and control-flow analysis to derive information such as def-use chain and liveness.

Subword-level parallelism (SLP) instructions that operate in a concurrent fashion on subsets of the underlying base word size. For example, one can use subword instructions to operate on four 8-bit elements on a 32-bit word performing operations such as masking or even averaging 8-bit integer values, taking into account subword boundaries for arithmetic operations, such as addition and subtraction.

Superlinear, sublinear, linear scaling terms used when analyzing a speedup metric. In the presence of multiple available processing elements, workload can be distributed across them. We can expect that, if we double the number of processors, the performance is also doubled if the workload distribution is properly balanced and all processors are working at peak capacity. In this case, we say that performance has scaled linearly. However, if the performance is less than double than we say that performance scaled sublinearly. This can happen if the increase in the number of processors, which leads to less workload per processor, results in memory or IO bottlenecks. On the other hand, the computation scales superlinearly if the performance more than doubles. This can happen, for instance, when the workload allocated to each processor fits in the cache memory, thus increasing the performance of individual processors. Furthermore, in the context of a distributed system, the reduction in workload size may also lead to reduce or hide network, memory, and disk storage bottlenecks in each machine.

Systolic array a homogeneous parallel computing architecture where each processing node is interconnected in a very regular fashion, typically in a two-dimensional grid. These architectures typically accomplish their computation by "waves" of data flowing and/or pulsating along one or more direction.

T

Task parallelism a form of concurrent execution where different tasks or code sections are executed concurrently by different processing elements, requiring explicit synchronization between them whenever tasks need to share data or to satisfy control and data dependences.

Task-level pipelining an execution mode in which different processors (or application-specific architectures) execute sequences of data-dependent tasks in a pipelined fashion. Synchronization and data communication between executing tasks is typically achieved via FIFO buffers or other communication channels.

Thread-level parallelism a form of parallelism in which tasks execute asynchronously within the same execution environment (address space) and communicate using specific synchronization primitives, such as semaphores and locks. The threading environment is managed by the operating system.

Timespan a time frame or a span of time in the context of execution time or scheduling.

Toolchain, tool flow, design-flow a generic name given to a set of synthesis and compilation tools that work together to produce an executable specification and/or a hardware design specification.

Trip count or iteration count (loop iterations) the number of times a loop body is executed. The trip count can be statically determined if loop bounds can be determined at compile time (e.g., they are constants).

U

Unit-stride accesses (stride-one accesses) a term used when successive accesses to array elements are performed on contiguous locations of memory.

Use-def chains a data structure that identifies for a program variable use (read) all definitions (writes) that can reach that use. Hence, a UD chain allows a compiler to determine which are the possible write operations (definitions) that can influence the result of a specific read operation.

V

Vector length the number of consecutive data items that a vector instruction can handle. Vector length supports the auto-vectorization process by providing the correct factor to unroll and strip-mine to derive suitable vector instructions.

Vector splats term used when assigning all elements of a vector to a certain value (the value can be given by a scalar variable, by a constant, or by an element of the vector).

Vectorization/auto-vectorization a feature supported by most compilers, which include program analysis and code transformations that automatically infer vector instructions from loop-based computations in order to maximize performance.

W

Worst-case execution time (WCET) a timing analysis that computes the worst-case execution time of a section of a code for all possible data inputs and possible environment conditions. This metric is key to perform scheduling analysis for real-time safety-critical systems.

Z

Zero stride a type of stride in which only a single element of the array (in a specific position) is to be used in all the computations. Conceptually, it can be used in a vector operation as a constant.

Index

Note: Page numbers followed by *f* indicate figures, *t* indicate tables, *b* indicate boxes, and *np* indicate footnotes.

Printed in the United States
By Bookmasters